RECONSTRUCTIONS IN EARLY MODERN HISTORY
Series Editors: John Morrill and Pauline Croft

The Stuart Parliaments
1603–1689

DAVID L. SMITH
Fellow and Director of Studies in History,
Selwyn College, Cambridge

A member of the Hodder Headline Group
LONDON • NEW YORK • SYDNEY • AUCKLAND

First published in Great Britain in 1999 by
Arnold, a member of the Hodder Headline Group,
338 Euston Road, London NW1 3BH

http://www.arnoldpublishers.com

Co-published in the United States of America by
Oxford University Press Inc.,
198 Madison Avenue, New York, NY 10016

British Library Cataloguing in Publication Data
A catalogue record for this book is available from the British Library

Library of Congress Cataloging-in-Publication Data
A catalog record for this book is available from the Library of Congress

ISBN 0 340 62502 3 (pb)
ISBN 0 340 71991 5 (hb)

1 2 3 4 5 6 7 8 9 10

Production Editor: Julie Delf
Production Controller: Helen Whitehorn
Cover Design: Mouse Mat

Composition in 10/11pt Sabon by Phoenix Photosetting, Chatham, Kent
Printed and bound in Great Britain by MPG Books, Bodmin, Cornwall

What do you think about this book? Or any other Arnold title?
Please send your comments to feedback.arnold@hodder.co.uk

In memory of Sir Geoffrey Elton

Contents

PART II: PARLIAMENTS AND POLITICS

Preface

This book attempts to fill a major gap in the existing literature about the Parliament of England. There are excellent single-volume syntheses on the Parliaments of sixteenth-century England, notably Michael Graves's *The Tudor Parliaments: Crown, Lords and Commons, 1485–1603* (Harlow, 1985) and Jennifer Loach's *Parliament under the Tudors* (Oxford, 1991), but nothing comparable has yet appeared for the seventeenth century. This book is intended to redress that by offering a synthesis of the massive literature on Stuart Parliaments. In the process, I have tried also to incorporate some of my own research and to advance a general interpretation of seventeenth-century parliamentary history that transcends both the 'Whig' and 'revisionist' positions. This book argues instead for an organic approach that integrates parliamentary history into the wider processes of government and the on-going relationship between successive rulers and their subjects. If it provides a useful overview of the Stuart Parliaments and in turn stimulates further research on this vast subject, then it will have fulfilled its purpose.

An introductory chapter analyses the nature of medieval and Tudor Parliaments by way of background, and then describes the main themes and surviving sources for the Stuart Parliaments. The remainder of the book is then divided into two main sections. The first consists of five chapters analysing how Parliament functioned as an institution: these examine in detail who sat in each House and how they were selected, how Parliament acted as both a High Court and a Great Council, Parliament's financial role, the nature of parliamentary procedure, and the changing relations, in both theory and practice, between Crown, Lords and Commons. The second section explores the history of parliamentary politics in this period. It comprises three chronological chapters, each of which locates the proceedings in both Houses in the context of broader political and constitutional trends. The final chapter looks ahead to the period after 1689 and concludes by assessing the extent to which Parliament had changed since 1603.

At the end of the book, after the notes, there is a glossary of technical terms and six appendices giving further factual information including the dates of parliamentary sessions, the number of acts passed in each session, and the names of the key officers of each House. After the appendices there is a select bibliography. Throughout the abbreviations, notes and bibliography, the place of publication of printed works is London unless otherwise stated. In all quotations from primary sources, I have extended contemporary contractions and modernised spelling, capitalisation and punctuation. All dates are given in Old Style, except that the year is taken as beginning on 1 January rather than 25 March. Public acts of Parliament are cited by regnal year and chapter number; private acts are cited by the regnal year and then the number given to the Original Act at the House of Lords Record Office.

Researching and writing this book has made me aware that parliamentary history is an even more complex and technical subject than I had previously realised. I am deeply conscious of the many debts that I owe to friends and colleagues who have helped me to make sense of some very difficult sources, and to negotiate some particularly hazardous historiographical minefields. All historical research is a collaborative endeavour, but this is perhaps especially true when the area has been as well worked by scholars as the Stuart Parliaments. I have been very fortunate to have John Morrill and Pauline Croft as my editors. I am most grateful for their invitation to write this book, and for their enormous encouragement, advice and support at every stage of its preparation. In particular, they both sent me extremely detailed and perceptive comments on the first draft which have immeasurably improved the final version. I owe a great debt to the following scholars who also read the whole of the first draft and made many helpful suggestions: Michael Graves, Chris Kyle, Patrick Little, Paul Seaward and Graham Seel. All of these generously shared their knowledge of seventeenth-century Parliaments with me, and between them they produced lists of comments and corrections that covered a total of nearly 30 pages of single-spaced manuscript or typescript. With most of them I have also had the added pleasure of discussing the Stuart Parliaments at length on a number of occasions during the past 12 months, including over some particularly enjoyable extended 'working lunches' in various Cambridge hostelries. Together with the series editors, they have all saved me from a very large number of errors, misconceptions and infelicities. However, as usual it goes without saying that none of them is in any way to blame for the shortcomings of the end product, responsibility for which rests entirely with me. Indeed, on several points I received flatly contradictory advice from different people: it is quite impossible to please everybody, especially on a subject like this, and conflicting suggestions afforded a salutary reminder of how open many of the questions addressed in this book remain.

I also owe a particular debt to my former research student, Harry Bowcott, whose M.Phil. thesis on a related subject I supervised while I was working on this book. Our discussions were a constant source of stimulus to me and have greatly influenced my thinking on the nature and role of Parliament in seventeenth-century England. I am very grateful for valuable advice and information on specific points to John Coffey, Kurt Fryklund, Mark Kishlansky, Alan Orr, Jon Parkin and Christopher Thompson. I am indebted to Chris Kyle and John Reeve for showing me papers prior to publication, to Christopher Thompson and Corinne Comstock Weston for sending me offprints of several papers, and to the Centre for Kentish Studies for providing copies of a number of documents among the Sackville Manuscripts. I wish to thank the staff at the House of Lords Record Office, and especially the Clerk of the Records, David Johnson, for their kind assistance during the research and writing of this book. I owe thanks as well to Christopher Wheeler and Elena Seymenliyska at Arnold who throughout this project have been unfailingly helpful, encouraging and supportive.

Ten years, almost to the day, since I was first elected to a Fellowship at

Selwyn College, Cambridge, I remain deeply grateful to the Master and Fellows not only for continuing to provide a wonderfully congenial and conducive working environment but also for granting me two terms of sabbatical leave in 1997 during which I was able to write most of the first draft of this book. I also owe a great deal to my undergraduate pupils and particularly to those students who attended a course of eight lectures on the Stuart Parliaments which I gave in the Cambridge History Faculty during the Lent Term of 1998. Their feedback and especially their questions, after lectures and in supervisions, have been far more valuable and important in shaping this book than they can possibly realise.

Finally, working on Stuart Parliaments has brought home to me just how much any study of this subject owes to historians of the Tudor Parliaments, and above all to the late Sir Geoffrey Elton. Reading and re-reading his voluminous writings on sixteenth and early seventeenth-century Parliaments (in turn only one aspect of his vast oeuvre) has made me more aware than ever of the magnitude of his achievement. Though never formally supervised by him, I had the privilege of attending his lectures and later his research seminar, and of benefiting greatly from his sympathetic guidance and generous encouragement. This book is dedicated to his memory, with gratitude and respect.

D. L. S.
Selwyn College, Cambridge
September 1998

Abbreviations

AHR	*American Historical Review*
AO	C. H. Firth and R. S. Rait (eds.), *Acts and Ordinances of the Interregnum, 1642–1660* (3 vols. 1911)
BIHR	*Bulletin of the Institute of Historical Research*
BL	British Library
CD, 1621	W. Notestein, F. H. Relf and H. Simpson (eds.), *Commons Debates, 1621* (7 vols., New Haven, 1935)
CHJ	*Cambridge Historical Journal*
CJ	*Journals of the House of Commons* (1803–)
CSPV	R. Brown *et al.* (eds.), *Calendar of State Papers Venetian* (40 vols., 1864–1940)
EcHR	*Economic History Review*
EHR	*English Historical Review*
Grey, *Debates*	Anchitell Grey (ed.), *Debates of the House of Commons from the year 1667 to the year 1694* (10 vols., 1763)
HJ	*Historical Journal*
HLQ	*Huntington Library Quarterly*
HLRO	House of Lords Record Office
HMC	Historical Manuscripts Commission
HR	*Historical Research*
JBS	*Journal of British Studies*
JMH	*Journal of Modern History*
LJ	*Journals of the House of Lords* (1846)
OA	Original Acts (at the HLRO)
PER	*Parliaments, Estates and Representation*
PH	*Parliamentary History*
PP	*Past and Present*
PRO	Public Record Office
Procs., 1628	M. F. Keeler, M. J. Cole and W. B. Bidwell (eds.), *Proceedings in Parliament, 1628* (6 vols., New Haven, 1977–83)
TRHS	*Transactions of the Royal Historical Society*
TT	Thomason Tracts
Wing	Donald Wing (ed.), *A Short-Title Catalogue of Books Printed in England, Scotland, Ireland, Wales and British America and of English Books Printed Abroad, 1641–1700* (2nd edition, 3 vols., New York, 1972–88)

|1|

Introduction

The problem

The exceptional durability of England's governmental institutions creates special problems for the historian. Precisely because so much of English constitutional change has occurred through evolution rather than revolution, particular institutions often measure their existence in centuries rather than decades or years. Yet the continuity of names such as Parliament or Privy Council or Chancery belies a process of piecemeal adaptation to shifting circumstances: though the labels endured, the realities they describe changed dramatically through time. Furthermore, those changes took place in complex ways and at variable speeds; an institution might remain similar for decades only to alter radically over a few years. This produces many hazards for the historian because it makes it exceptionally easy to underestimate the degree of change and to project later developments backwards onto earlier periods. It was no accident that a historical schema such as the Whig interpretation emerged in England, for the superficial continuities of English history make teleology unusually difficult to avoid. Yet those continuities are often more apparent than real, and scholars frequently find themselves analysing contrasted historical realities divided by a common language.

Nowhere have these problems proved harder to overcome than in reconstructing the history of the English Parliament. It is all too easy to assume that medieval or early modern Parliaments shared the characteristics and preoccupations of their modern successors. For many years, the most influential interpretation of parliamentary history envisaged a grand progression towards modern liberty and democracy in which Parliaments played a crucial role in defending the subjects' rights and freedoms against royal encroachment. The story led from Magna Carta through the conflicts of the late medieval and Tudor periods to reach a dramatic climax in the revolutions of the seventeenth century; thereafter, gentler and more gradual honing of the system took place until the late Victorian Parliament emerged in all its glory. To S. R. Gardiner, writing in the 1880s, 'the Parliament of England was the noblest monument ever reared by mortal man', and 'in all main points the Parliament of England, as it exists at this day, is the same as that which gathered round' Edward I.[1]

This view – of which Gardiner was by no means the most extreme exponent – had a number of unfortunate consequences. In the first place, it diminished the extent of change over time, with the result that Parliament was seen as essentially the same institution throughout its long history. This in turn meant that earlier Parliaments were assessed according to nineteenth- or twentieth-century criteria. Parliament was seen primarily as a political institution whose overriding purpose was to restrain the ambitions of overmighty monarchs and to safeguard the liberty and freedom of the subject. Particular importance was attached to Parliament as an arena for political activity, debate and often conflict. This provided the central themes for such celebrated works as Sir John Neale's history of Elizabethan Parliaments: during her reign, the House of Commons learnt what Neale called 'the art of opposition', and by the time of her death it had 'reached maturity . . . the instrument was tempered with which the Crown was to be resisted and conquered'.[2] More recently, a collection of essays entitled *Parliament and Liberty from the Reign of Elizabeth to the English Civil War* has provided the first volume in a series on 'The Making of Modern Freedom'.[3] This emphasis on politics and the defence of freedom obscures the fact that for centuries the principal functions of Parliament were not so much political as conciliar, financial and legislative: it gave counsel, voted taxes and passed laws. Furthermore, such verdicts typically impose another characteristic of modern Parliaments by assuming the dominance of the House of Commons. The House of Lords – throughout the medieval and early modern periods the more politically powerful and procedurally sophisticated House – is commonly relegated to the sidelines.[4] Above all, this interpretation imposes a teleological framework which organises accounts of earlier Parliaments in terms of modern categories, and assesses them according to how far they advance or retard progress towards the ultimate goal of the modern Parliament rather than examining them on their own terms and in their own right.[5]

This problem is especially acute for the seventeenth century. I will suggest in due course reasons why that century was a crucial period in the history of the English Parliament, and that it was not the same institution by the end as it was at the beginning. But if this was a pivotal period, it was not so for the reasons that Whiggish historians alleged. For much of the present century the most influential interpretation of early Stuart Parliaments has been that laid out by Wallace Notestein in his 1924 lecture 'The Winning of the Initiative by the House of Commons'. According to Notestein, the years 1604–29 'gave us in politics a new kind of Commons that was by and by to make inevitable a new constitution'.[6] The Commons 'gained the real initiative in legislation' that enabled it ultimately to defeat Charles I in the Civil Wars of the 1640s, and later to triumph over James II at the Glorious Revolution. Notestein's interpretation fitted neatly with the picture of mid and late seventeenth-century Parliaments found in the works of, among others, Gardiner, Firth, Trevelyan and David Ogg.[7] The underlying assumption was that Parliament (for which read 'the Commons') acquired greater institutional maturity and political power and, in a series of dramatic constitutional conflicts, defeated the authoritarian ambitions of the Stuarts. Perpetuated also through a number of readily accessible selections of source material,[8] this view remained remarkably pervasive until the 1970s, and still provided much of the framework for Lawrence Stone's *The Causes of the English Revolution, 1529–1642* (1972).[9] But since then, as we shall see, a massive body of research has so drastically revised this picture as to leave little of it intact. Even if some of that 'revisionism' has itself been challenged, there is no question of simply resurrecting the Whiggish interpretation that preceded it.

Before we begin to consider the revised view of Stuart Parliaments, it is also worth stressing that pious myths about the institution are by no means unique to the nineteenth and twentieth centuries. The seventeenth century had its own ideas of the origins and early history of Parliament, and these often assumed political significance because they could be manipulated for specific purposes. Two examples – one from early in the century, the other from late on – will serve to illustrate this point. During much of the Tudor period, the most widely accepted version of Parliament's origins was that advanced by Polydore Vergil and Holinshed who dated its existence from 1116. However, Pauline Croft has recently shown that at the end of Elizabeth's reign and into the early years of James I, there was a wave of antiquarian interest in the subject that advanced an altogether different story. Lawyers and antiquarians such as Sir John Doddridge traced Parliaments back to pre-Roman times, to 'those sages the Druids', whose yearly conventions were conducted without monarchs. This assertion of Parliament's great antiquity became politically charged under James I and especially Charles I because it offered a powerful defence of Parliament as more anciently established than the monarchy itself. At a time when many thought the Stuarts less favourably disposed towards Parliaments than the Tudors, and when Parliaments felt more and more insecure about their future, such a historical account provided an important 'sustaining myth'.[10]

An example from the later seventeenth century affords a further illustration of this link between a particular view of Parliament's origins and a specific political agenda. At the height of the Exclusion Crisis, another lawyer and antiquarian William Petyt published *The Antient Right of the Commons of England Asserted, or, A Discourse proving by records and the best historians, that the Commons of England were ever an essential part of Parliament* (1680). He argued that the Commons had existed since before the time of legal memory, from the days of the Britons and the Anglo-Saxons. He used this claim to assert that the immemorial House of Commons was an integral part of the English Parliament, and that the three elements in the Parliament – Crown, Lords and Commons – enjoyed equal and 'co-ordinate' powers. These ideas were not in themselves new,[11] but in the context of the attempt to exclude James, Duke of York from the line of succession they struck a powerful chord as a robust defence of Parliament's position against the Court. As with Doddridge, the supposed immemoriality of the Commons underlay a wish to defend it for very particular and immediate political reasons.[12] The historian of Stuart Parliaments thus faces a double challenge: not only to strip away the flawed perspectives of Whiggish historians, but also to allow for the myths espoused by contemporaries that in turn shaped their own political behaviour. Those seventeenth-century myths are interesting more for the political purpose they served during that period than for anything they tell us about earlier Parliaments. Indeed, recent research has produced a very different account of medieval and Tudor Parliaments, and it is essential to examine this if the Parliaments of the Stuart period are to be seen in their proper perspective.

The medieval and Tudor background

The origins of Parliament as an institution lay in the monarch's need to obtain counsel on matters of national concern and to secure the consent of leading subjects to laws and taxation. It was thus created as part of the monarch's government, not in opposition to it, and this fundamental fact coloured much of its subsequent history. As G. O. Sayles has written in his magisterial account of medieval Parliaments, 'Parliament was an expedient of government, to be summoned when the King desired a particularly full and representative Council.'[13] Parliaments were summoned and dissolved at the monarch's discretion, and they complemented other conciliar bodies. Parliaments evolved as an outgrowth of the King's Council, called on an *ad hoc* basis whenever the monarch felt the need to consult more widely among his subjects, most commonly in times of war or political instability. Parliaments existed alongside the King's Council of legal officers and magnates and the periodic meetings known as Great Councils (the King's Council enlarged by bishops and nobles), but they took place less regularly because the specific needs that they served were less constant.

The earliest known official use of the term Parliament was in 1236,[14] and the first formal calling of a Parliament took place in 1258 at the instigation of Simon de Montfort and the baronial opposition against Henry III. Subsequent monarchs, especially Edward I and Edward III, quickly saw the value of such assemblies as a way of periodically involving the political elite in the business of government, the creation of law and the dispensing of justice. By the fourteenth century Parliaments, comprising selected knights and burgesses as well as legal officers, nobles, bishops and abbots, were being referred to as both 'the community of the realm' and 'the High Court of Parliament'.[15] During the first half of the fourteenth century the institution began to crystallise: from at least 1332 onwards, the knights and burgesses deliberated separately from the others, and by 1340 it was recognised that these 'Commons' were an indispensable, although not co-equal, component of a Parliament. Parliament thus came to comprise two chambers: one consisted of the King's Council afforced by bishops and nobles (what later became the House of Lords), the other of representatives of the shires and boroughs (the future House of Commons). From 1340, the lower clergy ceased to attend Parliaments and instead joined the ecclesiastical Convocations of the provinces of Canterbury and York;[16] the higher clergy (bishops and, until the 1530s, abbots) continued to sit in Parliament as lords spiritual as well as in the Upper House of Convocation. The year 1340 also saw the beginning of an official record of Parliaments known as the Parliament Roll – essentially a list of petitions submitted to Parliament together with the King's response – that was kept in the Chancery.[17] Such a continuous official record was another clear sign of Parliament's emergence as a settled institution.

Medieval Parliaments developed a remarkable range of functions. They were in the first place conciliar bodies, intended to give the monarch a wider range of advice than the King's Council or the Great Council could do, and to allow direct contact between ruler and ruled. Such occasions served the interests of the subjects as well because they enabled the presentation of grievances or matters requiring a judicial hearing before the largest possible body. This meant that Parliament also operated as a court of record, answering petitions and settling legal cases. Because it was wider than the other law courts and conciliar bodies, Parliament became recognised by the later fourteenth century as the most authoritative means of making laws. During the first half of the fifteenth century, the Commons were gradually transformed from a body which submitted petitions for redress of grievances, with the King and Lords sitting in judgement, into a full partner in the law-making process. Bills could hence-forth be initiated by any of the constituent elements of the Parliament, a fea-ture that subsequently produced the distinction between public and private acts of Parliament.[18] The other central function of Parliaments was to vote taxes. The Hundred Years War that began under Edward III left the Crown with an urgent need for revenue, and it became accepted that whereas in peace-time the monarch was expected to live off the income generated by the royal demesne and its attendant feudal dues, during wars or in time of 'evident and urgent' need, taxes could be raised for the good of the realm provided that Parliament consented. The Commons' right to initiate such grants of taxation was firmly established by the mid-fourteenth century, and in 1407 they suc-cessfully protested against what they regarded as the Lords' encroachment on that right. This convention greatly helped to secure the co-operation of tax-payers and thus further increased the usefulness of Parliaments to the Crown.

The emergence of such assemblies took place across much of medieval Europe, but the Parliament of England was unusual in three important respects. First, it combined the roles of a court of law and a representative assembly that – with the important exceptions of the Aragonese Cortes and the Polish Diet (Sejm) – remained distinct elsewhere. Second, the bicameral struc-ture of the English Parliament was shared only with the Polish Sejm and the Diets of Hungary and Bohemia, and with the Irish Parliament which was heav-ily based on the English model. A more common pattern on the continent was for the three estates of nobility, higher clergy and commons to sit separately, whereas in the English Parliament the peers and bishops (lords temporal and lords spiritual) formed a single chamber – a fact that, as we shall see, made it extremely difficult to reconcile English parliamentary structures with custom-ary concepts of the three estates.[19] Another variation, closer to home, which again contrasts with the English bicameral structure was the unicameral Parliament of Scotland, in which peers, burgesses, bishops and officers of state all met in a single chamber. Finally, the opportunity for subjects to present peti-tions and thereby secure authoritative judicial resolution of grievances or dis-putes by the King and his extended Council – what ultimately developed into the legislative process of private bills – conferred immense benefits that extended the value of Parliaments to the nation at large. The adjudication of grievances was not uncommon in continental representative assemblies, but the mechanism of private bill procedure was a relatively unusual feature which the English Parliament shared with only a minority of other institutions, such as the Aragonese Cortes, the Sicilian Parlamento, and, closer to home, the Scottish Parliament.[20]

It was entirely to be expected that in performing these diverse functions Parliament should on occasion also become a forum for political deliberation and even conflict. This could involve the expression of criticisms against cur-rent royal policies and those advisers held responsible for them. However, it needs emphasising that this was not Parliament's main characteristic, but rather a secondary consequence of its primary functions as a judicial, legisla-tive and conciliar body. Co-operation rather than conflict was the normal rela-tionship between the various elements of a Parliament, and this was essential for it to work efficiently and productively as an institution. Only such a busi-ness-like institution could prove beneficial to Crown and subjects alike, and those very real benefits explain why successive monarchs called so many Parliaments during the Middle Ages: nearly 200 between 1272 and 1399, and over 50 between 1399 and 1485.[21] In all, between 1327 and 1485, there were only 42 individual years in which Parliament did not meet.[22] Monarchs were surely not going to summon assemblies that appeared to be hotbeds of nascent opposition to the Crown, although that is in effect how Whiggish historians often depicted them. The idea that Parliament was part of royal government rather than a counterweight to it ran directly contrary to the traditional interpretation associated with William Stubbs. It was first advanced as long ago as 1893 by F. W. Maitland when he edited the Parliament Roll for the 1305 Parliament,[23] and it has been borne out by much subsequent research.[24] Most recently, John Watts has argued that the centrepiece of public affairs lay not in Parliament but in the monarch and his on-going relationships with members of the political elite.[25] Parliament formed an organic, albeit intermittent, part of the machinery of government and should not be seen as separate from it, let alone as antithetical to it.

Likewise, it is important not to underestimate the institutional development and political effectiveness of medieval Parliaments. J. S. Roskell in particular has shown that medieval Parliaments sometimes asserted their strengths – especially the right to consent to taxation as a handle against the Crown – more frequently and successfully than did Tudor Parliaments.[26] By the latter part of the fifteenth century, although members of the Commons remained deferential to their social superiors in the Lords, they were accepted as an equal and indispensable partner in the making of legislation. Parliament had by then emerged as a fully bicameral institution, and in 1489 the judges could declare a certain act of attainder invalid on the grounds that 'nothing was said of the Commons'.[27] This equipollence was resoundingly confirmed during the Reformation Parliament of 1529–36. Despite all the qualifications and caveats that have been advanced to Sir Geoffrey Elton's thesis of a 'Tudor revolution in government', the significance of the 1530s in the history of Parliament was considerable. Institutional developments came in direct response to pressing political circumstances. The fact that the King and Thomas Cromwell exploited Parliament to push through the break with Rome and enact a series of other reforms had profound implications for the nature of Parliament as an institution.

First of all, the Reformation Parliament demonstrated more clearly and emphatically than ever before the omnicompetence of statute. Until then it had been generally accepted that although the scope of statute law was considerable, and that it was the highest form of human positive law in England, it could not override the dictates of natural or divine law. As Christopher St German put it in around 1528, a statute was 'not righteous nor obligatory but it be consonant to the law of God'.[28] As a result of the Reformation Parliament, these limitations fell away as the potentialities of statute law were explored more widely than hitherto. In particular, it was recognised – though not without much debate and some resistance – that statutes could regulate religious and spiritual matters, as well as property rights, and could also sweep away franchise jurisdictions where royal writs had hitherto carried at best only limited force. After the 1530s, the supremacy of parliamentary statute became an accepted principle that survived until the process of European integration during the closing years of the twentieth century.[29]

A second crucial implication derived from the fact that those statutes were enacted by the Crown-in-Parliament. Although the doctrine that statutes required the assent of Crown, Lords and Commons had become well established during the later Middle Ages, the notion had persisted that the King alone made law; indeed, as late as Henry VII's reign the monarch occasionally amended statutes unilaterally after they had passed both Houses and after he had given his consent.[30] The identification of King-in-Parliament as the supreme legislative authority (what Elton and Graves have called a 'mixed sovereign'[31]) was made more explicitly and self-consciously during the Reformation Parliament than ever before. Only from the 1530s did the enacting clause for statutes become generally established as: 'by the King's most excellent majesty, with the advice and assent of the Lords spiritual and temporal and the Commons in this present Parliament assembled, and by authority of the same'.[32] The senior partner within this mixed sovereign clearly remained the King, responsible for summoning and dissolving Parliaments at will; yet in 1542 Henry VIII acknowledged that the sovereign authority of King-in-Parliament was greater than that of the King alone when he told the Commons that 'we at no time stand so highly in our estate royal, as in the time of Parliament, wherein we as head, and you as members, are conjoined and knit together into one body politic'.[33]

This realisation that the Crown was actually more powerful when operating in partnership with Parliament as a 'mixed sovereign' than when acting alone steadily dawned on Henry's successors. Even during the troubled reigns of Edward VI and Mary, the essence of Parliaments remained a search for co-operation between ruler and ruled. Under Edward parliamentary authority was used to implement a more radically Protestant reformation, and Somerset's attempt to make large-scale use of proclamations proved a failure. Similarly, Mary grudgingly recognised the need to work with Parliament in order to revoke the Henrician and Edwardian religious reforms that she loathed.[34] As Michael Graves has written, throughout these years Parliament 'continued to be a communion of crown and governing elite, acting as partners in the management of the kingdom. ... It served the interests of both the monarchy and the wider community of the realm.'[35]

Graves's statement offers an ideal lead-in to the revised accounts of Elizabethan Parliaments that have emerged over the past two decades. Until the early 1970s, the orthodox interpretation was that associated with Sir John Neale. As noted above, Neale's work fitted perfectly with the Whig vision of English history. He saw the Elizabethan Commons as an institution growing in authority and political maturity, and increasingly willing to stand up to the Crown in defence of its privileges and liberties. This framework led him to concentrate mainly on episodes of political conflict over 'matters of state' between Elizabeth and members of the Commons spearheaded by a vociferous 'Puritan choir'.[36] Against this, 'revisionist' historians, most notably Elton and Graves, have advanced an interpretation that sees Elizabethan Parliaments very much as a continuation of medieval and early Tudor assemblies rather than as a prelude to the conflicts of the seventeenth century. They have argued that Neale's emphasis on political conflict is misleading and that we should instead focus on Parliament as an institution whose principal function was to advise the monarch and to vote legislation and taxation. In order to discharge this business effectively, it was essential for Crown, Lords and Commons to co-operate in a spirit of reasonable harmony. The Lords – largely neglected by Neale – were the socially superior and politically more influential House. Many of the occasions on which the Commons apparently 'opposed' the Crown in fact reflected divisions of opinion within the Court and Privy Council that extended into the Houses of Parliament: vertical divisions between different groups within Court, Council and Parliament were thus more important than horizontal divisions between the two Houses and the Crown. Elton and Graves have suggested that there was no organised 'opposition', and that the leadership of the Commons lay not with a 'Puritan choir' (the existence of which is doubtful) but with the Crown's nominees, the Speaker and Privy Councillors, and their 'men-of-business'. In other words, Parliament remained what it had always been: primarily a legislative rather than a political body, and a part of the royal government rather than a counter-balance to it.[37]

Much of this 'revisionism' is extremely persuasive, and the limitations of Neale's interpretation have become plainly apparent. The revised view of Elizabethan Parliaments makes far more sense in terms of what we now know about the nature of the institution during the Middle Ages and the early sixteenth century. It is important, however, not to throw the baby out with the bath water. No more than the traditional version can the revised interpretation stand alone as a self-sufficient account of parliamentary history. There is substantial evidence of ideological disagreement and even of principled conflict in Elizabethan Parliaments. Patrick Collinson has shown that a figure such as Thomas Norton, whom Graves regarded as an archetypal 'man-of-business', closely associated with patrons in the Privy Council and the City of London, did hold strong religious convictions and was driven by a genuine desire to advance the godly cause through Parliament.[38] Similarly, Terry Hartley has recently offered a moderate reassertion of at least some of Neale's arguments. In particular, he has downplayed the political significance of patron–client links between Privy Councillors, peers and members of the Commons; he has also emphasised the depth of unhappiness within the Commons over matters such as religion and monopolies, and refused to see Peter Wentworth, the vigorous defender of parliamentary free speech, as an isolated or unrepresentative figure.[39] Elton and Graves have given us superbly researched studies of Elizabethan Parliaments as a legislative institution, but there is a danger of losing sight of the very real political disputes that took place within them.[40]

One possible way of synthesising, and indeed transcending, these different interpretations is presented in the recent research of David Dean and Ian Archer on parliamentary 'lobbying'. Dean in particular has suggested that we should 'consider Parliament as an arena in which different "interest groups", "factions" or "lobbies" operated'. The interaction of such lobbies could easily lead to disputes, but 'within a framework which can be described as co-operative'.[41] This model has the advantage of seeing Parliament as *both* a political arena *and* a legislative body, and it thus avoids a false polarity between the Whiggish and revisionist interpretations. It also makes sense of 'puritan' calls for 'further reformation' in that the godly were one of the lobbies who sought to advance their cause through Parliament. In this they resembled other interest groups, such as individual boroughs or the City of London livery companies, who used Parliament as one of a number of channels – including the Court, the Privy Council, and the local and central law courts – through which they could press their claims and oppose conflicting interests.[42] Dean has recently published a detailed reconstruction of these processes during the second half of the reign.[43] His work not only goes beyond both the traditional and revisionist paradigms; it also underlines once again that Parliament cannot be understood in isolation from the other organs of government. Lobbies may have sought to resolve their problems through Parliament because statute was the highest form of law and therefore the one against which it was hardest to appeal. But if they could achieve a satisfactory outcome through other institutions that convened more regularly than Parliament, then that often afforded a speedier and cheaper method of redress. Parliaments allowed, so to speak, the pursuit of interests by other means.

Perhaps the most striking characteristic of Parliament as it had developed by the end of the sixteenth century was its distinctiveness and sophistication as an institution. It was exceptional among European assemblies in its organisation and diversity of function. Few other assemblies offered such a wide range of benefits to so many different constituents or displayed such precisely developed structures and procedures. The combination of a court of record and a representative assembly within a single institution had no parallel within the British Isles and on the continent was found only in Aragon and Poland. The provision for resolving sectional or personal grievances through private legislation (as distinct from the adjudication of private petitions) was not encountered widely elsewhere, with some notable exceptions that included Aragon, Sicily and Scotland. Also unusual was the bicameral structure of the English Parliament: apart from the Irish Parliament, which was modelled on the English, bicameral structures otherwise existed only in Poland, Hungary and Bohemia. In most of the rest of Europe, assemblies met either in plenary session, or by estates (often jealously guarding their own distinct privileges), or by *ad hoc* arrangements. The nature and extent of the English Parliament's role in both passing laws and granting taxes was also exceptional: probably the closest continental parallel in this respect was the Swedish Riksdag. The Scottish Parliament did not have any monopoly over the making of laws or the granting of taxation in that these were equally valid if they had received the consent of a convention of the estates. In the Irish Parliament, Poynings' Law (1494) stipulated that no bill could be introduced until it had been approved by the King and Privy Council in England. Certainly some assemblies, such as those in Saxony and Württemberg, exercised tighter financial control than the English Parliament, but – like the estates in France and Spain – they lacked its direct participation in law-making. The Cortes of Aragon was a far more effective curb on royal action, but that only encouraged the Crown to discard it as soon as it ceased to offer adequate financial support. That was a constant hazard for representative assemblies if they tried to pursue the principle of redress before supply, and one that we shall see faced the English Parliament at various times in the seventeenth century.[44]

During Elizabeth's reign, however, the exceptional attributes of English Parliaments continued to make them extremely useful occasions to both monarch and subject, and the war against Spain after 1585 only increased the Queen's need for parliamentary taxation. It is true that Parliaments sat less frequently under the Tudors than under their predecessors: no fewer than 55 years passed between 1485 and 1603 when no Parliament met, and during Elizabeth's 45-year reign Parliaments assembled on only 13 occasions. Yet the frequency of parliamentary sessions is not necessarily a reliable index of the health of the institution, and at the close of the sixteenth century Parliaments continued to form a flexible and valuable element among the agencies of government. The fact that they met irregularly did not diminish their importance in certain circumstances. When Lord Burghley drew up a 'bill for the Queen's safety' in 1584 making contingency plans in the event of Elizabeth's untimely death, he envisaged that royal authority would temporarily be wielded by a

Great Council, which would, after an interval of 20 days, recall the most recent Parliament; this could then legislate in the absence of a monarch.[45] An institution which could be entrusted with such powers can hardly be regarded as in decline.

Themes and sources

This brief overview of medieval and Tudor Parliaments provides a useful background against which the Stuart Parliaments can be examined. The perspective that it offers on the institution can be used as a kind of 'baseline' by which to assess developments after 1603. The research of medievalists and Tudor historians has given us a fresh and challenging agenda for the study of Parliament, different criteria to evaluate, new themes to investigate. It seems important to analyse Parliaments as working institutions that formed an integral part of the machinery of government; as bicameral bodies in which the Lords were at least as important as the Commons; and as occasions where the expectation was that the harmonious transaction of business would be the norm rather than the acrimonious debating of political issues. However, the extent to which these lessons can be applied to what happened after 1603 remains the subject of intense controversy, and the historiography of seventeenth-century Parliaments is far more diffuse and patchy than that of the Tudor Parliaments. The lines of debate are more varied and less clearly defined, and although some themes and topics have been investigated in great depth others remain relatively under-studied. Few areas of historical controversy are more embattled and cacophonous.

Clearly there is a major problem to be explained. The old Whig certainties of a rising House of Commons that protected the liberties of the people from the authoritarian ambitions of the Stuarts and thereby paved the way for a gradual advance towards the Victorian constitution may have been discredited; yet the seventeenth century remains a formative period in the history of Parliament. At the beginning of the century the institution exhibited recognisable continuities with its medieval and Tudor predecessors. By the end, although some of those continuities persisted, Parliament stood transformed. Parliaments no longer met intermittently but became a permanent part of government that met every year from 1689 onwards. Their existence was guaranteed not only by statute but by the Crown's financial necessity. Parliamentary grants provided not merely 'extraordinary' revenue in wars or other emergencies, but the entire tax base of the state. Whereas the expectation in the early seventeenth century was that members of the Commons would usually be 'selected' through a consensual process, by the end far more were being chosen through elections that reflected deep-rooted political and religious divisions. Within Parliament, a fluid political scene characterised by loose-knit factions and many 'non-aligned' individuals had given way to one in which two parties, the Whigs and the Tories, were emerging and could command the regular allegiance of a majority of members. Without resurrecting Whig teleologies, it would be true to say that by the end of the period Parliament had changed dramatically and bore a closer resemblance to the modern institution than it had in 1603.

This book will explore how and why that transformation came about during the course of the seventeenth century. The core of it is divided into two main parts. The first presents an anatomy of Parliament as an institution and comprises five thematic chapters. These chapters overlap to a considerable extent and their subject matter is inseparably linked: they need to be read together as a unit. Chapter 2 examines the membership of the two Houses – who was entitled to attend and by what right – and then considers the debates over how far members of Parliament were seen as 'representatives' of their constituencies, and the complex relationship between parliamentary proceedings and wider opinion. The third chapter explores how the English Parliament uniquely combined the roles of 'High Court' and 'Great Council'. It examines Parliament's place within the legal system, and the remarkable revival of impeachment and the appellate jurisdiction of the House of Lords that took place during the seventeenth century. The chapter then looks at legislative activity and procedure, and finally at how Parliament operated as an institution that offered counsel to the monarch. Chapter 4 addresses a particularly controversial topic, the 'power of the purse', and investigates the extent to which Parliament used its right to consent to taxation as a lever against the Crown. This chapter considers how Parliament's financial powers altered over the century, its changing place within the English State's fiscal system, and the political implications of this. Historians have also hotly debated the significance of parliamentary procedure, which forms the subject of Chapter 5. How far were procedural changes politically important? Did they represent efforts by the Houses to diminish the Crown's influence over their deliberations; or were they merely *ad hoc* attempts to improve the efficient transaction of business? Lastly, Chapter 6 examines the relationship, both in theory and practice, between the three components of the 'parliamentary trinity' – Crown, Lords and Commons – and assesses how far their relative powers and status changed during the course of the seventeenth century.

The first part of the book thus explores a series of parallel themes throughout the whole century – what might be called a longitudinal analysis. By contrast, the second part offers a lateral analysis: it consists of three chronological chapters covering the periods 1603–40, 1640–60 and 1660–89. Each chapter tries to reconstruct the changing nature of Parliament's role within England's system of government and its relationship with political life and culture. They are not so much blow-by-blow accounts of successive Parliaments as examinations of the principal areas of parliamentary concern and their significance for the political history of the period in question. These chapters thus attempt to locate the themes highlighted in the first part of the book within a sequence of contemporary contexts. The final chapter looks forward to subsequent developments during the reigns of William III and Anne, and ties the strands of the argument together by considering how Parliament had changed since 1603. The book as a whole thus attempts to see Parliament as part of the larger organism of seventeenth-century politics and government – what contemporaries referred to as 'the body politic'. In a sense, the very idea of a book devoted to Stuart Parliaments may seem to run counter to this and to reassert a Whiggish assumption about the centrality of Parliaments in national political life. Yet I hope to show that Parliaments are no less valid a subject of study even if the institution needs to be understood as part of a bigger whole rather than as a distinct entity in its own right.

In the last part of this introductory chapter, it is worth briefly describing the principal types of primary sources that help us to reconstruct parliamentary history. The 'revisionist' account of Tudor – and especially Elizabethan –

Parliaments rests not only upon contrasting interpretations but also on the use of different sources from those to which Neale and others devoted most of their attentions. Scholars such as Elton and Graves, keen to reconstruct the workings of Parliament as an institution, placed particular emphasis on the official records generated by Parliament's transaction of business, and these sources remain available throughout the seventeenth century and beyond.

Originally, the formal record of Parliament was the so-called Parliament Roll. In the Middle Ages this had been a fairly full record of parliamentary business and proceedings, but from 1484 onwards it included little more than the texts of acts passed. From 1540 the texts of private acts became progressively less comprehensive, until in 1593 only their titles were recorded on the Parliament Roll. By the end of the sixteenth century the Parliament Roll was thus a mere shadow of its former self: a derivative source that nevertheless was enrolled in Chancery and hence remained the document that formally gave Parliament its legal status as a court of record.[46] During the 1620s, however, the Clerk of the Parliaments, Henry Elsynge, began to produce Rolls that emulated their medieval predecessors in their inclusion of a narrative of parliamentary proceedings and extensive supplementary documentation. Elsynge's reversion to earlier practice stemmed from his conviction that the accurate recording of precedents was essential not only for Parliament's work as a court but also to inform the revival of medieval procedures such as impeachment.[47] However, Elsynge's fuller form of Parliament Roll was part of a 'painful labour' that his successors failed to emulate, and they reverted to the previous practice of listing public acts only.[48]

By the sixteenth century, the texts of the public acts in the Parliament Rolls were in fact copied from the list of statutes passed that was printed at the end of each session. First printed in 1484, and first issued for public use in 1510, these 'sessional prints' became the standard means of reference to acts of Parliament for law courts and for the nation at large. From 1547 the sessional prints, and the collected edition of *Statutes of the Realm* later compiled from them,[49] comprised only public acts; or rather, inclusion in the prints became the accepted definition of a public act.[50] The texts were copied from the Original Acts, the actual documents that were passed – often with visible amendments – by both Houses and then received the royal assent. From 1497 these Original Acts form an almost continuous series, kept at the House of Lords Record Office, and they are important not least because they provide the texts of all the private acts. They constitute the definitive record of all acts of Parliament.[51]

From the sixteenth century onwards, there also survive Journals kept by the clerks of both Houses.[52] These developed very much as a working tool of the clerks, designed to help them keep abreast of parliamentary business, the appointment of committees, the progress of bills and so forth. Here, as in many other matters, the Lords led the way, with a Journal that survives continuously from 1510 and achieved a settled format from 1536 onwards. The Commons Journal is extant only from 1547, and it was not until 1660 that it assumed a standardised form that ceased to reflect the vagaries of individual clerks. It needs stressing that these Journals are the clerks' records of matters discussed, decisions reached, orders and letters issued, and bills read and passed. What they seldom contain is a record of debates.[53] They bear a closer resemblance to the minutes of meetings. Because they omit virtually all mention of debate and therefore dispute, they naturally create an impression of agreement and co-operation, and this is a major reason why revisionist historians, with their concentration on institutional sources such as the Journals, have been so struck by a sense of harmonious decision-making. It is worth adding that the Lords Journal is somewhat fuller than that for the Commons, in that it helpfully includes a list of those peers who were present on any given day.

The Journals of the two Houses were published in printed editions in the late eighteenth and early nineteenth centuries.[54] But, although convenient, these printed versions cannot wholly take the place of the manuscripts from which they were derived. When the Manuscript Journals were printed the editors frequently introduced capitalisation, punctuation and lay-out not found in the originals. Even more disruptive is the fact that they sometimes changed the paragraphing, breaking up certain items of business or welding others together, and some items were omitted altogether. In the case of the Lords, there also survive the Draft Journals, from which the final version was prepared, and the even earlier stage known as the Manuscript Minutes (sometimes also called 'Scribbled Books'), which are the notes compiled by the clerks either during the actual sittings of the Lords or immediately afterwards. These earlier stages can sometimes give a more accurate indication of the order in which business was taken, and they can also contain deleted material omitted in the subsequent versions of the Journal.[55]

For the Commons, by contrast, we possess only the Manuscript Journals: the Minute Books were almost all lost in the fire that engulfed the old Palace of Westminster in 1834.[56] That fire destroyed a large part of the archives relating to the Commons, including a vast collection of sessional and judicial papers used by the House or arising from its work, although some of these can be partially reconstructed from other sources, especially the equivalent records for the House of Lords, known as the Main Papers. These survived because they were stored in a separate building across Old Palace Yard, the Jewel Tower, which escaped the fire. The Main Papers are arranged in a vast chronological sequence and, importantly, they include the records of the Lords' activities as a court of law.[57] These papers are highly significant for our period because the House resumed its judicial power in 1621 after a period of disuse, and they have only recently begun to receive the scholarly attention that they deserve.[58]

There is, unfortunately, no seventeenth-century equivalent of *Hansard* – no official transcripts of parliamentary debates.[59] Instead, for information about what was *said* in the Houses during the seventeenth century we are forced back primarily onto the private diaries kept by certain members. Here the records of the two Houses are the reverse of the situation regarding the Journals and sessional papers, in that we have far more diaries for the Commons than the Lords. For the Lords, such material is decidedly thin, and some of the most important sources remain unpublished.[60] By contrast, for certain seventeenth-century Parliaments we have numerous private diaries that record aspects of proceedings in the Commons.[61] Yet, as Sir Geoffrey Elton, Colin Brooks and especially John Morrill have cautioned us, these sources pose considerable problems for historians.[62]

In the first place, the diaries cannot be treated as accurate transcripts of what an individual speaker actually said on a given day. Their accounts of the same speech can often differ dramatically, and there is no straightforward way to determine whether one diary is likely to be closer than another to the original words spoken. Members kept diaries in a variety of ways and for a range of different reasons. In some cases we have the notes that they actually wrote – often in extremely cramped conditions[63] – during proceedings, whereas others probably made fair copies at some later date. Some kept diaries as sources of information that could then be shared with patrons, allies and friends; for others the main concern was to take down only such detail as seemed useful or interesting to them. Still others sought to create an *aide-mémoire* for their own later use, while some were motivated mainly by a fascination with the institution of Parliament. Each diary necessarily reflects the particular biases, attitudes and preoccupations of the member concerned, as well as the motives that led him to compile it.

Nor is there any guarantee that speeches recorded in these private diaries were even delivered. In the early 1640s, Sir Simonds D'Ewes' diary contains many long and finely-wrought speeches ostensibly by himself, but which are not corroborated by other sources: it is possible that much of his diary represents a retrospective fantasy of what he would have liked to have said had he had the nerve or opportunity to do so – that he was what John Morrill has called 'the Walter Mitty of the Long Parliament'.[64] Even in less extreme cases than D'Ewes, there was often a temptation for diarists to hone or embellish their own speeches. By the same token, the absence of references to a speech in the diaries does not necessarily prove that it was never given. Diarists tended, naturally enough, to focus on the most colourful, dramatic and memorable moments in Parliament. The more prosaic and routine business receded into the background, yet it was probably more representative of what proceedings were like most of the time: disputes and dramas were worth recording precisely because they were exceptional. This helps to explain why Neale, who based his account of Elizabethan Parliaments primarily on the surviving private diaries, drew such consistent attention to moments of conflict. More generally, when historians quote from the diaries they often select the most vivid or eye-catching version of a phrase, but that is not necessarily the most reliable.

The private diaries are thus more complex and problematic sources than they initially appear. Although at one level the difficulties resemble those inherent in all primary sources,[65] the diverse nature and provenance of the diaries, and the fact that they seem to offer such an appealingly direct contact with the words of the past, do generate distinctive obstacles of their own.[66] Yet these are not insurmountable, and provided that their complexities and limitations are remembered the diaries can still yield much useful information. Jack Hexter urged the importance of carefully collating the various recorded versions of speeches and applying existing scholarly conventions for quotation from primary sources: he suggested that difficulties were best dealt with on an *ad hoc* basis and should not deter us from quoting from the diaries.[67] More recently, John Morrill has provided a very helpful set of guidelines for the reconstruction of what was said in seventeenth-century Parliaments, drawing out the above problems and suggesting ways to guard against them. In particular, he has urged historians not to prefer one account to another unless there are very good reasons for doing so, and, when faced with several different versions, to collate and paraphrase rather than quote directly from a single source which may be misleading.[68]

A number of Morrill's guidelines are also applicable to the texts of particular speeches that circulated either in manuscript or, increasingly as the century wore on, in print. It was regarded as a breach of parliamentary privilege (which upheld the secrecy of proceedings) to publish reports of speeches and debates without special permission. However, these 'separates', together with growing numbers of newsletters and newsbooks, responded to considerable and widespread interest in parliamentary proceedings and had a significant impact on the formation of public opinion.[69] But precisely for that reason speeches reported in this way were often embellished and rewritten, and sometimes had never been delivered at all. This became even more of a problem after the early 1640s, when the abolition of existing controls on printing enforced through the Court of Star Chamber led to a proliferation of printed 'separates'. But, as Alan Cromartie has shown, a significant proportion of these items were fabrications.[70] To take one very important example, 15 of the 33 speeches attributed to John Pym between November 1640 and October 1643 were probably fabricated.[71] It is often extremely difficult to sort out which editions were actually authorised by the members who allegedly delivered them, let alone how closely they resembled the speeches as originally given.

Similar problems bedevil the vast assortment of material printed for Parliament during the 1640s and 1650s. Sheila Lambert has produced a magisterial listing of items printed either by order of Parliament or with Parliament's permission.[72] This differentiates such items from the many that appeared without any authorisation. Lambert shows that official printing for Parliament began in May 1641, and that it thereafter served a variety of purposes, from the dissemination of propaganda on behalf of the Parliamentarian cause to the recording of ordinances and public acts. Unfortunately, a reconstruction of such printing is hampered by the failure of the Journals of the two Houses to record all of the orders to print, and by the fact that no official collection of such material was compiled. Another very striking phenomenon is the marked decrease of printing for Parliament from the Restoration until well into the eighteenth century, a development possibly linked to the association of such material with the turmoil of the revolutionary decades.

An institution that related to so many different aspects of government and national life as did Parliament has naturally left many traces in a wide variety of other sources. So diverse and many-sided were its functions that material relating to the history of Parliament survives in a host of private and public archives and libraries. But the above account at least delineates the most salient categories of records: it shows something of their range and also the particular problems that they present. It is now time to turn to the history of the institution that can be reconstructed from them.

PART

I

THE PARLIAMENT OF ENGLAND

|2|

Membership, attendance and representation

One of the first steps in analysing any institution must surely be to identify the members who comprised it and to explain how they came to be there. This chapter will address four closely connected questions. First, who sat in the two Houses of Parliament during the course of the seventeenth century? Second, by what right did they do so and how, in the case of the Commons, did they come to be chosen? Third, how regularly did they attend? Finally, in the case of the Commons, how representative were they, and of whom, and what were their relations with their constituents? This last question will lead us into a broader consideration of the interaction of Parliament with the wider world: what was the relationship between parliamentary politics and trends in public opinion in the nation as a whole? The first three questions will be examined for the Lords and Commons in turn; the fourth problem will form the subject of a final section.

The House of Lords

Questions of membership and attendance are much more straightforward to answer for the Lords than the Commons. To attend the Lords required a personal summons from the monarch. This was normally extended to three categories of persons. The first were the lords spiritual: the Archbishops of Canterbury and York and 24 bishops. Secondly, there were the lords temporal, who comprised the hereditary peers, together with the greatest officers of state, the Lord Chancellor (or Lord Keeper), who presided over the Lords, the Lord Treasurer, the Lord President of the Council and the Lord Privy Seal. The Prince of Wales might also attend, as Prince Charles did regularly in the Parliaments of 1621 and 1624.[1] Finally, there were the senior judges and legal officers of the Crown, most notably the Masters in Chancery, the Judges of King's Bench and Common Pleas, the Attorney-General, the Solicitor-General, the Master of the Rolls, the Chief Baron of the Exchequer, and the King's serjeants-at-law. These judges and legal officers attended as 'assistants': they were entitled to contribute when called upon for advice and to act as advisers to committees, but they could neither speak (unless called upon to contribute) nor vote. Their expertise on legal matters often proved invaluable, especially in drafting and amending legislation and in conducting the judicial business of the House.[2]

The lords temporal were the most complex of these categories. They consisted of five degrees of nobility: in descending order, dukes, marquesses, earls, viscounts and barons. Although a summons to attend the Lords was seen as an essential attribute of noble status, it was usual for a few peers not to receive summonses by dint of being minors, insane, imprisoned, impoverished or overseas. However, by the early seventeenth century the peers regarded a summons as a matter not of the King's discretion but of right unless they fell into one of the above categories. It was, in Henry Elsynge's words, 'an essential point of inheritable honour'.[3] The Lords increasingly asserted their right to regulate their own membership, and Charles I's occasional attempts to withhold a writ of summons for political reasons – for example from the Earl of Bristol and Bishop Williams of Lincoln in 1626, or from Saye, Brooke and Mandeville in the Short Parliament – encountered fierce resistance as a breach of privilege.[4]

The membership of the Lords was, nevertheless, under the Crown's control to a far greater degree than the Commons. The lords spiritual, the officers of state, and the judges and legal officers, were all royal appointees. Although not servile placemen, the majority could reasonably be expected to support the Crown on many matters. Furthermore, monarchs could create new peers at will, or elevate existing ones within the peerage. Elizabeth I had been notoriously reluctant to make new peers, and there were only 55 lay peers by the time of her death in 1603. James I expanded the lay peerage to 81 by 1615 and to 104 in 1625. The early years of Charles I's reign saw further creations, and by 1628 the figure had increased to 126.[5] A significant number of these Caroline creations, especially before the Parliaments of 1626 and 1628, clearly reflected a desire to bolster support for the Crown within the Upper House: Sir Benjamin Rudyerd called them 'cardinals to carry the consistory'.[6] Likewise, in 1641 the King was alleged to have created several new barons in a bid to save Strafford's life.[7] The creation of new peers, together with the fact that over a quarter of peerage families became extinct in the male line roughly every 25 years, ensured considerable turnover in the families who sat in the Lords. In 1625, only 45 of the 104 lay peers held titles created before 1603; by 1640 the figure was 41 of 123. On the eve of the Civil War, Stuart creations thus constituted 66.6 per cent of the peerage.[8]

The political turmoil of the 1640s drastically affected the composition of the Lords. During the autumn of 1641, as opinion within both Houses became more and more polarised, Charles I tried to mobilise the bishops to form a nucleus of loyal supporters in the Lords.[9] But this only raised anti-episcopal sentiment to such a pitch that Charles was forced to assent to a bill excluding bishops from the Upper House in February 1642.[10] With their exclusion and the withdrawal of the Royalist peers, the Lords was reduced to a potential nucleus of around 30 by the end of 1642. By an ordinance of 29 June 1644, no member of either House who had once deserted the Parliamentarian cause could be readmitted without the consent of both Houses.[11] The upheavals of the Civil War thus significantly diminished the numbers who were regarded as eligible to sit in the Lords, quite apart from the question of how many of these actually attended.[12]

At the Restoration, the House of Lords was restored in exactly the same form as before the Civil War. The lords spiritual once again took their places in 1661,[13] as did all those lay peers created by Charles II or his father since May 1642 who were still living. In November 1661, 132 lords temporal were summoned to Parliament. In 1678, all but two of the 19 Catholic peers refused to comply with the terms of the second Test Act and were excluded from the Lords, leaving the total in that year at 147, but by 1685 the figure had risen to 153. The experiences of the revolutionary decades, and especially the abolition of the House for 11 years, understandably made the Lords even more defensive of their rights than before. Unlike his father, Charles II never tried to withhold a writ of summons from a peer, but when he twice attempted to summon minors whom he thought likely supporters, on both occasions the House debarred them from taking their seats. Roughly two-thirds of those on whom Charles conferred titles were former Royalists, or from Royalist families, and sympathetic to the established Church.[14] James II only created four new peers during his short reign:[15] his bid to 'pack' the Commons was not accompanied by the large-scale creation of new nobles, and a list of May 1687 indicates that 85 peers were hostile towards the proposed repeal of the penal legislation against Catholics, whereas 19 were doubtful and 57 (of whom 22 were Catholic) were supportive.[16] There were, it seems, secret plans to 'pack' the Upper House, but they never materialised.[17]

All the figures given above relate to the numbers of peers summoned to the Lords; the proportion who actually attended was much smaller. Relatively low attendances in the Lords had been an endemic problem during the Middle Ages and the early sixteenth century. However, from around the 1530s onwards, attendance seems to have improved somewhat.[18] In the first four sessions of James I's first Parliament, attendance never fell below 50 per cent, and was frequently higher.[19] There was apparently a slight tailing off in the Parliaments of 1621–9, when attendance in the Lords was rarely over 60, and often considerably less.[20] This trend continued into the Long Parliament, when even during the unprecedented crisis of 1640–1 the average attendance varied between 53 and 63.[21] From early 1642 onwards attendance declined steeply as the bishops were excluded and the Royalist peers left Westminster: the average attendance fell from 59 in January 1642 to 41 in March, and to 15 by December. After the outbreak of the Civil War, some peers took up arms for Parliament. By 1644 the average attendance in the Lords had fallen to 13–18.[22] The King was doing rather better: when he summoned an alternative Parliament to Oxford in January 1644, about 40 peers attended.[23] At Westminster, the Lords recovered slightly thereafter, reaching an average of 17–20 for most of 1646. However, during the second half of 1647 average attendance fell to between eight and 12. For most of the following year it hovered at around ten, but by December 1648 it had dropped to about six, prompting one newspaper to mock that the peers 'sit and tell tales by the fireside to drive away the time'. In the five or so weeks of 1649 prior to its abolition, attendance in the Lords averaged four or five.[24]

After the Restoration, the attendance of peers improved slightly, but on average rarely exceeded about half those summoned. The average attendance between 1660 and 1681 stood at 74.[25] As in earlier periods, there was a marked tendency for attendance to dwindle towards the end of sessions, as the business of the House shifted from public policy to judicial matters and private legislation. However, the number of peers who never attended the Lords at all remained fairly small, and the most common reason for absence – understandable enough in a House whose average age during Charles II's reign was 50 – appears to have been genuine ill health.[26]

As in most institutions, it fell to a relatively small core of 'regulars' to shoulder the main burden of business. In the Parliaments of the 1620s, only 14 peers were appointed to more than 30 per cent of the committees created during those sessions in which they participated.[27] Between 11 January and 10 April 1641, 31 committees were appointed, staffed by 66 individual peers. But only 16 peers were appointed to ten or more committees, 25 were appointed to three or less, and 24 of those known to have attended were not appointed to any. The situation between 29 November 1641 and 26 March 1642 was very similar: 64 committees appointed, staffed by 66 peers, of whom 16 sat on 15 or more. Twenty-seven were appointed to three or less, and 24 of those known to have attended were not appointed to any.[28] Throughout the century, Privy Councillors remained an important element within this core of particularly active members. The vast majority of members of the Privy Council sat in the Lords rather than the Commons: 18 out of 24 in 1604, 24 out of 30 in 1625, 24 out of 29 in 1660.[29] Privy Councillors frequently chaired committees and managed conferences with the Commons.[30] This meant that the Houses never sat on Sundays, when the Privy Council met, or during meetings of the Court of Star Chamber during the law terms.[31] Many peers, including some of the Privy Councillors, also held senior offices at Court, such as Lord Steward or Lord Chamberlain: of the 123 lay peers in 1640, 28 either held office at Court or were closely associated with the Court by personal attendance or friendship.[32] The membership of the Lords underlines the extent to which royal government in early seventeenth-century England was personal government: the same individuals wore a number of different hats and could be encountered as members of the Lords, Privy Councillors, officers of state or senior figures within the legal profession. This doubling up of roles greatly assisted communication between the different institutions of government and helped them to form a coherent whole.[33]

The House of Commons

The membership and attendance of the Commons are altogether more difficult to reconstruct. Its members did not represent constituents in any direct numerical sense. Rather, they represented particular communities, and can be divided into two groups. Every county in England sent two members (and every Welsh county one) known as knights of the shire, giving a total of 90 in 1603. This figure remained unchanged until 1673, when the county palatine of Durham gained the right to send two members.[34] Far more numerous were the so-called burgesses, two members sent by each borough (one for each Welsh borough) that had been enfranchised either by royal charter or by statute. The number of such boroughs grew considerably under the Tudors, so that the burgesses increased from 219 in 1485 to 372 in 1603. This expansion continued, though rather more slowly, throughout the seventeenth century, reaching 417 in 1640 and 421 in 1689. The overall size of the Commons thus increased from 462 in 1603 to 507 in 1640 and 513 in 1689.[35]

The traumas of the 1640s and 1650s profoundly affected the composition of the Commons. During the Civil Wars large numbers of members left Westminster to rally to the King or to return to their localities. Over a hundred attended the Oxford Parliament which Charles I summoned in January 1644.[36] In December 1648, the army purged what remained of the Commons at Westminster: Colonel Thomas Pride arrested 45 members and secluded 186, while a further 86 withdrew in protest. That left the so-called Rump

Parliament of just over 200 members which survived until 1653 (although only 60–70 were at all active).[37] After the brief interlude of the 144-strong Nominated Assembly,[38] three Protectorate Parliaments were called under the terms set out in the Instrument of Government of December 1653. These were unusual among seventeenth-century Parliaments in two respects. First, in a bid to secure the election of men loyal to the regime, they saw the partial introduction of reforms that drew on earlier Leveller proposals for parliamentary reapportionment. The distribution of seats was drastically rearranged in favour of the counties and away from the boroughs: of the 400 English and Welsh members, 259 were knights and only 141 burgesses. The county franchise was redefined to comprise all those who possessed real or personal property worth £200 or more except for Catholics, abettors of the Irish Rebellion and all others involved in any war against the Parliament since 1 January 1642.[39] Secondly, these Parliaments also included up to 30 representatives from each of Scotland and Ireland, in recognition of the formation of an integrated British Republic in 1652–4.[40] These reforms were partially abandoned for the elections to the third Protectorate Parliament,[41] and after 1660 the distribution of seats was restored to exactly what it had been immediately prior to the outbreak of the Civil War.[42]

The burgesses thus once again outnumbered the knights by over four to one. What were the reasons for this steady enfranchisement of new boroughs? For the sixteenth century, Norman Ball's research has recently gone some way towards reasserting the older argument advanced by Neale that the principal reason for most creations lay in the Crown's need to find seats for reliable members who could offer assistance and support.[43] Alastair Hawkyard, on the other hand, has shown that the large number of early sixteenth-century enfranchisements stemmed mainly from the Crown's wish to make the Commons representative of as many parts of England and Wales as possible. Hawkyard demonstrates that this coincided with a growing conviction among the local gentry that membership of the Commons should be regarded as an honour rather than a burden and, as Elton argued, Tudor enfranchisements were in part a response to a heightened demand for seats among the gentry.[44] This demand persisted after 1603, but it seems that the Crown's willingness to enlarge the Commons gradually diminished. Although James I enfranchised the Universities of Oxford and Cambridge and six other boroughs between 1603 and 1615, he called a halt there. In 1624 he declared that 'our number in the Lower House is already too great',[45] and argued that there were 'many burgesses that come to Parliament from boroughs quite decayed', such as Old Sarum 'where there is nothing but conies'.[46] Under the Stuarts the Crown and its advisers exerted much less pressure to create further seats than in the previous century. However, local nobility and gentry apparently pressed for further constituencies to be added, and they secured the assistance of antiquarians like William Hakewill in identifying towns whose medieval right to return members had fallen into disuse. No fewer than 15 such borough constituencies were restored between 1621 and 1641.[47] The situation was more stable during Charles II's reign, which saw the addition of only six new seats.[48] Thereafter, no further constituencies were created until the Great Reform Act of 1832.

All of these figures represent the maximum numbers of seats in the Commons; the actual numbers that attended were considerably lower. Unfortunately, we have no systematic way of measuring attendances because, unlike the Lords Journal, the Commons Journal does not list those present on a particular day. Instead, all we have to go on are the numbers indicated as voting in divisions. When the House voted on a motion, those in favour went outside into an antechamber while those against remained seated; there was thus no way of abstaining in this period, which means that the sum of 'ayes' and 'noes' gives the total present at that moment. Throughout the seventeenth century perhaps around a fifth of members never attended the House; and there were many more who arrived late or departed early. On two days during the 1621 Parliament there were more than 300 members present, but for the remainder of the time attendance never reached 170.[49] During the 1640s, it was rare for more than 250 members of the Long Parliament to be present, and the average attendance was probably in the region of 125.[50] In the Protectorate Parliaments, average attendances ranged between 28 and 49 per cent: the combined average for all three was 33 per cent.[51] The situation after the Restoration was fairly similar. Rarely were more than 300 members present, and then usually only for really significant or contentious votes.[52] As in the Lords, there tended to be a hard core of members who were particularly active. The joint committees that were so crucial to the organisation of the Parliamentarian war effort during the Civil Wars tended to be dominated by certain members who became almost full-time 'committee-men'.[53] During the 18-year Cavalier Parliament, more than half the members were appointed to few or no committees, and over two-thirds made no recorded speeches.[54] It is likely that the core of active members of the Commons who spoke regularly or served on committees became gradually less dominated by Privy Councillors and office-holders as the century progressed, and the readiness of non-officers to act in these ways bears out the continuing value of Parliament as a forum for advancing local or sectional interests.[55] It is also important to remember, when analysing the core of active members, that there were basic physical constraints on the numbers who attended the Lower House. St Stephen's Chapel within the Palace of Westminster, where the Commons met until 1834, could comfortably seat little more than 200 members.[56]

The processes by which members of the Commons came to be chosen have been the subject of vigorous debate between historians. The franchise varied considerably between constituencies. In the shires, the electorate had been defined since 1430 as the '40 shilling freeholders' – those who owned freehold land worth at least 40 shillings per annum. Although the numbers who fell above this threshold varied greatly from place to place, monetary inflation during the sixteenth and early seventeenth centuries had the effect of increasing the county electorate considerably. By contrast, the much greater number of urban constituencies possessed a wide range of different types of franchises. By 1641 the most common sort vested the franchise in the freemen of the borough; elsewhere, the electorate comprised the members of the corporation, or those who possessed certain levels of wealth or particular types of property (burgage tenures, for example); in a few cases it included all those actually resident in the borough.[57] This diversity of franchise meant that the actual number of voters in borough elections could vary from over two thousand to less than ten.[58]

Derek Hirst has argued that the early Stuart electorate was considerably larger and more politically volatile than was often supposed.[59] Totals are extremely difficult to estimate, but Hirst suggests that, in all, perhaps about one third of adult males, and a few widows who owned sufficient property, would have been enfranchised by the early 1640s. In particular, there was a trend for the franchises in many towns to become more 'open' and, as members remained in some measure accountable to their constituents, this meant that it became more difficult for patrons to control elections and increasingly candidates had to appeal directly to electors. As a result, the electorate became more politically aware and involved with national issues, and this brought an increase in the number of contested elections, especially in the counties and the larger boroughs where there were most electors. Hirst argues that the number of such contested elections increased from 13 in 1604 to 86 in the autumn of 1640.[60]

It is the nature and incidence of those parliamentary elections that proved to be the most controversial aspect of Hirst's thesis. Mark Kishlansky has argued strongly that actual elections, in the sense of a contest between candidates leading to a poll or vote among electors, were the exception rather than the rule in early seventeenth-century England. He suggests that the vast majority – perhaps well over 90 per cent – of members were chosen by a process of selection in which nobles, gentry and/or aldermen presented electors with candidates whom they were invited to acclaim. He argues that 'contested elections were the failures', which only occurred when the normative processes of selection by patrons and then endorsement by electors broke down. Electoral contests were regarded as highly undesirable: they brought dishonour upon the contestants and disrupted the harmony of communities. Instead, as in so many other aspects of early Stuart political culture, ideas of harmony and deference, and the role of patronage, were of crucial significance.[61]

This provides a context for John K. Gruenfelder's conclusion that between 1604 and 1628 perhaps 24–30 per cent of Commons seats were filled by nominees of the peerage.[62] Two case-studies will serve briefly to illustrate how this worked. First of all, John Pym owed his seat as a member for Tavistock (Devon) in the Parliaments of 1624, 1625, 1626, 1628–9 and in the Short and Long Parliaments to the patronage of Francis Russell, fourth Earl of Bedford. Pym came from a Somerset family and had no direct connection with Tavistock: it is doubtful whether he could have secured the seat, even in 1640, but for the fact that Bedford was Lord Lieutenant and Custos Rotulorum of Devon, and owned extensive lands in and around Tavistock.[63] Pym was thus, in John Morrill's words, 'a carpetbagger for a pocket borough'.[64] Similar points can be made about Sir Benjamin Rudyerd, who owed his return for Portsmouth (1621, 1624, 1625), and then for the Wiltshire constituencies of Old Sarum (1626), Downton (1628–9), and Wilton (1640–8) to William and Philip Herbert, third and fourth Earls of Pembroke. The third Earl was Lord Lieutenant of Wiltshire and Captain of Portsmouth Castle; after his death in 1630 he was succeeded in these offices by his younger brother who became fourth Earl. Their seat was at Wilton House, and during this period the Earls of Pembroke nominated both members for Wilton and at least one for each of the three other constituencies that Rudyerd represented.[65] Such electoral influence by peers was an important element in the process of parliamentary selection that Kishlansky sees as characteristic of the early Stuart period.

Kishlansky goes on to argue, however, that this pattern declined during the second half of the century as a result of the upheavals of the 1640s and 1650s. He suggests that during the revolutionary decades it became impossible to contain ideological divisions, and that as a result a different political culture emerged, one that tolerated conflict and accepted electoral contests as a legitimate way to choose members of the Commons. It was recognised that unanimity was very difficult to attain, and polling came to be seen as the normal means to settle a dispute. As a result, contested elections became much more common: on average, there were contests in about a third of counties in each general election between 1661 and 1689. Kishlansky sees this development as closely associated with the emergence of political parties and of a new culture which separated political competition from social relationships. He concludes that 'it is to the mid-seventeenth century that we must look to understand the origins of participatory democracy'.[66]

Kishlansky's thesis is very striking and persuasive, and it makes a great deal of sense of the overall shape of the seventeenth century. To some extent his dispute with Hirst may be more apparent than real, in that the latter always recognised that contested elections were in the minority. However, it would be fair to say that Hirst devoted a disproportionate amount of attention to them, and that Kishlansky offers the more satisfying survey of the ways in which early Stuart members of the Commons were chosen. He gets the contested elections into perspective, without in fact suggesting that their numbers were drastically smaller than had been supposed. He only refutes around 20 of the 300 or so contests that have been claimed for the period 1603–40, but he does offer a fundamental reinterpretation of their significance. Of course, some of these scholarly disagreements depend on how a contest is defined. Kishlansky uses the very clear definition of the presence of more than two candidates on the day of an election, necessitating a poll or vote. However, it was sometimes extremely difficult to distinguish between 'elections' and 'selections': patrons were generally well advised to select candidates who would be acceptable to voters, while at the election, a final assertion of unanimity for form's sake sometimes concealed earlier divisions. Some of these classifications become very ambiguous indeed.[67]

It is certainly possible that Kishlansky has somewhat overdrawn the contrast between the periods before 1640 and after 1660: in particular there may have been more signs of political contention and division under the early Stuarts than he allows. The elements of continuity may have been greater, the transformation less stark.[68] Nevertheless, electoral contests clearly did become more frequent, and attitudes towards them changed. Instead of being perceived as unfortunate breakdowns of the normative system of selection, used only as a last resort to resolve deadlock, they became accepted as an appropriate way to choose parliamentary representatives. Political culture was markedly different during the later seventeenth century: there was less expectation of consensus, more acknowledgement of division. The politics of party gradually began to emerge. All these shifts were closely reflected in the mechanisms by which members came to be chosen.

Representation and public opinion

Ultimately, the debate over elections and selections forces us to look more closely at the relationship between members of Parliament and their constituents. We need to examine the background and identity of members in order to assess how representative they were of the electorate. It is also important to get a fuller sense of the issues and concerns that mattered to electors: what did they expect of members, and how far were the latter held to account?

This in turn will lead us to examine the nature of public opinion and its interaction with parliamentary politics.

Although in one sense the Lords sat as the King's 'natural counsellors', and thus represented only themselves, many regarded the Upper House as no less representative than the Lower. Several peers expressed a belief that it was their duty to serve the public in Parliament, or at any rate the property owners among the nobility, gentry and 40 shilling freeholders. There were clearly a number who felt a strong public responsibility to safeguard property and liberties as well as to redress local and national grievances.[69] In 1667, the Bishop of Durham argued against the enfranchisement of that county on the grounds that he could quite adequately represent it from the Lords.[70] However strange such sentiments may sound today, they made sense in the hierarchical and patriarchal society of seventeenth-century England, and there is no reason to doubt the sincerity of those who uttered them.

It was, however, the members of the Commons who were most central to Parliament's claim to represent 'the body of the whole realm'.[71] Yet an analysis of the social profile of members immediately reveals that the Commons were an extension of the landed elite represented in the Lords rather than generically different from it. The proportion of members who were sons of peers remained fairly constant throughout the century at 8 or 9 per cent.[72] By far the largest category – which comprised around 50 per cent in Elizabethan Parliaments and about 53 per cent towards the end of the seventeenth century – were landed gentry.[73] The proportion of lawyers registered little change and remained consistently around 14–15 per cent, but the proportion of merchants declined slightly from 11 per cent in 1640 to 9 per cent after the Restoration.[74] Of course, a significant number of these lawyers and merchants were also members of gentry families, so that in all by the later seventeenth century over three-quarters of members can be classified as county gentry.[75] Thus, apart from a tendency for the dominance of the gentry to become even more marked, the overall social complexion of the Commons did not alter dramatically during the seventeenth century.[76] It is also worth adding that the members who were nominated to the Nominated Assembly and returned to the Protectorate Parliaments reflected a shift *within* the gentry – towards the lesser gentry – rather than *away from* the gentry altogether.[77]

An examination of the office-holding of members of the Commons provides further evidence of the continued dominance of the propertied elite. Of the 507 original members of the Long Parliament, 22 per cent held office at Court or in royal administration of some kind. At a local level, fewer than 1 per cent served as Lords Lieutenant, 15 per cent as Deputy Lieutenants, 24 per cent as sheriffs, and 43 per cent as JPs. Between 1660 and 1690, the proportion of government officials fluctuated considerably, between about 6 and 16 per cent. Four per cent were Lords Lieutenant, 47 per cent Deputy Lieutenants and 13 per cent sheriffs, while the proportion of JPs rose dramatically to 85 per cent.[78] For comparison, in the Elizabethan period, approximately 35 per cent of members had been government officials, 3 per cent Lords Lieutenant, 12 per cent Deputy Lieutenants, 10 per cent sheriffs, and 60 per cent JPs.[79] There was thus a gradual increase in the proportions of members who served as Deputy Lieutenants or JPs between the later sixteenth and later seventeenth centuries, and a corresponding decline in the proportion who held office in central government. These figures also underline the point that both central and local government in early modern England rested with a relatively small elite whose members combined a number of different roles. As Conrad Russell has written, 'the sort of men who assembled at Westminster were not widely different in character and outlook from the same men as they have become familiar to us as Justices of the Peace'.[80] The fact that they wore several 'hats' made their co-operation with the Crown all the more essential for the smooth running of government.

The residential relationship of members to their constituencies provides another useful yardstick for how representative they were. Here again the trend was for the county gentry to become even more dominant. Throughout the century, nearly all knights of the shire were resident in the counties they represented. By contrast, between 1603 and 1640 only about 23 per cent of burgesses actually lived in the boroughs for which they sat. Fifty per cent lived nearby, or at least in the same county, but no fewer than 27 per cent came from outside the county.[81] Although this proportion of 'foreigners'[82] may sound high, it is worth noting that it represented a significant drop from the Elizabethan Parliaments, when the corresponding percentages were 25, 34 and 41 per cent.[83] The later seventeenth century saw a decrease in the number of both the borough residents and the 'foreigners', to an average of about 18 per cent each. The dominance of the county gentry, on the other hand, reached a new high of around 64 per cent.[84] Possibly the most significant conclusion that can be drawn from these figures is that there was a long-term trend away from returning members who did not at least live in the same county.

There is plentiful anecdotal evidence to support this view. As the century progressed noble patrons found it harder and harder to secure the election of their clients where they were not residents of either borough or county. For example, when recommending candidates to boroughs in Sussex and Norfolk in the 1620s and in 1640, the Earl of Dorset went out of his way to stress that they were 'countrymen' of the borough inhabitants. But this strategy sometimes failed when, as at Great Yarmouth early in 1640, the candidate was not in fact resident within the county.[85] Those candidates who lived in the locality were highly valued as spokesmen for the 'country' (regularly used in this period as a synonym for 'county'), and the number of 'foreigners' returned to the Commons declined steadily from 132 in 1624, to 79 in the Long Parliament, to 68 by 1689.[86] Such concern to secure local representatives was entirely understandable: they were naturally better placed not only to express their constituents' grievances at Westminster but also to make use of all the opportunities that Parliament offered in the way of lobbying and promoting private legislation for the advancement of local interests. To take but one example from many: during the seventeenth century, the most pressing concerns of the voters at Rye in Sussex were to secure control of the lighthouse at Dungeness and to alleviate the progressive silting up of their harbour; local members were far more likely to appreciate the importance of these issues and to fight the town's corner in Parliament than someone from further afield.[87]

The corollary of this was that protégés of peers were more likely to be accepted when they were local, and such clients probably comprised about one quarter of the Commons during the seventeenth century.[88] But it was certainly wise for patrons to bear electors' concerns in mind during the selection of candidates if contested elections were to be avoided. In an important article, Richard Cust and Peter Lake have analysed Sir Richard Grosvenor's address as sheriff to electors before the uncontested Cheshire election of 1624. Grosvenor invited freeholders to approve the two recommended candidates, but did so

mainly on the grounds that they were committed Protestants, 'ripe in judgement, untainted in their religion ... without fear to utter their country's just
complaints and grievances'. Had the candidates been otherwise, then the freeholders would have been justified in rejecting them. For, as Grosvenor put it,
'freedom of voice is your inheritance and one of the greatest prerogatives of the
subject, which ought by all means to be kept inviolate and cannot be taken
away from you by any command whatsoever'.[89] Voters were thus acknowledged to be capable of making individual political choices: they were 'not simply voting fodder for the leading gentry'.[90]

Grosvenor's speech also indicates that it would be misleading to see the electorate as preoccupied mainly with local rather than national issues, or indeed
to erect a false dichotomy between the two. Richard Cust has shown how the
circulation of newsletters, copies of parliamentary speeches and verbal reports
of proceedings fostered a widespread awareness of national politics throughout early Stuart England.[91] He argues in particular that the later 1620s saw the
emergence of an intense anti-popery and a profound fear of religious innovation. From 1618 onwards, the European context of the Thirty Years War only
exacerbated anxieties that international Catholicism was rapidly advancing at
the expense of Protestantism. More generally, the political behaviour of
Charles I after 1625 raised fears that 'new counsels' were encouraging a more
authoritarian style of kingship. All these concerns can be discerned in the electoral politics of the later 1620s and in 1640; and although resentment of many
specific policies, such as the Forced Loan, reflected particularist grievances and
sensibilities, numerous private letters and diaries reveal a keen local interest in
the national scene.[92] Contemporaries usually did not draw a distinction
between local concerns and broader political issues: many people regarded the
two as interconnected, and saw the preservation of local interests as one aspect
of a more general defence of Protestantism and the subjects' liberties.[93]

The existence of informed and engaged public opinion is equally apparent
in the later seventeenth century. In 1665 it was reported that watermen
enquired about forthcoming business as they rowed peers to the Lords, while
eight years later a future Whig member of the Commons wrote that 'the common people talk anything, for every carman and porter is now a statesman'.[94]
Despite attempts to keep parliamentary proceedings secret, interest in them
was insatiable and became especially lively during periods of political turmoil,
such as the Exclusion Crisis of 1678–81. That crisis saw concerted efforts to
mobilise electoral opinion for or against exclusion: mass petitions were circulated and newsbooks proliferated.[95] By 1681 the embryonic Whig and Tory
parties were beginning to emerge. The Whig/Tory divide became steadily
sharper during the years that followed, and had a direct impact on the behaviour of the electorate. W. A. Speck has shown that in the growing number of
contested elections, 'the vast majority of voters cast their votes along party
lines'.[96] Although it would be anachronistic to see these parties as organised in
anything like a modern form, they nonetheless commanded the allegiance of
many within the electorate. Party issues thus served to integrate local and
national politics still further.

That process of integration raises the question of what happened after members had been returned. How accountable were they to their constituents?
Here again we should beware of imposing modern criteria upon the much
more fluid and diffuse reality of the seventeenth century. Nevertheless, there is
evidence that a number of members kept their constituencies informed of

parliamentary developments on both national and local questions. There was
clearly an expectation in some constituencies that members would send reports
of proceedings, although exactly how much bearing this practice had upon the
behaviour of members at Westminster is much less clear. The extent to which
they received explicit political instructions from constituents varied considerably from time to time, and probably only reached significant levels during
major crises. Thus, in the opening stages of the Long Parliament several members presented petitions or statements of grievances from constituents, while in
the elections for the Oxford Parliament of 1681 over 20 boroughs sent
addresses thanking their members for their services and recommending them to
support certain measures in the Commons.[97] But in less turbulent times, such
'instructions' were much less common. A good example of a constituency in
which they did occur was Great Yarmouth, where after each election a committee was appointed 'to advise and give instruction to the burgesses about
such matters as shall be holden to be dealt in . . . for the general good of the
town'.[98] However, the usual pattern was that members were not formally 'man-
dated', nor was their return ever conditional upon acceptance of such 'instructions'.[99] They always remained free agents able to speak or vote as their
consciences dictated: Edward Seymour declared in 1680 that 'gentlemen come
not here with resolutions, but to take them upon clear debate of things'.[100]

Rather, such 'accountability' as there was often worked in more informal
ways. There is some evidence that members who were consistently found
wanting as champions of local interests, or whose stance on national issues did
not accord with that of the majority of electors, were liable to suffer the consequences at the next selection or election. Another way in which local developments could indirectly influence the political behaviour of members was
simply by the information that came to them. For example, it is unlikely that
Sir Edward Dering would have 'defected' from supporting the campaign for
root-and-branch reform quite so suddenly during the summer of 1641 had he
not received reports from his Kentish constituents of spontaneous outbreaks of
iconoclasm that threatened an incipient collapse of public order if episcopacy
were to be abolished.[101] Dering's actions reflected a complex interaction
between local concerns and his own personal attitudes in a way that is impossible to separate.

In short, members of Parliament were in an unusually ambivalent position.
As we have seen, many of them held office at both local and national levels.
Just as the institution of Parliament provided a 'point of contact' between
Crown and subjects, so its members formed a linch-pin between centre and
locality. In Russell's words, they performed a 'dual role as champions of the
localities at the centre, and of the centre in the localities'.[102] Yet even this telling
aphorism does not quite capture the full complexity of members' activities, for
in Parliaments they were thought to have an obligation to the whole nation as
well as to their own 'country'. Sir Edward Coke once wrote that 'though [a
member] be chosen for one particular county or borough, yet when he is
returned and sit in Parliaments he serveth for the whole realm; for the end of
his coming thither, as in his writ of election appeareth, is general'.[103] This
Janus-faced role was the precise correlative of Parliament's function of welding
central and local government together into a single, organic whole. It was natural, therefore, that an inseparable blend of national and local concerns should
have guided the complex processes by which members of Parliament were
chosen.

John Miller has written that 'whatever its deficiencies, the House of Commons was more representative than almost any comparable institution in early modern Europe'.[104] Certainly much of Parliament's role in government, and perhaps especially its capacity to agree legislation and taxation with the Crown that were then binding on the subjects, depended on acceptance of its claim to be the 'representative of the people'. As we shall see, during the English Revolution such radical groups as the Levellers challenged this and demanded universal (male) suffrage.[105] But at other times, criticisms such as that of Sir Robert Sawyer – who declared on 28 January 1689 that 'we do not represent so many as the fourth part of the nation' – were generally voiced for immediate polemical reasons.[106] Far more prevalent was the view of Sir Edwin Sandys in 1607:

> the whole do join in making laws to govern the whole; for it is fit and just, that every man do join in making that which shall bind and govern him, and because every man cannot be personally present, therefore a representative body is made to perform that service.[107]

Conrad Russell, who has found 'no European equivalent' to Sandys' speech, observes that 'the English Parliament was highly unusual among European estates in that it was a national assembly and consequently enjoyed a hold on public and patriotic sentiment that many European estates would not enjoy'.[108] As we have seen, most members of the two Houses came from a common, landowning elite, united by family and patronage ties. Yet the fact that their claims to represent the whole realm could command widespread acceptance – and indeed be compared favourably with most continental assemblies – was of vital importance in underpinning Parliament's political authority and its relationship with the Crown.

|3|

Functions I: High Court and Great Council

Another striking contrast between the English Parliament and most continental institutions was the way in which it combined the role of a court of record with that of the monarch's Great Council. Parliament's activities as a court of law can be sub-divided into judicature (the administration of justice) and legislation (the creation of new statute law jointly by the two Houses and the monarch). Contemporaries perceived no clear distinction between judicature and legislation, and regarded the making and implementation of law as inseparably linked. Parliament thus formed the apex of the legal system as well as one of the councils that surrounded the monarch in overlapping concentric circles. As Sir John Doddridge put it, 'for the nature of a Parliament, it is *consilium*, and it is *curia*'.[1] This fusion of judicial, legislative and conciliar functions was virtually unique to the English Parliament, and is vital in explaining its political and constitutional role throughout the seventeenth century.

First of all, it is worth briefly examining how the physical layout of the Palace of Westminster reflected Parliament's functions as both High Court and Great Council (see the map on p. 33).[2] The central law courts met in and around Westminster Hall, the only part of the palace that survived the fire of 1834 and still stands today. The Courts of Common Pleas, Chancery and King's Bench met in their own designated areas within the Hall; the Court of Exchequer was housed in a building off the north-east end of the Hall, close to the Exchequer itself, while the Court of Wards lay at the south end of the Hall. Next door to the Court of Wards, running towards the River Thames, stood St Stephen's Chapel, where the House of Commons met from 1549 onwards. To the south, two further buildings housed the Court of Requests and the Painted Chamber, and beyond them was the House of Lords. The Court of Requests and the Painted Chamber were thus conveniently sited midway between the two Houses, and the latter was often used as the venue for joint conferences of the Lords and Commons. The High Court of Parliament was thus physically located in the same complex of buildings as the central law courts, a fact which underlined Parliament's status as a court of record and the highest court of appeal, and facilitated the transfer of cases between different courts.

The relationship between the monarch's Great Council and the Privy Council was also close. Until the sixteenth century, the Privy Council had often met in a building at the north end of the Palace of Westminster, standing on the east side of New Palace Yard and abutting the Thames. However, under the early Tudors this became used mainly for meetings of the Star

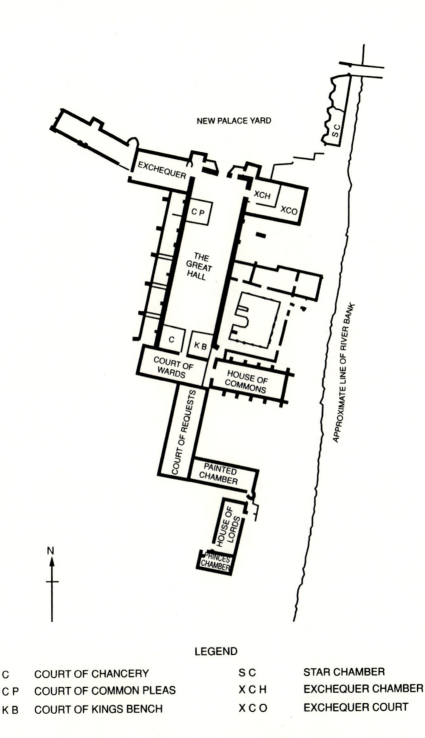

Outline map of the Palace of Westminster in the seventeenth century. Source: Willson H. Coates, Anne Steele Young and Vernon F. Snow (eds.), *The Private Journals of the Long Parliament* (3 vols., New Haven and London, 1982–92), I, 539.

Chamber (the Privy Council sitting as a court of law), and the Privy Council itself nearly always convened in the Council Chamber in the Palace of Whitehall. This was even more convenient for the monarch than the Palace of Westminster, and also reflected the considerable overlap of personnel between Court and Council. Nevertheless, the Privy Council still occasionally met in the Palace of Westminster in order to allow members to participate in parliamentary debates more conveniently. The central law courts and the three 'points of contact' thus met in close proximity to each other, a fact that underlines the symbiotic relationship between them which will emerge throughout this chapter.

Judicature

Contemporaries clearly recognised Parliament's identity as a court and referred frequently to the 'High Court of Parliament'.[3] In the 1570s Sir Thomas Smith called it the 'highest and most authentical court of England', while the serjeant-at-law, Sir Henry Finch, defined Parliament in 1613 thus:

> The Parliament is a court of the King and nobility and commons assembled, having an absolute power in all causes. As to make laws, to adjudge matters in law, to try causes of life and death, to reverse errors in the King's Bench, especially where any common mischief is, that by ordinary course of law, there is no means to remedy . . . And all their decrees are as judgements. And if the Parliament do err . . . it can no where be reversed but in Parliament.[4]

Similarly, Sir Edward Coke began *The Fourth Part of the Institutes of the Laws of England*, 'concerning the jurisdiction of Courts', with a discussion 'of the high and most honourable Court of Parliament'.[5]

The judicature of Parliament stemmed directly from its medieval origins as an extension of the King's Council. During the Middle Ages, one of the key functions of Parliaments was to hear petitions and to rule on legal cases. In the sixteenth century, however, the development of other law courts gradually eclipsed parliamentary judicature. In particular, the volume of business handled by Star Chamber, Chancery (the Lord Chancellor's Court, administering the system of law known as equity), and the common-law courts of King's Bench and Common Pleas expanded considerably and led to a corresponding decline in the number of cases brought before Parliament. Since these courts met regularly, litigants naturally preferred them to the occasional meetings of Parliament. However, the early seventeenth century saw a revival of parliamentary judicature which resoundingly demonstrated its continuing value and importance within the legal system.

That judicature can broadly be divided into two types, original and appellate, both of which were revived roughly simultaneously from 1621 onwards. Original judicature involved hearing cases that were being initiated for the first time, and could be exercised either by each House individually or by both Houses jointly. Each House could handle cases of privilege relating to its own members, and also had the right to try cases determining membership of that particular House. It was well established that members of the nobility charged with treason or a felony had the right to be tried by their peers. When Parliament was in session, this involved a trial by the full House of Lords presided over by the Lord High Steward; when Parliament was not sitting, the accused peer would be tried by a special court comprising the Lord High Steward and a body of peers chosen by the monarch. In such cases the Lords acted as both triers and judges.[6] The Lords could also hear petitions that involved deciding cases in the first instance, as well as receiving appeals from other courts.[7] The judicature of the Commons acting by itself was rather weaker because it lacked the power to hear evidence under oath. The Lower House could ensure the preservation of its members' privileges, but as far as trying criminal offenders was concerned, its judicial activity was restricted to procedures conducted by the two Houses jointly.

These joint criminal procedures took two main forms, attainder and impeachment. An attainder was an act of Parliament declaring an individual guilty of treason or some other felony. It had developed in the later fourteenth century and was employed with particular frequency during the second half of the fifteenth century and the first half of the sixteenth. In the Tudor period, attainders were invariably initiated by the monarch rather than the Houses.[8] The procedure was little used between 1603 and 1641, and especially during the 1620s it proved very difficult to secure the Lords' consent to several bills of attainder proposed by the Commons, including one against Roger Manwaring.[9] However, in 1641, attainder turned out to be the speediest and most appropriate way to remove Strafford, whose conviction under the existing law of treason was proving problematic.[10] Attainder had the particular advantage of bypassing common-law proceedings by a direct statutory imposition of the death sentence, and during the Civil Wars and Interregnum it provided Parliament with a valuable weapon against enemies as diverse as William Laud and John Lilburne.[11] However, this provoked a reaction after the Restoration in favour of upholding common-law rights of trial, and the last use of attainder to replace a common-law trial was in the case of Sir John Fenwick, who had plotted to assassinate William III, in 1696.[12]

The relatively infrequent use of acts of attainder during the early seventeenth century was closely related to the revival of the medieval procedure that came to be known as impeachment.[13] This procedure is thought to have originated in 1376, and the last medieval impeachment was that of Lord Stanley in 1459. Although exact proceedings varied to some extent from case to case, and the medieval precedents revealed diverse methods and procedures, the general pattern was for the Commons to present an accusation against an individual who would then be tried before the Lords. Impeachment fell into desuetude after 1459, but it was revived in 1621 and used against the monopolists Sir Francis Michell and Sir Giles Mompesson as well as against the Lord Chancellor, Sir Francis Bacon. In 1624 it was employed against Lord Treasurer Middlesex, and two years later Charles I dissolved Parliament in order to thwart an attempt to impeach Buckingham.[14] Between 1621 and 1805–6 there was a total of 54 cases of impeachment.[15] As Colin Tite has shown, the procedure was not definitively settled in 1621 and continued to evolve thereafter. However, from the late 1620s onwards the main stages of the impeachment process were pretty well established. The Commons would agree articles of impeachment and present them to the Lords; the accused made a formal answer, and the Commons then appointed managers to prepare evidence. A common-law trial would follow, presided over by the Lord High Steward (if a peer was accused) and otherwise by the Lord Chancellor or Lord Keeper. The Commons' managers presented their case, the counsel for the accused answered, witnesses were heard, and the peers then voted on the judgement to be given.[16]

Impeachment was particularly useful because it allowed the Houses to try to dislodge 'evil counsellors' and 'enemies of the commonwealth' without attacking the monarch personally. In part, it grew naturally out of the Commons' traditional role of identifying and reporting general grievances. The representative nature of the Commons, examined above,[17] helped to facilitate this process and lend it legitimacy. Coke argued in April 1624 that the Commons:

> appear for multitudes and bind multitudes . . . They are the representative body of the realm; for all the people are present in Parliament by person representative; and therefore, by the wisdom of the state, and by Parliament orders, the Commons are appointed the Inquisitors General of the grievances of the kingdom.[18]

Impeachment enabled the Commons to present their case against individuals who were accused of some grievance against the 'commonwealth', ranging from monopolies to 'evil counsel'. It also overcame the obstacle that the Commons could not hear testimony under oath. Although its common-law processes could not convict Strafford of treason – thereby necessitating recourse to attainder – in general during the seventeenth century the Houses found impeachment more flexible and widely appropriate than attainder. Another consideration may have been the fact that there were no sixteenth-century precedents for attainders being initiated by anyone except the monarch. It would be quite misleading to see impeachments as a vehicle for 'opposition' to the Crown or its servants: they often reflected conflicts between different factions within the Court and Privy Council, and they extended the politics of the Court and Council into Parliament.[19] This was particularly true of the attacks upon Bacon and Middlesex. However, when the King insisted on defending the accused – as Charles I did with Buckingham in 1626 and Strafford in 1641 – impeachment necessarily generated friction between the monarch and members of the Houses. To that extent, although this was probably not in the minds of the men who revived it in the early 1620s, impeachment could subsequently be used as a weapon against the Crown's servants, if necessary in direct contravention of the monarch's declared wishes.

James Hart, J. Stoddart Flemion and Allen Horstman have shown that the 1621 Parliament also saw the revival of the private party judicature of the House of Lords. This was very much in response to particular circumstances, and it encompassed both first instance judicature (in answer to petitions) and appellate judicature (the authority to hear and adjudicate appeals against the decisions of inferior courts). The latter had largely fallen into disuse during the later Middle Ages and under the Tudors,[20] but frustration with the chronic delays and high costs of the central law courts led a growing number of litigants to seek recourse to the Lords, which clearly emerged as the highest court of appeal in the period after 1621. The Lords heard appeals (on the basis of writs of error) from the common-law courts of King's Bench and Common Pleas, and also determined appeals from a range of other courts, including Chancery, Exchequer, Requests and the palatine Courts of Lancaster and Durham. The number of petitions and appeals that the House accepted for review increased rapidly, from 14 in 1621 to 86 in 1626. In all, 207 cases were adjudicated during the 1620s, 74 of them (by far the largest single category) relating to matters of property. The plaintiffs, and the nature of their cases, were remarkably diverse, and the Lords proved very willing and well equipped to handle this upsurge in business. It offered not only an authoritative and speedy ruling on cases but also a way of resolving jurisdictional conflicts between the common-law and equity courts. The Lords took their duties as a High Court extremely seriously, and during the 1620s succeeded in re-establishing the Upper House as a vital component within the legal system. The fact that much of this activity was conducted in co-operation with the Privy Council offered a reminder of the origins of both bodies in the councils of medieval monarchs, and the overlap in their membership greatly facilitated such co-ordination. By the end of the decade, judicial business had become the most time-consuming activity of the Lords.[21]

An even larger number of cases were brought before the Lords in the early 1640s. There were three principal reasons for this. First, the implementation of official policies during Charles I's Personal Rule – especially relating to the collection of non-parliamentary taxation and the prosecution of religious nonconformity – had frequently involved a 'careless disregard for legal propriety';[22] litigants saw the Lords as the easiest and most authoritative body to which to appeal, and over 400 such cases were submitted during the first six months of the Long Parliament. Once again, the Lords embraced its obligation to restore faith in the legal system and responded energetically to this particular crisis.[23] The second cause was more deep-rooted and lay in the manifold problems that continued to face litigants. Not only were the cost and the delays of lawsuits often intolerable; as in the 1620s, there were also frequent jurisdictional disputes between the common-law and equity courts. In particular, many litigants felt acutely the lack of an effective appeal procedure against the judgements of the equity courts, and there were regular complaints that Chancery was exceeding the bounds of its jurisdiction by deciding matters that should more properly have been determined at common law, especially issues of property. The final reason for the Lords' increased workload was the abolition in July 1641 of the Courts of Star Chamber and High Commission, and the suppression of the jurisdiction of the Privy Council, the Councils of the North and the Marches, and the palatine Courts of Lancaster and Durham. The result of this was that more litigants turned to the Lords. However, during the years of civil war, the credibility and authority of the Lords as a High Court became seriously tarnished. Attendances declined steeply,[24] and the ranks of senior legal officers at Westminster became badly depleted: by January 1643 the Lord Keeper of the Great Seal, the Master of the Rolls, and seven of the 12 common-law judges had all joined the King at Oxford.[25] The Lords also became associated with the major violations of legal propriety – especially the sequestration of property – that Parliament committed in order to defeat the King.[26] As a result, few mourned the demise of the Upper House in the wake of the regicide.

Yet the Lords undeniably fulfilled an extremely useful role within the legal system. During the Interregnum, the failure of proposals for a thoroughgoing reformation of justice, and uncertainties over how far the Commons alone could wield supreme judicial power,[27] demonstrated the need for such a court and in 1660 it was restored, complete with the same jurisdiction as prior to 1649.[28] Private litigants once again emerged in droves, and the Lords accepted their duty to them as readily as before. Approximately 1,200 petitions and writs of error were presented to the Lords between 1660 and 1681, roughly three-quarters of them in the Convention Parliament of 1660–1. However, during Charles II's reign there was growing disquiet in the Commons about the original jurisdiction of the Lords, possibly because some members of the Lower House felt that it might infringe their privilege of freedom from legal suits during time of Parliament.[29] The case of Skinner vs. the East India Company (1667–70) caused a major furore that effectively brought the first instance jurisdiction of the Lords in civil cases to an end. But the Upper House fought tenaciously to retain their appellate judicature. This issue resurfaced in the case of Shirley vs. Fagg (1675) when the Commons resolved that 'there lies no appeal to the judicature of the Lords in Parliament from courts of equity'.[30] The Lords retaliated with a robust resolution defending the King's:

> highest court of judicature in the kingdom, the Lords in Parliament; where His Majesty is highest in his royal estate, and where the last resort of judging upon writs of error and appeals in equity, in all causes, and over all persons, is undoubtedly fixed and permanently lodged.[31]

They won their point and the case eventually blew over. The Lords continued to hear appeals and to offer decisions to private litigants that were both final and relatively easily available. Although they had lost their original civil jurisdiction, they retained their original criminal and appellate civil jurisdictions.[32]

In short, during the course of the seventeenth century, as Elizabeth Read Foster has written, 'the High Court of Parliament became a working reality'.[33] It is important not to underestimate the competence or effectiveness of the Houses, and especially the Lords, as a court of record. Although only a minority of the members of either House had received legal training, they could draw on the expertise of the legal officers, and the procedures that they evolved were entirely in accordance with the practices of the common-law courts. Lord Holles wrote of the Lords in 1675 that 'in general it may [be] said of that House, that many among them are persons of honour and integrity that will not be biased, and [are] of experience to understand and judge a right of such matters as are brought before them'.[34] Perhaps the greatest weakness of Parliament as an element within the legal system was that unlike the other law courts it did not meet regularly.[35] Litigants always had to contend with the vagaries of parliamentary summonses, prorogations and dissolutions. However, in 1678 it was established that appeal cases could be carried over, if necessary, from session to session, and Parliament to Parliament.[36] This further enhanced the usefulness of the Lords as a court of appeal.

The High Court of Parliament thus performed a valuable and flexible role as an integral part of the legal system, a court with final authority to which litigants could turn if they failed to find remedy elsewhere. Here again, as in its other functions, Parliament should be seen as an agency of royal government rather than as any kind of counterweight to it. As during the Middle Ages, it acted as the King's High Court, dispensing justice in the King's name.

Legislation

The modern demarcation between the judiciary and the legislature was entirely alien to seventeenth-century England. Contemporaries regarded the judicial and legislative functions as part of a single process whereby the Houses collaborated with the Crown to redress grievances and resolve problems both general and specific. The making of legislation was another aspect of

Parliament's role as a High Court, and just as the Lords was the highest court of appeal, so the statutes passed by Crown, Lords and Commons constituted the highest form of human positive law. The assent of all three elements in this 'parliamentary trinity' was required for an act to be passed, and acts could only be amended or repealed by other acts. Nor was it possible to appeal against the terms of a statute unless it could be proven that these were based upon demonstrable error. The extent of the Houses' involvement in the formulation and enactment of legislation was highly unusual within Europe. In Scotland the monarch did not necessarily need parliamentary consent in order to create and enforce laws or to raise taxes – the consent of a convention of the estates was equally valid – while in the Irish Parliament no bill could be introduced without the prior approval of the English King and Privy Council.[37] Conrad Russell has observed that 'the firmness of [the English Parliament's] hold on the legislative function seems, in Europe, to be paralleled only in Catalonia'.[38] As J. P. Cooper argued, in Poland, Sweden and Bohemia, the Crown certainly needed the consent of the estates in order to legislate, but the more usual pattern, in France, Germany and much of Spain, was for the estates to submit 'grievances or demands to the prince, who then legislated about them'.[39] The tripartite legislative procedure of the English Parliament was among its most distinctive characteristics.

That procedure was clearly developed by the end of the sixteenth century.[40] Acts of Parliament began in the form of bills, written on paper, which were usually introduced by handing them to the Lord Chancellor (in the Lords) or the Speaker (in the Commons). Bills could be initiated in either House, except for subsidy bills, which always originated in the Commons, and estate bills and restitution bills,[41] which normally began in the Lords. The basic procedure was for bills to be read three times in each House. At the first reading the full text of the bill would be read. This was a formal occasion, and the bill was generally not debated at that stage. At the second reading, a summary ('breviate') of the bill was read, and general debate would take place. The majority of bills were then referred to a committee of members for consideration and amendment.[42] Counsel could be heard and witnesses examined; amendments were incorporated onto the paper text of the bill. The chairman of the committee then reported its findings: amendments were read, debated and agreed or disagreed. At that stage – or sometimes after the second reading, if the House decided to omit the committee stage – the bill would be engrossed on parchment. After the breviate of that 'engrossed bill' had been read a third time, the Lord Chancellor or the Speaker put the question of whether or not it should pass. If the bill was passed, the clerk wrote the transfer formula (or 'bail')[43] on the bill and forwarded it to the other House. There the process was repeated, and any amendments incorporated onto the engrossed bill. If the bill was passed unamended, it remained in (or was returned to) the Lords to await the royal assent, except for supply bills which were returned to the Commons. If it was passed with amendments, the bill would be returned to the House in which it had originated, together with a paper of amendments which that House then needed to agree. If it did not agree, then a conference (or if necessary several conferences) would be held between representatives of both Houses to try to resolve the disagreement. Bills that were finally agreed then awaited the royal assent at the end of the session.[44]

Both bills and acts were divided into two types, public and private. The correlation between the two categories was not exact, and it was possible for public bills to become private acts, or vice versa. Although it is broadly true that the benefits of private bills and acts extended only to certain individuals or to a specific locality or corporation, while public bills and acts addressed wider problems and issues, there were a number of technical differences which render the distinction more complex. The formal definition of a public act was that it appeared in the sessional print of statutes; those left unprinted were classified as private acts. The distinction between public and private bills was different and more complicated. Although the Speaker laid it down in 1607 that a bill affecting three counties or less was private, many exceptions can be found to this principle.[45] William Hakewill claimed that the key difference was that public bills received the royal assent in the form 'le roi le veult', whereas private bills were assented to in the form 'soit fait comme il est désiré'.[46] However, Sir Geoffrey Elton demonstrated that in fact the distinction between the two assent formulae lay not between public and private acts, but between local acts, which (like ones of national concern) got the form 'le roi le veult', and truly private or personal ones, benefiting only named individuals, which alone got the form 'soit fait comme il est désiré'.[47] The real distinction between public and private bills appears to have been that fees were payable to the Lord Chancellor or Lord Keeper, the Speaker, the Clerk and the serjeant-at-arms, among others, during the passage of private bills but not of public bills.[48] For example, every individual who derived benefit from a private bill paid £10 to the Lord Chancellor or Lord Keeper, and every corporation, town, company or society paid £4. The Clerk of the Parliaments, the Under-Clerk of the Parliaments (the Clerk of the Commons) and a number of other officials also received fees for every private bill, and these formed an essential part of their income.[49] It was also possible for a private bill to be included in the sessional print on payment of a further fee, and thus to become a public act.

The importance of private acts of Parliament should never be understated. Throughout the seventeenth century they slightly outnumbered public acts: in the period 1604–90, 535 (52 per cent) of a total of 1,024 acts passed were private, compared with a total of 489 (48 per cent) public acts. Because these totals include the periods of major political crisis during the early 1640s and late 1680s, when private acts were rather crowded out by urgent public business, they if anything slightly understate the relative proportion of private legislation in more stable times. Thus, during the period 1604–29, 188 (56 per cent) of the 337 acts passed were private, while between 1660 and 1685 the corresponding figures were 296 (55 per cent) of 534. The totals of private and public acts passed in each session between 1604 and 1689 are set out in Appendix 2 (pp. 239–40, below).

Private acts offered individuals, localities, corporations, companies and other lobbies an excellent opportunity to protect and advance their interests by statute – the most authoritative form of law and the one against which it was most difficult to appeal. Although private bills required the payment of fees, they could save the beneficiaries considerable expense in subsequent litigation. Here again we see the very close relationship between judicature and legislation. Private bill procedure and the appellate jurisdiction of the House of Lords both originated in the medieval practice of presenting petitions to the King's Council in Parliament. As a result, private acts display the same diversity as appeals and petitions to the Lords. They comprised, first of all, three types of bill that were always private. Estate acts formed probably the largest single category of private legislation. These offered an excellent way to resolve problems of ownership and to affirm legal title to land, although they were often a source of dispute between the interested parties. Less contentious were the acts of restitution in blood which restored individuals to full legal rights of which they had been deprived because an ancestor had been attainted of treason or another felony. Finally, acts of naturalisation granted full native rights to individual foreigners or to children born abroad to English fathers, as well as to any foreign wives that they had married.

In addition to these three categories, there were then numerous other acts relating to particular local or private interests which shed remarkable sidelights onto the people and problems of the age. A few examples will give a flavour of the range of subject matter: 'An Act for confirmation of letters patent made to the Governors of the Free Grammar School at Saint Bees, in the County of Cumberland' (1605–6); 'An Act for the assuring and establishing of the Isle of Man' (1610); 'An Act for the confirmation of His Majesty's letters patents to the town of Plymouth, and for dividing the parish, and building of a new Church there' (1641); 'An Act for making navigable the Rivers commonly called Brandon and Waveney' (1670–1).[50] There are also quite a few examples of acts which look equally local but were in fact classified as public acts, perhaps because their proponents were able to argue that their benefits (especially to trade) extended more widely, or just possibly because of clerical error in their classification. Such public acts include 'An Act for the making up and keeping in reparation of Chepstow Bridge' (1605–6); 'An Act for incorporating the makers of knives and other cutlery wares in Hallamshire in the County of York' (1624); 'An Act for the regulating of the trade of bay-making in the Dutch Bay-hall in Colchester' (1660); 'An Act for regulation of the pilchard fishing in the counties of Devon and Cornwall' (1661–2); 'An Act for the better repairing and maintaining the pier of Great Yarmouth' (1677–8).[51] There could be no clearer illustration of the 'omnicompetence of statute' than the sheer range of matters regulated by these acts of Parliament.

The provision of private acts was highly significant because it extended the usefulness of Parliament beyond the government to ordinary citizens. As a result, individuals and interest groups as diverse as livery companies, borough corporations, and Oxford or Cambridge colleges could seek to alleviate their problems by promoting a private act of Parliament. The term 'lobbies' has recently been applied to cover these various interests. Given that Parliaments sat only intermittently, these lobbies naturally pursued their interests in other arenas as well, by conducting litigation in the local or central law courts, or by petitioning the Privy Council, or by making informal approaches to influential figures in the Court and/or Council who were close to the monarch. Private bill initiatives were expensive and had to wait until Parliament was in session; as a result, they often represented only the most visible of a complex web of contacts and activities on behalf of diverse individuals and groups. As David Dean and Ian Archer have shown for the later Elizabethan period, there was the potential for serious conflict between competing lobbies, and this regularly spilled over into Parliament. The success of private bills often depended on enlisting the support of powerful sponsors in each House, and this required careful preparation and canvassing prior to a session.[52] Hostile interests would often engage in similar manoeuvres. If the drawback of Parliaments was that they were not in constant session, their two great advantages lay in the supreme authority of statute and the fact that the sheer range of interests represented in the two Houses made them a very appropriate forum in which to debate and arbitrate these conflicts of interest.

There is as yet no systematic study of how this process of lobbying operated in seventeenth-century Parliaments comparable with Dean's for the later sixteenth century. However, one example drawn from Clive Holmes's research will give a brief indication of how recourse to Parliament could help to resolve a prolonged local conflict.[53] During the reign of Charles I, five major drainage schemes were established in the fenlands of Lincolnshire, Bedfordshire and Cambridgeshire. These projects involved the drainage of many thousands of acres of fen. They disrupted the lives of fen-dwellers and reclaimed new lands at the cost (it was alleged) of worsening the quality of others. As a result, for nearly a century the drainers and fenmen battled with each other, launching suits in both local and central law courts, submitting petitions to Parliament, sometimes even resorting to violence. However, what appears to have distinguished those schemes that were ultimately successful is that the drainers managed – often after prolonged efforts – to secure the backing of parliamentary legislation. This not only set up a recognised administrative machinery for implementing the schemes and preventing sabotage; it also conferred legitimacy on the operations by the 'full and final confirmation' of statute. An act 'wherein all men's consents are included' was superior to any other form of edict – such as a Privy Council order – and it proved invaluable in overcoming the opposition of fen-dwellers. By contrast, those drainers who failed to obtain such legislation were forced to resort to lawsuits with such frequency that they became a standing joke. It was very striking that only those operations that lacked statutory authority were subjected to regular attack by the fenmen. This demonstrates that Sir Thomas Smith's claim that 'the consent of the Parliament is taken to be every man's consent'[54] was not empty rhetoric: there was a pervasive acceptance that whatever was decided by Parliament, 'the representative of the realm', was indeed binding upon the whole realm.[55]

There was thus a regular, but not constant, demand for legislation by many subjects as well as the Crown and its advisers, and the overall scale of legislative activity in seventeenth-century Parliaments was impressive. In all, the years between 1604 and 1690 saw the passage of no fewer than 1,024 acts (489 public, 535 private).[56] Yet these figures represent only a minority of the bills that were initiated. The proportion of bills that became acts, which stood at 23 per cent in the period 1571–97 and 22 per cent in 1603–25, increased to 34 per cent in 1660–85 and then jumped to 51 per cent in 1689–1714. The marked increase in the success rate of bills becoming acts after 1689 was probably due primarily to the fact that Parliament thereafter met each year, thereby significantly increasing the amount of available parliamentary time. These overall percentages conceal an interesting discrepancy between the two Houses. Fewer bills were initiated in the Lords than in the Commons: 38 per cent in 1571–97, 35 per cent in 1603–25, 32 per cent in 1660–85. However, bills that originated in the Upper House had a consistently higher success rate. In 1571–97, only 18 per cent of bills initiated in the Commons became acts, compared with 43 per cent for the Lords. The equivalent figures for 1603–25 were 18 and 39 per cent; and for 1660–85, 32 and 37 per cent.[57] These figures reflect the continuing importance of the Lords in the legislative process as well as the fact that it was less deluged by bills than the Commons. The Upper House was thus able to devote more of its time to considering and revising bills, as well as to other business such as judicature. It was also the more orderly and efficient House, not least because the legal assistants were on hand to advise on precedents and procedures.

Precisely because statute was such a flexible instrument, and could meet so many different public and private needs, demand for it was necessarily determined by a wide range of variables. It was natural that the total number of acts passed in successive sessions should therefore fluctuate considerably. In particular, under James I and Charles I there was a steady decrease in the number of acts passed. Whereas the five parliamentary sessions of 1604–10 produced no fewer than 226 acts, the seven sessions of 1614–29 yielded only 111. This compared with 260 acts during the 1530s and 259 during the 1550s, but then less than 100 in every decade of Elizabeth's reign except the 1580s. R. W. K. Hinton argued that this indicated a 'decline of parliamentary government' under Elizabeth and the early Stuarts.[58] Some contemporaries shared this concern. Pym was reported as saying in December 1621 that 'bills are the end of a Parliament', and there was considerable frustration and disappointment when a session failed to produce a reasonable crop of acts.[59] But however understandable such contemporary fears were, it is difficult to use these raw figures to quantify 'decline'. The number of acts passed was related to the perceived need for new laws to resolve problems. In the late sixteenth and early seventeenth centuries some people felt that there were enough statutes in existence. As Coke observed in 1593, there were 'so many [laws] already, that they were fit to be termed *elephantinae leges*, therefore to make more laws it might seem superfluous'.[60] There was no decline in the legislative efficiency of Parliament as such, and the number of bills initiated was slightly higher in the early seventeenth century than in the later sixteenth. The diminution in the number of acts passed was also a reflection of several occasions – especially in 1621 and 1626 – when the monarch dissolved Parliament precipitately and thereby aborted quite large numbers of bills as they neared completion of their passage through the Houses. That there was no long-term decrease in Parliament's capacity to pass numerous acts is demonstrated by the resurgence of legislation that followed the Restoration. A total of 372 acts were passed during the 1660s, the highest number in any decade of either the sixteenth or seventeenth centuries. As in the 1530s, a period of national reform and settlement generated an increased need for new acts, both public and private. Although periods of political instability certainly undermined legislative productivity, as was evident at times during the 1620s or 1680s, this was mainly because other circumstances sometimes impelled the monarch to dissolve Parliament very abruptly. The actual legislative machinery remained fully operational, and was available to successive monarchs and their subjects whenever problems or grievances emerged that were most effectively resolved by statute.

Council and counsel

The bringing together of the diverse elements of the political nation not only underpinned Parliament's legislative and judicial functions; it was also crucial to Parliament's role as the monarch's 'Great Council'. Parliament had originated as an enlargement of the medieval Great Councils, and although the latter term continued to be applied during the sixteenth century to *ad hoc* assemblies of the nobility, by the seventeenth it was almost always used as a synonym for Parliament.[61] Contemporaries spoke of 'the Great Council of Parliament' as much as of 'the High Court of Parliament'. No less than in earlier centuries, a wise monarch needed to take counsel to discover the grievances and pressing needs of the commonwealth, and to gain a sense of what policies were practicable to pursue. Among the worst traits of stereotypical bad rulers, like the Old Testament figure Rehoboam, was that they only took counsel from a small group of flatterers who told them what they wanted to hear.[62] By contrast, wise rulers listened, at least periodically, to a much wider circle of advisers, a service for which the 'representative of the whole realm' was ideally suited.

The term 'Great Council' was used in contradistinction to the Privy Council. By assembling a far wider range of representative individuals on a much less regular basis, Parliament directly complemented the inner body of (usually) 15–40 Privy Councillors who generally met weekly. Coke wrote that 'the King of England is armed with divers Councils, one whereof is called *commune concilium*, and that is the Court of Parliament'.[63] Similarly, Sir Francis Bacon described Parliament as 'the great Council of the King, the great Council of the Kingdom, to advise His Majesty of those things of weight and difficulty which concern both the King and kingdom',[64] while Oliver St John called it:

> '*commune concilium regni*', in respect that the whole kingdom is representatively there; and secondly, that the whole kingdom have access thither in all things that concern them . . . and thirdly, in respect that the whole kingdom is interested in, and receives benefit by the laws and things there passed.[65]

The monarch's sources of counsel thus surrounded him in concentric circles, spreading outwards from the Privy Council and the informal advisers of the royal Court, to 'the Great Council of Parliament'.

Those concentric circles were not mutually exclusive and intersected with each other. Their roles were complementary and intertwined, an interdependence neatly expressed by the author of *Fleta* (c. 1296) who wrote that 'in his parliaments the king in council holds his court'.[66] In particular, there was considerable overlap of personnel between these 'points of contact'. Many Privy Councillors were members of either the Lords or the Commons, and they often played an important role in guiding parliamentary business, especially in chairing committees. During Elizabeth's reign, roughly 35 per cent of committee chairmen in the Commons had been Privy Councillors. This proportion declined steeply under the early Stuarts as James ennobled the vast majority of his Privy Councillors leaving only two in the Commons in 1604. This figure rose to nine by 1621 but declined thereafter and stood at four in the Long Parliament: the average for the period 1604–40 as a whole was about five.[67] The pattern of most Councillors sitting in the Upper House continued after the Restoration. Of the 29 members of the Privy Council in 1660, only five did not sit in the Lords. Between 1660 and 1681, 64 of the 262 (24 per cent) peers eligible to sit in the Lords were Privy Councillors, whereas the proportion for members of the Commons was only about 2 per cent. Moreover, Privy Councillors were often among the most assiduous members. They chaired roughly half the Lords' select committees appointed during Charles II's reign, and presided over the Committee of the Whole House for more than 90 per cent of the time.[68] Above all, the Privy Councillors provided an excellent line of communication between the two Houses and the Crown, Court and Council.

The prominence of so many Privy Councillors in the Lords greatly assisted the Crown in guiding official legislation through the Upper House.

Furthermore, particularly after 1660 many of them also helped to mobilise support for the monarch, collecting proxies and gathering votes.[69] It would, however, be anachronistic to speak of their 'managing' the Houses. At hardly any time did the monarch have a legislative programme as such, and a model that envisages relations between the monarch and the two Houses in terms of competition or a battle for control is highly misleading. It would be truer to say that factional divisions existed within both the Privy Council and the Great Council. Throughout the century, differences of opinion apparent at Court or in the Privy Council were liable to spill over into Parliaments. This was hardly surprising given the overlap in personnel between these bodies, nor was it necessarily politically destabilising. After all, these conciliar structures were intended to allow the monarch to hear a wide range of opinions.[70]

How smoothly that process worked depended largely on how far the Houses' methods of presenting advice were in tune with the monarch's ways of receiving it. No hard-and-fast rules governed this interaction, and tensions always lurked within the idea of parliamentary counsel. Was it a duty, or was it a right? Were certain matters excluded? If the monarch barred discussion of some subjects, did the Houses have a duty or even a right to offer advice against the wishes of the Crown? These proved contentious issues throughout the seventeenth century. In 1621, James I and the Commons had a series of sharp exchanges on precisely this point.[71] The Commons wished to advise James on foreign policy, and specifically on the possible marriage of the Prince of Wales to the King of Spain's daughter. James warned the Commons not to 'argue and debate publicly of the matters far above their reach and capacity' or to 'presume henceforth to meddle with anything concerning our government or deep matters of state'. The Commons retaliated with a petition of right which claimed that 'the ancient liberty of Parliament for freedom of speech' was their 'ancient and undoubted right'. Furthermore, as the King's 'most loyal and humble subjects and servants, representing the whole commons of your kingdom', they had resolved 'out of our cares and fears truly and plainly to demonstrate these things to your Majesty which we were not assured could otherwise come so fully and clearly to your knowledge'. James replied, rather loftily, that he was 'an old and experienced King needing no such lessons', and again warned them not to 'meddle with things far above your reach'. He then argued that the intermittent nature of Parliaments necessarily limited the value of their advice on matters of state:

> These are unfit things to be handled in Parliament except your King should require it of you; for who can have wisdom to judge of things of that nature but such as are daily acquainted with the particulars of treaties and of the variable and fixed connexion of affairs of state.

The Commons responded with a forthright Protestation that 'the arduous and urgent affairs concerning the King, State, and defence of the realm' were 'proper subjects and matter of counsel and debate in Parliament', an assertion that so infuriated James that he tore the Protestation out of the Commons Journal and shortly afterwards dissolved the Parliament. In the Protestation, the Commons took care to incorporate the form of words traditionally employed in the summons to members of Parliament, that they assemble to advise the monarch on *'quibusdam arduis et urgentibus negotiis'*,[72] and they always held that their role – indeed their 'undoubted birthright' – was to counsel but not to determine. James by contrast asserted that the Commons' privileges 'were derived from the grace and permission' of his ancestors, and that the House had no right to advise but merely a duty to do so when he requested them to. There was no obvious solution to these intractable issues, and the political confrontation was only resolved in 1624 when James greeted the Houses with the promise that he would 'entreat [their] good and sound advice' and that they could 'freely advise' him.[73]

The situation deteriorated rapidly under James's successor. Charles I's attitude towards taking counsel was summed up in his comment to the Privy Council in 1627 that 'the question was of obeying the King, not of counselling'.[74] He had a very clear idea in advance of the kind of 'advice' that he expected from Parliament. A draft declaration for the 1628 Parliament stated that 'we hoped that all members of that great body, being the great council of this kingdom, would in these times of general danger have also brought with them minds so prepared for the advancing of the public good as no sinister respects whatsoever should have diverted them'.[75] He was bitterly disappointed by the sessions of 1628–9, and when, on 2 March 1629, several members tried to forestall an adjournment by physically holding the Speaker in his chair, Charles had Sir John Eliot, Denzil Holles and Benjamin Valentine arrested and charged with 'seditious words'. They pleaded the parliamentary privilege of free speech, but the Judges of King's Bench ruled that this did not extend to fomenting 'sedition and discord' and sentenced them to imprisonment.[76]

Charles's propensity to see any unwelcome advice as tantamount to sedition or even treason led him naturally towards a decision to rule without Parliaments. He was not, however, completely oblivious to advice; things might have proved less catastrophic if he had been. The problem was that he was prepared to listen to advice when it essentially confirmed his own views. During the later 1620s he turned increasingly to 'new counsels' and restricted appointments to the Privy Council and elevations to the peerage to those who affirmed his own preferences. He dispensed entirely with one of the three points of contact between 1629 and 1640, and effectively closed the other two to dissentient voices. This was the predicament that caused the Houses to demand, in the summer of 1642:

> That the great affairs of the kingdom may not be concluded or transacted by the advice of private men, or by any unknown or unsworn councillors, but that such matters as concern the public, and are proper for the High Court of Parliament, which is your Majesty's great and supreme council, may be debated, resolved and transacted only in Parliament, and not elsewhere.[77]

But what if – as happened in this case – the monarch still refused to listen? What if the Houses found that the monarch rejected their advice and turned instead to advisers they distrusted or regarded as evil? In those circumstances, the fact that Parliament combined the roles of High Court and Great Council provided the basis for a radical solution. On 6 June 1642, in a Declaration in defence of the Militia Ordinance, the Houses insisted:

> The High Court of Parliament is not only a court of judicature, enabled by the laws to adjudge and determine the rights and liberties of the kingdom, against such patents and grants of His Majesty as are prejudicial thereunto ... but it is likewise a council, to provide for the necessities, prevent the imminent dangers, and preserve the public peace and safety

of the kingdom, and to declare the King's pleasure in those things as are requisite thereunto; and what they do herein hath the stamp of the royal authority, although His Majesty, seduced by evil counsel, do in his own person oppose or interrupt the same; for the King's supreme and royal pleasure is exercised and declared in this High Court of law and council, after a more eminent and obligatory manner than it can be by personal act or resolution of his own.[78]

This remarkable statement demonstrates the radical constitutional potential contained within Parliament's fusion of the roles of court and council. The fact that it combined both functions lay at the heart of its claims to rule on the King's behalf and to pass ordinances which had the force of statute even though they had not received the royal assent. These claims, and the policies based upon them, will be discussed more fully in Chapter 8, but they are worth mentioning here because they grew directly out of the distinctive combination of Parliament's functions examined in this chapter.[79]

This radical development culminated in the Commons' resolutions of 4 January 1649 that the Commons, 'being chosen by, and representing the people, have the supreme power in this nation', and 'that whatever is enacted, or declared for law, by the Commons ... hath the force of law; and all the people of this nation are concluded thereby, although the consent and concurrence of king, or House of Peers, be not had thereunto'.[80] These resolutions provided the theoretical justification for the abolition of monarchy and the House of Lords the following March, and for the establishment of the Commonwealth.[81] But with the creation of the Protectorate in December 1653 there was a gradual retreat from such claims towards a more traditional commitment to government 'by a single person and a Parliament'. After 1660 Parliament's conciliar role remained essentially as it had been before 1642. A crucial constitutional guarantee of Parliament's ability to counsel the monarch continued to lie in the privilege of free speech, and in December 1667 both Houses affirmed that this formed a vital part of 'the ancient and necessary rights and privileges of Parliament'.[82] John Miller has suggested that although a minority of members argued that the King should do whatever the Commons advocated, the majority still felt that Parliament's role was to advise and persuade, but not to compel.[83] As in earlier decades, the subjects on which the Houses could counsel the monarch remained a potential source of dispute. This was especially true of foreign policy. In May 1677, for example, the Commons submitted an address to Charles in favour of alliances against France, arguing that this was 'so important to the safety of your Majesty and your kingdoms' that they could not do otherwise 'without unfaithfulness to your Majesty and those we represent'. Charles's robust reply echoed James I in 1621: 'you have intrenched upon so undoubted a right of the Crown that I am confident it will appear in no age (when the sword was not drawn) that the prerogative of making peace and war hath been so dangerously invaded'.[84] The fact that the Houses could advise but not determine was most graphically illustrated by the events of the Exclusion Crisis, when Charles successfully resisted the campaign to exclude James, Duke of York from the line of succession. This was a matter, Charles insisted, 'that in our royal judgement so nearly concerned us, both in honour, justice and conscience', that he could not possibly accept the exclusionists' demands. To have done so would, he claimed, have risked causing 'another most unnatural war'.[85]

The basis of Parliament's usefulness as an advisory body rested on its capacity to represent as broad a range of opinion as possible. Only in this way could the monarch gain a sense of attitudes in the realm at large and judge what policies were practicable. But in 1687–8 James II violated this principle by seeking the return of a 'packed' Parliament the majority of whose members supported the repeal of penal legislation against Catholics.[86] It had always been central to Parliament's function that its judicial, legislative and conciliar activities grew out of its role as the 'representative of the whole realm'. Although monarchs and their most senior advisers might sometimes try to 'manage' parliamentary business, to 'pack' Parliament would destroy its value as a 'point of contact'. As Thomas Mallett had observed in 1621, 'if elections [are] not free, we shall have packed Parliaments. Free elections [are] the foundation of our Parliament liberty.'[87] This issue played a crucial part in the origins of the Glorious Revolution, and William of Orange asserted that his intervention in 1688 was 'intended for no other design but to have a free and lawful Parliament assembled as soon as is possible'.[88] The following year, the Bill of Rights, which was enacted as a statute, stipulated that 'election of members of Parliament ought to be free', and that 'the freedom of speech and debates or proceedings in Parliament ought not to be impeached or questioned in any court or place out of Parliament'.[89] These customary privileges, which safeguarded Parliament's role as the monarch's Great Council, were thus enshrined in statute for the first time.[90] In this way, at the end of the century, the conciliar and legislative functions of Parliament, which embodied its dual role as both High Court and Great Council, became even more closely intertwined than before.

4

Functions II: the power of the purse

Of all the functions of Parliament, possibly the one that made it most immediately valuable to the Crown was its right to consent to the levying of taxation. Financial need was often the most important short-term reason why Parliaments were summoned. Their control over taxation was also closely linked to the functions analysed in the previous chapter, in that grants of supply were passed as legislation, and the Houses claimed the right to advise on those matters for which it voted taxes. Clearly this had important political implications for the relationship between successive monarchs and their Parliaments, not least because it also gave the Houses – and especially the Commons, which alone possessed the right to initiate grants of taxation – some opportunity to try to extract concessions from the Crown in return for supply.

Yet the precise nature of this 'power of the purse', the regularity and effectiveness with which it was deployed, and the extent to which it contributed to the origins of the Civil War, all remain highly contentious questions. It is also worth noting that Parliament's fiscal powers and practices changed considerably over time. During the course of the 1640s the Houses raised unprecedented levels of taxation on their own authority, and many of these levies were continued during the 1650s. After the Restoration the system was again overhauled. Prerogative sources of revenue were abolished and the Crown was granted certain taxes and other sources of revenue in lieu. But the outlines of the distinction between ordinary and extraordinary revenues survived, and it was only in the 1690s that the system was fundamentally reformed. As a result, we are not analysing a static situation, and it therefore makes sense to divide this chapter into three broadly chronological sections, covering in turn the periods up to 1642, 1642–60, and 1660 onwards.

The early seventeenth century

At the beginning of the seventeenth century, the English fiscal system remained essentially as it had been since the fourteenth century. Royal revenues were divided into two branches, 'ordinary' and 'extraordinary'. The 'ordinary' revenues comprised the Crown's own permanent income from its lands, from justice, customs duties, and feudal dues such as wardship. It was expected that for most of the time the monarch would live on these sources of income ('live of his own'). Only in times of emergency – of 'evident and urgent' need – was it anticipated that the Crown would seek 'extraordinary' revenue in the form of taxation or various kinds of loan. From the mid-fourteenth century the principle was established that direct taxation could only be levied with Parliament's consent. Furthermore, certain categories of the ordinary revenue, including customs duties such as tonnage and poundage, were traditionally also voted to the Crown in Parliament before they could be collected.[1] Unfortunately, the ordinary revenues, and especially those from the Crown lands, had failed to keep pace with inflation, with the result that between the death of Henry VIII and that of Elizabeth I they declined by about 40 per cent in real terms.[2] Such a drop put intense pressure on the existing fiscal system and made the issues of finance deeply controversial under the early Stuarts.

The grants of direct taxation made upon particular occasions consisted of the clerical subsidy (granted by the clergy in their Convocations[3] but confirmed by an act of Parliament), and of two taxes on the laity, the fifteenth and tenth and the lay subsidy. The fifteenth and tenth was a quota tax on movable property (rural and urban respectively) levied at rates originally fixed in 1334 but revised in the fifteenth century. The apportionment of payments was left to local discretion, and the tax was collected by commissioners drawn from the local gentry who were made personally liable to the Exchequer. Although quotas were sometimes adjusted in response to special pleading from particular localities, the yield remained approximately £30,000 throughout the sixteenth and early seventeenth centuries, when grants usually consisted of two or three in most sessions. The burden of the fifteenth and tenth often tended to fall quite heavily on the less well off – it was complained in July 1610 that it would 'pinch the poor'[4] – and this was the reason given for its abandonment after the mid-1620s.[5]

The lay subsidy was different in many respects. Introduced in the early sixteenth century, it was an assessed tax on every form of income that was collected, mostly effectively, in the same way as the fifteenth and tenth. The greatest weakness of the subsidy was the increasing inaccuracy of the assessments of wealth on which it was based. The subsidy was assessed by commissioners drawn from the gentry who often drastically under-assessed their friends, neighbours and dependants. As a result, the value of one subsidy declined not only in relative terms, as it failed to keep pace with inflation, but also in real terms, from £130,000 in the middle of Elizabeth I's reign to £70,000 by 1621 and £55,000 by 1628.[6] The more subsidies that Parliament voted, the more serious the under-assessment became. Sir Walter Raleigh observed in 1601 that 'our estates that be £30 or £40 in the Queen's books are not the hundredth part of our wealth'.[7] One Sussex JP, James Colbrand, complained that 'the rich were often rated ... much too low, at not a fortieth part of their wealth': in that county the average assessment of 70 leading families dropped from £61 in the 1540s to £14 in the 1620s. During the latter decade, for example, Sir Thomas Pelham, whose annual income exceeded £2,000 was rated at £50, and for the 12 subsidies voted during these years he paid only £100.[8] This problem was compounded by the fact that poorer taxpayers who died or moved away were not replaced on the subsidy rolls: whereas 6,700 subsidy payers were listed in Essex in 1566, by 1628 there were only 3,700.[9] In the opening decades of the seventeenth century, England was probably one of the most lightly taxed states in Europe.

This situation was very double-edged for the nobility and gentry who sat in

Parliament. The less they paid in subsidies the less bargaining power they had over the king, and the less reason he had to summon Parliament. The percentage of total revenue derived from parliamentary direct taxation fell from 16.38 in the period 1560–1602 to 9.28 between 1603 and 1625 and to a mere 3.96 in the years 1625–40.[10] This was bound to have profound political consequences for, as J. S. Roskell observed, 'the power of Parliament and especially of the Commons has always depended in the last resort upon control of taxation'.[11] Similarly, H. G. Koenigsberger, in his magisterial survey of European representative assemblies, concluded that 'it was important for a Parliament to establish the principle of redress of grievances before supply; i.e. a Parliament must not agree to grant taxes before the King has met its demands'.[12] How far was this true of early Stuart Parliaments, and to what extent did the declining value of direct taxation erode their bargaining power over the Crown?

In a series of highly influential books and articles, Conrad Russell has argued that early Stuart Parliaments insisted less often on the principle of 'redress before supply' than had previously been supposed, and that even less often did this tactic prove successful.[13] He suggests that the sums of supply offered generally 'fell so far short of the King's needs that they were simply not worth bargaining for'.[14] It was thus 'hard to see what, in financial terms, he stood to gain from calling future Parliaments'.[15] In short, by Koenigsberger's test, 'the English Parliament before 1629 was heading for extinction'; moreover, the fact 'that they came so close to extinction was in large measure their own doing' because of their refusal to be realistic about the Crown's financial needs.[16] Against this, Tom Cogswell has denied that Parliament was on a 'low road to extinction'. He argues that the Commons' 'response to the financial demands of war and its ability to extract redress of grievances only underscore the fact that we should be very careful about placing Parliament on any list of endangered institutions'. He insists that we should not underestimate 'the immense political leverage which came from linking redress to supply'.[17]

As in so many historical debates, there would appear to be right on both sides, and it may be possible to achieve some kind of synthesis between the two positions. It is worth stressing, first of all, that it would be misleading to equate the power of the purse simply with the principle of 'redress before supply'. It is certainly true that if we look for sessions in which supply was withheld until grievances were redressed, we do not find many examples. The session of 1628 is perhaps the plainest instance, when the vote of five subsidies was confirmed only after Charles I had agreed to the Petition of Right.[18] Other occasions when supply was withheld were the Parliaments of 1614 and 1626, and the Short Parliament of 1640. In each of these, the Commons insisted on redress of grievances before supply, and each time the King peremptorily dissolved Parliament rather than make concessions. The King went without his supply, and the Commons' grievances went unresolved. This clearly argues that the bargaining tactic of redress before supply was used relatively sparingly, and that in practice more often than not it failed to extract the desired concessions.[19]

At the opposite end of the spectrum, there were other occasions when supply was voted without any real attempt to ensure redress of grievances. In 1606, in a surge of loyalty following the Gunpowder Plot, three subsidies and six fifteenths were voted.[20] Grievances were only presented to the King the day before supply was voted, and the grants were not made conditional upon their redress. Much the same was true of the 1610 session, when one subsidy and one fifteenth were voted.[21] But the sessions of 1621, 1624 and 1625 were rather more complicated. In 1621 supply in the form of two subsidies was not tied to redress, although it was linked to the promise of future Parliaments. This outcome reflected the Houses' willingness to contribute to a military campaign to relieve the Palatinate, and also their concern for their own future. It was thus possible to make a grant while also securing a concession other than simply 'redress of grievances'.[22] Russell and Cogswell disagree most markedly over the 1624 Parliament. Russell argues that supply (three subsidies and three fifteenths) was granted before grievances were remedied. However, Cogswell points out that although this may be true of the Petition of Grievances presented towards the end of the Parliament, that document was limited in scope precisely because so many grievances had already been redressed over the preceding weeks.[23] He also shows that the Commons was able to use the promise of a subsidy bill to ensure that the session lasted a week longer than originally envisaged.[24] Against this, Chris Kyle has argued that the Crown was not forced into making significant concessions prior to the grant of supply, and that the Petition of Grievances was sufficiently important to be presented again the following year.[25] The subsidy act as finally passed was also notable for the fact that it tried to appropriate the supply to specific items of expenditure, namely the navy, aid to the Dutch, and the defence of the British Isles. However, there was no way of enforcing these appropriation clauses, and they were apparently ignored.[26] The 1625 Parliament was also complex, and it is important to distinguish between the London and Oxford sittings. In the first the Houses voted two subsidies without securing significant concessions; in the second, they withheld further supply until they were satisfied about Buckingham's conduct of future campaigns. Such guarantees were not forthcoming, and the King dissolved Parliament without gaining any more subsidies.

Altogether, it is a very mixed, complicated picture. On the one hand, Parliament's strongest card was the fact that it possessed the 'power of the purse' at all: it could always offer the monarch the possibility of supply as an incentive to summon Parliament. On the other hand, the value of that supply was a rapidly diminishing asset. Members thus faced a difficult dilemma. The withholding of supply afforded their best chance of exercising leverage over the Crown. Equally, given the declining value of what they could – or were prepared to – offer, the more concessions they demanded the more likely it became that the monarch would decide that parliamentary supply was simply not worth the political cost. As the 1620s progressed, members increasingly feared for their future. They were acutely aware that the lack of adequate supply might provoke the King to raise extra-parliamentary taxes and to dispense with Parliaments. Among the members who expressed such concerns most insistently was Sir Benjamin Rudyerd, who reportedly declared on 22 March 1628 that:

> This is the crisis of parliaments; by this we shall know whether parliaments will live or die . . . The way to show that we are the wise counsellors [is] . . . by giving the King a large and ample supply proportionable to the greatness and importance of the work in hand, for counsel without money is but a speculation.[27]

Such fears were clearly borne out by Charles I's decision to rule without Parliaments after 1629. Equally, the fact that he had summoned Parliament in four of his first five years on the throne suggests that he still saw the institution as at least potentially valuable. He may also have believed that he could manipulate Parliament, as he had to some extent been able to do in 1624.[28] Certainly without parliamentary taxation the King could survive in peacetime but it was difficult for him to wage a war without Parliament's co-operation:[29] the Personal Rule was founded on ending the conflicts against France and Spain. Non-parliamentary levies, such as the Forced Loan of 1627, were financially effective but constitutionally problematic. The Loan yielded over £240,000, the equivalent of between four and five subsidies,[30] but at the cost of raising tangled issues surrounding its legality and the relationship between the royal prerogative and the rule of law, issues which came to a head in the Five Knights' Case.[31] Parliamentary taxation was more constitutionally straightforward but difficult to secure without political concessions, whereas non-parliamentary taxation was constitutionally contentious but at least did not require negotiation with the Houses.

As with other difficult choices throughout his reign, possibly Charles I's greatest mistake was that he tried to pursue both options. The legality of extra-parliamentary taxation proved contentious in a polity where Parliament was widely seen as 'the ancient and royal way of aid and provision for the King with treasure'.[32] Or, as Secretary Conway put it in 1623, English monarchs 'having no other sure or good ways to aid themselves must do it by Parliament'.[33] This remained true despite the declining value of the subsidy: as some Privy Councillors observed, subsidies 'will not do all that is necessary, yet it will be a good help'.[34] Unfortunately, Charles – much more than James – jeopardised such grants of supply by regarding them as a test of loyalty. A draft declaration for the 1628 Parliament, which was vetted by Charles and offers a revealing insight into his mind, stated that in 1625 'we were presented from our people with the free gift of two entire subsidies, as a pledge of their love and as the first fruits of their dutiful affections unto us, which we lovingly and graciously accepted'. Richard Cust has argued persuasively that Charles's 'tendency to see a grant of supply in very personal terms' and his 'habit of reducing the whole issue to a matter of trust' were manifestations of his 'suspicion of his subjects' intentions'.[35] Yet Charles's own behaviour, especially his refusal to abandon Buckingham and his willingness to resort to non-parliamentary taxation, only made it more likely that Parliaments would mistrust him and therefore fail his test of their loyalty. This then set up a vicious circle by forcing him to rely more heavily on non-parliamentary sources of revenue.

Analogous problems affected parts of the Crown's ordinary revenue that traditionally received Parliament's consent before they were collected, especially customs duties. The so-called ancient, or great, customs, originally introduced in 1275, were recognised as the Crown's by right and required no renewal.[36] However, during the early seventeenth century, the extent of Parliament's control over two further categories of customs duties – impositions and tonnage and poundage – became hotly disputed.

The Crown had always possessed a theoretical right to levy extra import duties, known as impositions, in order to regulate trade and to protect native producers and manufacturers. The merchant community strongly resented them, and in 1606 the London merchant John Bate refused to pay impositions on currants imported from the Levant, a duty that had been introduced in 1601. When, at the instigation of Robert Cecil, Earl of Salisbury, and the Lord Treasurer, the Earl of Dorset, Bate was sued in the Court of Exchequer, the judges upheld the King's right to levy impositions on the grounds that this fell within his extraordinary (or absolute) prerogative – which operated outside but not contrary to the law – rather than his ordinary (or legal) prerogative.[37] Successive Lord Treasurers correctly perceived this as one of the few really effective ways to enlarge the Crown's ordinary revenues, and impositions were extended by revising the Books of Rates (which laid down the rates of customs duties) in 1608, 1613, 1615, 1622 and 1635. Impositions became ever more lucrative: their annual yield increased from £70,000 in 1614 to nearly £250,000 by 1640.[38] They surfaced as a grievance in most parliamentary sessions between 1606 and 1629, but the Crown nevertheless continued to raise them.[39] The essential point of dispute was whether they should be classed under the absolute prerogative (the Crown's extraordinary powers which could be exercised to regulate trade or foreign policy) or under the ordinary prerogative (exercised through Parliament and the common law).[40] This was a genuinely grey area, but behind the Houses' concern clearly lay a fear that such a valuable and flexible source of income would increase the Crown's capacity to rule without Parliaments.

Anxieties about impositions also help to explain why tonnage and poundage became so controversial in the later 1620s. Tonnage and poundage was imposed on every tun of wine imported, and every pound's worth of goods that was either imported or exported: since Richard III's accession in 1483, the first Parliament of each reign had granted these duties to the new monarch for life. However, in 1624, Solicitor-General Heath provoked a furore by citing the 1604 act granting tonnage and poundage to James as a justification for raising impositions. To prevent a recurrence of this, the following year the Commons passed a bill granting tonnage and poundage to Charles for one year only pending a full-scale review of customs revenues in general. The Lords, however, let this bill sleep after the first reading, and the Parliament was dissolved before the general review could be conducted. Charles nevertheless continued to collect tonnage and poundage for the next 15 years, despite protests from the Commons that this was illegal without parliamentary consent.[41] Although the Commons' initial attitude may well have been far from hostile, they became steadily more insistent on their right to assent to tonnage and poundage, and on 2 March 1629 resolved that anyone who paid it was 'a betrayer of the liberties of England'.[42] To Charles, on the other hand, the Commons' behaviour appeared merely perverse: that a majority of members had called for a war which they then refused to finance properly seemed to him to reflect the pernicious influence of a minority of 'ill-affected persons'.[43]

This sort of misunderstanding was characteristic of a fiscal system in which the gap between the Crown's needs and the Houses' willingness to give became steadily wider. During the mid and late 1620s, the costs of war were such that the Crown probably needed in the region of £1 million a year. Parliamentary supply amounted to £353,000 in 1624, £140,000 in 1625, and £275,000 in 1628. Small wonder, then, that Charles felt that the Houses were 'enforcing us to new courses for the necessary defence of ourself and people'.[44] Yet the Houses believed that they were acting generously: after all, five subsidies in 1628 was an unprecedentedly large number. Unfortunately, most members failed to take sufficient account of the combined effects of inflation, the declining value of the subsidy, and the escalating costs of war. The King was better placed than they were to understand these effects, but their mistrust of his advisers, especially Buckingham, was so great that they were reluctant to listen. Hence, as Russell has argued, 'the gulf between the maximum politically possible and the minimum administratively viable' gradually widened.[45]

Given that the essential outlines of this fiscal system had existed for nearly three centuries, it was hardly surprising that serious problems were emerging. Unfortunately, early seventeenth-century attempts at financial reform all proved to be failures. The most radical scheme was Salisbury's Great Contract of 1610. This envisaged that the Crown would surrender such unpopular feudal dues as wardship and purveyance in return for an annual parliamentary grant of £200,000 and a lump sum of £600,000. However, both the King and the Houses came to the view that they preferred the existing system.[46] The King listened carefully to Sir Julius Caesar's warning not to surrender 'the fairest flowers for profit and command in all his garland', and his calculation that the Crown's actual gain would have been only about £85,000 a year, still leaving a substantial deficit.[47] Many members of the Houses, on the other hand, were horrified by the prospect of an annual supply of £200,000 generated by permanent taxation. Sir Roger Owen thought this a 'colossal sum'; others believed – quite incorrectly – that it amounted to 'the eighth part of all the kingdom's possessions'.[48] The anxieties of James and the Houses caused the scheme to founder, and the opportunity for a fundamental overhaul of the fiscal system was lost.

Conrad Russell has shown that during the 1620s there was a marked contrast between the majority of members, who insisted that the Crown had sufficient revenues provided they were correctly managed, and a small minority – led by Sir Nathaniel Rich, Sir Benjamin Rudyerd, Sir Dudley Digges and John Pym – who sought permanent reforms that would both enlarge the Crown's income and safeguard the future of Parliaments. That might mean reforming the assessment of subsidies, or revising the customs, or allowing the Crown to sell licences or monopolies. But such ideas were unable to overcome the ingrained conviction of the majority that the removal of 'evil counsellors' and the restoration of efficient administration would solve the Crown's financial problems.[49]

The only significant reforms of the period before the Civil Wars took place in 1641. The Personal Rule had proved two things beyond doubt. The first was that the Crown could generate enough revenue by means of fiscal feudalism (wardship, purveyance, forest fines, knighthood fines) and prerogative levies (impositions and above all Ship Money) to achieve an annual income of approximately £1 million and thus balance its peacetime budget.[50] However, the second lesson was that it was still effectively impossible to fight a major war – and certainly not an unpopular war – without parliamentary supply. In October 1636 the Earl of Dorset had noted Charles's determination 'not to come to Parliaments in necessity or upon necessity',[51] yet it was precisely such necessity which forced him to recall Parliament in 1640. In such a context, it was not surprising that the Short Parliament should have insisted very starkly on the principle of no supply before redress of grievances,[52] or that the Long Parliament should have taken advantage of Charles's defeat in the second Bishops' War to dismantle much of the financial machinery which had underpinned the Personal Rule. The King was in no position to resist a series of statutes in the summer of 1641 which declared illegal impositions (22 June), Ship Money and forest fines (7 August), and knighthood fines (10 August).[53] Yet alongside these negative measures, a group associated with Bedford devised a programme of constructive reforms that would have involved Parliament paying off the King's existing debts and assuming control over the customs. They would also have placed royal revenues on a more secure footing by voting fixed sums in taxes, and by confiscating the lands of 'delinquents' and of Deans and Chapters. There was even a possibility that the Great Contract might be revived. This scheme would have involved several 'bridge-appointments', headed by those of Pym as Chancellor of the Exchequer and Bedford as Lord Treasurer, but the latter's death in May 1641 was a serious blow to these proposals.[54]

Negotiations nevertheless continued over tonnage and poundage, which the Houses granted to the King for a series of short fixed terms in 1640–2.[55] Many members were reluctant to make a more permanent grant, thereby enhancing Charles's financial independence, without obtaining further political concessions from him.[56] Charles's financial estimates for 1642 indicate gross revenues of £334,480, as compared with an annual figure of £899,368 when the Long Parliament met. Some of his most lucrative sources of revenue had been declared illegal. As Russell has written, 'Charles simply could not make a settlement with the Long Parliament unless a new revenue settlement, and a proper grant of tonnage and poundage in particular, were part of the bargain.'[57] But by the summer of 1642 it was clear that the Houses would only contemplate such a settlement, including a revised Book of Rates, in return for major political, constitutional and religious concessions regarding such matters as the King's choice of advisers, his command of the militia, the reformation of the Church, and the punishment of 'papists' and 'delinquents'.[58] The Houses wished to bring Charles, in Lord Brooke's striking phrase, to 'a necessity of granting'.[59] Such a strategy clearly indicates that they still saw mileage in the 'power of the purse'; what Brooke and his allies did not fully anticipate was that faced with necessity Charles would prefer fighting to granting. By 1642, the Houses had so reduced the King's revenue as to leave him with only two choices: to accept their terms, or to raise forces against them. Given his personality and beliefs, he naturally opted for the latter. The Houses had used their financial powers to manoeuvre him into a corner in which he could neither afford to make a settlement with them nor contemplate making the concessions they demanded. They offered so little in the way of revenue that Charles finally concluded that he was better off fighting than negotiating further. Here, then, was the immediate contribution of the 'power of the purse' to the outbreak of the English Civil War.

The Civil Wars and Interregnum

From the fourteenth century until 1642, Parliament's right to vote taxation had formed part of an organic fiscal system. It provided for the monarch's extraordinary needs just as Crown lands, feudal dues and the profits of justice generated the ordinary revenue. But with the outbreak of Civil War those members of the Houses who remained at Westminster found themselves in the wholly unaccustomed role of having to assume executive powers. This meant not only passing ordinances which had the force of law even though they had not received the royal assent, but also raising taxes on the Houses' own authority in order to support troops. In doing so, they imposed a tax burden on England that vastly exceeded anything that the early Stuarts had ever implemented, and that would not be equalled again until the 1690s.

Two contrasted taxes formed the basis of Parliamentarian finance. The first was the weekly assessment, introduced by an ordinance of 24 February 1643.[60]

This became monthly from 1645, and it continued until the Restoration.[61] The assessment was a quota tax, and the key to its success lay in the fact that it combined the most effective features of three earlier taxes without any of their weaknesses. Like the fifteenth and tenth and Ship Money, but unlike the subsidy, it was based on a quota rather than on assessments, and the quota was then divided up between and within the localities. Like the subsidy, but unlike Ship Money, local disputes over the division of the quota were arbitrated by local commissions.[62] The prototype for the assessment lay in a proposal advanced by Bedford and his allies in 1641, which had in turn formed the basis of an assessment of March 1642 to raise £400,000 for troops to quell the Irish Rebellion.[63] Although attempts were made to include income from personal property and from income and fees, the assessment effectively became a land tax. It proved very efficient and produced remarkably high yields: the quotas introduced in February 1643 were roughly the equivalent of a parliamentary subsidy every fortnight. By 1645-6, Kent was paying more in assessments every month than it had paid in any one year for Ship Money.[64]

The other great Parliamentarian tax, the excise, worked on altogether different principles. Before the Civil War there had been no indirect taxation in England granted by Parliament, with the exception of tonnage and poundage.[65] An excise – a tax on consumables, paid at the point of retail on certain commodities – had been mooted by Pym and others in the 1620s and in 1641, but it was only in an ordinance of 22 July 1643 that the Houses established a 'new impost' on such goods as tobacco, wine, cider, beer, imported silks, furs, hats, leather and linen.[66] Further items were added over the years that followed: soap, paper, cloth and imported glassware in September 1643; meat and salt (the principal preservative) in January 1644; alum, hops, saffron, and English-made hats and silks in July 1644.[67] A tax on so many essential commodities was bound to be deeply unpopular, and by the summer of 1647 riots against the excise had become sufficiently serious for the duties on meat and salt to be revoked.[68] However, the salt duty was reintroduced in August 1649, and in March 1654 Cromwell extended the excise to virtually all saleable commodities.[69]

The Houses also employed a range of other expedients to raise money. Each was administered through a central committee consisting of members of both Houses who were responsible for collecting (but not spending) particular revenues.[70] The Committee for the Advance of Money was established in November 1642 to raise loans and to impose assessments on those who would not contribute to the Parliamentarian war effort voluntarily.[71] The following March the Committee for Sequestrations was created to administer the estates confiscated from Royalists and Catholics. In all, nearly 5,000 people suffered the loss of their estates in this way. When the yield from sequestrations proved disappointing, the less active Royalists ('delinquents') were allowed to regain their estates in return for taking oaths of loyalty and for paying heavy fines ('compositions'); but a minority of hard-line 'malignants' were exempted from any form of redress.[72] Most ironically of all, the Houses continued to collect tonnage and poundage.[73]

This was emblematic of a war effort which saw the Houses commit many of the heinous acts for which they had earlier denounced Charles I. The massive financial cost of war was only part of a wider picture in which the Houses breached many of the clauses of Magna Carta and the Petition of Right. Martial law, arbitrary imprisonment, billeting of troops and manifold violations of due process of law were justified by the argument that Lord Wharton voiced in 1643, that 'they were not tied to a law for these were times of necessity and imminent danger'.[74] Yet such flagrant breaches of the rule of law were bound to generate a backlash, especially when accompanied by such a crushing tax burden.[75] By the summer of 1648, many areas were demanding an end to such policies: over 10,000 inhabitants of Dorset, for example, signed a petition calling for 'a speedy and just account of all our monies and estates cheated or wrested from us by loans, contributions, taxes, fines, excise or plunder'.[76] Such feelings contributed to the outbreak of the second Civil War, not least because by that stage many perceived the King as a more convincing champion of the rule of law than the Houses. Many of Charles's financial expedients were modelled on those of Parliament. The Royalist 'contribution' was similar to the assessment, and there was also a Royalist excise. It is, however, notable that Charles delayed the introduction of the latter until it could be approved by the Oxford Parliament.[77] This suggests that he recognised the value of being seen to respect the principle of taxation by parliamentary consent, an attitude that was consistent with the image of a defender of popular liberties which he projected at his trial and execution.[78]

The story of parliamentary taxation during the Interregnum presents an interesting mixture of change and continuity. The principal sources of public revenue remained the same as during the 1640s, and indeed sometimes faced the same objections as early Stuart taxation. The monthly assessments produced an average of £1.4 million a year during the period 1648–53 (a higher level than Charles I's annual revenue had ever attained) and although this figure fell to below £1 million thereafter the assessments remained unpopular.[79] The discrepancies between the quotas for different counties were especially resented.[80] The excise raised less money – on average about £350,000 a year – but was even more widely hated. Although the practice of farming the excise after 1650, and the dropping of the excise on meat and beer, helped to ensure that the excise riots of the 1640s did not continue into the following decade, there could be no doubt about continuing popular hostility.[81] For instance, in 1657 a rather grim *Dialogue betwixt an Excise-Man and Death* concluded with the moral: 'Let all Excise-men hereby warning take / To shun their Practice for their Conscience sake'.[82] William Prynne refused to pay the excise levied under the Cromwellian ordinance of March 1654 on the grounds that it had not yet been ratified by Parliament. In *A Declaration and Protestation against the illegal, detestable, oft-condemned new tax and extortion of excise*, Prynne accused Cromwell of 'an arrogation of a super-transcendent jurisdiction' and thought it 'strange . . . that any of those who . . . remonstrated against the late King, and justify the bringing of him to justice . . . should before and since imitate or exceed him in all and every of these particulars'.[83]

In 1654 the legality of customs duties on imported silk received a very similar challenge from a London merchant, George Cony, on the grounds that they were being collected under the Cromwellian ordinance of March 1654 which had not yet received parliamentary consent.[84] Against this, Cromwell claimed that the Instrument of Government had empowered him to issue ordinances which had the force of law until Parliament assembled, and that the raising of taxes was essential on grounds of necessity. However, the subsequent imprisonment of Cony and his lawyers appeared to many contemporaries to epitomise Cromwell's authoritarianism. These included Lord Chief Justice Rolle, whose brother's goods had been seized for refusal to pay tonnage and poundage in 1628, and who resigned his office in 1655. Cony was eventually persuaded to drop his suit. But his case not only posed uncomfortable questions about the relationship between protectoral powers and Parliament's right to consent to taxation; by raising the argument of necessity it also came dangerously close to Charles I's defence of the Forced Loan and Ship Money.[85]

The surfacing of such issues was indicative of the gradual drift back towards traditional institutions that took place during the 1650s. In some ways, relations between Cromwell and his Parliaments on financial matters closely resembled the situation under the early Stuarts. The costs of military campaigns against Spain prompted Cromwell's decision to call the second Protectorate Parliament in September 1656,[86] and as in earlier decades, the ruler's financial needs enabled Parliament to extract concessions in return for supply. The particular targets of the first sitting were the Major-Generals and the Decimation Tax, a levy on former Royalists that had been introduced without Parliament's consent. This hostility left Cromwell with no alternative but to abandon both experiments in January 1657 as the price for securing a parliamentary grant of £400,000 to finance the war against Spain.[87] In both Protectorate Parliaments, members were very reluctant to grant Cromwell too generous a financial settlement lest this become 'a means to keep off Parliaments'.[88]

Possibly the biggest departure from earlier practice was the concept of a fixed annual income granted to the head of state by Parliament. In December 1653, the Instrument of Government provided for the raising of 'a constant yearly revenue' to maintain a standing army of 10,000 horse and 20,000 foot, together with £200,000 a year 'for defraying the other necessary charges of administration of justice, and other expenses of the government'. This was not to be altered 'but by the consent of the Lord Protector and the Parliament'.[89] Likewise, in the summer of 1657, the Humble Petition and Advice made provision for a yearly revenue of £1.3 million, of which £1 million was tied to the armed forces and £300,000 to the costs of government. There followed the revealing provisos that none of this money was to be 'raised by a land tax', that these arrangements were not to be 'altered without the consent of the three Estates in Parliament', and that 'no charge be laid, nor no person be compelled to contribute to any gift, loan, benevolence, tax, tallage, aid, or other like charge without common consent by act of Parliament, which is a freedom the people of these nations ought by the laws to inherit'.[90] Thus was the 'power of the purse' enshrined in the second of the written constitutions of the Interregnum. Furthermore, the principle of a fixed parliamentary grant of revenue to the ruler survived after 1660 and formed the foundation of the Restoration financial settlement.

The later seventeenth century

The Restoration Settlement sought to ensure a monarchy that was strong enough to rule effectively but not so strong as to repeat the grievances of Charles I's reign. In steering between anarchy and tyranny, the settlement's guiding principle was to turn the clock back to 1641, not to either 1640 or 1642. In the financial sphere, this meant affirming the abolition of all feudal dues (such as wardship and purveyance) and the illegality of prerogative taxation (like Ship Money, impositions and Forced Loans). In their place, the

Convention Parliament voted a permanent, ordinary revenue – derived from the customs and the excise[91] – which was then supplemented by periodic grants of parliamentary supply. The basic distinction between ordinary and extraordinary revenues thus continued, except that the former were now based on parliamentary grant as well.[92]

It was anticipated that the ordinary revenue would total about £1.2 million a year, but this soon turned out to be wildly over-optimistic. The ordinary revenue reached only £544,911 in 1661-2, whereupon a new hearth tax of one shilling on every hearth or chimney was introduced in 1662. In the event, however, this raised less than half the required sum.[93] The ordinary revenue did not exceed £1 million until 1671-2, and only in the last four years of Charles's reign did it consistently reach between £1.2 and £1.3 million.[94] It was supplemented by temporary grants of direct taxation either through subsidies (four in 1663, one in 1671) or more commonly in the form of assessments modelled on those of the 1640s and 1650s.[95] Parliament also granted the Crown various indirect taxes including the Wine Duties of 1670 (renewed in 1678) and the Additional Excise of 1671 (renewed in 1677).[96] Nevertheless, except in his final years Charles II was always short of money,[97] and although it is unlikely that the Convention had deliberately contrived to place Charles in this predicament, few members of subsequent Parliaments showed any desire to alleviate it lest this weaken their financial hold over him. For, as Sir Thomas Meres put it bluntly in February 1677, "twill be a mighty mischief to give an additional revenue. Your Parliament by it is of no effect nor use . . . 'Tis money that makes a Parliament considerable, and nothing else.'[98] Danby similarly discerned a feeling in the Commons that 'the Crown ought from time to time to be beholding to them for those additions which may be wanting at the year's end'.[99]

Restoration Parliaments were no less conscious of the 'power of the purse' than their early Stuart predecessors. In 1660 the Speaker told Charles 'that it was never the custom of Parliaments to charge the people with payments, until their liberties and grievances were first confirmed and redressed'.[100] Yet, as John Miller has argued, the use that they made of this power, and the extent to which they were successful, varied considerably during the course of the reign. Much depended on how they perceived current royal policies, especially in the areas of religion and foreign policy. During the 1660s the Commons sometimes succeeded in delaying supply, but their attempts to appropriate grants to specific purposes named by Parliament were a failure. Where they supported a war, as in 1665-6, they were prepared to vote extra supply to meet the costs.[101] After 1672, however, growing hostility towards Charles's pro-French, anti-Dutch foreign policy and his support for religious toleration at home made members much more intransigent. In 1673-4 they used the threat to withhold supply to force Charles to withdraw the Declaration of Indulgence, accept the Test Act, and make peace with the Dutch. These were the most notable successes for the principle of 'redress before supply' during the entire reign.[102]

However, as in earlier decades such a strategy was much more likely to succeed in wartime (notably in 1672-4), not least because the profits from trade that formed the basis of the ordinary revenues necessarily depreciated during wars. In the late 1670s, by contrast, the Houses signally failed to secure the disbandment of the army with the money they had voted for that purpose.[103] The 'power of the purse' was further diminished by a trade boom which increased the net yield from customs duties from an annual average of £372,440 during the 1660s to £560,000 in the period 1675-85.[104] It was this, above all, which gave Charles the financial independence to weather the Exclusion Crisis because it enabled him to dissolve Parliament when it suited him politically. Furthermore, an ordinary revenue which averaged £1,310,000 a year between 1681 and 1685, combined with a pacific foreign policy, allowed Charles to violate the Triennial Act by not recalling Parliament in 1684.[105] Thus, if the extent to which the Houses asserted the principle of 'redress before supply' depended largely on their perception of royal policies, the effectiveness of their strategy remained a function of the Crown's financial position. By voting the Crown a permanent revenue derived from customs duties and the excise, the members of the Convention had overturned the pre-Civil War situation and left the bargaining power of their successors crucially dependent upon the vagaries of trade.

Just how little safeguard this system offered against a ruthless monarch in a favourable economic climate became glaringly obvious during the reign of James II. When James's first Parliament assembled in May 1685 it voted him all the revenues that had been settled on his brother.[106] In order to aid the King in suppressing the revolts led by Monmouth and Argyll, it also granted him additional customs and excise revenues for a period of five (in some cases eight) years.[107] Such was the buoyancy of trade that James's ordinary revenue reached an annual average of £1,580,000 over the next three years, and his net income an annual average of £2,066,300.[108] This made James, in J. P. Kenyon's words, 'the first monarch since Henry VIII to enjoy financial independence',[109] and left him free to dissolve Parliament whenever he wished. He had obtained exactly what he wanted, for, within 48 hours of his accession he had confided to the French ambassador that he intended to enjoy:

> the same revenues the King my brother had . . . It is a decisive stroke for me to enter into possession and enjoyment. For hereafter it will be much more easy for me either to put off the assembling of Parliament or to maintain myself by other means which may appear more convenient for me.[110]

James knew exactly how to defuse the power of the purse and he succeeded admirably. He was financially independent for the rest of his reign, and his bid in 1687–8 to secure a 'packed' Parliament was motivated by a wish to repeal the penal laws against Catholics, not by any financial need. However, the attempt to 'pack' Parliament proved disastrous and was one of the key reasons that William of Orange gave for his intervention in November 1688.

The members of the Convention which assembled in the wake of James's flight to France were determined not to make the same mistake again. This was a sentiment that united members of all political persuasions. In January 1689, William Sacheverell, a Whig, urged the Commons to 'secure this House, that Parliaments be duly chosen and not kicked out at pleasure, which never could have been done without such an extravagant revenue that they might never stand in need of Parliaments'. The following year Paul Foley, a Tory, expressed similar views: 'If you settle such a revenue as that the King should have no need of a Parliament, I think we do not our duty to them that sent us hither.'[111] Gilbert Burnet detected a belief among 'many that [William] would grow arbitrary in his government, if he once had the revenue; and would strain for a high stretch of prerogative, as soon as he was out of difficulties and necessities'.[112] The result was that in March 1689 Parliament granted William a revenue of £1.2 million. Furthermore, it was stipulated that half of this sum was to be used for the civil administration and the other half for war.[113] This grant was decided without any investigation of the Crown's financial position. It could not possibly meet even the peacetime needs of the Crown, and William fumed that 'the Commons used him like a dog'.[114] The Bill of Rights also explicitly ruled out non-parliamentary sources of revenue: 'the levying of money for or to the use of the Crown by pretence of prerogative, without grant of Parliament, for longer time, or in other manner than the same is or shall be granted, is illegal'.[115]

However, what really necessitated a fundamental overhaul of the fiscal system was not this financial settlement but the fact that England was involved in almost constant warfare during the 25 years that followed the Revolution of 1688–9. The Nine Years War (1689–97) cost about £5.5 million a year, the War of the Spanish Succession (1702–13) about £8.5 million a year.[116] This, together with the deliberate weakening of the Crown's permanent revenue, rendered obsolete the ancient distinction between the ordinary and extraordinary revenues which had persisted in a modified form after the Restoration. Instead, England was definitively transformed, as Michael Braddick has argued, from a 'demesne state' to a 'tax state'.[117] The proportion of national revenues derived from non-parliamentary sources shrank from 76 per cent in 1626–40 to 10 per cent in 1661–85, and to only 3 per cent in 1689–1714.[118] By the 1690s virtually all revenue was being raised by direct or indirect taxation granted by Parliament.

The fact that these taxes were voted by Parliament gave them a legitimacy in the eyes of taxpayers which allowed their yields to increase dramatically during this period. Between 1688 and 1714 a total revenue of £122 million was raised, an average of nearly £5 million a year. Of this total, roughly £35 million came from customs duties and £30 million from the excise. The hearth tax was abolished in 1689, and four years later a new direct tax, the land tax, was introduced. The fact that the land tax, like the assessment, was a quota tax was crucial in tackling the problem of under-assessment, and helps to explain why it yielded as much as £46 million by 1714. Another experiment was the window tax, established in 1696. These taxes generated even higher yields than those of the 1640s and 1650s, and were much less widely resisted. The result was that from being one of the most lightly taxed nations in Europe in the early seventeenth century, by the close of the century the English were paying a level of taxation per head exceeded only by the Dutch Republic.[119]

This necessarily had profound implications for the relationship between Crown and Parliament, which will be examined more fully in the final chapter.[120] The important point to make here is that the Crown's dependence upon Parliament was greater than ever before, and as a result Parliament became a permanent institution of government, sitting every year from 1689 onwards. This greatly strengthened the 'power of the purse'. During the 1690s, parliamentary supply was regularly 'appropriated' to specific areas of expenditure; it also became quite common for the Lower House to 'tack' clauses redressing constitutional grievances onto revenue bills which the Crown could ill afford to refuse. From 1690 a Commons Commission of Public Accounts monitored the government's financial management with far more effect than the committee briefly established in the late 1660s. In particular, the Commission enabled Parliament to exercise a power of audit which meant that 'appropriation' of revenue – unsuccessfully attempted in 1624, in the mid-1660s and in the late 1670s – could henceforth be implemented in practice.[121]

The triumph of the 'power of the purse' was particularly apparent in two developments. First, the government's fiscal credit became directly dependent upon parliamentary guarantees. There had briefly been an attempt, in a scheme proposed by Sir George Downing in 1665, to provide statutory guarantees that loans would be repaid through a system of credit orders. However, a run on such orders forced the government to stop honouring them in January 1672 (the so-called Stop of the Exchequer), and the order system collapsed.[122] It was not until the 1690s that vast sums were borrowed on long-term public loans, by means of such credit instruments as mortgages, insurance and stocks and shares, and in 1693 a funded 'National Debt' was established. This replaced the personal debts of the monarch and was underwritten by Parliament. The following year saw the foundation of the Bank of England, a joint-stock company in which subscribers lent a total of £1.2 million to the government at an interest rate of 8 per cent in return for incorporation as a bank. The Bank was also given the authority to issue notes and discount bills on the security of parliamentary taxation. Such public borrowing raised the government's spending power by nearly 34 per cent in the 1690s, and its viability rested on parliamentary guarantees and public confidence in Parliament's capacity to ensure the regime's fiscal probity.[123] The second development was the Civil List Act of 1698, which granted the Crown tax revenues worth about £700,000 a year 'to meet the costs of the civil government and the royal establishment'. The Crown was not permitted to retain any surplus yield on the taxes allocated for this purpose 'without the authority of Parliament'. This established the principle – which still exists today – that parliamentary revenue should meet the costs of civil government, and it definitively ended the medieval tradition that the King should 'live of his own'.[124]

The old financial system had survived from the fourteenth century, and in many ways the wonder is that it endured so long. By the end of the seventeenth century it had finally been abandoned, and Parliament's 'power of the purse' had assumed a wholly new importance in the management of public finance. That outcome was far from inevitable, and it grew out of complex historical circumstances, not least the wars of the late seventeenth and early eighteenth centuries. All that perhaps was inevitable was the demise of the ancient system, which by the seventeenth century was unlikely ever again to meet the demands made of it, and which contained the potential for frequent misunderstandings between successive monarchs and their Parliaments. For as the Earl of Clarendon wryly observed, 'Parliaments do seldom make their computations right, but reckon what they give to be much more than is ever received, and what they are to pay to be as much less than in truth they owe.'[125]

|5|

Procedure

Various aspects of parliamentary procedure, particularly those governing the passage of legislation, have already been discussed earlier in this book. This chapter will examine more closely a number of procedural matters that have so far been treated only in passing, if at all. Parliamentary procedure grew up piecemeal over time, in response to the needs of the moment. It was a hotch-potch produced by the institution's historical development rather than the embodiment of any coherent vision or principle. For the sake of imposing some semblance of order upon a far from orderly subject, the following sections will examine the material under five main headings: privilege and liberties; the appointment and role of the Speakers and clerks; committees; the structure of parliamentary days and sessions; and what may be called the 'theatre of Parliament'.

One central theme of the chapter will be the extent to which procedural developments were of political and constitutional significance. In recent years several scholars, most notably Sheila Lambert, have challenged older accounts which saw procedural change as an attempt, especially by the Commons, to strengthen its position in relation to the Crown. Lambert and others argue instead that the amount of procedural innovation in seventeenth-century Parliaments has been exaggerated, and that such innovations as did occur were intended to enhance the Houses' capacity to transact the business for which they were called. Far from heralding the 'winning of the initiative by the House of Commons', procedural changes were designed to increase the Houses' effectiveness to offer advice, to represent opinion, to pass legislation, and to cope with the sheer volume of bills. Procedure thus constitutes another important dimension of Parliament's role as an agency of royal government.[1] That said, once in place procedural devices could be utilised for political purposes that had not been in the minds of their original instigators. This theme of unintended consequences will emerge regularly in what follows.

Privilege and liberties

In order for Parliament to function effectively as a legislative, deliberative and conciliar body, its proceedings were safeguarded by a range of privileges that had grown up during the medieval and Tudor periods. These should, more precisely, be divided into privilege and liberties. They were broadly similar in the two Houses, except that members of the Lords also enjoyed certain further privileges accorded to them as peers of the realm. By the beginning of the seventeenth century, both Houses could legitimately regard these privileges and liberties as theirs by right, although the origins, nature and scope of them all left plentiful room for dispute both between Lords and Commons and between the Crown and the two Houses.

At the beginning of each session, the Speaker of the Commons[2] petitioned the monarch for the granting of four 'ancient' privileges: free access to the monarch and to the Upper House in order to convey the opinions of the Commons; the right to correct mistakes or misunderstandings that might be prejudicial to the Commons; 'liberty of speech for the well debating of matters propounded'; and freedom from arrest and legal suits for members of the Commons and their servants.[3] Conventionally, the Lord Chancellor or Lord Keeper would then reply on the monarch's behalf, granting these privileges. By the end of the sixteenth century the Speaker's petition and the monarch's grant had become formalities, although it was possible for certain caveats to be added. In 1614, for example, Lord Chancellor Ellesmere requested the Commons not to use freedom from arrest to 'protect debtors'.[4] By contrast, the Lords were not expected to petition for their privileges: it was assumed that they enjoyed these by right, much like the similar powers and entitlements of the Privy Council.[5]

Strictly speaking, the term 'privilege' referred only to members' privilege of freedom from arrest and from legal suits. Peers enjoyed freedom from arrest (though not from suits) at all times, but for members of the Commons it applied only while Parliament was sitting and for 20 days after the end of each session.[6] The rationale behind this privilege was that when a man was summoned to Parliament, he had to be free to obey without being hindered by the actions of private individuals. Those serving in the High Court of Parliament were not to be called by lesser courts, except in cases of treason, felony or a breach of the peace. As John Selden wrote in 1629: 'Privilege of Parliament is to keep a Parliament man free from any disturbance, that he may freely attend the business of Parliament.'[7] This privilege extended also to a member's servants and attendants on the grounds that their service was essential if he was to fulfil his duties properly.[8]

The privilege of freedom from arrest was emphatically confirmed in 1604 when Sir Thomas Shirley, newly elected member for Steyning, was imprisoned in the Fleet for debt. Eventually, the Commons prevailed upon the Warden of the Fleet to grant his release. In the wake of Shirley's Case, a statute safeguarded the privilege, and James I took care to respect it.[9] However, he observed crisply that 'the Parliament not sitting, the liberties are not sitting', and in 1621 he even claimed that he was 'very free and able to punish any man's misdemeanours in Parliament, as well during their sitting as after'.[10] But in practice, James wisely did not put this to the test, and he bided his time before moving against those most hostile towards Buckingham. In 1621, for instance, he waited until the parliamentary recess before detaining Sandys together with the Earls of Oxford and Southampton, while in January 1622 Coke, Hakewill, Phelips, Mallory and Pym were arrested immediately after the dissolution of Parliament.[11] By contrast, during the 1626 Parliament Charles I violated the privilege of each House in turn by ordering the arrest of several of Buckingham's most outspoken critics. The Earl of Arundel was detained on the rather flimsy pretext that he had allowed his son to marry into the royal family without permission. This was, Charles claimed, a 'personal misdemeanour ... which had no relation to the Parliament'. The House repeatedly petitioned for Arundel's release, and ultimately declined to proceed with other business until he resumed his seat, at which point Charles finally capitulated.[12] In the Commons, meanwhile, Sir Dudley Digges and Sir John Eliot had also been imprisoned while Parliament was sitting, prompting Sir Nathaniel Rich to declare that 'our liberties now suffer in a higher manner than ever they did in the memory of man'.[13] Charles's characteristic belief that a minority of troublemakers were disrupting Parliaments, combined with his authoritarian temperament, led him several times to breach parliamentary privilege by seeking the arrest of those he regarded as 'ill-affected'. This strategy culminated in the King's attempted arrest of Lord Mandeville along with five members of the Commons on 4 January 1642, a personal intervention that was greeted by cries of 'privilege, privilege'.[14]

The later 1640s and 1650s saw the privilege of freedom from arrest violated several times far more flagrantly than it had been by Charles I. Most famously, on 6 December 1648 Colonel Thomas Pride arrested 45 members of the Commons and secluded 186 more in a bid to secure a majority in favour of bringing the King to trial. The secluded members denounced this 'high violation of the rights and privileges of Parliament, and of the fundamental laws of the land'.[15] About a dozen elected members were denied admission to the first Protectorate Parliament on the grounds that the Council of State did not regard them as 'persons of known integrity, fearing God, and of good conversation'. This figure rose to as many as 100 in the second Protectorate Parliament.[16] The Interregnum also saw the abolition of the Lords and the loss of peers' immunity from arrest or civil litigation.[17]

After the Restoration, the perceived threats to freedom from arrest and legal suits were transformed. That members of the Commons viewed Charles II very differently from his father was strikingly revealed when, in December 1661, the new King arrested a member, John Lovelace, for preparing to fight a duel outside the House. Charles notified the Speaker of the arrest, whereupon the Commons took Lovelace into their own custody and recorded their 'humble thanks' to the King 'for his grace and favour, in being so tender of the privileges of this House, as to acquaint Mr Speaker therewith'.[18] However, after 1660 this privilege became a major source of dispute between Lords and Commons. Perhaps as a result of their experiences during the Civil Wars and Interregnum, both Houses became even more protective of their privileges than hitherto. Charles II wisely stood clear while the Lords and Commons locked horns in the cases of Skinner vs. the East India Company (1667–70) and Shirley vs. Fagg (1675). In both, the Commons challenged the Lords' jurisdiction and argued that it infringed the immunity of their members from legal suits during parliamentary sessions. Here, as on earlier occasions, a privilege that originated in the need to free members to attend parliamentary sessions could be exploited for political purposes. Some 'Country' members of the Commons deliberately took advantage of these two cases to foment discord between the two Houses.[19]

A similar malleability is evident in a further aspect of this privilege, namely the right of each House to determine who should enjoy it, and thus to decide the membership of the House. The Commons' right to determine whether an individual was qualified for membership of the House was recognised by the mid-sixteenth century,[20] and in 1621 the case of the monopolist Sir Robert Floyd established the Commons' right to expel one of its own members.[21] More problematic was the Commons' claim to decide disputed elections. It used to be thought that the Buckinghamshire election case of 1604 (Goodwin vs. Fortescue) established this right unambiguously, but more recent research has shown that it was not the constitutional landmark once supposed. The dispute reflected factional tensions within the Court and Privy Council, and entrenched rivalries at county level, more than any heightened consciousness of privilege on the part of the Commons. Certainly from 1604 disputed elections were referred to the Committee of Privileges nominated by the Commons, which had developed under Elizabeth I; after 1672 this was constituted as a Committee of the Whole House.[22] But there is no evidence that Lord Chancellor Ellesmere's ruling in 1604 was intended to be a definitive settlement, and agencies other than the Commons, notably Chancery, continued to interfere in some election disputes thereafter without necessarily causing complaint. Here again procedural developments were very much an *ad hoc* response to particular situations.[23]

If the term 'privilege' was technically restricted to the freedom from arrest and legal suits enjoyed by members, the other rights and freedoms which were loosely bracketed together under the heading of 'liberties' were regarded as belonging to the Houses collectively. Of these the most famous was liberty of speech, which was examined in detail in Chapter 3.[24] Here it is just worth observing the twofold theme that is emerging in this chapter: first, that this liberty had originated as a way of enhancing the usefulness of Parliament to the monarch by ensuring that members offered counsel as freely as possible; and second, that the limits of free speech were sufficiently vague to leave scope for political dispute between successive monarchs and their Parliaments. One common way of trying to avoid conflict was for the Speaker's petition to promise that speech would be decorous and 'not pass the latitude of duty and discretion'.[25] But that distinction was so subjective as to offer no reliable solution. It was, furthermore, only in 1689 that parliamentary freedom of speech acquired statutory authority when it was affirmed by the Bill of Rights.

Many of Parliament's liberties were so flexible and vaguely defined as to permit a range of possible applications in practice. For this reason, even the most learned lawyers shied away from composing any definitive guide to privilege and liberties. As Sir Edward Coke admitted, 'the laws, customs, liberties and privileges of Parliament are better to be learned out of the rolls of Parliament, and other records, and by precedents and continual experience, than can be expressed by any one man's pen'.[26] Quite often, the terms 'privilege' or 'liberties' were loosely applied to any procedural practice which protected the independence of either House, especially the Commons. Both Houses had control over their own procedures and managed their own affairs.[27] They were also entitled to safeguard the secrecy of their deliberations, although attempts to achieve this were often unsuccessful.[28] The plasticity of the idea of privilege – and the extent to which it could be exploited for political purposes – was apparent in 1629 when John Rolle claimed that members' privilege extended to their property as well as their persons. This followed the seizure of his goods after he refused to pay tonnage and poundage without Parliament's consent. The Commons agreed that he should be allowed the immunity of privilege for his possessions, but the King's dissolution of Parliament precluded any grant of compensation until the Long Parliament.[29] Equally flexible was the Commons' right to punish non-members who offended them. Established in the later sixteenth century and affirmed by the case of Edward Floyd in 1621,[30] this right was invoked relatively infrequently, but in it lay the seeds for the Long Parliament's punitive policies during the 1640s.[31]

In addition, the Lords possessed several other rights unique to the Upper House. As we saw in Chapter 2, by the early seventeenth century, peers regarded a summons to Parliament as a right rather than at the monarch's discretion. When Charles I tried to exclude the Earl of Bristol and Bishop Williams by not summoning them to the 1626 Parliament, the House condemned this as a breach of privilege.[32] An extension of the peers' right to attend the Lords was the custom whereby those peers who were unavoidably absent were entitled to appoint another to act as their proxy.[33] Peers usually chose colleagues of broadly similar religious and political attitudes as their proxies. It cost £2 to register a proxy with the Clerk, who recorded it in the Proxy Book. In 1626 a standing order was passed that no peer could hold more than two proxies, a decision consciously directed against Buckingham who in that Parliament held no fewer than 13.[34] A further order stipulated that 'all proxies from a spiritual lord shall be made unto a spiritual lord, and from a temporal lord unto a temporal lord'.[35] In some Parliaments as many as 40 peers appointed proxies: illness, age or official business elsewhere were as likely reasons for their absence as lack of interest in parliamentary proceedings. Proxies had to be renewed at the beginning of each new session, and they were nullified if the absentee actually attended the Lords. The House was able to decide when proxies were to be used, and they were usually deployed only when a vote was expected to be close. This was sometimes crucially important, as for example in March 1645 when Saye's use of the Earl of Mulgrave's proxy ensured the passage of the officer list for the New Model Army, which included a number of well-known Independents, in a House divided 11:11. When, the following year, Mulgrave transferred his proxy to Saye's opponent Essex, this was enough to give the Presbyterian peers a small majority in the Upper House for much of 1646.[36] Another practice distinctive to the Lords was that peers were entitled to record their 'dissent' in the Journal below a vote of which they disapproved. This right was extended in 1640 to allow peers to enter written 'protests' against the decision of the majority, a procedure that those voting among the minority especially valued.[37]

Finally, peers enjoyed a number of rights as individual nobles.[38] In cases of treason or felony, they were entitled to be tried by their peers. During trials they testified on their honour rather than under oath. Peers were protected by a special statute known as '*Scandalum Magnatum*' against anyone who spread false stories about them or caused dissension between the Lords and Commons.[39] By virtue of their traditional role as royal counsellors, peers enjoyed by right the personal access to the monarch for which the Speaker of the Commons had to petition. Most picturesquely of all, by a right dating from the reign of Henry III, a peer journeying to Parliament could take two deer in the royal forest.[40] This ancient right illustrates once again how parliamentary privileges and liberties were a complex blend of the old and the new, a constantly developing series of responses to changing situations and circumstances.

Speakers and clerks

Analogous points may be made about the role of the Speakers and clerks of each House. They played a crucial part in ensuring the smooth and effective functioning of Parliaments as agencies of royal government. Although they were all – with the theoretical exception of the Speaker of the Commons – Crown appointees, it would be anachronistic to see any inherent conflict of interests between their duties to the monarch and to the Houses: they were simultaneously the servant of the Crown and the servant of their House, and perceived no incompatibility between the two. Occasionally such conflicts could occur, but only when relations between the Crown and the Houses were already strained for some other reason. In this organic system of government, the Speakers acted as pins linking the different elements together, while the clerks gave them invaluable assistance in planning parliamentary business and keeping records.

The Speaker of the Lords was the Lord Chancellor or the Lord Keeper of the Great Seal.[41] Only one or other of these officers existed at any one time. They exercised identical authority, except that the dignity of the Lord Chancellor's office was greater. The Lord Chancellor was the Crown's servant: he spoke and acted for the monarch except on those occasions (commonest under James I and especially Charles II) when the monarch was personally present in the House. He would relay messages from the monarch, adjourn, dissolve or prorogue Parliament on the monarch's behalf, and at the end of the session he would pronounce the form of words bestowing or withholding the royal assent to bills that had passed both Houses. The position was potentially of immense influence, above all because – together with the Clerk – the Lord Chancellor arranged the agenda for each day and could thus favour certain bills or matters of business over others. To the monarch it was vitally important that the Lord Chancellor should be effective at forwarding business that the Crown supported and delaying matters of which it disapproved. The individual personalities of successive Lord Chancellors, and the extent to which they enjoyed the confidence of both the Crown and the House, were therefore crucial. It was striking that when the Lord Chancellor or Lord Keeper had alienated either the monarch (like Lord Keeper Williams in 1625) or a significant proportion of the House (like Lord Keeper Finch in 1640), the sessions proved turbulent and divisive.[42] On the other hand, an experienced officer, with a strong position at Court – such as Ellesmere or Clarendon – could prove an invaluable servant of the Crown and play a critical role in guiding legislation through the House.[43] In August 1641, the Lords asserted its right to choose its own Speaker in the absence of the Lord Chancellor or Lord Keeper, a claim that was reiterated in 1660.[44] But otherwise the position of the Speaker of the Lords as a Crown appointee was a straightforward one that underlined Parliament's status as a 'high court' and an institution of royal government.

The choice of the Speaker of the Commons was somewhat more complex. In theory, the Lower House chose the Speaker from among its number, but in practice the nomination was made from the Court.[45] This pattern was well established by the beginning of the seventeenth century, and resumed after the Restoration. For example, on the first day of the Cavalier Parliament, the senior Privy Councillor present nominated the Speaker (Sir Edward Turnor, an established Crown spokesman), and was seconded by another Councillor. The House raised no objection.[46] In 1673 several members expressed the view that it was inappropriate for Sir Edward Seymour, as a Privy Councillor, to be Speaker.[47] Seymour remained in office, however, and indeed the Commons came to hold him in sufficient esteem that when Charles rejected the House's nomination of him as Speaker in March 1679, there was such a furore that the King had no alternative but to prorogue Parliament.[48] The following year he accepted Sir William Williams as Speaker, but the appointment of so radical a Country figure indicated that this particular manifestation of Court influence was beginning to decline.[49] In 1695 the Commons forthrightly rejected a royal nominee for Speaker, and thereafter the Speaker was chosen by whichever party enjoyed a majority in the House.[50]

As in the Lords, the Speaker exercised control over the agenda and was responsible for determining the order in which items were taken. However, the Commons did possess the power to overrule the Speaker's choice of business.[51] How far this was used depended on the prevailing political mood and the degree of harmony that existed between the Crown and the Commons. During the early seventeenth century the Commons tended to treat the Speaker more robustly, a trend that culminated in the extraordinary scene on 2 March 1629 when the Speaker was physically restrained in his chair in order to prevent him from dissolving Parliament.[52] There emerged, as seldom before, a stark conflict between the Speaker's duties to the Commons and his role as a servant of the Crown. In a powerful phrase that signalled how far the workings of the constitution had become dislocated, William Strode told Finch that he was either a servant of the House or of the Crown, to which Finch sadly replied 'I am not less the King's servant for being yours.' Unable to contemplate making the choice that Strode laid before him, Finch was held down while the House passed three resolutions against innovation in religion and the collection and payment of tonnage and poundage.[53] In 'normal' times the Speaker would never have faced such a conflict of loyalties; that it arose at all demonstrated how deeply Charles and some of his subjects mistrusted each other by 1629. Such mistrust inevitably disrupted the smooth running of the points of contact between them, and placed the Speaker in a peculiarly difficult position.

The Speaker's dual allegiance to Crown and House was put to further severe tests during the 1640s. The events of 4 January 1642 dramatically illustrated that it was by now impossible to serve two masters. When Charles attempted to arrest five members of the Commons, and pointedly asked Speaker William Lenthall where they were to be found, Lenthall replied:

> I have neither eyes to see, nor tongue to speak, in this place but as this House is pleased to direct me, whose servant I am here; and I humbly beg your Majesty's pardon that I cannot give any other answer than this to what your Majesty is pleased to demand of me.[54]

Charles's action had forced the Speaker to make an unprecedented choice between his two allegiances. The fact that he had to choose at all indicated how far the workings of government had broken down, and later monarchs wisely avoided pushing matters to a point where the issue of the Speaker's loyalties became explicit.

The Speakers of each House received vital assistance from a steadily expanding clerical staff. The senior clerk, known as the Clerk of the Parliaments, was principally concerned with the Lords.[55] A Crown appointee, the Clerk was responsible, with the Lord Chancellor, for preparing agendas, and for suggesting which bills might be read, which committees report, and what business be introduced. He was responsible for recording the proceedings of the House in the Journal, and subsequently for compiling the Parliament Roll. At the end of the session, he would send public acts to the King's printer for the production of the sessional print of statutes.[56] It was also expected that he would be able to provide guidance on precedents and to locate relevant parliamentary records at short notice. All of these duties became steadily more onerous during the course of the seventeenth century, especially during the 1640s. Furthermore, the preservation of records and the provision of copies of orders or acts for interested parties meant that the Clerks' work continued even when Parliament was not sitting.[57] From around 1610 Clerks appointed two assistants: Owen Reynolds and Henry Elsynge acted as assistants to Robert Bowyer, for example. From the Restoration, the senior of the two was known as the 'clerk assistant', the junior as the 'reading clerk'.[58] The House of Commons had since the fourteenth century possessed its own Clerk – sometimes called the Under-Clerk of the Parliaments – who was appointed by the Crown. The first known official appointment of a Clerk Assistant (by the Crown, on the Speaker's recommendation) was in 1640, although some earlier Under-Clerks had had assistants, for example John Wright's son assisted him in the Parliament of 1624.[59]

Among the most important duties of the Clerk of each House was the preservation of a parliamentary archive.[60] By the start of the seventeenth century this had begun to assume the characteristics of a record office, and this trend was reinforced by two outstandingly gifted and assiduous Clerks under the early Stuarts. During the tenures of Robert Bowyer (1609–21) and Henry Elsynge (1621–35) it became established practice for the working papers of the Lords (including what became the Main Papers) to be preserved as the nucleus of a parliamentary archive rather than as the Clerk's personal property, although there was a partial relapse under John Browne (1638–49; 1660–91). Elsynge also secured the acquisition in 1621 of the ancient Jewel Tower across Old Palace Yard as a suitable repository for the Lords' archive – a stroke of good fortune that ultimately ensured that these sources survived the fire of 1834.[61] It is interesting that this move took place roughly simultaneously with the revival of the Lords' judicature,[62] and also with the first attempts to codify aspects of Lords' procedure in a series of standing orders which were then added to thereafter.[63] The formation of the Lords' archive was thus closely associated with the House's need to retrieve accurate precedents and its wish to impose order upon its own proceedings.

Committees

The committee structure of each House was complex and registered a number of significant changes during the seventeenth century. In addition to the *ad hoc* committees appointed to consider specific bills, several standing committees were appointed to review matters relating to general areas such as privileges or petitions. A procedure also developed known as the Committee of the Whole House, in which all those present could participate without being constrained by the usual rules governing debate. Here again, recent research has challenged the view that some of these developments reflected the growing assertiveness of the Commons in particular, and that they were intended to diminish the Crown's control over the Houses. Instead, it has been suggested that they were a series of piecemeal devices, adopted to expedite business and improve the efficiency of the Houses. Such arguments offer a persuasive explanation of the reasons why these procedural innovations were introduced, but there is a danger of overlooking the political uses to which they could be put once established. Here it is worth examining the different categories of committee in turn.

Ad hoc committees were appointed in each House to consider particular matters and to prepare business for the House. Most commonly, they were set up to discuss and amend the majority of bills after their second reading. When a committee was ordered in the Commons, the Speaker would invite the House to shout out the names of those members whom they wished to be appointed as 'committees' (members of the committee).[64] The Clerk took down the names, an important responsibility that was potentially open to manipulation, notably in the early years of the Long Parliament.[65] Within the smaller Upper House a rather more decorous procedure was possible. In the opening decades of the century, it was first determined how many members of each 'bench' (bishops, earls, barons, etc.) should serve, and individual peers were then nominated. In the early Stuart period, it was increasingly common for committees to be composed of an equal number of earls and bishops and double that number of barons.[66] However, this practice appears to have been abandoned by the time of the Short and Long Parliaments, and by the late 1670s it had become usual for all those present in the House at the time a committee was ordered to be appointed to it.[67] The members of the committee would then determine exactly when and where they met, normally at eight o'clock in the morning and/or two o'clock in the afternoon. Commons committees most frequently met in the Court of Exchequer, the Court of Wards, or the Court of Star Chamber, whereas Lords committees usually met in the Painted Chamber or the Prince's Chamber.[68] Committees of the Upper House were chaired by the peer who was first in order of precedence, although during the latter part of the century this gave way to the election of a peer of appropriate ability, knowledge and availability.[69] Commons committees chose their own chairmen throughout the century. Chris Kyle has shown that attendance at committees was often extremely poor, due partly to apathy and partly to the fact that because there was no centralised control of committees it was common for several of them to arrange to meet simultaneously. As a result, they were often subject to innumerable adjournments. In a bid to offset the problem of low attendance, the size of the average committee increased exponentially during the early Stuart period. Attempts to impose a quorum (either a minimum of seven or eight, or half those appointed) were generally not observed in practice, and additional members were often added to the original committee.[70] Once the committee had reported back to the House – often but not invariably through its chairman – it would normally cease to exist. When the House adjourned itself, all the committees then in existence remained in being, and some continued to meet; when the King adjourned Parliament all committees ceased until Parliament reconvened; and when Parliament was prorogued or dissolved the existence of all *ad hoc* committees was automatically terminated.[71]

By taking a great deal of business, especially relating to individual bills, off the floor of the Houses, *ad hoc* committees undoubtedly saved a lot of time and accelerated the passage of legislation. Any member could be appointed to a committee, although it was established practice in the Lords that no absentee member could be appointed unless his role as an officer of state directly impinged on the committee's business.[72] As we saw in Chapter 2, attendance in each House and appointment to committees tended to fall to a core of active members, and there was at times some evidence of an approximate link between activity and political alignment. In the Lords during the 1620s, certain peers who were hostile to Buckingham, such as Southampton, Saye, Bedford and Essex, were disproportionately likely to attend the House and therefore to be appointed to committees.[73] This connection between attendance and committee membership became much closer from the later 1670s onwards when it became normal practice for all those then present in the Lords to be appointed to *ad hoc* committees. The presence of Privy Councillors in each House, and their appointment to committees, could advance the Crown's interest whereas their paucity – for example in the Commons under the early Stuarts – could give those members critical of royal policies greater influence. The workings of committees could thus assume political significance.[74]

Much the same was true of standing (or 'grand') committees. Like *ad hoc* committees, these were appointed from among members of the relevant House; unlike *ad hoc* committees, they were established at the beginning of each session, continued to meet until the end of the session, and handled any matters that arose within a broad subject area. Standing committees first came into general use in the Lords in 1621, and the two most important over the years that followed were the Committee for Privileges and the Committee for Petitions. The latter effectively took over the role of a medieval body known as the Receivers and Triers of Petitions, who continued to be appointed but ceased to serve any real purpose.[75] In the Commons, three standing committees – for privileges/elections, grievances and religion – had grown up during the sixteenth century, and they were joined in 1621 by committees for trade and courts of justice. These standing committees retained their separate identities, although during the early seventeenth century an increasing proportion of their discussions took place under a new procedure called the Committee of the Whole House.[76]

The main lines of this procedure were soon established, and both Houses employed it with increasing frequency after 1606. Any member could propose discussing a matter in Committee of the Whole House, and if this was agreed the Speaker would vacate the chair. In the Commons another chairman would be chosen, but in the Lords this practice was not adopted until after the Restoration. When either House was sitting as Committee of the Whole House it followed the procedures of committees rather than the standard rules of debate. This meant, above all, that the normal restriction that each member could speak only once on the same matter in any given day was waived, thereby allowing much freer and more expeditious debate. Furthermore, when a House was sitting in Committee of the Whole House its proceedings were not recorded in the Journal. It seems that the procedure was originally introduced on the initiative of Privy Councillors who wished to increase their opportunity to answer questions and rebut counter-arguments to their proposals.[77] It also saved time by taking a great deal of debate off the floor of the House, and was certainly not intended as a weapon against the Crown.[78] Nevertheless, although the Lord Chancellor or Speaker could participate as a member, the fact that he was not in the chair necessarily diminished the extent to which he could steer discussion. Once the procedure became established, it was often especially welcome to those members who found themselves in a minority. Certain members could exploit the device to circumvent the Speaker, such as William Mallory who proposed doing so for the debate on the Commons' Protestation of 1621, 'that we might not be troubled this day with the Speaker'. In June 1628, Charles I's order to the Speaker to prevent the Commons from referring to Buckingham by name was bypassed in similar fashion.[79] The procedure thus permitted members to exert pressure on the

Crown and its advisers, as for example in such diverse circumstances as Strafford's trial in 1641 or the promotion of the Irish Cattle Act of 1666.[80]

In addition, joint committees comprising members of both Houses were set up from time to time to handle a variety of business. They could be requested by either House to discuss matters of mutual concern, and in legal cases they had the advantage of enabling members of the Commons to hear evidence under oath.[81] By the reign of James I, the established practice was for the Commons to nominate twice as many representatives as the Lords. Such committees were invariably chaired by a peer and they usually met in the Inner Court of Wards. Initially, meetings were very formal and emphasised the social inequality between the Houses, with peers seated and wearing their hats while members of the Commons stood in their presence, without their hats. However, it is likely that some of these formalities were abandoned during the 1640s, when the Long Parliament made very extensive use of joint committees. Eighteen such committees were established in 1641, and no fewer than 60 the following year. Joint committees were given wide-ranging responsibilities to raise money, manage the war effort and govern the realm: among the most important were the Committee for the Advance of Money, the Committee for the Sequestration of Delinquents' Estates, the Committee for Compounding with Delinquents, and the Committee for Plundered Ministers. Most powerful of all was the Committee of Both Kingdoms, created in 1644 to co-ordinate the Parliamentarian war effort and civilian government, which became almost independent of the Houses that had established it.[82] The Long Parliament really saw the zenith of the joint committee, and they became much rarer after the Restoration.[83] Only three such committees were appointed during Charles II's reign and the system was abandoned altogether after 1695.[84]

Another way in which members of the Lords and Commons could meet formally was in conferences of the two Houses. These had been held from time to time since the fourteenth century,[85] and in earlier records are sometimes difficult to distinguish from joint committees. Like joint committees, conferences could be requested by either House, and they can broadly be divided into two categories: formal conferences, at which information was exchanged, and free conferences at which free debate and discussion took place. When a request was agreed to, each House would appoint a delegation of 'managers' to represent them at the conference. Conferences were normally held in the Painted Chamber and they were chaired by one of the managers of the House that had made the initial request. As at joint committees, there would be twice as many representatives of the Commons as of the Lords. Other members who were not 'managers' could attend but not speak. At conferences, the convention was always observed that the peers sat with their hats on while members of the Commons stood bareheaded in front of them. Most conferences were concerned with legislation (especially after the Restoration), although other matters such as privilege or judicature were sometimes considered as well. The Houses did not sit while a conference was meeting, and afterwards the 'managers' would select one of their number to report back to the House. Although they facilitated communication between the two Houses, conferences were not always harmonious occasions. Members of the Commons sometimes felt intimidated by the peers (whose managers often included a significant number of Privy Councillors) and some resented the formal deference that they were expected to display; some of the older members in 1604 'found themselves sick and lame long after' a conference.[86] For their part, the peers at times felt outnumbered and overawed by the eloquence and legal learning of many of the Commons managers. Conferences occasionally became very heated. In 1661, for example, the rival managers disagreed so strongly over a bill that the conference broke down and they stormed out of the Painted Chamber.[87] Both Houses grew increasingly wary of the acrimony that free discussion could cause, and as a result during the later seventeenth century formal conferences grew more common (approximately ten were held each session between 1660 and 1681) whereas free conferences became less frequent and disappeared entirely by 1704.[88]

The structure of days and sessions

When Parliament was sitting the structure of the day's business was governed by a number of conventions which the Houses were able to revise as necessary. The Houses usually assembled at nine o'clock in the morning and rose before noon, although on occasion the time of meeting was advanced to eight o'clock. Committees normally met at eight o'clock in the morning and/or two o'clock in the afternoon. Sometimes the Houses would then reconvene at two or three in the afternoon and work on through the afternoon. Private bills were often dealt with during the afternoon, in an attempt to prevent them from crowding out more public matters.[89] As the pressure of business increased during the early seventeenth century, and especially after 1640, the Houses at times worked later. Under Elizabeth the Commons had never sat later than three o'clock in the afternoon,[90] but a new record was set on 22–23 November 1641 when the debate on the Grand Remonstrance continued until two o'clock the following morning.[91]

The frequency of afternoon sittings varied considerably during the course of the century, and was determined primarily by the volume of business and the gravity of the political situation at any given moment. For example, during the first session of James's first Parliament, the Commons sat 95 times, 8 (8 per cent) of them in the afternoon, while the Lords sat 69 times, 6 (9 per cent) in the afternoon.[92] In 1628, the session dominated by the Petition of Right debates, 17 (17 per cent) of the Commons' 102 sittings were in the afternoon while the proportion in the Lords was 13 (14 per cent) of 94.[93] In the first two months of the Long Parliament, only 6 per cent of the sittings of each House took place in the afternoon.[94] By contrast, in November 1641, the month of the Grand Remonstrance, the Commons sat 37 times, 10 (27 per cent) of them in the afternoon, while for the Upper House – which was not involved in drafting the Remonstrance – the proportion was 3 out of 27 (11 per cent).[95] The same general pattern persisted after the Restoration. In the relatively quiet session of 1664, for example, the Commons only met in the afternoon for 3 (7 per cent) of its 42 sittings, while the Lords only did so for 1 (3 per cent) of 36.[96] In the 1685 session, which faced the threats of the Monmouth and Argyll rebellion as well as the need to settle the finances of a new King, the proportions of afternoon sittings were 5 (12 per cent) of 41 for the Commons and 3 (9 per cent) of 34 for the Lords.[97]

Members of both Houses had numerous other commitments in the capital that made it difficult to sustain the work load associated with a parliamentary session over more than relatively short periods. Many members took advantage of being in London to attend to other business such as pursuing their own needs or those of their localities in the law courts, or to visit old friends, or to enjoy the opportunities for social occasions, or sight-seeing or shopping. Attendance tended to decline during the course of a session, and many members were probably glad that Parliaments only sat for a small proportion of the time. During James I's 22-year reign, parliamentary sessions lasted a total of about 148 weeks (approximately 33 months). From Charles I's accession until the dissolution of the Short Parliament, the figure was 48 weeks (roughly ten months and three weeks). The average length of sessions was 16 weeks under James I and 9 weeks under his successor. This trend continued after the Restoration: although the Cavalier Parliament met for a total of 18 sessions in as many years, the average length of a session during Charles II's reign was still only eight to ten weeks, and during James II's reign Parliament sat for a total of less than eight weeks.[98] In all, Parliaments were thus sitting for rather less than 10 per cent of the time, a statistic which dramatically highlights that although Parliament was a settled institution whose meeting place, records and procedure had continuity from session to session, its meetings were very intermittent.[99]

These overall figures conceal the fact that Parliaments varied considerably in length. Some lasted for only a single session and could be extremely brief, such as the Short Parliament (three weeks) or the third Exclusion Parliament (one week). Others comprised more than one session, although only three seventeenth-century Parliaments lasted for more than two sessions: that of 1604–10 (five sessions), the Long Parliament (in almost constant session between 1640 and 1653, and only finally dissolved in 1660), and the Cavalier Parliament (18 sessions from 1661 to 1678). There was no necessary link between the number of sessions and the degree of political instability prevailing during a Parliament, although it is noticeable that those years that saw several new Parliaments called in quick succession (especially 1625–9, 1640 and 1679–81) were periods of particularly tense relations between the Crown and the Houses.

During the early seventeenth century the royal powers to summon, dissolve and prorogue Parliament became politically contentious in a way that partly reflected the fears of some members – especially of the Commons – that the future of Parliaments was in danger. Until 1640–1 there was little challenge to the monarch's right to summon and dissolve Parliament at will.[100] However, from 1621 onwards many members of the Commons claimed that the House could only be adjourned by itself. It was accepted that monarchs could *prorogue* Parliament, which meant that they could bring the current session to an end without dissolving the Parliament. A prorogation terminated all unfinished bills and committees, so that they had to begin again from scratch in the next session. An adjournment, by contrast, merely froze them in their tracks so that they could be resumed when Parliament reassembled following the recess. Adjournments could last for anything from a single day to several months, and the resumption of business represented a continuation of the same session. Furthermore, members' privileges – especially their freedom from legal suits – continued throughout a recess, whereas after a prorogation or a dissolution they lapsed after 20 days. As G. A. Harrison has shown, during the 1620s an assertion of its right to adjourn itself became the Commons' preferred way to safeguard incomplete legislation, protect its privileges, and prolong the Parliament's existence. It was claimed that whereas dissolution and prorogation lay within the royal prerogative, adjournments were determined by the

Commons itself (just as other law courts had authority to adjourn themselves). These claims culminated in the events of 2 March 1629, when several members claimed that the House alone could decide whether and when it should be adjourned.[101]

By 1640, heightened suspicion of the monarch led members to adopt a different strategy. From early in the century there had been sporadic but fairly muted calls that Parliaments should be summoned annually.[102] As fears grew for Parliament's future, members cited two statutes of the reign of Edward III that stipulated that Parliament should meet every year.[103] In 1610 there were several calls for Parliament to meet regularly – possibly every five or seven years, if not annually – but the idea attracted little support. At some time between 1614 and 1621, an anonymous author composed a lengthy manuscript tract entitled 'Motives to induce an annual Parliament': this tract, which was widely circulated, advocated that Parliament should become a permanent institution no longer dependent upon royal summons.[104] By 1641 many members so mistrusted Charles I that they passed two radical measures to safeguard their own future. The first, which received the royal assent on 15 February, was a Triennial Act modelled on that passed in Scotland in June 1640.[105] This 'Act for the preventing of inconveniences happening by the long intermission of Parliaments' stipulated that henceforth a new Parliament should meet at least every third year: if the King failed to issue writs, an elaborate mechanism was established to ensure that Parliament would convene automatically. The second measure, to which Charles assented on 10 May, was 'an Act to prevent inconveniences which may happen by the untimely adjourning, proroguing, or dissolving this present Parliament'.[106] This required that the Long Parliament could only be dissolved by another statute, to which it would of course have to consent.

These two acts marked an unprecedented encroachment on the royal prerogative to summon and dissolve Parliaments at will. Although the Triennial Act invoked the statutes of Edward III's reign, these had never been implemented. The two acts of 1641 protected the Long Parliament from royal action but not – as Pride's Purge and the expulsion of the Rump plainly demonstrated – from army intervention. Only on 16 March 1660 did the Long Parliament finally vote its own dissolution.[107] The Triennial Act technically remained in force after the Restoration, but to the overwhelmingly loyalist Cavalier Parliament it appeared 'in derogation of His Majesty's just rights and prerogative inherent to the imperial crown of this realm for the calling and assembling of Parliaments'. A new Triennial Act of April 1664 repealed that of 1641 and stated merely that 'there may be a frequent calling, assembling and holding of Parliaments once in three years at the least' without establishing any administrative machinery to ensure this.[108] An attempt by Sir Richard Temple in 1668 to restore the 1641 sanctions ended in ignominious defeat.[109] In 1684–5, this lack of safeguards enabled Charles II to evade the 1664 Triennial Act by not summoning a Parliament, a failure that prompted remarkably little outcry.

Only after the revolution of 1688–9 did annual Parliaments become a permanent feature of government. In December 1694 another Triennial Act (an 'Act for the frequent meeting and calling of Parliaments') stated that 'from henceforth a Parliament shall be holden once in three years at the least' and created the necessary administrative arrangements to guarantee that this would indeed happen.[110] Parliament actually met every year from 1689 onwards, a fact that initially owed less to the 1694 Triennial Act than to the

Crown's desperate need for money in a period of almost incessant warfare and to the constitutional changes that this brought in its wake.[111] It was that very practical development, founded on the massively strengthened 'power of the purse', that finally dispelled fears for Parliament's future and guaranteed its permanence as an institution.

The theatre of Parliament

Ritual accompanied many aspects of parliamentary proceedings, and the opening and closing ceremonies in particular presented colourful and dramatic spectacles. Historians have only recently begun to appreciate the political significance of public ceremonial in early modern England, and this dimension of Parliament has yet to receive the detailed treatment it deserves. The following brief discussion will focus on the rituals that marked the beginning and end of parliamentary sessions, and will argue that they expressed two central themes that have already emerged in this book: the continuities between seventeenth-century Parliaments and their medieval predecessors, and the role of Parliaments in bringing together the diverse elements of the body politic.

The ceremonies at the opening of Parliament were divided into three stages. First, there was a royal procession from the palace of Whitehall to Westminster Abbey. Elizabeth Read Foster has described such a spectacle during the reign of James I:

> First came messengers and trumpeters, then royal judges and Privy Councillors, bishops in ecclesiastical robes, peers in their Parliament robes of velvet trimmed with ermine. There followed the prince in his Parliament robes, with cap and coronet, and at last the King, preceded by his cap of estate and sword, wearing his Parliament robes and crown, flanked by gentlemen pensioners and followed by his guard. Heralds, splendid in ceremonial attire, marshalled each group.[112]

It is striking that members of the Commons were not included in this procession unless they were Privy Councillors or royal officials. This was very much the extended royal household and Council in procession, a fact which underlined the medieval origins of Parliament in which the Commons came as petitioners to the monarch and his permanent advisers.[113]

The procession was followed by a service in Westminster Abbey in which God's blessing upon the new parliamentary session was sought. During the course of this ceremony the monarch received the sceptre of St Edward, symbolising the royal supremacy over the Church. While the service was being conducted in the Abbey, the Lord Steward was supervising another ritual in the Palace of Westminster whereby those who were about to become members of the Commons took the oath of allegiance to the monarch.[114] This was the essential preliminary to the third and final stage of the opening of Parliament, which took place in the House of Lords.

The monarch was led to the throne at the far end of the House of Lords and the peers then took their seats. On the monarch's right sat the archbishops and bishops in order of appointment, while on the left sat the lay peers by rank (dukes, marquesses, earls, viscounts, barons) and thence by date of creation. The clerks, judges and legal assistants sat on woolsacks in the middle of the chamber, and it was on one of these immediately below the throne that the

Lord Chancellor sat when the monarch was not present.[115] The members of the Lower House were then summoned to assemble by the bar at the opposite end. The Lord Chancellor delivered a speech in which he set out the main reasons why the monarch had called Parliament, and then invited the Commons to elect a Speaker. The Clerk of the Parliaments then read out the names of the Triers and Receivers of Petitions in the Lords, after which the monarch departed. The opening ceremonies were not fully concluded until the second or third day, when the monarch returned to the Upper House and the members of the Commons presented their 'chosen' Speaker. This was, as we have seen, a fiction in that the Speaker remained a Court nominee. By custom, the Speaker pleaded his unworthiness for the office. He was answered by the Lord Chancellor, and then requested the traditional privileges of the Commons.[116] The Lord Chancellor granted these on the monarch's behalf, after which the monarch left the Palace of Westminster escorted by the nobility. The members of the Commons meanwhile returned to their House where the reading of a bill 'pro forma' signalled their right to initiate new legislation. This formally concluded the opening ceremonial, and the Houses could turn to the actual business of Parliament.[117]

If the opening procession had underlined Parliament's medieval origins, the ensuing ceremonies in the House of Lords served to highlight the unity of the three components of Parliament – Crown, Lords and Commons – as the expression of the body politic. As Conrad Russell has written, 'the most important symbolism of a Parliament was that of unity. It was part of the conventional wisdom of the seventeenth century that the king and his people, like head and body, had no true independent life: their strength was in their interdependence.'[118] The rituals at the opening of Parliament presented a powerful visual symbol of this interdependence of the monarch and the two Houses.[119]

Much the same was true of the rather less spectacular ceremonial that marked the closing of a parliamentary session. The monarch – or the Lord Chancellor on the monarch's behalf – would meet members of both Houses in the Lords. The Speaker made a general speech of thanks to the monarch, after which the monarch (or Lord Chancellor) replied and then gave – or occasionally withheld – the royal assent to those bills that had completed their passage through both Houses. The use of Law French for the formulae of assent or rejection further emphasised the continuities with the medieval past.[120] Finally, the Speaker presented any subsidies that had been voted, and the monarch responded with thanks. The Lord Chancellor then announced the dissolution or prorogation of Parliament on the monarch's behalf, thus formally bringing the session to a close.[121]

It is worth adding one final point about the political importance of parliamentary ceremonial that will serve to draw the threads of this chapter together. Traditional forms of ritual at times belied the novel political contexts in which they took place. For example, although Sheila Lambert is quite correct to stress that the opening of the Long Parliament assumed an entirely customary form, John Morrill has observed that it took place against a background of unprecedented crisis, with a Scottish army in the north-east of England, and a widespread determination to end forever the policies associated with Charles I's Personal Rule.[122] Equally, ceremonies, like parliamentary procedure in general, could sometimes be more politically significant than at first sight appears. Pauline Croft's recent examination of the parliamentary installation of Henry, Prince of Wales on 4 June 1610 clearly illustrates how a public ceremony could be consciously manipulated for political purposes. Salisbury hoped that the installation might serve to rally the loyalty of both Houses to the Crown during the delicate negotiations that surrounded the Great Contract. Although this was the first installation of a Prince of Wales since 1504, precedents could be produced dating back to the reign of Henry III. The ceremony thus drew out the continuity of English kingship in ways that helped to emphasise the legitimacy of the Stuart dynasty. The ceremony was in part modelled on the state opening of Parliament, but with the highly significant differences that it was held in the Court of Requests and that seating was provided for all members of both Houses. This served to flatter the Commons in ways that the traditional opening ceremonies – in which they stood at the bar of the Lords – conspicuously did not. Of course, the installation failed to have the effect that Salisbury desired: the Great Contract floundered, and in 1616, four years after Henry's death, Charles was installed as Prince of Wales in a private court ceremony that set the tone for his whole reign. Yet even this was significant for, as Croft has argued:

> The reversal in 1616 to a court ceremony, with little public participation, can be seen as one of the milestones in the gradual emergence of a new set of monarchical attitudes and assumptions, the distance and remoteness of which led eventually to the Personal Rule, and ultimately perhaps to the scaffold outside Whitehall.

The political import of such ceremonial – as of the other procedures examined in this chapter – should never be underestimated.[123]

|6|

The parliamentary trinity

Just as the ceremonial analysed at the end of Chapter 5 symbolised the unity of Crown and Parliament as head and members of one 'body politic', so the institutional reality was that Parliament consisted of a trinity comprising monarch, Lords and Commons. This had several important theoretical and practical implications that will be explored in this chapter. In the first place, the components of the parliamentary trinity did not fit at all easily with the conventional definition of the three estates (spiritualty, nobility, commonalty). This generated a confusion which became politically significant during the 1640s when it mattered greatly whether or not the Crown was itself regarded as one of the three estates. The controversy was still not entirely resolved by the end of the century. Second, the fact that Parliament was a 'mixed sovereign'[1] meant that much of its effectiveness as an institution depended upon reasonably harmonious relations between the three component parts. Many older accounts often treated 'Parliament' and 'House of Commons' as though they were synonymous, and thus overlooked the fact that Parliament was a bicameral institution in which the Lords played at least as important a role as the Commons. Terminology subtly reflects this. For example, members of the Commons are today called Members of Parliament, but for the seventeenth century the term is anachronistic and best avoided.[2] The three elements of the trinity were all members of Parliament and need to be accorded equal weight. Furthermore, the nature of their interactions varied considerably over time and crucially influenced political developments during the course of the century.

Theory: the three estates

The discrepancy between the structure of the English Parliament and the customary definition of the three estates really became apparent during the early sixteenth century, and especially as a result of the changes that took place during the 1530s.[3] The conventional idea that emerged during the Middle Ages identified the three estates as spiritualty, nobility and commonalty: those who pray, those who fight and those who labour.[4] All these elements were indeed present in the English Parliament as it had developed by the later Middle Ages, but they cut across the institutional structures of the two Houses. The English Parliament was relatively unusual, at least in Western Europe, in the division of peers and gentry between the Lords and Commons.[5] The more common pattern was for clerics, landowners and burgesses to sit separately as three 'estates'. The second of these comprised the 'nobility' ('nobilitas'), a single

category that amalgamated what in England were divided into peers (nobility)
and gentry.[6] The English Parliament, by contrast, had evolved as an extension
of the King's Council and had as a result developed a bicameral structure. It
owed nothing to concepts of the three estates, yet those ideas were so pervasive
that commentators naturally sought to reconcile them with the institutional
reality. The result was profound confusion. The spiritualty sat in the Lords,
those who on the continent would have been classified as 'nobility' were
divided between Lords and Commons, and the third estate (the burgesses)
were members of the Commons. To complicate matters further, the English
Parliament was indeed a tripartite body, comprising three equipollent members; Crown, Lords and Commons. Some observers therefore concluded that
the three estates in England were in fact the monarch plus the two Houses,
while others insisted that the three estates were lords temporal, lords spiritual
and commons, with the Crown (not itself an 'estate') presiding above them.

It was all rather messy, but during the sixteenth and early seventeenth centuries the unresolved confusion remained benign and was not of great political
moment. Following Henry VIII's famous pronouncement in Ferrers' Case in
1542,[7] Tudor doctrine, in the hands of writers such as John Hooker, William
Lambarde and Sir Thomas Smith, tended to focus on the parliamentary trinity
of Crown, Lords and Commons and to regard those as the three estates (when
they used the term at all).[8] This concept of the parliamentary trinity had the
further advantage that it coincided very neatly with the classical theories of
Aristotle and Polybius which identified the pure types of government as
monarchy (the rule of one), aristocracy (the rule of a few), and democracy (the
rule of many). When correlated with these theoretical categories, the English
system could be said to combine elements of all three, and Tudor writers such
as John Aylmer rejoiced in the blessings of such mixed government.[9]

During the early seventeenth century, however, there was a tendency to deny
that the monarch was one of the three estates. This was a point on which both
James I and Sir Edward Coke could agree. James argued in 1621 that
Parliament was composed of a head and a body: 'the head is the monarch and
the body the three estates of the realm'.[10] In Coke's view, similarly, Parliament
consisted of the King 'sitting there in his royal politic capacity' together with
'the three estates of the realm': those four parts collectively formed 'the great
corporation or body politic of the kingdom and sit in two Houses'.[11] In practice, it did not greatly matter how the estates were defined, and whether or not
the Crown was regarded as one of them, as long as relations between them
remained reasonably amicable.[12] But when their relationship deteriorated and
the Civil War loomed, the theoretical definition of the three estates suddenly
acquired considerable political importance.

In order to justify taking up arms against the King and passing legislation
without his assent, Parliamentarian writers utilised the concept of the three
estates as Crown, Lords and Commons to assert that they possessed 'co-ordinate' powers. This theory, most eloquently advanced by Charles Herle, Philip
Hunton and William Prynne, led logically to the principle known as *rex sin-
gulis major, universis minor*: that the King, although the chief member of
Parliament, could be outnumbered and bound by the two Houses. As Prynne
put it, 'one of the three estates is lesser than the three estates together; who in
Parliament . . . are not subordinate, but co-ordinate parts of the great Common
Council of the kingdom'.[13] Herle took this argument a stage further. He
asserted not only that the two Houses outnumbered the King but also that if

the King were prevented from exercising his official powers (for example by malign advice), the Houses could if necessary discharge them on his behalf even if this contravened his personal wishes.[14] This claim ultimately produced a theory of parliamentary sovereignty that reached its logical culmination in the voluminous writings of Henry Parker.[15]

In responding to these arguments, some Royalists retained the definition of the three estates as Crown, Lords and Commons. For example, Charles I's *Answer to the Nineteen Propositions*, drafted on the King's behalf in June 1642 by Viscount Falkland and Sir John Culpepper, asserted that the Houses' demands would disrupt the 'ancient, equal, happy, well-poised, and never enough commended constitution of the government of this kingdom'. Falkland and Culpepper claimed that the essence of England's uniquely well-balanced system of government lay in the fact that it blended the best features of absolute monarchy, aristocracy and democracy. These three elements were represented within the constitution by the monarch, the Lords and the Commons, which formed the three estates. The result was a 'regulated monarchy' in which the monarch was 'a part of the Parliament'. From this premise, it was then argued that the powers 'legally placed in both Houses' were already 'more than sufficient to prevent and restrain the power of tyranny', and that the *Nineteen Propositions* would bring 'this splendid and excellently distinguished form of government' into 'a dark, equal chaos of confusion'.[16]

During the Civil Wars a number of moderate Royalist pamphleteers like Dudley Digges followed the *Answer to the Nineteen Propositions* in depicting the King as one of the three estates. However, not all Royalists accepted this definition and some regarded it as a disastrous mistake. Edward Hyde felt that such a view was not only 'prejudicial to the King' but also implicitly acknowledged the exclusion of bishops from the Lords in February 1642. He insisted that the three estates were lords spiritual, lords temporal and commons, with the monarch standing above them.[17] His position was shared by many other Royalists including such writers as John Maxwell, Griffith Williams and Peter Heylyn, who argued that to identify the monarch as one of the three estates effectively robbed him of sovereign powers.[18]

The crucial problem that many moderate Royalist writers faced during the 1640s was how to prevent an identification of the three estates as Crown, Lords and Commons from sliding into the doctrine of co-ordinate powers. They attempted to resolve this problem in different ways. Henry Ferne, for example, apparently abandoned the estates theory associated with the *Answer to the Nineteen Propositions* and in his later works argued that 'properly the prelates, Lords and Commons are the three estates of this kingdom, under His Majesty as their head'.[19] Other writers adopted a more subtle approach. Sir John Spelman asserted that the King's powers were limited but that he nevertheless remained 'a supreme head, a sovereign'. The two Houses were 'merely instruments of regulation and qualification of the King's legislative absoluteness', and they were 'no sharers with him in the sovereignty'.[20] Thus, although he accepted that the Houses co-operated with the monarch in the passing of legislation, Spelman rejected the doctrine of co-ordinate powers.[21] In similar vein, Dudley Digges accepted that the monarch had 'his hands bound up from using the legislative power without the concurrence of the peers and commons', but thought that he nevertheless remained 'our sovereign lord'.[22] Digges regarded England as 'a restrained and limited monarchy' in which the monarch wielded 'supreme' but 'not absolute power'.[23] In this way, writers such as

Spelman and Digges could continue to identify the three estates as Crown, Lords and Commons without endowing them with co-ordinate powers.

Amidst the revolutionary events of the late 1640s, these distinctions appeared increasingly irrelevant. There seemed little point in deliberating over the exact definition of the three estates at a time when the monarchy and the Lords were abolished and the Commons was drastically purged. The Commonwealthsmen developed the idea of unicameral sovereignty, and in January 1650 all males aged over 18 were required to take an Engagement pledging loyalty to the Commonwealth 'as it is now established, without a King or House of Lords'.[24] The political thought of the 1650s was dominated by the republicanism of Harrington and the naked authoritarianism of Hobbes. Disputes over the precise extent of royal powers and their relationship with Parliament and the rule of law were submerged by fundamental debates over the nature of political authority and of civil society.[25] Yet the constitutional impact of such ideas was relatively transient, and when the monarchy was restored in 1660 the controversies surrounding the monarch's relationship with the Houses of Parliament, and the definition of the three estates, returned along with it.

Conscious of where the idea that the monarch was one of the estates had led during the 1640s and 1650s, the Restoration regime made every effort to repudiate it. The King and his advisers were particularly anxious that the Convention's resolution of 1 May 1660 that 'according to the ancient and fundamental laws of this kingdom, the government is, and ought to be, by King, Lords, and Commons'[26] should not imply the doctrine of co-ordination. Sir Matthew Hale wrote of 'the "three estates of the realm" assembled in Parliament, viz. the lords spiritual, lords temporal and commons'.[27] In the trial of 29 regicides that began in October 1660, the royal judges affirmed that the King was the head of the three estates and refuted the principle of co-ordinate powers within Parliament.[28] When Sir Henry Vane the younger came to be tried in 1662, an anonymous diarist recorded that his assertion of 'the co-ordinate, and, in some cases, superior authority of Parliament, with the uncourtly position, that all power is derived from the people, were treasons of too high a nature to be uttered with impunity'.[29] From 1660 the enacting clauses of statutes assumed a standard form that made the same point: 'Be it enacted by the King's most excellent majesty by and with the advice and consent of the lords spiritual and temporal and the commons in this present Parliament assembled and by the authority of the same.'[30] The return of bishops to the Lords in 1661 made the definition of the estates as lords spiritual, lords temporal and commons seem all the more plausible. The revised Prayer Book of 1662 contained a telling change to the service of thanksgiving for the foiling of the Gunpowder Plot that reinforced this idea. Whereas the service had formerly referred to 'the happy deliverance of His Majesty, the Queen, Prince and states of Parliament', the revised wording gave thanks for 'the happy deliverance of the King, and the three estates of the realm'.[31] Just as it was Hyde who became Lord Chancellor in 1660, so it was his definition of the three estates that triumphed at the Restoration.

Yet the doctrine of co-ordinate powers was not so easily vanquished. As the Parliamentarian polemicists of the 1640s had realised, it offered a formidable lever to use against unpopular royal policies, all the more so because – to the embarrassment of the Crown's supporters – it possessed the endorsement of Charles I's *Answer to the Nineteen Propositions*. In May 1679, Shaftesbury and his allies reproduced a lengthy extract from the *Answer* to support their demand for Danby's impeachment.[32] During the Exclusion Crisis, the doctrine of co-ordination made a remarkable comeback in the writings of such Whigs as William Petyt.[33] By contrast, the heirs of Clarendon, sometimes designated 'Friends of the Constitution in Church and State' – those who emerged in the 1680s as Tories – bitterly condemned the idea of co-ordinate powers and the estates theory associated with it. Among the most forceful critics of co-ordination, and a fierce opponent of Petyt, was Robert Brady.[34] With the defeat of the Whigs, Tory beliefs gained ascendancy, and were epitomised by Oxford University's denunciation in 1683 of the proposition – left over from 'the heat of the late troubles' – that 'the sovereignty of England is in the three estates, viz. King, Lords, and Commons. The King has but a co-ordinate power, and may be over-ruled by the other two.'[35] This attitude held sway during the Tory Reaction and persisted into James II's reign.[36] In his massive *Vindication of the Antient and Present Establish'd Government of the Kingdom of England*, published in 1687, Fabian Philipps asserted that:

> our Kings of England in their voluntary summoning to the Great Councils and Parliaments some of the more wise, noble and better part of their subjects . . . did not thereby create, or by any assent, express or tacit, give unto them an authority, co-ordination, equality or share in the legislative power.[37]

In the light of the events of the following year, such an elevated view of royal authority soon took on a deeply ironic quality.

It has been suggested, most notably by C. C. Weston, that the Revolution of 1688–9 saw the triumph of the doctrine that the three estates of Crown, Lords and Commons possessed co-ordinate powers.[38] However, this argument may need some qualification. By the 1680s, the definition of the three estates was in large measure a party issue. Whigs generally held to the idea of co-ordination between monarch, Lords and Commons. This view, ultimately derived from Parliamentarians such as Hunton and Herle, provided a powerful constitutional legitimation for resistance to James during the Exclusion Crisis and the Revolution of 1688–9. Most Tories, on the other hand, still espoused the definition of the three estates as lords spiritual, lords temporal and commons. Like Hyde and other Civil-War Royalists, they adhered to this concept out of respect as much for the bishops as for the Crown. One of the constitutional issues dividing the two parties was thus the composition of the three estates. The significance of the Revolution was not so much that it marked the victory of the first doctrine over the second as that it achieved a skilful compromise that most advocates of either doctrine could accept. In fact, the Bill of Rights, far from espousing the idea of co-ordinate powers, was much closer to the Tory position. It began: 'Whereas the lords spiritual and temporal and commons assembled at Westminster, lawfully, fully and freely representing all the estates of the people of this realm . . .'.[39] In the revised coronation oath, William and Mary swore to govern 'according to the statutes in Parliament agreed on' (rather than the laws granted by their predecessors), but this merely brought the oath into line with the legislative supremacy of King-in-Parliament that was already well established.[40] The Tory view of the monarch as standing above the three estates did not disappear. It was found well into the eighteenth century and was expressed, for example, in Sir William Blackstone's *Commentaries on the Laws of England*.[41] It would therefore be misleading to say that the doctrine of co-ordinate powers, and the vision of the three estates on which it rested, had 'triumphed either in the revolution of 1689 or very shortly afterwards'.[42]

What can be said, perhaps, is two things. First, it seems that the Revolution of 1688–9 did not so much resolve the issue of the three estates as take the political sting out of it. There was, in a sense, a return to the situation that had obtained prior to 1642, in which different views of the three estates co-existed without causing much controversy or political instability. This was very much of a piece with the Revolution Settlement, the great strength of which was that it enabled different people to believe different things about the events of 1688–9 and their aftermath. Just as Whigs could maintain that James II had broken his contract and been lawfully resisted, so Tories could hold the exact opposite; but most members of both parties could live with the settlement. Similarly, it was possible to hold either view of the three estates while still subscribing to the broad lines of the settlement. The result was that as in the sixteenth and early seventeenth centuries the three estates could be variously defined without becoming a politically live issue.

Second, as the revised coronation oath reveals, the settlement enshrined the principle of the legislative supremacy of the monarch working with the two Houses. This had the effect of elevating the legislative function above Parliament's other roles to a greater extent than ever before. As the Whig lawyer Sir John Hawles informed the peers during the trial of Henry Sacheverell in 1710:

> although your lordships are the supreme court . . . from whom no appeal lies to any other court of judicature, yet your lordships, as you are part of the legislature, are greater than you are in your judicial capacity, in which you are subject to the law though in your legislative capacity, in concurrence with two other powers, you are above the law.[43]

Such ideas opened the way to what would later on emerge as the doctrine of parliamentary sovereignty.[44] Because the legislative function embodied the equipollence of Crown, Lords and Commons, some commentators have thought that the corresponding concept of the three estates carried the day in 1688–9. In fact the belief that the monarch was not one of the estates remained alive and well. However, because it elevated the monarch above the three estates, that Tory view actually sat much more easily with the conciliar and judicial roles of Parliament. As more and more attention was paid to the legislative role, the Tory concept naturally began to lose ground to the Whig concept. Without succumbing to Whiggish teleology, in the very broadest terms this can be seen as part of a gradual shift of emphasis away from those parliamentary functions that most pre-eminently derived from its medieval origins (its conciliar and judicial roles) towards those that ultimately defined it as the sovereign legislature of modern times.

Practice: relationships within the trinity

It will be apparent from the first section of this chapter that the theory of the three estates was most liable to cause controversy during periods when political relations between Crown, Lords and Commons had become destabilised over other issues. The Civil War and the Exclusion Crisis are the most striking examples of this. When relations were more harmonious the existence of contrasted views of the three estates did not in itself cause serious problems. Reasonably good relations between Crown, Lords and Commons were crucial for the effective operation of Parliament as an institution, and it is therefore important to assess how far these existed in practice. This is a very wide-ranging subject that will form a central theme of Part II of this book, and the present section is intended only to survey some of the characteristic features of relations between members of the Upper and Lower Houses, and between the Crown and the two Houses, during the course of the seventeenth century.

An appreciation of the importance and vitality of the House of Lords has been among the most significant features of recent research on early modern Parliaments, and previous chapters have already given some indication of the variety of forms that this took. We have seen that in some areas – most obviously judicature – the Lords could exercise considerable powers independently of the Commons.[45] Much of the symbolism and ritual associated with Parliaments expressed the social superiority of the 'Upper House', a fact which was of considerable importance in the hierarchical society of seventeenth-century England. The peers were the monarch's natural advisers and their chamber was an extension of the monarch's council that pre-dated the formation of the Commons.[46] The Lords was in many ways the more efficient of the two Houses.[47] It remained throughout the century a powerful source of political influence, while its importance in the production of legislation was evident in the number of bills that originated in the Upper House, and in the fact that a higher proportion of those bills became acts than was the case for the Commons.[48]

Equally, few historians would assert that the Lords acted as puppet-masters, pulling strings to make members of the Commons do their bidding. Rather, the links between members of the two Houses highlight the nature of Parliament as a bicameral institution. Parliament's conciliar, judicial, financial and legislative activities all involved frequent and intensive collaboration between the two Houses. There were regular formal meetings between members of the Houses in conferences and joint committees.[49] But informal links were no less significant. As we have seen, the vast majority of the members of both Houses in fact came from a common, propertied elite, united by family and patronage ties: the Earl of Arundel once referred to the Commons as the Lords' 'younger sons'.[50] A significant proportion of members of the Lower House were either directly related to peers or received their patronage, not least in the form of electoral influence.[51] As Jason Peacey has argued, seventeenth-century patronage took the form not so much of a hierarchical ladder of patrons and clients as of a series of 'networks' that brought together nobles and gentry of similar political and religious attitudes and extended throughout the worlds of government, the Church and the law.[52]

Certain members of the Commons may have owed their seats to noble influence, but this did not make them subservient to their patrons in the Lords once Parliament was sitting, as the careers of the two members, John Pym and Sir Benjamin Rudyerd, who were discussed in Chapter 2 as case-studies of the electoral influence of peers serve to illustrate. Pym and his patron the Earl of Bedford clearly shared similar political and religious attitudes, and on several occasions they can be found collaborating closely in Parliament, for example in promoting the impeachments of Manwaring and Buckingham, in seeking a fundamental overhaul of royal finances, and in developing a scheme of 'bridge-appointments' in 1640–1.[53] Such a pattern reveals the way in which patronage typically took the form of bicameral co-operation rather than a hierarchical relationship in which clients deferred to patrons. Similarly, throughout his parliamentary career, Rudyerd co-operated closely with his patrons, the third and fourth Earls of Pembroke, and his stance, especially on issues such as foreign policy, Buckingham's impeachment and the Petition of Right, was carefully co-ordinated with theirs.[54] An alignment between Rudyerd and Pembroke was also evident in the Long Parliament, and in the summer of 1642 both remained at Westminster while continuing to urge an 'accommodation' between the King and the Houses.[55] Cases like Rudyerd and Pym were far from unusual and help to explain the scale and sophistication of bicameral collaboration between members of the two Houses.

It is also worth observing that many members of the Lords had served for varying lengths of time in the Commons before their elevation to the Upper House. Prominent among these were often the Lord Chancellor (or Lord Keeper), the Lord Treasurer, the Lord President of the Council and the Lord Privy Seal, as well as the senior judges and legal officers of the Crown who attended the Lords as 'assistants'. Such prior experience reinforced the close ties between the two Houses.[56]

It is against this background that the political relations between the Lords and Commons need to be analysed. Like their Tudor predecessors,[57] seventeenth-century Parliaments were notable less for conflicts between the two Houses than for rivalries between factions operating within each House. 'Faction' was a pejorative term in the seventeenth century, associated with subversion and sedition.[58] Nonetheless, in its modern sense it helps to catch the loose-knit nature of groupings that wholly lacked the cohesive organisation of political parties today. These factions commonly spilled over from divisions within the Court and Privy Council, a phenomenon encouraged by the extensive overlap of personnel between these institutions. Once again, the organic nature of the body politic was strikingly apparent. One of the most crucial determinants of relations between the Lords and Commons lay in the relative strength of the various factions within each House. Political alignments were highly fluid and could change significantly during the course of a single session. It is worth examining a few examples that illustrate the workings of such bicameral factions.

In the early decades of the century, the links between members of the two Houses were mainly personal: more organised co-ordination was relatively unusual, although there are signs that it began to develop during the later 1620s. In particular, the Crown ceased to be able to rely on the support, or at least acquiescence, of a majority within the Lords. The attempted impeachment of Buckingham in the 1626 Parliament demonstrated the intense hostility that many members of both Houses felt towards the Duke. The agenda for the Commons' proceedings against Buckingham was set out when Dr Samuel Turner posed six queries relating to the Duke's conduct of the war and his mismanagement of government. Turner was a close associate of one of Buckingham's most eminent opponents in the Lords and the Privy Council, the third Earl of Pembroke, and other members of the Pembroke connection, including Sir John Eliot, soon joined in the attack. During April, May and June 1626, as the campaign against Buckingham gathered momentum, a hard core of peers emerged who actively sought his disgrace. It is true that the attack on

Buckingham was never as fierce in the Lords as in the Commons, and that many peers were more exercised by the King's violations of their privileges by his confinement of the Earls of Arundel and Bristol (two outspoken critics of Buckingham) than they were by the fate of the royal favourite as such. Nor should the extent of co-ordination between members of the Houses be exaggerated: just when the impeachment trial was nearing completion in the Lords, the Commons voted to proceed against Buckingham by remonstrance. Nevertheless, the lack of positive support for the Duke within the Lords, and the fact that peers like Pembroke were in touch with vigorous critics in the Commons, undoubtedly strengthened the campaign against Buckingham, and seems to have been crucial in persuading Charles that he had no alternative but to dissolve the Parliament.[59]

The debates over the Petition of Right two years later provide an interesting illustration of how bicameral disagreements, arising from the ascendancy of different groupings within the two Houses, could ultimately be overcome. From the beginning of the session, a majority of the Commons wished to declare the illegality of such recent royal policies as the Forced Loan, imprisonment without trial and arbitrary billeting of troops. When it became clear that the King would not assent to a statute, they decided to submit a petition of right. In the Lords, however, the majority of peers were initially hostile to such a petition, prompting Joseph Mead to observe that 'the greater part of the Lords stand for the King's prerogative against the subjects' liberties'. Only after prolonged consultation and debate during April and May 1628 were sufficient moderate peers won over to the Petition as it stood to enable it to pass the Lords. In this process, personal links between members of the two Houses were important in co-ordinating strategy and rallying support behind the Petition. Many members of the Commons realised the crucial importance of winning over the Lords: Sir Thomas Wentworth allegedly urged 'that the Lords join with us, else all is lost'. Frequent joint conferences were held in which members worked closely to reach agreement over the Petition. These manoeuvres ultimately had the effect of isolating Buckingham and his closest allies and achieving majorities in both chambers in favour of the Petition.[60]

These bicameral connections became stronger and better organised during the years of Civil War. In July 1642, the Houses' resolution to raise an army and to appoint the Earl of Essex as Lord General was the result of careful advance planning by like-minded peers (led by Essex and Northumberland) and commoners (especially John Pym and Denzil Holles).[61] During the years that followed, various factions can be seen at work in both Houses as well as in the many joint committees created to manage Parliament's war effort. By the mid and late 1640s, two rival groupings dominated Parliamentarian politics. The first, sometimes labelled the 'Presbyterians', was led in the Upper House by the Earl of Essex and Lord Willoughby of Parham. Among their leading allies in the Commons were Denzil Holles, Bulstrode Whitelocke, Sir Henry Mildmay, Robert Reynolds, Sir John Meyrick and Sir Philip Stapleton. These people, who commanded a narrow majority in both Houses for much of the 1640s, sought a Presbyterian national church, modelled on the Scottish Kirk, and a political settlement that placed relatively lenient limitations on the King's powers. The other grouping, sometimes called the 'Independents', was led in the Lords by peers such as Viscount Saye and Sele, the Earls of Northumberland, Salisbury and Nottingham, and Lords Wharton and Howard of Escrick; and in the Commons by Saye's son Nathaniel Fiennes, Oliver Cromwell, Oliver St John,

Sir Henry Vane the younger, Sir John Evelyn, William Strode, Samuel Browne, Henry Darley and John Gurdon. These people generally sought tighter controls on the King's powers and an Erastian church settlement that provided some toleration for Independent congregations.[62]

The rivalry between these groupings was evident not only over such major issues as the establishment of the Committee of Both Kingdoms, the Self-Denying Ordinance and the creation of the New Model Army, but also in the workings of joint committees like the Committee for the Advance of Money and the Committee for the Sequestration of Delinquents.[63] The political and religious attitudes of these bicameral connections were also apparent in the terms that each wished to see presented to Charles. The Presbyterian majority in both Houses stamped its outlook clearly upon the Propositions of Oxford (1643), Uxbridge (1644) and Newcastle (1646),[64] whereas the Independents, in collaboration with allies in the Army, expressed their ideals in the *Heads of the Proposals* (1647).[65] In all these political manoeuvres, it is misleading to suggest that the peers were the dominant patrons, the commoners their obedient clients. Rather, individuals of similar outlook on national issues collaborated to advance their shared ideological agenda. It is also important to remember that, as David Underdown has argued, despite a 'gradual acquisition of party characteristics', neither 'the Independents nor the Presbyterians ... were homogeneous entities. Both were loose coalitions of groups, shading off into the grey mass of the uncommitted, which might support one or other on the merits of particular issues.'[66]

This pattern broadly continued after the Restoration. The ideological element in such groupings is again evident in the debates surrounding the Church settlement of 1662. The religious outlook of the restored House of Lords was remarkably diverse. Alongside the bishops and committed Anglican peers were others who supported as broad a Church as possible with a generous measure of toleration for those who felt unable to conform to it. The King hoped to mobilise as much support as possible for the latter position in order to realise his pledge in the Declaration of Breda to introduce 'a liberty to tender consciences'.[67] The main obstacle to this goal lay in the Commons which, following the return of the Cavalier Parliament in May 1661, was strongly in favour of a narrow, intolerant Church and deeply hostile towards dissent. The result was that, during 1661–2, the Upper House tempered the severity of the religious legislation prepared by the Commons. In particular, the Lords ensured that the penalties against dissenters imposed by the Act of Uniformity were significantly lessened, even though the basic outlines of the settlement remained as the Commons wanted.[68]

A further example from Charles II's reign that illustrates the workings of bicameral factions is the emergence during the mid and late 1670s of a 'Country party' in both Houses. This grouping was led in the Lords by those disgruntled former members of the Cabal, the Duke of Buckingham and the Earl of Shaftesbury, and in the Commons by such figures as William Cavendish, William Lord Russell, Sir Robert Howard and Sir Thomas Meres. They favoured greater toleration for Protestant dissenters and stronger measures against papists. They also advocated the dissolution of the Cavalier Parliament which they thought too deferential to the Crown and an inadequate defence against the perceived threat of 'popery and arbitrary government'. They hoped in the process to discredit the King's chief minister, Danby, and to secure high office for themselves. Like-minded peers and commoners can be found, for example in February 1677, attending secret meetings and then pursuing a co-ordinated strategy within each House to promote their goals. The second half of the 1670s also saw Danby adopt increasingly systematic techniques in order to counter this bicameral opposition. He mobilised the Crown's natural allies in the Lords, especially Anglican-Royalists and bishops, and he used patronage to build up an extensive body of support in the Commons where he could probably rely on a hard core of about 120 to 150 loyal members by 1677–8.[69] Only the extraordinary hysteria sparked off by allegations of a popish plot dissipated this support and generated a majority in each House in favour of Danby's impeachment.

One final example of the difficulties that arose when different groups held sway in each House came in the aftermath of the Revolution of 1688–9. Most of the Whigs, who formed a majority of the Commons in the Convention Parliament, felt that James II had broken his contract with his subjects. They argued that by fleeing he had 'abdicated the government' and left the throne 'vacant', and they secured a Commons resolution to this effect on 28 January 1689. Such wording was unacceptable to many Tories, who formed a majority in the Lords. They still clung to the view that James remained the rightful King even after his flight, and they objected to the words 'abdicated' and 'vacant' which implied that the Convention might have the right to fill the throne and thus determine the succession. They preferred instead the more neutral term 'deserted'. The two Houses reached deadlock, and the impasse was only resolved when William, who urgently needed to return to his military commitments on the continent, declared that unless he was made King he would go home immediately. This threat greatly strengthened the Whigs' hand, and the Tory majority in the Lords began to crumble. Some Tory peers slipped away, as did a number of bishops, and the remainder of the Lords passed a resolution agreeing with the Commons.[70]

In their different ways, these various episodes all illustrate the crucial importance of relations between members of the two Houses, rather than between the two Houses as such. It is very important to avoid seeing the Houses as monolithic bodies or the views of their members as static. There were many 'floating' members and quite often the decisions taken in each House reflected which political grouping had proved more successful in mobilising support. Only for a fairly brief period during Charles II's reign can we see sustained conflict between the two Houses as anything like collective entities. This dispute was focused around the celebrated cases of Skinner vs. the East India Company (1667–70) and Shirley vs. Fagg (1675), two suits that had serious constitutional implications because they raised issues of the Lords' judicature and the privileges of both Houses.

The case of Skinner vs. the East India Company arose when Thomas Skinner, having allegedly infringed the Company's monopoly of the Indies trade, protested that the Company had seized his goods.[71] The King referred the dispute to the Lords, who awarded damages against the Company. The directors of the Company petitioned the Commons, challenging the Lords' jurisdiction in the case and pointing out that some of the damages would fall on those Company directors who were members of the Commons. In May 1668 the Lower House voted the Lords' ruling 'a breach of privilege'. The Lords replied that the Commons had itself breached the Upper House's privileges, and acted 'contrary to the fair correspondency which ought to be between the two Houses'.[72] The Commons stood their ground, and the case dragged on until

February 1670, when Charles urged the Houses to drop the case and to expunge all references to it from their Journals. The case blew over although it did effectively mark the end of the Lords' first instance jurisdiction in civil cases.

The Upper House nevertheless successfully defended their appellate jurisdiction in the case of Shirley vs. Fagg (1675). Thomas Shirley appealed to the Lords against a Chancery decree in favour of Sir John Fagg, who was a member of the Commons. The Lower House argued that it was a breach of privilege for the Lords to hear appeals involving a member of the Commons in time of Parliament. The Lords retorted that 'it is the undoubted right of the Lords, in judicature, to receive and determine, in time of Parliament, appeals from inferior courts, though a member of either House be concerned therein, that there may be no failure of justice in the land'.[73] At one point the Lords declined to proceed further with any business until they obtained satisfaction. Eventually the case lapsed during the long prorogation of Parliament from November 1675 to February 1677, and there was no further challenge to the appellate jurisdiction of the Lords.[74]

These two cases became particularly bitter because a majority in both Houses felt that their privileges were at stake. This generated intercameral conflict in a way that was relatively unusual. It is also worth noting that here again relations between the Houses were complicated by the fact that different groupings held sway in each. The 'Country party' enjoyed an ascendancy in the Commons whereas the 'Court party' dominated the Lords. Both these groupings were far looser and more diffuse than modern parties. Nevertheless, they reflected different political outlooks, and their leading exponents harnessed the issues of privilege and jurisdiction as a way of attacking their political opponents in the other House. Had there not been two contrasted majorities in Lords and Commons it is doubtful whether the cases would have become quite so enflamed.[75] They were undoubtedly the most striking instances of hostility between Lords and Commons during the seventeenth century. Viewing the century as a whole, it would probably be true to say that the relative *political* powers of the two Houses as bodies changed comparatively little. What did shift over time was the relative strength of the members who held sway in each House. It was the operation and interaction of those bicameral groupings that most crucially affected the relationship between the two Houses at any given moment.

Parliamentary politics were not of course conducted in isolation, and most of the episodes examined above did not simply reflect relations between members of the two Houses. Frequently, they marked an extension of political manoeuvres being conducted, often by many of the same individuals, within the Court and the Privy Council. This was a process already familiar from earlier periods. In Elizabethan Parliaments the campaigns within Court and Council to urge the Queen to marry, or to designate a successor, or to execute Mary Queen of Scots, all spilled over into the Lords and Commons in time of Parliament. Thus the attack on Buckingham in 1626 was an extrapolation of a campaign that was already in progress within Court and Council. Conrad Russell has argued that:

> the impeachment of Buckingham was not a confrontation between 'government' and 'opposition': it was a confrontation between two groups within the Council, in which both sides enjoyed support within the Lords and the Commons, but the less influential group in the Council enjoyed majority support in the Commons.[76]

Parliament thus enabled Buckingham's opponents to extend their attack to another forum, to open a 'second front' so to speak, just as proponents of particular bills could turn to Parliament as one of a variety of arenas in which they pursued their goals. Once again Parliament, despite its intermittent meetings, needs to be seen as part of an integrated, organic system of government.

Two other notable examples of the way in which Court politics spilled over into Parliament were the impeachment of Middlesex in 1624 and the attempted impeachment of Clarendon in 1667. Since his appointment as Lord Treasurer in 1621, Middlesex had made himself widely unpopular at Court by his successful campaigns for retrenchment which upset a great many vested interests. Unfortunately, his financial caution led him to oppose the war against Spain that Buckingham and Prince Charles ardently supported after their disastrous expedition to Madrid in 1623. Determined to be rid of Middlesex, the Prince and the Duke rallied a loose-knit coalition of war supporters in both Houses who were only too pleased to impeach the Lord Treasurer on trumped-up charges of corruption.[77] The parliamentary proceedings against Middlesex make no sense unless the context of machinations within Court and Council is borne in mind. Equally, such machinations might have dragged on for considerably longer were it not for the decisive resolution that parliamentary impeachment provided.

The attack on Middlesex reflected disputes not only within the Court but also between James on the one hand and the Prince and Duke on the other. James thought their tactics highly dangerous: he told Buckingham, 'you are making a rod with which you will be scourged yourself', while he warned Charles, 'you will live to have your bellyful of Parliaments'.[78] Subsequent history, including the attempted impeachment of Buckingham and the attainder of Strafford, certainly bore this out. However, the attempted impeachment of Clarendon in 1667 presents an interesting variant on the more usual pattern. For here Charles II sided with the Commons in their attack on Clarendon, and against the Lords, who wished to protect him.[79] The King and the Privy Council saw Clarendon as an ideal scapegoat for England's defeats in the second Dutch War that would deflect blame from some of their own strategic decisions. However, the Lords refused to imprison Clarendon on a general charge of treason lest this create a precedent for the indiscriminate imprisonment of peers before the Commons had delivered specific written charges. The result was a pragmatic alliance between Crown and Commons despite the fact that, as Samuel Pepys observed, 'neither of [them] care[d] a fig for one another'.[80] The difficulty was only finally resolved when Clarendon learnt that the King was planning to try him outside Parliament in a court packed with his enemies, whereupon he fled to France. The interactions within the parliamentary trinity were thus very flexible, and there was no necessary reason why the Crown should be more closely aligned with a majority in the Lords than a majority in the Commons, although in practice that tended to be the case more often than not.

The politics of Privy Council and Great Council, of Royal Court and High Court, were thus inseparably intertwined. In such a context, the Crown's capacity to 'manage' the two Houses effectively was of crucial importance. This certainly does not mean that the Crown was trying to coerce the Houses; still less does it imply a model of parliamentary politics as a struggle between royal tyranny and the subjects' rights and liberties. But as a member of the parliamentary trinity, it was very much in the Crown's interests to mobilise support within the two Houses for issues and causes that it sought to promote. We have seen the very significant role that Privy Councillors and the presiding officers of both chambers played in this respect. They in turn could harness the services of other members known to be reliable and effective in advancing the Crown's views, those sometimes referred to in the Commons as 'men-of-business'.[81] It would be anachronistic to identify a conflict of interests between the Crown and the Houses, and indeed early seventeenth-century political thought offered an intricate rationale for why such a conflict should not occur. Nevertheless, Parliaments were intended to bring the monarch into contact with a range of opinions, and in promoting the Crown's preferred solutions and priorities amidst the wide variety on offer, some form of 'management' was vital.[82] How far this proved successful, and the occasions when it broke down, will be a theme of the remaining chapters of this book.

Another group of Crown appointees is also worth discussing at this point; namely the bishops in the House of Lords. We have noticed that they occupied an ambivalent position in theories of the three estates because whereas one theory identified them as an estate in their own right, the other potentially excluded them entirely. Certainly one of the advantages of the doctrine of co-ordination for those who sought to contain royal powers – such as the Parliamentarians of the 1640s and later the Whigs – was that by ignoring the bishops it implicitly removed some of the Crown's most reliable supporters. Although the bishops never formed a cohesive bloc, and remained individuals with minds of their own, most were more likely than not to ally with the Crown on major points of policy. This remained true throughout the century. For example, in 1628, the primary concern of most prelates was that the Petition of Right should not infringe the King's prerogative.[83] Similarly, after the Restoration the bishops were consistently among the Crown's most reliable allies in the Upper House. This was especially valuable in the years 1675–81, when they played a crucial part in ensuring that the 'Court' possessed a majority in the Lords.[84] As the number of lay peers increased, the size of the lords spiritual as a proportion of the whole diminished, from over 30 per cent in 1603 to less than 20 per cent by 1685.[85] Nevertheless, opinion in the Lords was often quite closely divided and the bishops therefore remained an important element in the Crown's 'management' of the Upper House.

The fact that the bishops' attendance rate was usually higher than that of the lords temporal further enhanced their value to the Crown.[86] Sometimes this was the result of deliberate attempts by the monarch and his advisers to mobilise the lords spiritual. Perhaps the most crucial instance of this was in the autumn of 1641, when Bishop Juxon of London rallied the bishops as part of a broader strategy, masterminded by Sir Edward Nicholas, to mobilise Royalist support in the Lords. Juxon's efforts produced a regular attendance of 10 to 15 bishops during the last three months of 1641, and his strategy gave a decisive spur to the campaign against the 'prelatical party' which culminated in the act excluding bishops from the Upper House in February 1642.[87] Later, after this act was repealed and the bishops were restored to the Lords in 1661, successive Archbishops of Canterbury regularly sent circular letters to ensure that as many bishops as possible attended the Lords.[88] In the bishops the Crown thus possessed a loyal group of allies in most of its policies except, as James II discovered, where these flagrantly undermined the established Church.

If the two Houses persisted with courses of action that the monarch found unpalatable, he could if necessary deploy three discretionary powers as last resorts. He could prorogue or dissolve Parliament; he could refuse the royal assent to bills that had passed both Houses (the royal veto); and he could dispense (exempt) named individuals from the force of a particular statute, or suspend the operation of a statute entirely. The use of these powers was another important element in the Crown's relations with the two Houses, and all of them had been significantly eroded by the close of the seventeenth century.

The first power, that of prorogation and dissolution, has already been examined in the previous chapter.[89] Until the Long Parliament it went largely unchallenged, and Charles I was able to state loftily but quite correctly in March 1626 that 'Parliaments are altogether in my power for the calling, sitting and continuance of them. Therefore as I find the fruits either good or evil, they are for to continue or not to be.'[90] Conrad Russell has observed that until 'the arrival of the Scottish army in 1640, the weapon of dissolution conferred almost complete power on the King in any contest with a Parliament'.[91] However, the Triennial Acts of 1641, 1664 and above all 1694 reduced the Crown's power in this respect. As we have seen, the third of these acts, together with the Crown's financial dependence upon Parliaments during the wars of the 1690s and 1700s, meant that by the end of the century the monarch could no longer dissolve Parliaments at will. Nor could prorogations be used to avoid meeting Parliament – as Charles II had done with great effect during the later 1670s and early 1680s – if that infringed the principle of triennial assemblies.[92] The Crown's powers in relation to the timing and sitting of Parliaments were thus considerably weakened.

The use of the royal veto was less constitutionally significant than might be supposed. Sir Geoffrey Elton showed that in the early Elizabethan Parliaments, far from indicating any conflict between monarch and Houses over matters of principle, the veto was mainly 'a last defence against ill-considered, partisan or even corruptly obtained acts of Parliament'. Most commonly, it was used to kill off private bills that were judged inimical to other powerful interests. Only on five of the 34 occasions when Elizabeth used the veto in the seven sessions from 1559 to 1581 can she be said to have blocked the manifest wishes of the two Houses.[93]

This interpretation seems to hold good for the Stuart Parliaments as well. In all, Elizabeth had vetoed 72 bills during the 13 sessions of her reign, but its use apparently diminished under the Stuarts.[94] It seems that James I only vetoed seven bills during his entire reign, two in 1604 and five in 1624. At least one and possibly both of those vetoed in 1604 were very much of the type that Elizabeth had vetoed quite regularly. James's decision to veto a bill 'concerning garbling of spices and drugs' probably reflected his strong support for the Apothecaries' Company, while the second vetoed bill, 'for reformation of brokers and pawntakers', again related to a particular interest group.[95] Of the five bills vetoed in 1624, two subsequently became acts in later Parliaments.[96] The other three were a bill to enfranchise County Durham (James claimed the Commons was too large already);[97] a bill to stop Catholic recusants from evading forfeitures by making their estates over to trustees (vetoed as a diplomatic sop to the French); and a bill for the naturalisation of a merchant, Philip Jacobson (on the grounds that the King could not afford to lose the double custom imposed on aliens).[98] Charles I used the veto only once in his entire reign: a remarkable fact which gainsays any attempt to see the veto as a weapon of royal authoritarianism. In 1628 he once again vetoed the bill to stop Catholic recusants from evading forfeitures by making their estates over to trustees.[99]

Charles II vetoed a total of five bills. Four of these were private bills vetoed because other interested parties managed to win the King's approval: Briscoe's estate bill (1662), the Earl of Derby's estate bill (1662), the Pawnbrokers' bill (1662), and Sir Trevor Williams' estate bill (1677). The only case of any constitutional significance was the Militia bill which Charles vetoed in 1678.[100] This bill sought to raise new militia on parliamentary authority at the time of the Popish Plot hysteria, but Charles insisted that this infringed the 1661 Militia Act which vested military authority in the Crown alone.[101] James II did not use the veto at all during his short reign. William III initially vetoed several constitutionally significant measures, including the Triennial Act and a place bill, but the latter elicited a Commons' resolution that those who advised the King to do so were 'enemies to your Majesty and your kingdom'.[102] In the end, financial necessity forced William to assent to the Triennial Act, and to accept a series of place clauses.[103] The veto was last exercised by Queen Anne in 1708. In the main, it provided a final long-stop to block legislation that would damage the interests of other groups or individuals. The veto thus played an integral role in reconciling the different interest groups affected by parliamentary bill procedure, and lobbying by those groups took place in a variety of arenas, of which Parliament was only one. Here again, Parliament's role as part of an interlocking system of government was usually more apparent than constitutional conflict within that system.

One reason why the Crown may have used the veto fairly sparingly was that it possessed another way round unwelcome statutes. This was the power to grant dispensations (exemptions) from the force of a particular statute to named individuals. These grants were made by letters patent known as *non obstante*. The Crown could also suspend the operation of certain statutes.[104] The customary constraint on these powers was that they could not be used to license any action that was intrinsically evil (*malum in se*), in other words contrary to the law of God, but only actions that happened to have been prohibited by statute for the common good (*malum prohibitum*). Since it was assumed that royal powers should also be exercised for the common good (*pro bono publico*) and not for the monarch's personal benefit (*pro bono suo*), in theory the supremacy of statute was entirely compatible with the royal dispensing power.[105]

This issue became increasingly contentious after the Restoration, largely because of the tension between the religious preferences of Charles II and James II and the nature of the restored Church of England. Charles II's desire for greater toleration of Catholics and Protestant dissenters led him in 1662–3 to request an act that would enable him to 'exercise with more universal satisfaction that power of dispensing which we conceive to be inherent in us'. But the Houses, fearing that this might involve wholesale dispensations from the Act of Uniformity, rejected the idea.[106] In March 1672, Charles tried again, issuing a Declaration of Indulgence in which he invoked his 'supreme power in ecclesiastical matters' to suspend all penal laws in religious matters. The Commons retorted that:

> no such power was ever claimed or exercised by any of your Majesty's predecessors; and if it should be admitted might tend to the interrupting of the free course of the laws, and altering the legislative power, which hath always been acknowledged to reside in your Majesty, and your two Houses of Parliament.[107]

Faced with concerted hostility in both Houses, the King backed down, cancelled the Declaration, and accepted the Test Acts against Catholics in 1673 and 1678. For the remainder of his reign he continued to make use of the dispensing power, which unlike the suspending power had not been seriously challenged, and he worked within the recognised convention that this could not be used to dispense excessive numbers or whole categories of people.[108]

There the matter rested until James II attempted to make vigorous use of the dispensing and suspending powers on behalf of his Catholic co-religionists. In 1686, following Parliament's refusal to sanction the dispensing of Catholic army officers from the Test Acts, James consulted the judiciary on the validity of the dispensing power, and after sacking no fewer than five judges he secured a favourable verdict in the collusive action Godden vs. Hales.[109] Emboldened by this, James made sweeping use of the dispensing power to promote Catholics in both national and local government as well as the army. Then, in April 1687, he issued a Declaration of Indulgence suspending the operation of the penal laws, although this was made conditional upon Parliament's subsequent approval. The following autumn, James set about securing the return of a sympathetic Parliament. But when, in April 1688, he instructed the clergy to read the Declaration from their pulpits on two successive Sundays, Archbishop Sancroft and six bishops petitioned against this order on the grounds that Parliament had declared the suspending power illegal in 1673. When the seven were tried for seditious libel, judicial opinion was mostly against the suspending power. One of the puisne judges, Sir John Powell, for example argued that if it were acknowledged then 'there will need no Parliament; all the legislature will be in the King', and the Catholic judge Sir Richard Alibone, who defended the power, found himself outnumbered.[110]

In 1689, the Bill of Rights finally resolved the issue when it declared that 'the pretended power of suspending of laws or the execution of laws by regal authority without consent of Parliament is illegal'. However, the clause on the dispensing power was more guarded, that 'the pretended power of dispensing with laws or the execution of laws by regal authority, *as it hath been assumed and exercised of late, is illegal*'.[111] This clause, introduced at the Lords' request, avoided the outright abolition of the dispensing power. Nevertheless, the power thereafter remained firmly under the control of the Houses and subsequent monarchs made no attempt to re-open the question.[112] The effect of these changes was to diminish any sense of the monarch as a sovereign law-maker, and strengthen the force of statutes made by Crown-in-Parliament.

This shift was part of a significant pruning of the Crown's powers in relation to the two Houses that followed the Revolution of 1688–9. Other aspects of this, such as Parliament's enhanced 'power of the purse', have been examined above, and the process as a whole will be surveyed in the final chapter. Collectively, the changes served to underline Parliament's nature as a trinity more clearly by the 1690s than had been the case in 1603. Although the legislative supremacy of Crown, Lords and Commons was acknowledged from the 1530s onwards, the royal powers to summon, dissolve and prorogue Parliament at will, to suspend or dispense from statutes, and to veto bills, all helped to sustain a concept of the monarch as standing above the two Houses, or outside the three estates. The fact that Parliament administered justice in the monarch's name, and acted as the monarch's Great Council, reinforced the same perception. In the first section of this chapter we saw that although this view survived long after 1689, especially in Tory circles, it gradually lost ground to the doctrine of legislative supremacy which affirmed the co-ordinate powers of Crown, Lords and Commons. This formed the theoretical counterpart to, and legitimation for, such practical developments as the abolition of the suspending power, the constriction of the dispensing power, and the 1694 Triennial Act. All these measures were part of a process that involved diminishing the Crown's discretionary powers in relation to the two Houses, and establishing more secure safeguards that protected Parliament from the whims of individual monarchs. The result was that, in both theory and practice, the parliamentary trinity had become a more concrete reality by the end of the seventeenth century than it had been at the beginning.

PARLIAMENTS AND POLITICS

|7|

Early Stuart Parliaments,
1603–1640

Early Jacobean Parliaments, 1604–1610 and 1614

No aspect of James I's kingship reveals his paradoxical blend of strengths and weaknesses, of wisdom and misjudgement, more plainly than his relations with his English Parliaments. On the one hand, his understanding of the nature of the institution and his capacity to defuse tension and controversy deserve much more credit than they have often received. But, on some occasions, he had himself sparked off those controversies either by his own tactlessness or by failing to pay sufficient attention to the managing of Parliaments. In his earlier years he had the advantage of an able team of advisers inherited from Elizabeth and led by Robert Cecil, Earl of Salisbury from May 1605. By contrast, in his later years James had the disadvantage of a widely unpopular favourite. Yet James's own distinctive political persona nevertheless remained clearly evident and formed a consistent thread running throughout the Jacobean Parliaments.

James delighted in addressing Parliament regularly and at considerable length, and these speeches tell us much about his attitude towards Parliaments. First of all, they show his awareness, from quite soon after his arrival, of the complex and multifaceted role of the English Parliament. Here, for example, is an account of his speech on 9 November 1605, four days after the discovery of the Gunpowder Plot:

> As to the nature of this High Court of Parliament, it is nothing else but the King's Great Council, which the King doth assemble either upon occasion of interpreting, or abrogating old laws, or making of new, according as ill manners shall deserve, or for the public punishment of notorious evil doers, or the praise and reward of the virtuous and well deservers ... And as to the end for which the Parliament is ordained, being only for the advancement of God's glory, and the establishment and wealth of the King and his people.[1]

Deeply aware that royal powers should be exercised for the public good (*pro bono publico*) and not for the monarch's personal good (*pro bono suo*), James went on:

> I never shall propose anything unto you, which shall not as well tend to the weale public, as to any benefit for me. So shall I never oppose myself to that which may tend to the good of the commonwealth, for the which I am ordained, as is often said.[2]

In such passages James sounded less like a foreign monarch, perplexed and irritated by the institutions of his new kingdom, than a newly arrived and slightly self-conscious *émigré* seeking to show off his intimate knowledge of institutions with which he was only recently acquainted. Contemporaries were often struck by James's Scottish accent and companions from north of the border, yet in his keenness to describe the English Parliament there is a sense in which he wished to become more English than the English.

James's parliamentary speeches also throw light on his often criticised tactlessness. In fact, the problem was not so much that he was tactless as such, but rather that this same urge to analyse an institution to which he came from outside sometimes led him to hit the wrong note or to advance descriptions that jarred with his listeners. Usually this was because he managed to emphasise the powers of the Crown in relation to the Houses rather more than many members found palatable. Perhaps the most famous example of this was his assertion that Parliament's rights were the gracious, and therefore revocable, gift of his ancestors rather than an immemorial birthright. He first asserted this in 1604, in a speech which prompted some members of the Commons to draw up the Form of Apology and Satisfaction setting out 'the rights and liberties of the whole Commons of [the] realm of England which they and their ancestors from time immemorable have undoubtedly enjoyed under your Majesty's most noble progenitors'.[3] A very similar exchange occurred over the Commons' privilege of free speech in 1621. As we saw in Chapter 3, there was scope for considerable disagreement over what subjects the Commons could advise upon, and whether this was a duty or a right. James's insistence in 1621 that they should only discuss matters of state when he asked them to, and his claim that their privileges were not an 'undoubted birthright' but 'derived from the grace and permission' of his ancestors served to enflame a highly contentious issue.

Such disputes undoubtedly reflected significant dissensus between the King and some members of the Commons. However, it is important not to see the Commons as a united entity, self-consciously defending itself against an aggressive monarch. Sir Geoffrey Elton showed that the Apology was drafted by a Commons committee set up to respond to the King on the specific issue of wardship.[4] When it was presented to the full House, a majority of members found its tone too provocative: the Commons did not adopt it and it was never formally presented to James.[5] Another feature of these exchanges was that they took place on a fairly high theoretical plane and within a framework that was notable for a broad level of agreement. It is important to remember that there was never any question of James trying to get rid of Parliaments. In his speech to both Houses on 21 March 1610 he made a fundamental distinction between 'Kings in their first original' and 'the state of settled kings and monarchs'. He clearly included himself among the latter, who were bound 'to the observation of the fundamental laws of his kingdom', and he promised to 'rule my actions according to my laws'.[6] In the creation of law, James accepted that insofar as he was absolute, it was in conjunction with Parliament. The making, amending and reforming of the law was to be carried out 'always by the advice of Parliament: for the King with his Parliament here are absolute (as I understand) in making or forming of any sort of laws'.[7]

That parenthetical 'as I understand' is another instance of James self-consciously feeling his way with the English Parliament, and he was receptive enough to adapt his ideas in the light of experience. For example, in 1610 the Commons complained that he was abusing his right to issue proclamations by using them to create new crimes or transfer crimes from one jurisdiction to another. James consulted the two Chief Justices, Sir Edward Coke and Sir James Altham, and accepted their decision against him. This marked a retreat from his claim in *The True Law of Free Monarchies* (1598) that 'the King make[s] daily statutes and ordinances, enjoining such pains thereto as he thinks meet, without any advice of Parliament or estates',[8] although it is important to remember that this work had been written in Scotland and referred to specifically Scottish conditions in which it was possible for the monarch and his Council to create and enforce laws that had not received parliamentary consent.[9] James recognised that the situation in England was rather different, and in March 1610 he acknowledged that he was 'a King by the common law of the land', and accepted that 'he had no power to make laws of himself, or to exact any subsidies *de jure* without the consent of his three Estates'.[10] Such flexibility suggests a political intelligence that was constantly learning and absorbing, and belies the older view of James as 'a foreign king' who 'imperfectly understood' England's 'constitutional customs'.[11]

Above all, James was not aiming at any kind of rule without Parliaments. At the end of the period covered in this first section, in the wake of the Addled Parliament of 1614, James had a private conversation with the Spanish ambassador, Sarmiento, later Count of Gondomar. James lamented that:

> The House of Commons is a body without a head. The members give their opinions in a disorderly manner. At their meetings nothing is heard but cries, shouts, and confusion. I am surprised that my ancestors should ever have permitted such an institution to come into existence.

However, he then added: 'But I am a stranger, and found it here when I arrived, so that I am obliged to put up with what I cannot get rid of.'[12] It was simply not on James's agenda to try to rule without Parliaments, and he remained willing to persist with them in the face of occasional disputes. His aggression towards Parliaments was usually rhetorical rather than practical, and if his words on occasion generated needless controversy, his actions often tended to defuse tensions rather than escalate them. The story of his relationship with successive Parliaments is rather like that of a rocky, at times verbally violent, yet essentially resilient marriage; despite the ups and downs a divorce was not on the cards.

However, when they speculated about their future, many members of James's Parliaments were haunted by intimations of mortality. The European context only increased such fears for, as Pauline Croft has written, 'members of the Commons were aware that representative institutions in other countries had not fared well during the later sixteenth century'. In France the Estates General had effectively lost the power to withhold taxation by the 1580s, and after 1614 they did not sit again until the eve of the Revolution. Philip II had limited the powers of the Cortes of Aragon after 1592.[13] Against such a background it was hardly surprising that the Houses, and especially the Commons, reacted touchily whenever James suggested that their privileges were merely the gifts of his predecessors, or that monarchy was of far more ancient origin than Parliaments. This prickliness took many different forms ranging from the assertion of Parliament's antiquity by lawyers such as Sir John Doddridge, discussed earlier,[14] to the statement in the 1604 Apology that 'the prerogatives of princes may easily and do daily grow; the privileges of the subject are for the most part at an everlasting stand'.[15]

We saw in Chapter 4 that the privileges and liberties of Parliament were sufficiently vaguely defined as to permit a variety of interpretations. Certainly fertile ground existed for parliamentary fears, but how well grounded were they in reality? It is difficult to accept some arguments that have been advanced for seeing Parliament as a declining institution in early seventeenth-century England. As was described in Chapter 3, notwithstanding R. W. K. Hinton's claims, the legislative achievement of Jacobean Parliaments did not register any significant overall decrease: measured by the very important yardstick of producing statutes, there was no pattern of decline. Faith in the power of statute to remedy a wide range of public and private grievances remained justifiably high. James I shared that faith and cannot be portrayed as the natural enemy of Parliaments against whom they had constantly to defend themselves. His management of Parliaments may not always have been very effective, but this owed more to indolence and to his frequent absences from the capital on hunting trips than to any active dislike of Parliaments. Insofar as James's relations with his early Parliaments were troubled, this was a manifestation less of royal hostility or institutional decline than of two particularly thorny and complex problems: the Anglo-Scottish Union, and royal finance. Unfortunately, on both these issues confidence in Parliaments as a panacea outstripped their capacity to provide a solution.

The question of the union dominated two of the first three sessions of James's first Parliament, in 1604 and 1606–7. His goal was both simple and vague, to develop the union of the crowns into a full-scale union of the kingdoms. He explained his view in his opening speech on 19 March 1604:

> What God has conjoined then, let no man separate. I am the husband, and all the whole isle is my lawful wife; I am the head and it is my body; I am the shepherd and it is my flock: I hope therefore no man will be so unreasonable as to think that I, that am a Christian King under the Gospel, should be a polygamist and husband to two wives; that I, being the head, should have a divided and monstrous body; or that I, being the shepherd to so fair a flock (whose fold hath no wall to hedge it but the four seas) should have my flock parted in two.[16]

Yet, as Jenny Wormald has recently argued, James's understanding of what such a union involved, and his plans for achieving it, were not defined at all clearly. Indeed, this may have been a conscious political strategy to disarm opposition to it.[17] His fullest public statement on the subject came in his speech of 31 March 1607, by which time the extent of English hostility to union had already become plain. James expressed his desire for 'a perfect union of laws and persons, and such a naturalising as may make one body of both kingdoms under me your king'. By this he meant 'such a general union of laws as may reduce the whole island, that as they live already under one monarch, so they may all be governed by one law'. That in turn involved three specific reforms: 'taking away of hostile laws', 'community of commerce', and naturalisation not only of those Scots born since March 1603 (the *Post-Nati*), but also those born prior to that (the *Ante-Nati*). Ultimately, he hoped 'to reconcile the statute laws of both kingdoms', although it is likely that this meant something closer to the congruity he sought between the two Churches than complete uniformity. The 'great and evident' benefits that would flow from such a union of the kingdoms were, he said, 'peace, plenty, love, free intercourse and common society of two great nations'.[18] Ultimately, he wanted a union of hearts and minds in which the two nations would grow to like each other and finally merge into one.

It was natural that James should seek to accomplish so fundamental a change through Parliament. A matter such as naturalisation was the exclusive preserve of private acts of Parliament,[19] and James recognised that it 'only lieth in your hands' and was a point 'so precisely belonging to Parliament'.[20] Furthermore, as he later acknowledged, 'an act of Parliament can do greater wonders: and that old wise man the Treasurer Burghley was wont to say, he knew not what an act of Parliament could not do in England'.[21] Furthermore, Parliament was the natural instrument to effect a union of hearts and minds. Unfortunately, it was in Parliament that those hearts and minds revealed their entrenched hostility towards James's proposals. On 1 May 1604 James complained of the Commons' 'jealousy and distrust, either of me the propounder, or of the matter by me propounded'.[22] All that was achieved by the end of the first session was the creation of a joint Anglo-Scottish commission to prepare more detailed proposals for union and report back to the next Parliament.[23]

As it turned out, the union issue was largely ignored in the session of 1605–6, when debate concentrated on the Gunpowder Plot, on purveyance and on matters of finance, and it was not until the 1606–7 session that there were further lengthy debates on the union. At this point, the depth of English hostility became brutally clear.[24] The joint Anglo-Scottish commission had generated proposals relating to trade, naturalisation and the border laws, but the Commons proved obstructive on all but the last. The reasons were essentially threefold. First, many members felt that a 'community of commerce' would damage English prosperity. Nicholas Fuller turned James's metaphor of the two flocks against him:

> One man is owner of two pastures, with one hedge to divide them; the one pasture bare, the other fertile and good. A wise owner will not pull down the hedge quite, but make gates, and let them in and out etc. If he do, the cattle will rush in in multitudes, and much against their will return.[25]

Closely linked to this was a second fear that naturalisation of the *Ante-Nati* would cause an influx of Scots into England who would monopolise James's person and take a disproportionate amount of patronage for themselves. Finally, reverence for the English common law and for the supremacy of statute made most members deeply suspicious of any 'union of laws'. It was by no means clear how the supreme authority of statutes, which has emerged in earlier chapters as a very distinctive feature of the English Parliament,[26] could be reconciled with a union of the kingdoms.[27] One of the most vociferous critics, Sir Edwin Sandys, even used James's term 'perfect union' to advocate an incorporative union in which Scottish law would be subsumed into English. It is notable that the overwhelming resistance among members of the Commons also received some support from within the Lords and Privy Council. Interestingly, the new procedure of the Committee of the Whole House which, as we have seen, was developed initially as a device to enable Privy Councillors to offer replies and counter-arguments at a time when they were very sparse in the Commons, was harnessed by the opponents of union to make their own resistance even more powerful.[28] James became more and more politically isolated until eventually, with great sadness, he abandoned the attempt to achieve a union of the kingdoms by statute.

Parliament's only tangible contribution to the cause of union was an act abolishing the hostile laws.[29] In the end, the wrangles over the union of the kingdoms revealed both the strengths and weaknesses of the early Stuart Parliament. It clearly failed to be the instrument of fundamental constitutional reform for which James hoped. Such gradual reforms as did subsequently occur (such as the introduction of JPs in Scotland and reforms of the Scottish Kirk) were implemented, mostly quite successfully, by extra-parliamentary means. Yet such reforms were only piecemeal changes introduced over time, and parliamentary statute would still have been the most effective way to enact an overall, coherent programme of change. The fact that James tried so hard to achieve that, while his opponents devoted equal energy to obstructing it, indicates that supporters and critics alike recognised the continuing power of statute. Although he ultimately gave way, James could be in no doubt as to Parliament's effectiveness in transmitting opinion from the realm at large and making him conscious of what was politically practicable. If Parliament failed to produce a union of hearts and minds, it at least left him painfully aware of what English hearts and minds were feeling. It was a frustratingly double-edged weapon, but a useful and potent one nonetheless.

If the union issue was barely mentioned after the 1606–7 session, questions of finance dogged all these sessions and subsequent ones as well. Chapter 4 analysed the intractable problems posed by a fiscal system little changed in essentials since the fourteenth century.[30] At the heart of these difficulties lay the ancient distinction between the ordinary and extraordinary revenues, neither of which was buoyant in the early seventeenth century: the former had declined by 40 per cent in real terms during the sixteenth century, while the latter was drastically under-assessed and dwindling rapidly. In an effort to keep his coffers as full as possible, James exploited such traditional dues as wardship, while also looking out for other valuable sources of revenue that might be levied under the royal prerogative. The Houses were particularly suspicious of the latter, especially impositions, and disputed whether these could be raised by prerogative powers. Equally, they were reluctant to grant more parliamentary supply to a monarch widely regarded as extravagant. Yet the less supply they voted the less incentive the monarch had to call them and the more necessity he had to look to non-parliamentary sources of revenue. The result was a vicious circle in which frustration and mutual incomprehension mounted between Crown and Parliament and turned finance into the most vexatious issue of Jacobean parliamentary politics.

These questions surfaced in James's first Parliament with regard to the ancient rights of wardship and purveyance. Wardship was the monarch's right to assume the guardianship of those of its tenants-in-chief who inherited estates as minors, and it included the lucrative right to manage the wards' lands. Purveyance was the Crown's traditional right to purchase transport, food and other supplies for the royal household at prices well below market level. The 1604 Apology listed both wardship and purveyance as grievances, and indeed the drafting of this document was precipitated by a debate on the issue of wardship.[31] Neither grievance was a novelty: both had existed since the fourteenth century and both were open to abuse, especially purveyance. Yet the Crown and the Houses utterly failed to agree on how best to resolve the problem. Salisbury consistently favoured composition, whereby the Crown would renounce wardship, purveyance and other feudal dues in return for a fixed parliamentary grant. This proposal found extensive support in the Privy Council and the Lords. But although some members of the Commons were initially sympathetic to composition (especially for wardship) their attitude gradually hardened, not least because they suspected that the grant would be set at too high a price. Many members disliked the prospect of regular taxation that it would necessarily entail, and wanted instead to introduce bills that would reform specific abuses. This unfortunately led them into disputes with the judges, who questioned whether statutes could regulate such royal powers. Throughout the first three sessions these issues were batted around in an increasingly desultory series of debates.[32]

These discussions culminated in the Great Contract proposal which dominated both sessions of 1610. Salisbury's scheme, discussed in Chapter 4, envisaged that the Crown would surrender such unpopular feudal dues as wardship and purveyance in return for an annual parliamentary grant of £200,000 and a lump sum of £600,000.[33] The adoption of such a reform depended crucially on the ability of the King and his advisers to reach agreement with majorities in the Lords and Commons, but instead the episode revealed a widening gulf between the assumptions of the Crown and the two Houses, and a growing inability to relate to the other's viewpoint. When Salisbury requested an annual grant of £200,000, together with a one-off supply of £600,000 to pay the King's debts, the sums 'much amazed the Commons'.[34] As a result, Parliament wholly failed to live up to Salisbury's hopes that it would be the one instrument that could overhaul the financial system. As James told him in December 1610: 'you see there is no more trust to be laid upon this rotten reed of Egypt, for your greatest error hath been that you ever expected to draw honey out of gall'.[35] Parliament had conspicuously failed to be the panacea for which James and Salisbury had hoped.[36]

The Houses' caution over the Great Contract was reinforced by the fact that another major financial grievance had emerged by 1610 in the form of impositions. We have seen earlier how James's levying of these raised fundamental constitutional questions over how far they came under the ordinary or the extraordinary prerogative, and therefore over whether they required parliamentary consent.[37] The legality of impositions became a highly contentious issue in most of the Jacobean Parliaments and the disputes over them – like those over the Great Contract – revealed a disturbing lack of financial understanding between the Crown and the Houses. To James, the £70,000 that impositions brought into the Exchequer annually as a result of the revised Book of Rates of 1608 helped considerably to reduce the royal debt. He could also point out that their legality had been upheld in Bate's Case (1606).[38] The Commons, by contrast, never really accepted either the verdict in Bate's Case or the financial necessity of impositions.[39] This inability to understand each other's positions was crucial, for, as Conrad Russell has written:

> The central disagreement of James's reign was about the true cost of government, and James's central failure was his failure to convince the House of Commons he needed as much as in fact he did. From that single failure all the constitutional problems of the reign stemmed.[40]

The Commons' lack of empathy for James's position stemmed partly from an inability to realise that the costs of government had increased dramatically while the ordinary and extraordinary revenues had declined. But their position was undoubtedly hardened by James's personal extravagance. James never quite grasped this. He lamented to the Privy Council in October 1607 that 'the only disease and consumption which I can ever apprehend as likeliest to endanger me is this eating canker of want'.[41] Earlier that year he had insisted that his exceptional generosity to suitors during his first three years in England was now over, and he hoped that the Commons would recognise their responsibility to help him financially.[42] But, as the Crown's net debt soared from only £100,000 in 1603 to nearly £600,000 by 1608,[43] most members joined Thomas Wentworth in asking 'to what purpose is it for us to draw a silver stream out of the country into the royal cistern, if it shall daily run out thence by private cocks?'[44] James was a genuinely needy King who was extravagant, and unfortunately his extravagance made the Commons more reluctant to acknowledge his genuine needs.

These perceptions guided the Commons' behaviour in 1610 and 1614. They refused either to recognise the Crown's right to levy impositions or to grant sufficient subsidies for the Crown to manage without impositions.[45] Each side was locked into its own assumptions. The Commons believed that James could be solvent if only he curbed his expenditure, and they were therefore reluctant to give him more revenue until he did. James, on the other hand, thought that his need for money was so self-evident that he interpreted the Commons' actions as a deliberate bid to weaken the Crown.

This dispute came to a head in the Addled Parliament of 1614. The Howards, who had risen to prominence after Salisbury's death in 1612, were far from friendly towards Parliaments, and it is possible that they fuelled false rumours that 'undertakers' were packing and managing the Commons, and that the Crown might exploit impositions as a way of dispensing with Parliaments thereafter.[46] In such a tense atmosphere, the Houses' use of direct redress-supply bargaining[47] was understandable. As emerged in Chapter 4, this tactic was used relatively sparingly in early Stuart Parliaments, and in 1614 it proved fatal because it led the King to retaliate by threatening dissolution. In Russell's words:

> James was leaving [the Commons] no alternative but to accept impositions or be dissolved, that is to be powerless in whichever way they chose. Equally, they were leaving James with no alternative but to be insolvent in whichever way they chose. There was no great incentive to concession on either side.[48]

This lack of financial understanding was perhaps the most disturbing feature of the early Jacobean Parliaments. For it meant that Parliament was failing to fulfil one of its central purposes, the provision of satisfactory royal revenues. The 'power of the purse' was, as we saw in Chapter 4, the parliamentary function that was potentially most useful to the monarch, and the fact that it was not working smoothly therefore had serious implications for the political relationship between the Crown and the Houses. The Addled Parliament demonstrated this very plainly because the issue of impositions ensured that the Parliament was dissolved before a statute could be passed (the parliamentary meaning of the term 'addled'). For a monarch and his Great Council to hold such divergent assumptions as to make dialogue virtually impossible on so central a matter as finance was an alarming development. Nevertheless, the extent of the breakdown of trust must not be exaggerated. In particular, these disputes tended to be confined to specific issues, and although they disrupted James's relations with his Parliaments, they were not as yet extrapolated into a wider debate on the nature of royal powers in other areas. That was to remain true throughout the rest of James's reign.

Late Jacobean Parliaments, 1621 and 1624

James's last two Parliaments met in very different circumstances, both at home and abroad, and this was clearly reflected in their proceedings. Perhaps the most important change since the time of the Addled Parliament was the outbreak in 1618 of an international religious conflict on the continent that ultimately split much of Europe into Protestant and Catholic camps. This not only made religion a live issue (effectively for the first time since 1603–4); it also plunged England into a serious trade depression which in turn heightened Parliament's concerns about finance.[49] In such a context, Parliaments needed particularly careful management, but this was not assisted by the growing influence of Buckingham, James's last and most disastrous favourite, who had risen rapidly to prominence in the years after 1616. Deepening mistrust of Buckingham henceforth bedevilled the Crown's relations with Parliaments until his assassination in August 1628.

The circumstances in which the 1621 Parliament was summoned reflected both the international situation and the workings of Court politics. Buckingham and Prince Charles, who were on increasingly friendly terms, urged James to threaten the use of force unless the Emperor withdrew his troops from the Rhenish Palatinate by the spring of 1621. Such a threat had to be backed up, and when a benevolence raised barely £35,000 it became clear that only a Parliament could supply the necessary revenue.[50] When it assembled on 30 January 1621, the Crown and both Houses were in a conciliatory mood and keen to avoid any repetition of the Addled Parliament. In his opening speech, James pledged his commitment to reducing Court expenditure and to preserving peace abroad, but stressed that contingency plans for war were necessary in the meantime.[51] For their part, members of the Lords and Commons were less vociferous on the issue of impositions throughout this Parliament, which was instead dominated by two issues: monopolies and foreign policy.

The Houses' amenable attitude was evident when they voted James two subsidies within a few weeks of Parliament's meeting.[52] They left the way open for further grants, and turned to investigate the royal grants of patents and monopolies. These grants were widely blamed for the 'decay of trade', and the Commons' investigations concentrated particularly on the right to license inns and alehouses and the patent for the manufacture of gold and silver thread. This was the context in which impeachment was revived,[53] for it provided a conveniently flexible and effective means to deal with two notorious monopolists, Sir Francis Michell and Sir Giles Mompesson.[54] However, the Houses had to tread warily, for Buckingham's brother Christopher Villiers and his half-brother Sir Edward Villiers were also involved in various monopolies, and Mompesson was Sir Edward Villiers's brother-in-law. Already there were signs of the bicameral hostility towards Buckingham that was to develop so strongly during the course of the decade, and his enemies in the Lords, especially the

Earl of Southampton, certainly encouraged the Commons' enquiries into monopolies as a way of attacking the Villiers family.[55] This so annoyed James that during the summer recess he briefly arrested Southampton and Oxford along with Sandys, one of their most vociferous allies in the Commons.[56] Meanwhile, the assault on monopolies led the Commons to investigate the 'referees' who had authorised these grants in the first place. Sir Edward Coke and Lionel Cranfield, later Earl of Middlesex, used this as an opportunity to promote the impeachment of the Lord Chancellor, Sir Francis Bacon, on the grounds that he had corruptly accepted bribes from Chancery litigants.[57] As on other occasions Parliament thus allowed factional rivalries within the Council to be pursued in a wider forum. Throughout all these proceedings, James stood back and made no attempt to protect either the monopolists or Bacon.[58] He seems to have been genuinely concerned to protect the interests of the commonwealth, and on 10 July issued a proclamation cancelling 18 monopolies and allowing 17 more to be challenged at common law.[59] The one subject that was not really discussed during the Parliament's first sitting was the ostensible reason for which it had been called, namely the possibility of war on the continent.

That all changed dramatically when Parliament reassembled on 20 November. The 12-year truce between Spain and the Dutch Republic had expired the previous April, and over the summer the Emperor flatly refused to withdraw Imperial troops from the Palatinate: as a result, by the autumn the clouds of war were gathering.[60] But what sort of war? The second sitting of the 1621 Parliament lasted barely four weeks and led to one of the most spectacular confrontations between James and any of his Parliaments, focused on the Commons' privilege of free speech. The cause of this conflict seems to have been a misunderstanding between James and the Houses over exactly what he wished them to discuss. James subsequently claimed that he wanted the Houses to consider an expedition to relieve the Palatinate, but to avoid the subjects of a Spanish campaign and Prince Charles's marriage (for he was still hoping for a 'Spanish match'). However, neither Buckingham's clients nor the Privy Councillors ever made this clear to the Commons, and this failure of management ensured that members were genuinely astonished when James forbade them to discuss these matters.[61] His behaviour enflamed the already touchy question of the Commons' privilege of free speech and the subsequent exchanges over this issue, examined earlier,[62] culminated in the extraordinary scene on 30 December when James tore the Commons' Protestation from the Journal.

There was no doubting James's fury. A week later he dissolved Parliament, thereby depriving himself of further supply, and at the same time imprisoned several members of the Commons, including Coke, Sir Robert Phelips, William Mallory and John Pym, whom he called 'fiery and popular spirits'.[63] It is possible that the King's show of temper owed something to declining health, and also that Gondomar was encouraging him to take a strong line against an overtly anti-Spanish Parliament.[64] Yet James's behaviour was untypical, and it is notable that his proclamation dissolving Parliament also stressed the 'harmony' that had characterised the first sitting, and concluded with the hope that it would 'not be long' before he could again 'assemble our Parliament with confidence of the true and hearty love and affection of our subjects'.[65]

That essentially conciliatory attitude was evident when James summoned another Parliament in 1624. The previous year, the disastrous trip by

Buckingham and Prince Charles to Madrid to win the Infanta had left them determined to start a war against Spain. For once their views chimed in with the popular mood, and they soon assembled a bicameral 'patriot' coalition in support of war that included such erstwhile critics of the Duke as the Earls of Essex, Southampton, Oxford, Pembroke and Warwick, along with the likes of Digges, Coke and Sandys.[66] They persuaded the King to call another Parliament, and when it met James elegantly defused the memory of 1621 by inviting the Houses to advise him on 'matters of greatest weight and importance'.[67] He declared:

> I am so desirous to forget all rends in former Parliaments that it shall not be my default if I be not in love with Parliaments, and call them often, and desire to end my life in that intercourse between me and my people for the making of good laws, reforming of such abuses as I cannot be well informed of but in Parliament, and maintaining the good government of the commonwealth.[68]

The 1624 Parliament was in many ways the most successful of James's reign. In a single session it produced no fewer than 73 statutes, more than any other Jacobean session. Some of this legislation completed work begun in 1621, notably the Monopolies Act which declared grants of monopolies to individuals illegal.[69] Indeed, the fact that of the 185 bills that received at least a first reading in 1624, 107 had previously been examined in the 1621 Parliament provides an excellent illustration of the legislative continuity that could exist between successive Parliaments.[70]

Even more than in 1621, the Parliament of 1624 was dominated by the war and its implications. James had hoped to avoid an open breach with Spain and preferred an overland expedition to relieve the Palatinate. However, Buckingham and Charles mobilised their allies in both Houses to insist that the grant of three subsidies and three fifteenths was tied to the anti-Spanish war for which it had been voted. It was thus through their efforts that the 'appropriation' clause was inserted in the 1624 subsidy act, a point that shows how what might seem a bold constitutional claim by the Commons actually represented an extension of political machinations within the Court and Council.[71] This pattern was also evident in the way in which the Duke and Prince orchestrated the impeachment of Lord Treasurer Middlesex, who strongly opposed the war on grounds of cost. Once again, this needs to be understood in terms of the workings of the bicameral groupings within Parliament examined in the previous chapter. The attack on Middlesex was a notable instance of political conflict within Court and Council spilling over into Parliament, and as James presciently warned Buckingham and Charles, to foment such parliamentary pressure was a dangerous game.

One other worrying development that was clearly linked to the context of the Thirty Years War was a perceptible growth of religious anxieties within Parliament. It was one of James's most striking achievements as King of England that religious issues figured so little in most of his Parliaments: that was a real tribute to his management of the Church of England and his capacity to defuse religious controversy.[72] But in 1624 the Houses submitted a complaint against Richard Montagu's tract *A New Gag for an Old Goose*, which Pym thought 'full fraught with dangerous opinions of Arminius'. Montagu argued that the points of difference between the Churches of Rome and England were far fewer than had often been supposed. This view appealed to

James's ecumenicism, and he declared, rather rashly, 'If that is to be a papist, then am I a papist!' In fact, James's Calvinist credentials remained sound, as evinced for example in his sending of representatives to the Synod of Dort that condemned Arminius's views in 1619.[73] But the Montagu furore served as a warning that Catholic successes on the continent were making some English Protestants increasingly nervous. Under James, a ruler whom Pym tried to include in a list of 'Fathers of the Church' in 1629,[74] such fears remained fairly muted. But under a monarch less adept at balancing opinions and more willing to promote committed anti-Calvinists the potential clearly existed for intense religious controversy.

James prorogued the Parliament on 29 May 1624 with a magnanimous speech in which he praised 'the obedience and good respect of the Commons in all things this Parliament' and rejoiced at 'the happy conclusion of this session'.[75] He had apparently intended to recall Parliament in the autumn but in fact never did so. Although the reasons for this remain obscure, there is no evidence to indicate that James was reluctant to meet Parliament again. As Russell has written, 'the story of 1621 and 1624 suggests that not very much was wrong with relations between Crown and Parliament'.[76] There was relatively little polarisation of political or religious opinion, and no real continuity of opposition from the earlier Jacobean Parliaments. Throughout James's reign, the groupings within both Houses remained highly fluid and transient, and the majority of members were not consistently aligned with any one particular circle of associates. There was no organised 'opposition' as such, but instead loose-knit and shifting groups that converged to promote a specific view on a certain issue and then diverged again. Such groupings were often extensions of alignments within the Court and Privy Council: they existed within both Houses, and we have seen instances of bicameral co-operation, for example in the Union debates of 1604–7, over the impeachments of 1621, and in the 'patriot' coalition of 1624.[77] This meant that both Houses were regularly divided, and much depended on whether the exponents of a particular policy were able to achieve a majority in both Lords and Commons. Where they were, as in these three examples, there was little that the Crown could do to resist and James was sensible enough to realise the need for concessions.

This lack of any consistent 'opposition' group, wedded to a coherent ideological platform, ensured that there was no 'fault-line' running through Jacobean parliamentary politics. Various issues generated specific disagreements between the Crown and particular members, but the Parliaments proved able to resolve them or to brush them aside and start afresh. Although the revival of impeachment would later be used against the Crown's wishes, in this period James's willingness to sacrifice unpopular ministers undoubtedly helped the doctrine of 'evil counsellors' to be implemented effectively and to protect the monarch from direct criticism. He also showed a marked instinct for knowing when to compromise and to appeal to a consensual framework in order to defuse moments of tension. His principal weaknesses in his treatment of Parliaments were twofold: firstly his tendency to lecture members on the nature of their institution periodically caused offence, especially on the delicate matter of parliamentary privilege; and secondly at certain times he failed to take sufficient care over the management of Parliament in order to clarify his preferred policies and smooth the way for them. Management was not constantly needed, and it would be anachronistic to suggest that this was something that the Crown and the Privy Councillors in the Houses had to do routinely as a matter of course. But on some occasions, such as during the foreign policy debates in the second sitting of 1621, a clearer lead from the Crown and its advisers might have helped to avoid the subsequent confusion and confrontation.

It needs stressing, however, that James remained willing to work with Parliaments and did not entertain the possibility of ruling without them. His handling of Parliaments revealed the same basic resilience and good sense that, notwithstanding occasional moments of temper or tactlessness, characterised his conduct of government as a whole. In this respect, the continuities between Jacobean Parliaments and their Elizabethan predecessors should not be underestimated. The fact that during both reigns disagreements and misunderstandings occurred from time to time did not indicate anything fundamentally or permanently wrong with the relationship between Crown and Parliament. Although certain underlying problems within the structures of government, such as the financial system, were not rectified, there were limits to how far they were made worse, and if Elizabeth was more successful than James in restraining expenditure, for most of his reign James defused tensions in the Church more completely than his predecessor, a fact that was plainly reflected in parliamentary proceedings. The relationships between the Houses, and between them and the monarch, did not in essence change all that much between 1603 and 1625. But under James's successor it would be a very different story.

Early Caroline Parliaments, 1625–1629

Charles I's opening words to his first Parliament, that it did not 'stand with my nature to spend much time in words', immediately marked a profound contrast with his loquacious father.[78] Charles's essentially authoritarian temperament and style of government were plainly reflected in his relations with Parliaments, and often it was not so much what he *said* as what he *did* that mattered. The view of Parliaments that he expressed in various declarations during the later 1620s was in many ways a traditional and unexceptionable one.[79] The problem lay rather in Charles's handling of Parliaments in practice. Although he was not averse to Parliaments in principle he tended, far more than James, to regard them as tests of his subjects' loyalty, and he was acutely sensitive to the slightest sign of disobedience. He attributed any such disloyalty to a minority of 'malevolent' and 'ill-affected' members whom he blamed for misleading the 'sincerer and better part of the house', 'the wise moderate men' who formed the majority. Unfortunately, the sterner the measures he took against that perceived 'faction of discontented, seditious persons', the more he lost support within the moderate majority whose loyalty he wished to safeguard.[80] The result was that during the later 1620s many members of the Commons became more and more fearful about the future of Parliaments. The European conflict, and the general retreat of representative assemblies in much of the continent, fuelled such anxieties, and Sir Robert Phelips expressed the view of many when he reportedly declared in August 1625 that 'we are the last monarchy in Christendom that retain our original right and constitutions'.[81] The mentality of many members of the early Caroline Parliaments was an edgy and embattled one.

To make matters worse, Charles's policies and style of government aggravated many of the most delicate areas within the body politic. The war against Spain between 1625 and 1630 placed considerable strain on the financial system, a burden worsened during the years 1627–9 by the fact that, thanks to Buckingham's inept diplomacy, England was at war with France as well. The heavy costs of war gave new urgency to the already complex problems surrounding the royal finances, and also posed very starkly the thorny question of how far the Houses could influence the nature and management of a conflict for which they had granted supply. Buckingham's disastrous expeditions to Cadiz in 1625 and La Rochelle two years later made the Houses extremely reluctant to vote sufficient supply until he was removed. But whereas they blamed the failures on incompetent leadership, Charles blamed them on inadequate funding. He felt let down by the Houses and, encouraged by 'new counsels', he turned to non-parliamentary sources of revenue such as the Forced Loan of 1627, and imposed harsh punishments on those who refused to pay. These policies in turn raised complex and fundamental questions about the legality of prerogative taxation, the relationship between royal authority and the rule of law, and the protection of the subjects' rights and liberties. The later 1620s also saw the systematic promotion of anti-Calvinists to senior offices in the Church which awakened fears within Parliament that the nation's safeguards against popery were being weakened. These problems were all intertwined, and collectively they fomented growing mistrust between Charles and both Houses that culminated in his decision to rule without Parliaments after 1629.

Charles's first Parliament assembled in June 1625 amidst a severe outbreak of plague in London that eventually caused it to be adjourned to Oxford in August. In his opening speech, Charles told the Houses that the conflict against the Habsburgs had come about 'by your intreaties, your engagements', and urged them to vote supply as soon as possible.[82] But throughout the Parliament, members were once again left uncertain about what sort of war they were being asked to support. As a result, they voted two subsidies but refused any more until they received clarification about the war.[83] They voted tonnage and poundage to Charles for one year only pending a fuller review of royal finances, but when the Lords allowed this to fall asleep after one reading the King subsequently continued to collect tonnage and poundage without Parliament's consent.[84] Another disturbing development was the fact that for much of the Parliament the Commons devoted nearly half its time to religious concerns, a pattern that was in marked contrast to most Jacobean Parliaments. In particular, the Commons renewed its attack on Montagu,[85] and many members were horrified when the King appointed him a royal chaplain and instructed the Commons to drop their charges.[86] Charles could scarcely have done anything more likely to raise parliamentary suspicions about his own religious sympathies. Ignoring the King's request for further supply,[87] the Houses instead drew up a petition to Charles complaining of the recent 'animating of the popish party' and urging a range of measures including the enforcement of the recusancy laws.[88] The Commons also launched an enquiry into the sale of offices and honours that led them into criticism of Buckingham. It was at this point that Charles despaired of obtaining more subsidies and dissolved the Parliament.[89]

As the war developed, with Buckingham's disastrous expedition to Cadiz in the autumn of 1625,[90] Charles's financial position grew more dire and he called another Parliament for February 1626. Before it met, however, he tried to remove six members of the Commons whom he regarded as 'ill-affected' by having them pricked as sheriffs and thereby made ineligible for election.[91] Charles also created a number of new peers in order to bolster support in the Upper House.[92] These manoeuvres, together with Buckingham's defence of Montagu and other anti-Calvinists at the York House conference in mid-February, reinforced the anxieties of many members about the direction of official policies.[93] As a result, the Commons voted three subsidies and three fifteenths, but made them conditional on the redress of grievances.[94] The greatest of these was Buckingham, and the 1626 Parliament was dominated by the attempted impeachment of the Duke.[95] We saw in Chapter 6 how this became a genuinely bicameral campaign,[96] and, despite his creation of new peers this Parliament really marked the point at which Charles I ceased to be able to rely on the acquiescence of the Upper House. Given the extent of the monarch's control over the membership of the Lords, and the fact that throughout the seventeenth century most of the Upper House were normally willing to support the Crown, this was a very alarming development.[97] Charles's exclusion of Arundel and Bristol, in what was a manifest breach of privilege, aroused deep indignation in the Lords. The arrest of Digges and Eliot had a similar effect in the Commons, and in the end both Houses passed a 'forbearance' declining to proceed with further business until their members were reinstated.[98] Charles's actions represented a practical authoritarianism that went far beyond anything his father had done, and they reflected a much more high-handed attitude towards parliamentary privilege than James had ever displayed. The Commons blamed Charles's behaviour on Buckingham and became even more determined to destroy the King's favourite. Realising that he had to choose between gaining supply and protecting Buckingham, Charles opted for the latter and dissolved Parliament.

James I, like Charles II later in the century, never tried to obstruct an impeachment. This was very wise, because although it often meant abandoning loyal ministers, it did allow Parliament to attack those whom they regarded as 'evil counsellors' without criticising the monarch directly.[99] Charles I's approach was the exact opposite. However attractive his loyalty to his servants may have been as a personal trait, politically it made it extremely difficult for the Houses to sustain the doctrine of 'evil counsellors'. When, as part of the Houses' attempts to ensure that Charles was 'rightly advised', Eliot likened Buckingham to Sejanus, the hated adviser of the tyrannical Emperor Tiberius, Charles responded by arresting Eliot rather than Buckingham.[100] Instead of removing the Duke, the experience of the 1626 Parliament led Charles to turn to 'new counsels'. That summer, many of those who had defended Buckingham were promoted to the Privy Council or to senior Court offices. Buckingham's hold on patronage and promotion became ever tighter and he harried his critics relentlessly: Arundel, for example, was dismissed from the Council while Pembroke was systematically marginalised.[101]

Following the dissolution of Parliament in June 1626, Charles's 'new counsels', led by Buckingham, urged him not to recall Parliament and instead to raise prerogative taxation in the form of the benevolence (1626) and then the Forced Loan (1627). They also supported harsh punishments for those who refused payment, such as the billeting of troops on Loan refusers: around 70 individuals were imprisoned without cause shown, and when five of these sought a writ of habeas corpus, Charles used the suit as a test of his right to imprison without giving a reason whenever he alleged reasons of state security.[102] Nervous of such a claim, the judges returned only a 'rule of court' that could not be used as a binding precedent, whereupon Charles instructed the Attorney-General Sir Robert Heath to amend the record into a full verdict. As hostility towards these policies mounted, England's military fortunes plummeted still further when Buckingham made a disastrous attempt to relieve the French Protestant colony at La Rochelle in the summer of 1627. The £240,000 yielded by the Loan were soon exhausted, and its legality had been so widely queried (even if outright refusal was relatively rare) that there was no possibility of raising further revenue in that way. So, reluctantly, Charles summoned another Parliament for March 1628, a move once again preceded by the creation of several new peers.[103]

For the many in both Houses who were excluded from royal counsels, Parliament provided the only arena in which to influence royal actions and statute the only protection against their adverse effects. Charles's recent policies, especially the Loan, billeting and imprisonment without cause shown, had generated deepening mistrust of the King and the use that he was making of his discretionary powers. Members assembled in an atmosphere of urgency and tension, captured in Sir Benjamin Rudyerd's feeling that this was 'the crisis of Parliaments'.[104] Fearful of a dissolution, members deliberately steered clear of contentious subjects like Buckingham, tonnage and poundage or impositions. Instead, on Coke's advice, they decided to draw up a Petition of Right which, once it had received the royal assent, would possess the same legislative force as a statute. Such a petition was distinct from a petition of grace, in that it requested justice against grievances regarded as illegal, whereas the latter simply appealed for royal mercy or favour. The Petition of Right made no claim to enact new law. Rather, it reflected an intense reluctance to trust Charles with the Crown's traditional discretionary powers. It did not try to abrogate those powers, but to spell out more clearly than ever before the statutory safeguards that should have prevented their abuse. Virtually everyone agreed that the King possessed certain powers in an emergency. The dilemma was how to prevent him from using those powers in non-emergency situations without destroying the powers themselves or defining them so precisely that they ceased to be discretionary.

The Petition of Right was a very ingenious attempt to resolve the conundrum. It recited Magna Carta and a series of medieval statutes to demonstrate that non-parliamentary taxation, the imposing of martial law, billeting of troops on civilians without their consent, and imprisonment without cause shown were all contrary to the 'laws and statutes of this realm'.[105] It was a very practical document, born of mistrust of one particular monarch and prompted specifically by the royal policies of 1626–7. It was thus quite different from the 1604 Apology or the 1621 Protestation, texts which had discussed the origins and nature of royal powers at a very abstract level. The closest analogies would be the Commons' petitions of 1610 (on impositions) and 1621 (on freedom of speech), although these were much less wide-ranging than the 1628 Petition. All of these parliamentary documents need to be located within the particular circumstances in which they were written: they were responses to particular royal statements or policies, and they cannot be treated as a single series of constitutional signposts marking a 'high road to civil war'. Whereas Jacobean Parliaments generally engaged with James on his own theoretical level, because that was the plain on which he addressed them, the Petition of Right was an attempt to counter the far more practical (and therefore more dangerous) authoritarianism of Charles I. In that sense, each monarch got the Parliaments he deserved.

The prolonged discussions between the two Houses over the Petition during April and May 1628 provide a good illustration of the bicameral politics discussed in Chapter 6.[106] We saw there that initially a majority within the Upper House, mobilised by Buckingham, opposed the Petition and that only delicate negotiations by some of the Petition's leading supporters in the Commons, conducted in a series of joint conferences, eventually dispelled the hostility of enough peers for the Petition to be passed in the Lords.[107] When the Petition was presented to the King, his first answer (2 June) was evasive in that he did not actually accept the Petition as such, but merely stated that:

> The King willeth that right be done according to the laws and customs of the realm; and that the statutes be put in due execution, that his subjects may have no cause to complain of any wrong or oppressions, contrary to their just rights and liberties, to the preservation whereof he holds himself as well obliged as of his prerogative.[108]

The Commons were not satisfied with this and refused to confirm their grant of supply until, five days later, Charles gave a second answer using the conventional formula of assent to such a petition: 'soit droit fait comme est désiré'.[109] The Commons were delighted and shortly afterwards voted a grant of five subsidies.[110]

However, Charles's subsequent behaviour undid much of the good that his acceptance of the Petition might have achieved. Certainly neither the King nor the Petition's supporters had any doubts about the capacity of statute to guard against the abuse of royal powers. The Petition was enrolled as a statute on the Parliament Roll, but Parliament later discovered that when it was printed Charles ordered his unsatisfactory first answer to be printed as well as his formal assent, and also instructed the removal of the statute number. This was a deliberate bid to cause uncertainty about whether the Petition had the force of a statute.[111] That issue crucially affected whether it could be invoked in the law courts as a protection against royal actions. Furthermore, notwithstanding the Petition, many members of both Houses believed that there were many other important grievances still to be tackled. Led by Eliot and Coke, the Commons drew up a Remonstrance against Buckingham's conduct of the war, which they presented to Charles on 17 June.[112] The King expressed his surprise that they should have drawn up the Remonstrance so soon after the Petition and added haughtily that its subject matter was more appropriate for him to consider than for them.[113] The Commons nevertheless pressed ahead with another Remonstrance declaring Charles's continued collection of tonnage and poundage to be contrary to the Petition and 'a breach of the fundamental liberties of this kingdom'.[114] The next day the King asserted that this was a 'false construction' of the Petition, a claim that the Court of Exchequer subsequently upheld.[115] Insisting that the Petition was never intended 'to intrench upon my prerogative', Charles then prorogued Parliament.[116]

The closing weeks of the 1628 session showed how far apart the attitudes of the Crown and many members of both Houses remained despite the Petition of Right. Nor had things improved by the time that Parliament reassembled in January 1629. Buckingham's assassination on 23 August 1628 removed the 'grievance of grievances', but it also served to bring to the fore two other issues that had been rumbling on since the beginning of the reign. Charles had continued to collect tonnage and poundage, which he regarded as 'one of the chief maintenances of the Crown',[117] and he ordered those merchants who refused payment to be imprisoned. He personally authorised the goods of one of them, John Rolle, to be confiscated; since Rolle was a member of the Commons, the House subsequently tried to protect his property by claiming privilege. Such a claim illustrates the plasticity of the concept of parliamentary privilege in this period and the political uses to which it could be put.[118] Equally alarming was the wave of promotions of prominent anti-Calvinists to bish-oprics during the summer and autumn of 1628, including William Laud to London, John Howson to Durham and, most controversially of all, the notori-ous Richard Montagu to Chichester. Charles also granted a full pardon to Roger Manwaring, whom the 1628 Parliament had attempted to impeach for supporting the Forced Loan.[119] Such actions compounded the fears already expressed in the 1628 session about the growth of Arminianism.[120] As a result, when Parliament reconvened in January 1629, the two grievances of tonnage and poundage and religious innovation stood at the top of the agenda.

Charles's main motive for summoning the session was to secure a bill resolv-ing the matter of tonnage and poundage.[121] This he regarded as simply the rat-ification of a grant that was rightfully his. Many members of the Commons, however, were reluctant to appear to condone what they regarded as his illegal collection of it. Instead, they investigated the printing of the Petition of Right and the confiscation of Rolle's goods, and in the process uncovered the evi-dence of Charles's covert authoritarianism described in the previous para-graphs. It is noticeable that the Lords stood back from all these debates. Buckingham's death had removed a major grievance for many peers, and in 1629 the Upper House went about its own low-key business (such as a bill for apparel) without becoming overtly involved in the Commons' concerns.[122] However, it is likely that some peers, especially Pembroke and Warwick, encouraged the Commons' stand, especially on religion, as an extension of their own campaign against Laud's growing influence at Court, but did not wish to antagonise Charles any further themselves.[123] This provides a good indication of the different forms that bicameral consultation and collaboration between the Lords and Commons could take from session to session.

The Commons meanwhile appointed a committee to consider the state of the Church, and on 24 February this committee proposed a series of resolu-tions, condemning the 'subtle and pernicious spreading of the Arminian fac-tion' and requesting that the King 'be graciously pleased to confer bishoprics, and other ecclesiastical preferments, with the advice of his Privy Council, upon learned, pious and orthodox men'.[124] These proposals illustrated the increasing link in some members' minds between Parliaments and the prevention of reli-gious innovation. Charles, however, deeply resented what he took to be an encroachment on the royal supremacy, and the next day he adjourned Parliament for a week. The Houses reassembled on 2 March amid rumours of an imminent dissolution, and in a bid to forestall this, Eliot, Denzil Holles and Benjamin Valentine held the Speaker Sir John Finch in his chair while the House passed three resolutions declaring anyone who brought in 'innovation in religion', or who paid or collected tonnage and poundage, to be a 'capital enemy to this kingdom and commonwealth'.[125] This extraordinary episode revealed the desperation that at least some members felt by 1629; it also made up Charles's mind to dissolve the Parliament on 10 March.

In his closing speech, the King blamed the dissolution exclusively on 'the undutiful and seditious carriage in the Lower House', a recognition of the extent to which the Lords had remained quiescent during this session. He remained convinced that 'some few vipers amongst them did cast this mist of undutifulness over most of their eyes'.[126] That same day he issued a declaration in which he promised to maintain 'the true religion and doctrine established in the Church of England' and the 'ancient and just rights and liberties of our subjects'. He attributed all his problems with the Parliament to 'ill-affected men' who stirred up 'causeless jealousies'. These people, he believed, encouraged the Commons to try to 'extend their privileges' and to make claims whose drift was 'to break ... through all respects and ligaments of government, and to erect an universal over-swaying power to themselves, which belongs only to us and not to them'.[127] This highly characteristic belief in a minority of ringleaders led Charles to imprison nine members of the Commons for their part in the events of 2 March. He subsequently violated habeas corpus by moving the members to different gaols to give the law officers time to draw up charges that would get round the claim of parliamentary privilege. They were later charged with conspiring to 'raise sedition and discord between the King, his peers, and people'. Some were subsequently released, but Charles regarded Eliot as particularly culpable and detained him until his death in 1632.[128]

Charles did not call another Parliament for 11 years. It is not certain that he initially intended so long an interval, and it may be that his commitment to non-parliamentary government only hardened into a firm resolve by about 1632.[129] As so often, contemporaries found his intentions difficult to fathom. He left the matter deliberately open-ended, and on 27 March issued a proclamation 'for the suppression of false rumours touching Parliament' which declared it 'presumption for any to prescribe any time unto us for Parliaments, the calling, continuing and dissolving of which is always in our own power'. The proclamation concluded, enigmatically:

> we shall be more inclinable to meet in Parliament again when our people shall see more clearly into our intents and actions, when such as have bred this interruption shall have received their condign punishment, and those who are misled by them, and by such ill reports ... shall come to a better understanding of us and themselves.[130]

Such words were indicative of a very different political atmosphere between Charles and his Parliaments than anything known under James. Since Charles's accession, Parliament had met every year except 1627. But ironically this frequency, far from allaying fears about the future of Parliaments, had allowed a continuity of opposition to develop without there being sufficient time for anxieties to calm down between sessions. This was especially true of the remarkable escalation of religious tensions during this period. Although there was still no organised 'opposition', and groupings within the two Houses remained very fluid, a perceptible shift had occurred since 1625. Most notably in the Petition of Right, criticism of royal policies assumed a far more specific and practical form than had generally been the case under James. This was reinforced by hatred of Buckingham, which reached a greater intensity during the first three years of Charles's reign than hitherto. Partly because of the Duke's deep unpopularity, the later 1620s also saw a marked decline in the Crown's support within the Upper House. This was an ominous development, and it enabled those most critical of royal policies and advisers to make increasingly determined and co-ordinated use of bicameral collaboration, a phenomenon that we have seen most clearly revealed in the attempted impeachment of Buckingham in 1626 and over the Petition of Right two years later. It is probable that these debates also witnessed a hardening of attitudes and the emergence of political alignments based on deeper divisions of principle than had existed earlier in the century.[131] Yet these developments were not necessarily irreparable, and particularly after Buckingham's assassination there were widespread hopes that relations between Crown and Parliament might improve in the longer term. In the years that followed, Charles had the freedom to recall Parliament or not as he saw fit. He still held the political initiative: much would depend on the use that he made of it.

The Short Parliament

Parliaments were certainly not forgotten during the 11 years of Personal Rule. The perception of Parliament as a valuable conciliar body and a remedy for grievances remained especially strong in the popular memory. Although there is relatively little surviving evidence of individuals expressing regret at the absence of Parliament or pressing for its recall, we shall see that widespread anger against the lack of Parliaments for 11 years was forcefully expressed in 1640, and it prompted a series of reforms during the opening months of the Long Parliament intended to prevent such a prolonged period of non-parliamentary government from happening again.[132] It is possible that, with the peacetime budget balanced, the Personal Rule might have continued almost indefinitely had Charles avoided military entanglements. However, this speculation is in the end academic because the Scottish rebellion that necessitated the recall of Parliament in 1640 was not a *deus ex machina* but the direct consequence of one of Charles's most cherished policies, his drive to reform the Scottish Kirk. The same authoritarian style of government that had destabilised Charles's relations with Parliaments during the 1620s ultimately produced the circumstances that obliged him to summon another Parliament.

In many ways it makes sense to see the Short Parliament as a continuation, indeed a finale, of the Parliaments of the 1620s. The issues and the structure of proceedings probably had more in common with the sessions of 1625–9 than with the Long Parliament. Complaints of grievances took up where the Parliament of 1628–9 had left off. Furthermore, although the Short Parliament was much closer chronologically to the Long Parliament, it differed from it fundamentally in the crucial respect that the King's position relative to Parliament remained much as it had been in the 1620s. In the spring of 1640 Charles still had genuine political options, one of which was to dissolve Parliament whenever he chose. We shall see that by the time the Long Parliament met his military and financial circumstances had changed so dramatically that this was no longer true.

As in the 1620s, Charles summoned Parliament for one reason above all: money. He assumed that his cause against the Scots was so self-evidently strong that the Houses would naturally support him. At the opening of Parliament, the Lord Keeper reportedly said that 'upon these pressing and urgent reasons' the King expected supply to be granted 'with all speed', and that he would then call another session towards winter to consider what was thought 'to be good for the commonwealth'.[133] However, a minority of members were sympathetic to the Scots, and many more were unwilling to grant supply until their grievances were heard. Although a majority of the Lords accepted that supply should precede redress,[134] in the Commons – which, as we have seen, retained the right to initiate grants of supply – most members preferred, as in 1614, 1626 and 1628, to engage in direct redress-supply bargaining.[135] A number of speakers – including both future Royalists, such as Sir Francis Seymour, and future Parliamentarians like John Pym – began their accounts of grievances with the arrest of members in 1629.[136] The Commons' debates concentrated particularly on the long intermission of Parliaments, and on the fiscal expedients and religious innovations of the Personal Rule. Increasingly frustrated, Charles complained to the Lords on 24 April that the Commons 'have put the cart before the horse', and insisted that 'my necessities are so urgent that there can be no delay'.[137] However, on 29 April the Commons blithely embarked on a debate about ecclesiastical grievances which amounted to 'a comprehensive condemnation of the Laudian church, and one which came from almost all quarters of the House'.[138] By 4 May the King's patience was clearly running out. The Speaker, Sir John Glanville, warned: 'Let us ... use that course that may draw the being and subsistence of Parliaments rather than look to privilege of Parliament, which is nothing without being.' But Sir Henry Vane the elder was nearer the mark when he likened present events to the final stages of the Addled Parliament,[139] for the next day Charles dissolved the Parliament. Characteristically, he asserted that 'it hath been some few cunning and some ill-affected men, that have been the cause of this misunderstanding'.[140]

The Short Parliament certainly showed that mistrust between Charles and the Houses, and especially the Commons, had not dissipated since the 1620s. The Personal Rule had only added to the lengthy list of grievances that many members wished to discuss and deepened their desire to secure redress. For Charles the dissolution was a disaster, for it marked the point at which he began to lose control of events. In the summer of 1640 he could either have granted concessions to Parliament in order to gain supply, or concessions to the Scottish Covenanters in order to end the conflict. The only option that was not viable was to grant concessions to neither and launch a second campaign against the Scots without parliamentary supply.[141] Yet that was exactly what Charles did, precipitating the second Bishops' War which culminated in a Scottish invasion of the north-east of England. This military disaster drastically reduced the King's political options and created the unprecedented circumstances in which he was forced to recall Parliament. In late August, 12 peers submitted a petition urging Charles 'to summon a Parliament within some short and convenient time'. Among the grievances that they listed was 'the great grief of your subjects by the long intermission of Parliaments, in the late and former dissolving of such as have been called, without the hoped effects which otherwise they might have procured'.[142] Charles responded by summoning a Great Council of Peers to York, and when they met on 24 September he announced that he would call a new Parliament to assemble on 3 November. That Parliament was not finally dissolved until 1660, and it turned out to be quite different from any of its predecessors.

8

Revolutionary Parliaments, 1640–1660

The Long Parliament I: 1640–1642

The meeting of the Long Parliament marked a watershed in the institution's history. For over 12 years, until 20 April 1653, Parliament sat in continuous session, with no prorogations and only one adjournment (9 September – 20 October 1641). Although Parliament would later meet each year after 1689, the sessions only lasted a few months at a time for much of the eighteenth century,[1] and this phenomenon of sitting continuously throughout the year was not seen again. Also unique was the claim that a portion of the Houses made, from 1642 onwards, to exercise the King's executive powers on his behalf and to issue ordinances that they asserted had the force of statute. Instead of being an instrument of the King's government, Parliament became an alternative government, claiming to defend the King's office even if this meant waging a war against the person of Charles I. The Parliamentarians eventually defeated Charles and the purged 'Rump' of the Commons then assumed sovereign powers and appointed a High Court that sentenced him to death. In the wake of the regicide, the Rump abolished the monarchy and the House of Lords and declared England a republic for the only time in its history. The final irony came in April 1653 when the Army that had enabled the Houses to defeat Charles in turn dispersed those members of the Commons who were still sitting at Westminster.

None of these extraordinary events could have been foreseen when the Long Parliament assembled in November 1640. No member imagined that a section of the Houses would end up fighting the King, let alone executing him. The circumstances in which the Parliament met were certainly unique, for the King had agreed in October to pay the Scots £850 a day until he reached a permanent settlement with them that was acceptable to Parliament. Such urgent financial need had in practice removed Charles's discretionary power to dissolve or prorogue Parliament at will long before legislation was passed to that effect in 1641. The presence of 18,000 Scottish troops in the north-east of England in effect provided security for the Parliament's existence and members were keen to take advantage of this exceptional opportunity to remedy the nation's ills. To that extent, the conventional vision of Parliament as a panacea remained much as before. Sir Francis Seymour, for example, called Parliament 'the great physician of the commonwealth' and regarded the dissolution of previous Parliaments and the long interval between them as 'the cause of all mischief'.[2] Sir Henry Slingsby likewise hoped for a 'happy Parliament' in which 'the subject' would at last secure 'a total redress of all his grievances'.[3] However, the resolution of those grievances soon led the Houses into uncharted waters.

The most remarkable feature of the opening months of the Parliament was the almost unanimous hostility evinced towards the policies and personnel identified with Charles I's Personal Rule. The Parliament's first few days saw a sequence of speeches denouncing recent royal policies and presenting manifold grievances ranging from non-parliamentary taxation to innovations in the Church. Individuals who ended up on opposite sides in the Civil War were at this stage able to make common cause. The future Royalist Sir John Culpepper offered a lengthy statement of the 'grievances of the Church and Commonwealth', while the future Parliamentarian John Pym condemned a 'design to alter the kingdom both in religion and government'.[4] There was widespread agreement that, as in the late 1620s, Parliament's first step in combating such policies should be the removal of those 'evil counsellors' who were blamed for leading the King astray. It was against what Sir Benjamin Rudyerd reportedly called the 'subverting, destructive counsels', who rang 'a doleful, deadly knell over the whole kingdom', that the Houses therefore directed their energies first of all.[5]

As during the 1620s, impeachment provided them with a valuable weapon against 'evil counsellors'. During November and December, Lord Keeper Finch and the six other judges who had upheld Ship Money were impeached, although Finch and several other prominent Catholics fled abroad to avoid punishment.[6] The Commons voted to impeach Laud on 18 December 1640,[7] although he was not finally tried, attainted and executed until 1644–5.[8] Above all, the Houses were desperate to destroy Strafford, whom they feared might bring an army of Irish troops to be deployed on the mainland. Even more disturbingly, Strafford had apparently advised that in fighting the Scots Charles should be 'loosed and absolved from all rules of government'.[9] In November, impeachment articles were drawn up accusing Strafford of 'endeavouring to subvert the ancient and fundamental laws and government of England and Ireland'. The problem was that when Strafford's trial got under way in March 1641 it soon became clear that his actions, especially in Ireland, enjoyed the King's full support. An attempt to charge him with 'cumulative treason', whereby his actions were treated as amounting to treason collectively even though they did not do so individually, was a complete failure. The Houses therefore used a bill of attainder to declare him guilty as charged: as we saw earlier, this procedure had the particular advantage of speedily bypassing common-law proceedings.[10] In the end, 204 members of the Commons voted for the attainder, and only 59 'Straffordians' against. The bill then passed a very poorly attended House of Lords: many peers probably stayed away rather than risk offending Charles if they voted against Strafford, a further indication of the King's declining support within the Upper House.[11] Intimidated by crowds outside the Palace of Whitehall that made him fearful for his family's safety and his own, Charles reluctantly assented to the bill on 10 May and Strafford was executed two days later.[12]

This was a characteristic example of Charles's capacity to grant a concession just too late for it to do any good. Nine days before Strafford's execution, on 3 May, the Houses had been shocked to learn of a plot by a group of army officers to release Strafford and to raise troops to threaten Parliament with a dissolution. The King's involvement could not be proved at the time, although it was widely suspected and has since been demonstrated beyond reasonable doubt.[13] The Houses were terrified of a sudden dissolution, and this fear may help to explain their decision to attaint Strafford rather than persist with the slower procedure of impeachment.[14] The previous February, in the only significant piece of constitutional legislation of the first six months of the Long Parliament, the Triennial Act had been passed 'for the preventing of inconveniences happening by the long intermission of Parliaments'.[15] This act, like the wave of petitions from individuals to the Lords during 1640–1,[16] grew directly out of the deep and widespread anger felt at the absence of Parliaments for 11 years. The Triennial Act was, however, no protection against a snap dissolution of the present Parliament, so the Houses passed an act precluding a dissolution without the Parliament's own consent, and this received the royal assent on 10 May.[17] Deeper worries persisted, however. By mid-May 1641, over half of Charles's Privy Councillors of November 1640 had been imprisoned, exiled or disgraced. Yet the first Army Plot suggested that the removal of 'evil counsellors' might not have resolved the problem, and there was a feeling that more permanent constitutional reforms were needed to prevent any repetition of the Personal Rule. Such was the prevailing mistrust of Charles I that the Houses now set about dismantling the machinery of prerogative government.

The constitutional reforms of June–August 1641 all passed the Houses with large majorities, and all received the royal assent, albeit with transparent bad grace. They removed a number of long-standing grievances, and in particular many of those associated with the Personal Rule. On 22 June an act declared the collection of impositions and tonnage and poundage illegal without Parliament's consent.[18] This act, together with six subsequent ones,[19] granted tonnage and poundage to the Crown for fixed periods pending a more permanent settlement of the Crown's finances.[20] Two acts of 5 July abolished the Court of Star Chamber (thereby stripping the Privy Council of its judicial powers) and the Court of High Commission, both of which had been responsible for the draconian implementation of religious policies during the 1630s.[21] The Houses then turned to the unpopular fiscal expedients that had enabled the Crown to survive financially without Parliament in peacetime. Ship Money and forest fines were declared 'unlawful' on 7 August, as were knighthood fines three days later.[22] All of these institutions or levies were of medieval or Tudor origin, but Charles's use of them persuaded majorities in both Houses that they had to be abolished. This King simply could not be trusted with the same instruments of government as his predecessors.

If these statutes embodied a largely consensual programme of reform, the debates over three other issues during the summer of 1641 saw the initial unity of the two Houses begin to crumble. The first was the intractable problem of the royal finances, explored in Chapter 4.[23] The best chance for a long-term settlement probably lay in the schemes proposed by Bedford and his allies, but these suffered a setback when the Earl died suddenly in May 1641. Although some members, such as Sir John Culpepper, urged a new Book of Rates and a grant of tonnage and poundage for three years, the majority of the Commons were reluctant to vote such revenues until they had secured further political concessions from the King.[24] This matter was closely related to the second divisive issue, namely the choice of royal advisers. Here again Bedford's death was a blow to the chances of a settlement, for he was the linch-pin of a projected package of 'bridge-appointments' in which he would have been Lord Treasurer, with Pym as Chancellor of the Exchequer, and Oliver St John as Solicitor-General.[25] After the Earl's death, Pym and his allies adopted a more forceful approach. They drew up the Ten Propositions, which in a sense represented 'the minimum terms on which Pym would agree to a permanent grant of tonnage and poundage'.[26] They included requests that the King delay his projected journey to negotiate a settlement in Scotland, that Catholic priests be dismissed from the Queen's service, and that Lords Lieutenant and Deputy Lieutenants be 'such as may be faithful and trusty, and careful of the peace of the kingdom'. Most radical was the third proposition, that the King remove those advisers who 'have been active for the time past in furthering those courses contrary to religion, liberty, good government of the kingdom', and that he henceforth appoint 'such officers and counsellors as his people and Parliament may have just cause to confide in'.[27] This was the first appearance of what became one of the most intractable issues of the Civil War period, namely the extent of parliamentary control over the King's appointment of advisers. The Lords accepted the propositions with only minor amendments, mainly regarding the presence of Catholics close to the Queen. The Lords' willingness to go along with the greater part of the Propositions was further evidence of Charles's declining support among members of the Upper House: as Conrad Russell has written, it was 'a remarkable example of how far they were prepared to go in taking power out of the King's hands'.[28] But when the Lords sent a deputation to discuss the proposition about 'ill counsellors' with the King, Charles simply replied that he knew 'no ill counsellors'.[29]

Even more divisive was the subject of religion and Church government. There was virtual unanimity within Parliament that Laudian policies should be abandoned and Charles – in what proved to be an astute move – accepted this, doing nothing to rescue Laud and appointing instead a number of mainstream Calvinists to bishoprics. The problem lay in how far the actual institutions of the Church should be reformed. During the summer of 1641, as the Commons debated a bill proposing the abolition of episcopacy 'root and branch', a gulf opened up between those who wished to preserve bishops, even if in a modified or 'primitive' form, and those who would settle for nothing less than their outright abolition. The defenders of episcopacy shared Lord Digby's feeling that 'the grievances had grown from the abuse of the government and not from the government itself',[30] whereas its opponents believed that an office that could have been occupied by the Laudians was so intrinsically flawed that it had to be removed. They felt that the English Reformation had been incomplete, and that 'further reformation' was now essential to draw the English Church closer to the reformed churches of Scotland and the continent. Just how controversial this issue was is shown by the fact that on 27 May the Commons only agreed to a second reading of the root and branch bill by 139 votes to 108.[31]

This polarisation of religious opinion was all the more dangerous because it soon generated a corresponding political division. Conrad Russell and others have shown how members' attitudes towards the Church were usually an accurate predictor of Civil-War allegiance. This was also true for that minority of members of the Long Parliament who had sat in Parliaments of the 1620s.[32] Similarly, it was during the debates over whether to commit the London root and branch petition on 8–9 February 1641 that subsequent political alignments in the Long Parliament can first be glimpsed.[33] Once he had abandoned Laudianism, Charles was able to emerge as the natural rallying-point for the exponents of a reformed episcopacy. In his speech to both Houses on 25 January 1641, Charles declared: 'I make a great difference betwixt reformation and alteration of government; though I am for the first, I cannot give way to the latter.' He promised to 'reduce all matters of religion and government to what they were in the purest times of Queen Elizabeth's days', and to protect episcopacy as 'one of the fundamental institutions of this kingdom'.[34] To the many members who had opposed Laudianism primarily because of its authoritarian violations of custom and the rule of law, the King increasingly appeared a less threatening figure than those more radical members of the Houses who sought far-reaching structural change.

Developments in the provinces greatly exacerbated these divisions at Westminster. The links between parliamentary politics and the wider world were never more evident than during the summer and autumn of 1641. The previous January, the Commons had ordered the destruction of 'images' and 'superstitious pictures, monuments and relics of idolatry'.[35] However, as reports came in from all over the country of spontaneous outbreaks of iconoclasm, more and more members became anxious that such orders, and especially the campaign against episcopacy, would eventually bring the collapse of public order and the rule of law.[36] Sir Edward Dering's 'defection' from the cause of root and branch reform following disorders in his native Kent is an excellent and representative example of this shift in opinion.[37] Events in the country at large reinforced fears such as those of Sir John Culpepper, that people might 'speak and preach what they would' against the Prayer Book and even resort to 'open force and blows',[38] or of Sir Thomas Aston, that 'the removing of this order of bishops would shake a great part of the foundation of our common laws'.[39] Members at Westminster were acutely aware of wider developments, and only by recognising this can we explain why so many in both Houses thought Pym and his allies deeply irresponsible for pushing through a resolution on 1 September against altar rails, 'scandalous pictures', candlesticks and crucifixes.[40]

The Houses' awareness of opinion outside Westminster was enhanced by the fact that the early 1640s saw petitioning to Parliament on an unprecedented scale. These petitions were broadly of two kinds. First, the Lords received many petitions from individuals seeking remedies from the various legal proceedings and arbitrary practices that had been used to enforce the official policies of the Personal Rule. Such petitions reflected a deep resentment at the prolonged absence of Parliaments and a genuine belief in the institution's capacity to provide redress.[41] Second, there were the mass petitions, signed by large numbers of people from a particular county and often tabled by one of its members. The London root and branch petition of December 1640, allegedly bearing 15,000 signatures,[42] sparked off a wave of similar petitions against episcopacy: no fewer than 19 county petitions calling for the 'abolishing of the bishops with their hierarchical government' were submitted to Parliament during 1641.[43] But gradually, as fears of radical religious reform grew, petitions were produced in defence of bishops, the Prayer Book and the established Church. Such petitions are known to have circulated in at least 22 English counties between September 1641 and May 1642, and as many as 16 counties experienced clashes as rival groups of petitioners gathered signatures.[44] Later, during the first eight months of 1642, all but two of the 40 English counties submitted petitions to Parliament calling for a resolution of the crisis and an 'accommodation' between the Crown and the Houses.[45] Never before had members been made quite so forcibly aware of trends in public opinion.

In the late summer of 1641 much opinion, both inside Parliament and more widely, seemed to be moving Charles's way. By September he had reached a settlement with the Scots by which he abandoned his attempts to reform their Kirk in return for the withdrawal of their army, thereby removing at a stroke both the massive subvention he had to pay them and the security for the Long Parliament's existence. True, Charles could only dissolve the Parliament with its own consent, but given how many members were rallying towards him by the autumn that was not an unreasonable hope. Charles's advisers noted that Pym and his allies commanded less support than hitherto and felt increasingly optimistic about the chances of a dissolution.[46] Then, quite unexpectedly, the Irish Rebellion transformed the political landscape. Suddenly members faced what appeared to be the reality of a 'popish plot'; to make matters worse, the Catholic rebels claimed to be acting on a commission from the King. That claim was probably false, but this was less important than the fact that it appeared to confirm all the worst fears of Charles's leading critics. How, they asked, could Parliament possibly entrust such a King with an army to suppress the rebellion?

By posing that question, the Irish Rebellion had a dramatic impact on English parliamentary politics and raised the issue that later became the immediate cause of the Civil War. In an attempt to press home the case against Charles, on 8 November Pym and his allies tabled the Grand Remonstrance, a document that had been drafted by various Commons committees over the previous year. The Remonstrance was a comprehensive indictment of Charles's kingship.[47] It blamed all England's 'evils' on 'a malignant and pernicious design of subverting the fundamental laws and principles of government, upon which the religion and justice of this kingdom are firmly established'. Then followed 98 articles listing manifestations of this design, none of which predated Charles's accession, 65 articles listing the remedies already introduced by the Long Parliament, and finally 41 articles proposing further reforms. Throughout, the framers of the Remonstrance insisted that they sought nothing that 'should weaken the Crown either in just profit or useful power'. But, they believed, the only way to guarantee that Charles did indeed govern *pro bono publico* was to ensure that he was rightfully advised, and the Remonstrance requested him to 'employ such counsellors, ambassadors and other ministers in managing his business at home and abroad as the Parliament may have cause to confide in'. This was a direct challenge, as in the Ten Propositions, to the monarch's discretionary power to choose his own advisers. Another clause called for the creation of a 'general synod' to 'effect reformation' of religion. The Remonstrance polarised opinion in the Commons still further. When, on 22 November, it was eventually passed, it was only after a debate lasting about 12 hours and by a margin of 159 votes to 148.[48]

Such a division was a far cry from the high level of unity that had characterised the opening months of the Parliament. Many future Royalists were appalled that the Remonstrance was addressed 'downwards' rather than to the King. They were also concerned at the decision to present the Remonstrance without involving the Lords, and the Remonstrance revealed a growing divergence between the two Houses as well as within each of them. Preliminary discussions had probably taken place between the King's leading critics in both

Houses, and although Charles's support within the Upper House was far from solid, only a minority of peers actively promoted the Remonstrance. It is likely that this minority encouraged its allies in the Lower House to press ahead with the Remonstrance as a way of putting pressure on their colleagues in the Lords. Indeed, Charles later described the Remonstrance as 'an attempt to incense the people against us and the House of Lords'. It was, as Conrad Russell has written, 'intended as a reproach as much to the Lords as to the King'. However, the reluctance of the majority of the Lords to join in weakened the Commons' hand, for as the Remonstrance itself acknowledged, 'what can we the Commons, without the conjunction of the House of Lords?'[49]

It was in this context that Charles, predictably, rejected the Remonstrance on 23 December, insisting that his free choice of advisers was 'the undoubted right of the Crown of England'.[50] Then, on 4 January, in a characteristic bid to remove what he regarded as a hard core of troublemakers, he tried to arrest five members of the Commons and one of the Lords on a charge of treason. This flagrant breach of privilege caused a furore, and opinion in London became so hostile that on 10 January Charles and his family retreated from the capital. The attempted arrest seemed further evidence of Charles's high-handed attitude towards parliamentary privilege, and of his willingness to use force against Parliament. It prompted the Houses to establish a committee to draft what became the Militia Ordinance.[51] This ordinance, which completed its passage of both Houses on 5 March, argued that if the King were misled by 'the bloody counsels of papists and other ill-affected persons', the Houses could 'in this time of imminent danger' take over the King's military authority and appoint Lords Lieutenant and Deputy Lieutenants of whom they 'approved'.[52] These were quite unprecedented encroachments on the Crown's traditional powers, and many members of both Houses found them repellent. During the opening months of 1642, many either returned home or joined the King. The average daily attendance in the Lords fell from nearly 60 in January 1642 to around 40 in February and March,[53] while in the Commons, the average attendances revealed in division lists fell from 276 in January to 159 in April, 123 in July and 76 in August.[54] This rapid decline in attendance further escalated the crisis, for as more and more members left Westminster it became easier for those who remained to raise their demands even higher.

Behind the formation of parties within the two Houses during the opening months of 1642 lay two symmetrical and ultimately self-fulfilling conspiracy theories. On the one hand was what might be called the Puritan–Parliamentarian theory, as expressed in the Grand Remonstrance, which blamed all England's troubles on a 'popish plot'. According to this view, Charles had been systematically led astray by evil advisers who encouraged him to adopt authoritarian methods, including the use of force against the Houses. On the other side was an Anglican–Royalist theory which attributed the crisis to radicals in both Houses (sometimes called the 'Junto') and their 'schismatic' allies outside Parliament. Beyond these general positions, however, there were significant differences of emphasis between the two Houses. Many of the King's leading critics in the Commons seem to have been driven primarily by religious motives, and those who remained at Westminster had almost invariably displayed a strong commitment to 'further reformation' of the Church.[55] In the Lords, by contrast, those who favoured curtailing the King's powers apparently did so for mainly secular reasons. Although many of the Parliamentarian peers were sympathetic to godly reformation, their political

behaviour often appears to have been guided by a belief in aristocratic concil-
iarism and a conviction that the King's 'natural advisers' should regain control
of royal counsels through the Privy Council and the Great Council.[56] Among
the Royalists, it is rather more difficult both to isolate a religious motive and to
discern any characteristic differences between the members of the two Houses.
A commitment to the rule of law and to the preservation of the established
Church as a crucial part of settled structures of government was certainly a
strong motive. So too were a sense of honour and a desire to protect the
Crown's 'rightful powers'. These motives were probably felt with particular
intensity by many Royalist peers, and the passing of the Militia Ordinance
appears to have been the single most decisive moment in prompting an exodus
from the Upper House to join the King.[57]

During the spring and summer of 1642 the two sides became gradually
more entrenched, and every step that each side took to defeat the other only
confirmed the other side's worst fears and therefore made it raise its own
demands. Thus, Charles retaliated against the Militia Ordinance by raising
troops on his own prerogative authority by commissions of array. The
Houses in turn appointed Essex as Lord General and authorised the raising
of an army. By the summer of 1642 opinion was so divided that both sides
were convinced of two things: that a further threat of force might well face
down their opponents; and that if their bluff were called they had a good
chance of victory. Each invoked the other's military preparations to justify its
own, and each believed that the use of force could give it a strategic superiority that would strengthen its hand at the negotiating table. In the end, on
18 August the Houses declared all those who supported Charles 'traitors',
and four days later the King raised his standard against the Parliamentarian
'rebels'. So it came about that the King was at war with a section of his own
High Court and Great Council who demanded unprecedented restrictions on
his powers and who claimed to be able to exercise his office 'after a more
eminent and obligatory manner than it can be by personal act or resolution
of his own'.[58]

The Long Parliament II: 1642–1649

The year 1642 thus saw two major departures in the history of Parliament.
First, its membership was considerably diminished. The bishops had been
excluded from the Lords and many lay peers had left of their own volition,
leaving an average attendance that never rose above 20 between the autumn of
1642 and the House's abolition in 1649, and was often much lower. The
Commons similarly was reduced to an active membership of well below 200.
However, between 1645 and 1648 the Commons organised a series of
'recruiter' elections to replace those who had died, departed or been expelled.
In all, these elections returned about 275 new members and brought the total
size of the Commons back to 460: by 1648, 'recruiters' thus formed a majority of the House. These 'recruiter' elections frequently saw tussles between the
favoured candidates of rival groups within the Long Parliament, with radicals
on each side often taking an active role in election management. Pressure from
local county committees, and even the use of military power, were important in
determining the outcome of many of these elections, and very often this
worked in favour of localist interests. By contrast, more traditional influences,

notably that of the peerage, became much less significant and John Morrill has observed that 'carpetbaggers had never had such a thin time'.[59]

The second novelty was that in 1642 Parliament suddenly assumed executive powers to which it was wholly unaccustomed. From being an instrument of the King's government, with legislative, judicial and conciliar functions, the Houses now became an alternative to that government. This fundamental change inevitably had a dramatic effect on the nature of parliamentary business, bringing with it the innovatory concept of the ordinance, new taxes, and a proliferation of executive committees. The Houses' construction of an executive machinery was achieved remarkably swiftly and effectively. They claimed that ordinances passed by the two Houses had all the attributes of statutes,[60] and ordinances, which could be 'private' as well as 'public', were used to regulate a similarly vast range of matters.[61] As we saw in Chapter 3, the legislative and judicial functions of Parliament were closely related,[62] and in November 1643 the Houses also claimed control over the judicial system by ordering a new Great Seal to be made (Charles having taken the existing one to Oxford). The Great Seal was the ultimate symbol of sovereignty and Hyde saw this move as nothing less than the Houses' bid to assume 'sovereign jurisdiction in civil matters'.[63] During 1643 the Houses established two new taxes, the excise and the assessment, which yielded far greater sums than any previous parliamentary tax and played a crucial role in Parliament's ultimate victory.[64] The war effort was co-ordinated by a series of committees of both Houses that were invested with extensive powers and took a great deal of routine business out of the Lords and Commons. Such committees wielded far more sweeping powers than the joint committees which the Houses had customarily appointed, and they show how an existing procedure could be radically reworked to meet the new circumstances of war.[65] In those areas controlled by the Houses (initially mainly the south and east of England) county committees were appointed, most of whose members were nominated by the Houses.[66] When Scotland entered the war in support of the Houses, a Committee of Both Kingdoms was established to 'order and direct whatsoever doth or may concern the managing of the war'.[67] The breadth and vagueness of this remit meant that the committee became largely independent of the Houses. Its autonomy was further strengthened by an oath which required members to maintain the secrecy of its proceedings, a practice that the Lords regarded as unconstitutional.[68]

Among the most intractable problems that the Houses faced was the need to establish their own legitimacy. There was a long-standing tradition that the King could summon Parliament to wherever he chose, and that the monarch's presence was as indispensable for a legitimate Parliament as that of the Lords and Commons. Royalists were able to argue that the parliamentary trinity was indivisible, and that the withdrawal of the King and of so many members of both Houses had effectively deprived those who remained at Westminster of any right to term themselves a Parliament. They were simply, in Hyde's words, 'those few men who called themselves the two Houses of Parliament'.[69] The King's *Declaration* of 12 August 1642, drafted by Hyde, pledged his commitment to Parliaments as 'an essential part of the constitution' without which he could 'attain to no happiness', but insisted that the Junto had infringed 'the dignity, privilege and freedom of Parliaments'.[70] The King and his supporters argued that by the end of 1641 the large crowds of demonstrators at Westminster so intimidated the Houses that they no longer constituted a free

Parliament. Throughout the Civil Wars, Charles reiterated his desire for 'a free and full Parliament', and claimed to defend this concept far more authentically than the Houses. Thus, just as they claimed to defend the office of King by fighting Charles I, he claimed to defend the privileges and freedom of Parliament by fighting the Houses.

In December 1643, arguing that the only way to achieve a free Parliament was to adjourn to another location, the King summoned the members of both Houses to Oxford. About 40 peers and over 100 members of the Commons assembled the following month, and Charles promised that they could 'use all that parliamentary freedom which would be due to them if they were with him at Westminster, and which with all their other privileges they should enjoy at Oxford, though they could not in the other place'.[71] The members of the Oxford Parliament claimed that the Junto had 'speciously pretended the defence of the rights and privileges of Parliament' while in fact 'cancelling all the liberties and privileges of Parliament'. They regarded themselves as 'the true and lawful members of Parliament', whereas those who remained at Westminster were 'not a full nor free convention'.[72] The Oxford Parliament sat for two sessions (22 January – 16 April 1644 and 8 October 1644 – 10 March 1645), but unfortunately very little is known of its deliberations because all the records relating to it were burnt before Oxford surrendered in June 1646. It is, however, clear that the Parliament displeased Charles by persistently urging the continued search for an 'accommodation' with the Houses at Westminster, and that Charles ultimately came to dislike what he called 'our mongrel Parliament here'.[73] That phrase implicitly challenged the assembly's status and legitimacy, and the King's contempt was ironically shared by the members at Westminster who consistently refused to acknowledge the Oxford Parliament: some even allegedly called it 'the mock Parliament at Oxford'.[74] In 1646 the Houses demanded that those 'who have sat in the unlawful assembly at Oxford, called or pretended by some to be a Parliament', be 'removed from His Majesty's counsels'.[75] The question of which, if either, was the legitimate Parliament greatly complicated the successive peace negotiations of the 1640s.

The basic positions of the two sides in those negotiations had emerged in 1642 and in essentials did not change greatly thereafter. The Houses presented their terms in the *Nineteen Propositions* (1 June 1642), and subsequently refined them in the Oxford Propositions (1643), the Uxbridge Propositions (1644), the Newcastle Propositions (1646), and finally the Four Bills (1647).[76] The common denominator of all these terms was a belief that Charles I could not be trusted with many traditional royal powers, and that these had instead to be transferred to the two Houses. This principle of parliamentary restriction of royal action was applied to many different aspects of government. Charles was required to accept the permanence of the Triennial Act, to enforce the laws against papists, to dismiss specified individuals from his counsels, and to exempt certain named Royalists from any general pardon.[77] The Houses demanded the right to approve appointments to key offices of state, and from 1644 onwards this was extended into a demand to nominate them. Any settlement of the Church had to have parliamentary approval, and especially after the Scots entered the war in 1643 the Houses insisted on the abolition of episcopacy. The Houses also demanded that Charles accept the Militia Ordinance or settle the militia with parliamentary advice. But their basic concern was with Charles I rather than with the monarchy *per se*, and from 1646 onwards they required simply that the Houses control the militia for 20 years, which was the rest of Charles's presumed lifespan. Although some of these measures were undoubtedly envisaged as permanent changes, the nature of them was shaped primarily by mistrust of Charles and a perceived need to restrain his use of royal discretionary powers by transferring authority to the Houses.

The King's response to these terms remained absolutely consistent from the *Answer to the Nineteen Propositions* onwards. Charles insisted that the Houses' demands would rob him of powers that were lawfully and rightfully his, and thereby unbalance the constitution by transferring authority from the Crown to the Houses. The King and many of his supporters emphasised particularly that the Crown enjoyed certain discretionary powers by the laws of the realm as well as by God's law: they argued that such regal powers were essential for the safety of the nation and the protection of the subjects' liberties, and that the rule of law held both in equilibrium. The King promised to respect due process of law just as he pledged to defend the privileges of the High Court of Parliament. These obligations, he insisted, compelled him to reject the Houses' propositions. In May 1642, Charles had claimed that the Houses were in the grip of a 'faction of malignant, schismatical and ambitious persons' who wished to establish 'their own lawless arbitrary power and government';[78] and he maintained this position throughout the years that followed.

The management of the war effort against Charles, and from 1646 the search for a post-war settlement, inevitably raised many controversial questions that had a profound effect on the internal dynamics of the two Houses. In particular, contrasting outlooks on these issues fostered the emergence of rival bicameral groupings committed to different strategies for conducting the war and constructing a settlement. Certainly many members remained non-aligned, motivated as much by personal or local interests as by national concerns. But very broadly speaking, from the mid-1640s onwards two main 'interests' can be identified in each House. Contemporaries increasingly applied the ecclesiological terms 'Presbyterians' and 'Independents' to these groupings, although these terms are problematic because members' political and religious attitudes did not always synchronise or remain consistent.[79] Nevertheless, as we saw in Chapter 6, the labels do provide a convenient shorthand for two discernible groupings with hard cores of committed members, and characteristic views on national issues.[80] Although these groupings were highly fluid, and shaded off into the large mass of less committed members, they nonetheless managed to co-ordinate their activities more systematically and on a much greater scale than anything seen in earlier Parliaments.[81] This was accomplished, in particular, through the points of contact afforded by the unprecedented proliferation of joint committees, bodies that were all the more significant because of the way in which they took a great deal of business off the floor of the Houses.[82]

For much of the time, the small caucuses of committed members contrasted with a large and amorphous body of non-aligned members. Often it is impossible to detect any clear-cut party lines, but during certain periods some key issue brought differences of opinion into focus and the committed members vied with each other to secure backbench support. One such time was the winter of 1644–5, when the Independents, associated with figures like Viscount Saye and Sele, the Earl of Northumberland and Lord Wharton in the Lords, and Nathaniel Fiennes, Oliver Cromwell, Oliver St John, Sir Henry Vane the younger, and William Strode in the Commons, promoted the establishment of the Committee of Both Kingdoms, the Self-Denying Ordinance and the formation of the New Model Army. These measures were a deliberate bid to dislodge Essex as Lord General and to promote a more determined prosecution of the war. They were carefully co-ordinated with an attempted impeachment of Essex's leading ally in the Commons, Denzil Holles, for allegedly supplying the Royalist Council with secret parliamentary information.[83] Such political manoeuvres illustrate the extent to which these bicameral coalitions were personal as well as ideological networks. Like-minded members of the two Houses collaborated to advance common ends: the ties of patronage formed only one aspect of the workings of these networks, or 'interests', and cannot be separated from personal ties and shared religious and political attitudes.[84]

At the time of the Royalist surrender in June 1646, the Presbyterians enjoyed a slight majority over the Independents in both Houses. During the months that followed, the key issue dividing these two dominant groups became the nature of the post-war settlement. Tensions came to a head during the spring and summer of 1647, when attempts by the Presbyterian majority to disband the Army without guaranteed payment of arrears led the Army to protest that it was not a 'mere mercenary army', and that it was a more authentic bulwark of the 'fundamental rights and liberties' of 'the free-born people of this nation' than the Houses.[85] In religious and constitutional outlook, many officers felt most closely aligned with the Independent minority in both Houses, and demanded the impeachment of 11 leading Presbyterians, including Holles. These members fled in late June and the impeachment was in fact never proceeded with. However, on 26 July a mob of London apprentices and disbanded soldiers sympathetic to the Presbyterians invaded both Houses, whereupon both Speakers and many Independents (eight from the Lords and 57 from the Commons) sought refuge with the Army encamped outside London. Ten days later the Army occupied London and, in its first direct intervention in parliamentary affairs, reinstated those members who had fled.[86] Meanwhile, a coalition of Army officers and Independents collaborated in drawing up their own propositions for a peace settlement, the *Heads of the Proposals*. These envisaged a much less extensive transference of authority from the King to the Houses than the various sets of terms which the latter had officially adopted.[87] The Houses were to nominate the officers of state and control the militia for ten years, only seven Royalists were exempted from pardon, and those lately in arms against Parliament were to be excluded from public office for five years. The Triennial Act was to be repealed and Parliaments elected biennially on a redistributed franchise. These terms clearly reflected fears within the Army and among Independents that Parliamentarian tyranny was as dangerous as Royalist.

Such anxieties had become very widespread by 1647–8 and many people deeply resented the frequent violations of legal and constitutional propriety that the Houses had committed in order to defeat the King.[88] Lord Wharton had memorably expressed the outlook that motivated such behaviour when he declared, in the summer of 1643, that 'they were not tied to a law for these were times of necessity and imminent danger'.[89] Over the years that followed, ordinances blithely sanctioned the kind of illegal actions that had been denounced in the Petition of Right or the Grand Remonstrance, including the seizure of property, arbitrary arrest without trial, and the imposition of martial law. The central committees enjoyed quasi-judicial powers and those they tried and sentenced had no remedy at law. Such a novel extension of Parliament's existing judicature, against which there was no right of appeal, was widely unpopular.[90] So too was the unprecedentedly heavy fiscal burden of the excise and assessment, described in Chapter 4.[91] Ironically, Royalist government (though not always the behaviour of individual commanders) in practice displayed a much greater respect for settled institutions and established patterns of justice than the administrative machinery erected by the Houses.[92]

The belief that the Long Parliament had introduced a remedy worse than the original disease ultimately led many counties to submit petitions, of which that sent from Dorset in June 1648, allegedly signed by 10,000 of the county's inhabitants, was typical.[93] Its central demands were that 'the common birthright of us all, the laws, may be restored to their former purity, and that we may enjoy them without corrupt glosses and comments of their arbitrary power, or unequal ordinances and practices between them and their committees', and that 'our ancient liberties may not lie at the mercy of those that have none, nor enlarged and repealed by votes and revotes of those that have taken too much liberty to destroy the subjects'.[94] Such petitions were a devastating indictment on those who had claimed to protect England's laws and liberties from the arbitrary rule of Charles I.

Similar hostility greeted the Houses' attempted religious reforms. In 1643 the Houses had established the Westminster Assembly of Divines to plan the reformation of the Church along Presbyterian lines; thereafter, a sequence of ordinances banned use of the Prayer Book, replaced it with a new *Directory of Public Worship*, abolished episcopacy and ordered the sale of bishops' lands.[95] But efforts to enforce these changes on the ground, and to create a new Presbyterian order modelled on that of Scotland, proved a failure and revealed instead a widespread attachment to the worship and liturgy of the old Church. The Houses appointed a Committee for Scandalous Ministers to remove those who resisted these changes, but although this committee eventually ejected nearly a third of England's 9,000 or so parish clergy, many were secretly reinstated by their parishioners. Use of the Prayer Book remained common, and attempts to suppress the festivals of Christmas and Easter often sparked off riots, most famously at Canterbury in December 1647. By the late 1640s Presbyterian structures were only fully functioning in a handful of counties, whereas the remarkable resilience of what John Morrill has called 'folk Anglicanism' demonstrated the severe practical limitations on the Houses' capacity to reshape national religious life.[96]

If the most common response to 'parliamentary tyranny' was a conservative yearning for the 'known laws',[97] as the 1640s progressed minority groups emerged who demanded fundamental reforms of Parliament as part of a radically reshaped constitution. The most notable of these were the Levellers, who between 1647 and 1649 produced numerous pamphlets, petitions and manifestos culminating in the three *Agreements of the People*.[98] Arguing from the premise that 'all power is originally and essentially in the whole body of the people of this nation', they denounced the tyranny of existing institutions and demanded instead that a unicameral Parliament be established, elected annually or biennially on the principle of universal male suffrage. The second *Agreement* proposed a major redistribution of seats away from the boroughs and in favour of the counties in order to make the Commons as genuinely representative as possible.[99] The principle of regular *elections* thus provided a safeguard on the powers of a House of Commons that would wield 'supreme power and trust as to the making of laws, constitutions and offices, for the ordering, preservation and government of the whole'. The Levellers also urged that the present Parliament set a date for its own dissolution, 'by which time that great and supreme trust reposed in you shall be returned into the hands of the people, for and from whom you received it'.[100] This was another, more radical, manifestation of the pervasive disillusionment with the Long Parliament.

During the spring and summer of 1648, that disillusionment blended with surviving pockets of Royalist activism to produce the series of provincial risings known as the second Civil War.[101] This conflict was a direct consequence of Charles's refusal to come to terms with either the Houses or the Army, and his decision instead to sign an Engagement with those Scots who had turned to him out of disenchantment with the Houses' failure to implement far-reaching Presbyterian reforms. His role in causing the second Civil War convinced many Army officers that Charles was a 'man of blood' who had to be brought to account if further bloodshed was to be prevented.[102] In mid-November 1648 they demanded that Parliament bring Charles, 'the capital and grand author of our troubles . . . to justice for the treason, blood and mischief he is . . . guilty of'.[103] Yet, even at that stage, the majority of members of both Houses saw no alternative but to conduct further talks with Charles along the lines of all previous negotiations since 1642. It was at this point that, in order to prevent a betrayal of all that they had fought for, the Army purged the Commons of those most likely to oppose bringing the King to trial. On 6 December, Colonel Thomas Pride stood at the entrance to the Lower House with a body of troops: he arrested 45 members and secluded a further 186; 86 others promptly withdrew in protest.[104]

With the Commons reduced to an effective membership of barely 200,[105] events moved swiftly towards a climax. When the Lords rejected an ordinance creating a High Court to try Charles, the Commons passed the following remarkable resolutions on 4 January 1649:

> That the people are, under God, the original of all just power . . . that the Commons of England in Parliament assembled, being chosen by and representing the people, have the supreme power in this nation; and . . . that whatsoever is enacted and declared for law by the Commons in Parliament assembled has the force of law . . . although the consent and concurrence of the King and House of Lords be not had thereunto.[106]

This marked a complete redefinition of the nature of Parliament. If 1642 had established the principle that the Lords and Commons could issue ordinances without the King's consent, 1649 ushered in the concept of a sovereign Commons with the power to pass acts unilaterally. Backed by the Army, this Rump of the Commons set up a High Court which sentenced Charles to death as a 'tyrant, traitor, murderer and public enemy to the good people of this nation'.[107] The following March, the Rump passed an act abolishing monarchy as 'unnecessary, burdensome, and dangerous to the liberty, safety, and public interest of the people', and another abolishing the Lords as 'useless and dangerous to the people of England'.[108] On 19 May, a further act declared England to be a Commonwealth, governed 'by the supreme authority of this nation, the representatives of the people in Parliament'.[109]

With the abolition of the monarchy and the House of Lords, the parliamentary trinity was reduced to just one of its component parts: for the first and only time in English history, Parliament now became synonymous with the House of Commons alone. So revolutionary a step would have been unthinkable without the dramatic events of the Civil Wars, and impossible without the intervention of the Army. Yet, although the Rump of the Commons now wielded sovereign powers, its survival ultimately depended upon military support. By a profound irony, the outcome of the Civil Wars was to make Parliament's privileges – and indeed its very existence – a hostage not to the King but to the Army which Parliament had originally created to protect itself from the King.

The Commonwealth: the Rump Parliament and the Nominated Assembly

The extraordinary events of the 1640s had thus led to the destruction of the parliamentary trinity and the mutilation of the traditional body politic. The conflict between Charles I and the Houses reflected the profound mistrust that had grown up between the King and a section of his subjects. This mistrust acted like an infection within the body politic, and the members of both Houses became bitterly divided over how best to cure it. In the end, Parliament in its traditional form proved unable to overcome the infection, with the result that radical surgery proved necessary – so radical that it involved the amputation of the head and some limbs of the body politic, and the purging of others. But the republican torso that was left faced a fundamental problem that dogged it for the rest of its life: how, having cut itself adrift from traditional concepts of the polity, could it establish its own legitimacy? In fact, it never satisfactorily answered that question and remained reliant on the life support system provided by the Army. When, in 1660, that support system was finally switched off, the republican body politic died.

The Rump Parliament, which continued to sit until April 1653, faced a constant struggle both to establish its right to govern and to ensure its own survival. In January 1650 it imposed an Engagement on all adult males requiring them to promise to be 'true and faithful to the Commonwealth of England, as it is now established, without a King or House of Lords'.[110] Although many Presbyterians, including William Prynne, objected to this as an attempt to search men's consciences, a number of '*de facto* theorists', such as John Dury, Anthony Ascham and Marchamont Nedham, asserted that subjects were bound to obey whichever sovereign could impose order and give them protection. They thus argued that the possession of *de facto* powers in itself conferred legitimacy.[111] However, for much of the period 1649–53, the Rump's actual survival was far from assured. It confronted a series of threats both at home and abroad, including a Leveller mutiny in the summer of 1649, the subjugation of Ireland in 1649–50, a Royalist invasion through Scotland in 1650–1, and a war against the Dutch in 1652–4. None of these hazards could have been defeated without the Army's support, but by 1653 the Army leaders, and above all Oliver Cromwell, felt that the Rump had given very little in return for their military efforts.

For all its claims to be the 'representative' of the people, the Rump was actually a very small body. In all, around 210 members sat at some stage between January 1649 and April 1653. However, only about 60 or 70 of these were at all active, and the average attendance was usually between 50 and 60. Members represented a wide range of opinion and shared little beyond a belief in the Commonwealth and a willingness to sit in the Rump. Apart from a few clearly identifiable groups, such as the professional lawyers or those members associated with the City of London, no tightly defined factions existed, and groupings within the Rump were shifting, ephemeral, and rarely mutually exclusive.[112] From the outset, the Parliament was beset by divisions, and these differences, together with diminishing energies and a sense of lurching from crisis to crisis, brought a steady decline in the Rump's legislative productivity, from 125 acts in 1649 to 78 in 1650, 54 in 1651, 44 in 1652, and 10 in 1653.[113] The drop in committees appointed to draft new legislation was even steeper, from 152 in 1649 to 98 in 1650, 61 in 1651, 51 in 1652, and 12 in 1653.[114]

Positive reforms were few. In religion, the Rump was anxious to dissociate itself from the more radical sects and passed acts against adultery and blasphemy in 1650.[115] It seems to have felt rather embarrassed by its solitary concession to religious radicalism, the Toleration Act of September 1650, which abolished compulsory attendance at parish churches. In fact, the terms of the act were quite limited, not least because everyone was still obliged to attend some form of religious service on Sundays, and most members of the Rump were increasingly hostile towards the radical sectaries.[116] In the long term, one of the Rump's most significant reforms was probably the appointment of a commission for the propagation of the gospel in Wales.[117] This had some success in improving the provision of education, Welsh Bibles and Welsh-speaking preachers, and helps to explain the subsequent strength of nonconformity in Wales.[118] But, more often than not, urgent matters took priority over fundamental reforms. The lawyers in the Rump strongly resisted the far-reaching overhaul of the legal system that a special commission chaired by Sir Matthew Hale proposed in 1652.[119] A sample of 123 acts passed in three periods selected from throughout the Rump's existence, January–June 1649, January–June 1651, and January–April 1653, demonstrates this overriding concern with day-to-day survival: 74 acts dealt with matters of security, finance or taxation, 43 with local government or the Army, and 14 with social problems. Only six enacted economic and social reforms, and three legal reforms, while a mere five addressed religious issues.[120]

To Cromwell, who had written to the Speaker of the Rump, William Lenthall, the day after the Battle of Worcester hoping that this 'crowning mercy' would 'provoke' Parliament to 'do the will of Him who hath done His will for it',[121] the Rump's record was a terrible disappointment. He had wanted it to 'proceed vigorously in reforming what was amiss in government, and to the settling of the Commonwealth upon a foundation of justice and righteousness',[122] and had urged members to 'be mindful of their duty to God and men, in the discharge of the trust reposed in them'.[123] Gradually, however, he concluded that the Rump 'would never answer those ends which God, His people, and the whole nation expected from them'.[124] The Rumpers agreed in November 1651 to a dissolution not later than 3 November 1654, but when, on 20 April 1653, they voted to hold fresh elections without any means of 'screening' candidates, Cromwell led a body of troops to Westminster and expelled them. He later claimed that the Rumpers had wished to 'perpetuate themselves' by holding recruiter elections, but this was almost certainly incorrect.[125] His underlying fear was probably that fresh elections might produce a Parliament of 'Presbyters' and 'Neuters' who would be hostile to the godly reforms advocated by the Army. So, convinced that the Rump was no longer a 'Parliament for God's people', Cromwell destroyed it.[126] The remarkable irony of his action was not lost on contemporaries such as Dorothy Osborne, who observed: 'If Mr Pym were alive again I wonder what he would think of these proceedings, and whether this would appear as great a breach of the privilege of Parliament as the demanding [of] the five members.'[127]

Having abandoned a Parliament that he felt had betrayed the godly, Cromwell then sought a Parliament consisting exclusively of the godly. The Nominated Assembly, sometimes called the Little Parliament, or Barebone's Parliament after one of its most prominent members, was a radical departure from traditional Parliaments in concept and structure.[128] Modelled on the ancient Jewish Sanhedrin of Saints, and inspired by the ideas of the Fifth Monarchist Thomas Harrison, it comprised 139 'persons fearing God, and of approved fidelity and honesty'.[129] These individuals were not elected, but were selected by the Army officers who adopted and added to nominations made by the separatist congregations. On 4 July 1653, an exhilarated Cromwell welcomed the Assembly as a 'door to usher in things that God has promised, which have been prophesied of', and reminded members of the 'series of providences' that had called them to 'supreme authority'.[130] But he was bitterly disappointed. The Assembly's social composition did not differ greatly from other seventeenth-century Parliaments in that four-fifths of its members were gentry, 44 had some legal training, and 119 had served as JPs.[131] Such backgrounds explain why the Assembly combined religious radicalism with an underlying social conservatism. It passed no fewer than 29 acts, including such significant reforms as the legalisation of civil marriages performed by a JP, the compulsory registration of births, marriages and deaths, the relief of creditors and debtors, and tougher measures against thieves and highwaymen.[132] But the more moderate members were deeply alarmed by other proposals, such as the abolition of Chancery and the suppression of lay rights to nominate ministers of parishes.[133] When the Assembly voted by 56 to 54 to abolish tithes (many of which were paid to the laity), the moderates decided they had had enough; two days later, on 12 December, they got up early and, while the radicals were at a prayer meeting, dissolved the Assembly and surrendered power back to Cromwell.[134]

The Army, just possibly with Cromwell's prior knowledge, had an alternative constitution to hand in the form of the Instrument of Government, drawn up by Major-General John Lambert.[135] The central principle of this, England's first written constitution, was government by 'a single person and a Parliament'.[136] Cromwell was to become Lord Protector for life and rule with a Council of State and with Parliaments that would be elected triennially and sit for a minimum of five months. Beyond those basic requirements the Protector could summon or dissolve them as he pleased. The first Parliament would meet on 3 September 1654, and until then the Protector could issue ordinances with the force of law, but which required Parliament's subsequent ratification. Following the conquests of Ireland and Scotland, and their incorporation into a single Commonwealth with England, these Parliaments were to comprise 400 English members and 30 each from Ireland and Scotland. Members were to be 'persons of known integrity, fearing God, and of good conversation', and the Council of State was empowered to exclude those whom it believed did not fulfil this requirement. The Army Council of Officers formally adopted the Instrument of Government on 15 December and Cromwell was installed as Lord Protector the next day.

The Protectorate Parliaments

The story of the Protectorate Parliaments in many ways reflected the gradual drift back towards more traditional structures and institutions that characterised the later 1650s in general. After 13 years of sitting almost continuously, Parliaments once again became more intermittent. They did meet for a greater proportion of the time than under the early Stuarts, for a total of about 90 weeks between 1654 and 1659, but that was still very different from the days of the Long Parliament. Many contemporaries welcomed this development, and shared Marchamont Nedham's view that 'Parliaments always sitting are no more agreeable to the temper of this people than it is to a natural body to take always physic instead of food.'[137] As the Protectorate developed, Cromwell effectively became king in all but name, and his failure to establish harmonious relationships with successive Parliaments lay at the heart of the Republic's instability.

Cromwell certainly believed that Parliaments had a central role to play within any constitution. He told the first Protectorate Parliament on 12 September 1654 that 'the government by a single person and a Parliament is a fundamental. It is the *esse*, it is constitutive.'[138] Equally, he believed that Parliaments were entrusted with a powerful obligation to the people, and especially the godly, and that if they betrayed that trust they had to be dissolved. This was his primary motive for expelling the Rump, and the pattern was repeated in the first two Protectorate Parliaments. Cromwell remained committed to the principle of Parliaments and to the belief that they could serve as an instrument to promote a godly commonwealth. His conviction that Parliaments had a vital role to play in reconciling the interests of the godly with those of the whole nation helps to explain why he was so keen to work with Parliaments, and why there was not a single calendar year throughout the Commonwealth and Protectorate when a Parliament did not meet at some point. Yet in practice he could never find a Parliament that fulfilled his expectations. The crux of the problem was that he was trying to use an institution designed as the 'representative of the realm' to further a godly agenda that commanded the enthusiastic support of only a minority. As we saw in Chapter 2, the social composition of the Protectorate Parliaments did not differ dramatically from that of their predecessors,[139] and in their fears of religious radicalism, reluctance to introduce greater 'liberty of conscience', and mistrust of the Army most members reflected prevailing attitudes within the political elite. Cromwell desperately tried to avoid seeing any incompatibility between the interests of the godly and those of the nation as a whole. As he told representatives of the second Protectorate Parliament on 21 April 1657:

> I think you have provided for the liberty of the people of God and for the liberty of the nation; and I say, he sings sweetly that sings a song of reconciliation betwixt these two interests, and it is a pitiful fancy, and wild and ignorant, to think they are inconsistent.[140]

Yet Cromwell's dealings with successive Parliaments repeatedly demonstrated their inconsistency, and his attempts to create an identity between the interests of the nation and those of the godly ensured that he was never able to achieve a stable working relationship with any of the Interregnum Parliaments.[141]

The first Protectorate Parliament illustrated this problem very plainly. Cromwell's opening speech on 4 September 1654 stressed the trust imposed upon members, 'having upon your shoulders the interests of three great nations ... [and] the interest of all the Christian people in the world'. He believed that the Parliament represented 'a door of hope opened by God to us'.[142] But his hopes were quickly dashed. Many members were gentry or lawyers of Presbyterian sympathies, and in the opening days they demanded strong measures against the sects, together with revisions to the Instrument of Government that would enhance Parliament's powers. Cromwell responded on 12 September with a lengthy speech in which he outlined four 'fundamentals' of government: that the country should be governed by 'a single person and a Parliament'; that Parliaments should be elected frequently and not be perpetual; that there should be liberty of conscience in religion; and that control of the militia should be shared between Parliament and the Lord Protector.[143] Members were then required to take a Recognition affirming their loyalty to the Lord Protector and to the principle of government by 'a single person and a Parliament', whereupon around a hundred withdrew in protest.[144] But their departure did not make the Parliament any more 'pliable to [Cromwell's] purposes'.[145] After 12 September, Cromwell apparently felt that he should intervene as little as possible in the Parliament's deliberations.[146] However, by failing to manage the Parliament or to set a co-ordinated lead, Cromwell and his councillors gave members a chance to pursue their own preferred agendas which proved to be quite different from what he had hoped.[147]

During the weeks that followed, over 40 bills were prepared, on subjects as diverse as probate of wills and the management of saltpetre.[148] But members' energies were principally directed towards two ends: to augment Parliament's powers, especially in relation to the Army, and to enact measures against what they perceived as religious 'errors' and 'blasphemies'. To achieve these goals, they began to draft a lengthy 'constitutional bill' amending the Instrument of Government.[149] This bill introduced the provision that Parliaments could not be adjourned, prorogued or dissolved without their own consent.[150] It also increased parliamentary control over the militia, and demands for a considerable reduction in the size of the Army were only narrowly defeated.[151] In addition, the Parliament launched a frontal assault on the principle of liberty of conscience so dear to Cromwell and many of his Army colleagues by proposing legislation 'for the restraining of atheism, blasphemy, popery, prelacy, licentiousness and profaneness'.[152] Members' deep-rooted fears about the spread of religious errors, heresies and blasphemies were particularly evident in their imprisonment of the Socinian John Biddle for denying the Trinity and the divinity of Christ. Although Cromwell did not prevent Biddle's punishment, it was characteristic that he ensured that Biddle was imprisoned on the Scilly Isles, beyond Parliament's reach, and also granted him a weekly allowance of ten shillings.[153] Cromwell was appalled that the majority of members preferred to denounce religious sectaries and amend the Instrument of Government rather than confirm the 82 ordinances that he had issued during his first nine months as Lord Protector, among them the creation of 'triers' and 'ejectors' to improve the quality of the clergy.[154] Determined to block the 'constitutional bill', he dissolved the Parliament at the earliest possible opportunity, after five lunar rather than calendar months, on 22 January 1655. In his closing speech, he accused members of 'throwing away precious opportunities committed to' them, and condemned the 'weeds and nettles, briers and thorns' that had 'thriven under' the Parliament's shadow. He particularly regretted the Parliament's failure to grant 'a just liberty to godly men of different judgments', and lamented: 'is there not upon the spirits of men a strange itch? Nothing will satisfy them unless they can put their finger upon their brethren's consciences, to pinch them there.' It was, he concluded, his 'duty to God and the people of these nations, to their safety and good in every respect', to dissolve the Parliament.[155]

We noted in Chapter 4 that when Cromwell decided to call another Parliament, in September 1656, it was for the eminently traditional reason that he needed money.[156] The previous year, England and Wales had been divided into regions each governed by a Major-General with the assistance of new militias funded by a Decimation Tax on former Royalists. Cromwell had also launched a largely unsuccessful military campaign against Spanish possessions in the West Indies (the 'Western Design') and begun to plan an attack on the Spanish in Flanders. The parliamentary elections, held during August 1656, revealed intense hostility towards 'swordsmen' and 'decimators', and returned many members who were unsympathetic to the Army's religious outlook. When the second Protectorate Parliament assembled, the Council excluded over a hundred 'ungodly' members, including many prominent republicans, such as Thomas Scot and Sir Arthur Hesilrige.[157] A further 50 or 60 members then withdrew in protest. Although Cromwell carefully distanced himself from this purge, the Parliament had got off to an acrimonious start.

Like the members of the first Protectorate Parliament, most of those who remained in the second Protectorate Parliament had two immediate objectives: to prevent the spread of what they regarded as religious errors, heresies and blasphemies, and to strengthen Parliament's influence while diminishing that of the Army.[158] The first issue came to a head with the case of James Nayler, a Quaker who in October 1656 re-enacted Christ's entry into Jerusalem on Palm Sunday by riding into Bristol on a donkey, while his supporters threw palms at his feet. He was arrested and brought to London, where Parliament convicted him of 'horrid blasphemy'. Some members initially wished to sentence him to death but this was later reduced to severe corporal punishments.[159] Cromwell once again did not interfere in the House's discussions but he did query the 'grounds and reasons' of 'such proceedings (wholly without us)', thereby raising the ancient issue of the Commons' lack of unicameral judicature.[160] As in the earlier case of Biddle, although Cromwell abominated Nayler's actions and beliefs,[161] he was deeply apprehensive about where the Commons' religious intolerance might lead if it remained unchecked. Speaking to Army officers on 27 February 1657, he declared:

> That a House of Lords, or other check upon the arbitrary tendencies of a single House of Parliament, may be of real use. See what they, by their own mere vote and will, I having no power to check them, have done with James Nayler: may it not be any one's case, some other day?[162]

The House of Lords' judicature, so effectively revived from 1621 onwards, clearly fulfilled an important role within the legal system, and its absence raised serious concerns about the untrammelled powers of the Lower House.

If Cromwell was concerned about the lack of checks on the Commons, many members were increasingly anxious about the influence of the Army. In January 1657 they revived the strategy of redress-supply bargaining and refused to vote £400,000 for the war against Spain until a Militia Bill, introduced by Major-General Desborough to perpetuate the Major-Generals and the Decimation Tax, had been defeated.[163] A similar tension between the swordsmen and the civilians also lay behind the most controversial episode of this Parliament, the offer of the kingship to Cromwell. Many members feared that because the office of Lord Protector was unknown to the laws of England, Cromwell could in practice exercise more extensive powers than a king. Some of his utterances were extremely authoritarian and, ironically, all too reminiscent of Charles I, as when Cromwell justified emergency protectoral powers on the grounds that 'if nothing should be done but what is according to law, the throat of the nation may be cut while we send for some to make a law'.[164] Cromwell's civilian advisers, many of whom were of Presbyterian sympathies such as Bulstrode Whitelocke and Lord Broghill, therefore orchestrated the presentation of a new constitution, the Humble Petition and Advice, in February 1657, which offered Cromwell the kingship. This new constitution was a carefully calculated bid not only to strengthen Parliament's position but also to weaken the Army officers' influence over Cromwell and to impede their promotion of radical religious reforms, especially liberty of conscience. Not surprisingly, it was from the Army, and especially from such leading officers as Lambert, Desborough and Fleetwood, that the principal resistance to the kingship arose. The debates on this matter in Parliament directly reflected divisions between swordsmen and civilians among Cromwell's close advisers, and thus continued the well-established pattern in which parliamentary dynamics represented an extension of conciliar politics.[165]

Cromwell agonised for over two months before finally deciding to decline the offer on 8 May,[166] ostensibly on the grounds that the monarchy had been destroyed 'providentially' and that he 'would not build Jericho again'.[167] It is certainly possible that he realised that he was more powerful as Lord Protector.[168] However, the considerations that probably weighed most heavily with him were a reluctance to antagonise the Army – whose trenchant opposition he equated with God's disapproval – and also a fear that to accept the kingship would strengthen the hand of those civilians within the Council and Parliament who were least sympathetic to the godly 'cause', and especially to extending liberty of conscience more widely. This was particularly so in the wake of the Nayler case, which had heightened Cromwell's concerns about how parliamentary judicature could be harnessed to persecute the more radical sectaries. The episode of the kingship was thus yet another manifestation of the continuing tension between civilians committed to safeguarding Parliaments and the rule of law, and swordsmen wedded to greater religious toleration. Cromwell's agonised delay reflected the fact that he was being forced to choose between these two priorities, both of which he regarded as 'fundamentals'.

Once the issue of the kingship had been resolved, the remaining clauses of the Humble Petition and Advice proved much less controversial and were adopted with only minor revisions on 25 May.[169] Cromwell was to remain Lord Protector with the right to nominate his successor, but he was required to rule 'according to the laws of these nations', and to ensure that Parliament's 'ancient and undoubted liberties and privileges' were 'preserved and maintained'. With the memory of recent purges still fresh, it was stipulated that freely elected members could henceforth only be excluded 'by judgement and consent' of Parliament. These clauses all marked a revival of rights and privileges enjoyed by early Stuart Parliaments. Cromwell was also allowed to nominate an 'Other House' of between 40 and 70 people, although these had to be approved by the Commons. The creation of a second chamber was particularly welcome to Cromwell and partly stemmed from his own fears of an unrestrained Commons as manifested in the cases of Nayler and Biddle. On 26 June, in another striking move towards more traditional forms, Cromwell was again installed as Lord Protector, wearing a robe of purple velvet lined with ermine, and carrying a gold sceptre. The same day, Parliament was adjourned until the following January.[170]

There were further echoes of earlier Parliaments when members reassembled for their second sitting on 20 January 1658. Cromwell's main short-term concern was once more the need for money to fight the Spanish, and the beginning of the sitting was accompanied by ceremonial that resembled Tudor or early Stuart openings.[171] Cromwell had high hopes that this sitting would safeguard 'the honest and religious interest of the nation', but yet again these were dashed.[172] Only 42 of the 63 individuals summoned to the 'Other House' actually attended.[173] Those invited included seven peers but all except two declined: Viscount Saye, for example, refused to join what he called 'a stalking horse and vizard to carry on the design of overthrowing the House of Peers' by 'picking out a company to make another House of in their places, at the pleasure of him that will rule'.[174] But if Saye thought the 'Other House' a poor shadow of the Lords, some of the more hard-line republicans, including Scot and Hesilrige, saw it as far too like the old Upper House and challenged its legitimacy.[175] The Humble Petition and Advice had affirmed Parliament's right to judge the eligibility of its own members:[176] the Commons used this power to restore those members purged in September 1656, many of whom were republicans, and this had the effect of swelling the ranks of those hostile to the 'Other House', and indeed to the Protectorate itself. The nomination of some of Cromwell's most effective supporters to the 'Other House' further reduced any chance that the Commons would fulfil his hopes.[177]

Those hopes were most plainly expressed in a lengthy speech to both Houses on 25 January 1658 in which Cromwell urged members to remedy the 'calamities and divisions among us in respect of the spirits of men', to provide for the Army and for further campaigns against the Spanish, and not to tamper with the constitution.[178] But instead, Hesilrige, Scot and the other republicans pressed ahead with their attacks on the 'Other House'. They also co-operated with discontented elements among the soldiery and sectaries in London to promote a mass petition demanding the abolition of the Protectorate and the 'Other House', and the restoration of a unicameral sovereign Parliament in which 'the people (the original of all just power)' would vest 'supreme power and trust'.[179] The petition gained several thousand signatures and it was planned to present it to Parliament on 4 February. However, alarmed at this direct challenge to the government and at the signs of growing disunity within the Army's ranks, Cromwell pre-empted the petition by dissolving the Parliament on the morning of 4 February. Its sitting had lasted barely two weeks, and Cromwell's speech of dissolution concluded bitterly: 'let God be judge between you and me.'[180] That phrase, with its stark antithesis between Cromwell and the members, summed up his failure to achieve an harmonious relationship with any Parliament. The conflict between Cromwell's goals of government by 'a single person and a Parliament' and liberty of conscience ultimately thwarted the achievement of either. He wished to embrace as 'fundamentals' two objectives that in the end remained incompatible. His promotion of a minority agenda brought him into constant friction with the 'representative of the realm', and underlined the basic irreconcilability between the military leadership and the civilian politicians that ran like a fault-line through the Interregnum.

Cromwell's unique personality and achievements alone bridged the military and civilian camps, and after his death in September 1658 the tension between them destroyed the Republic within two years.[181] That tension immediately disrupted the third Protectorate Parliament which Richard Cromwell, facing a total debt of nearly £2.5 million, summoned in January 1659. Because no Parliament had ever approved the Instrument of Government, and no full Parliament had adopted the Humble Petition and Advice, the Council of State decided to abandon the revised system of representation and revert to the old franchise,[182] which produced a Parliament even less sympathetic towards the Army than its predecessors. The Parliament once again contained a strong republican element led by Hesilrige and Scot, and these members immediately launched a concerted attack on key parts of the Humble Petition and Advice, including the scope of the Lord Protector's powers and the provision for the 'Other House'. They managed to delay the formal recognition of the latter until 28 March.[183] The republicans, in collaboration with disaffected soldiers and sectaries within the City of London, also revived the petition against the Protectorate due originally to be submitted to Parliament on 4 February 1658: this time, the petition's promoters collected between 20,000 and 40,000 signatures and it was presented on 15 February 1659. The republicans welcomed it but most members were much more frosty.[184] In general, Parliament remained deeply mistrustful of the swordsmen and was much slower to make provision for the payment of soldiers' arrears than the Army had hoped. Like its predecessors, this Parliament was also opposed to extending liberty of conscience and on 5 April it passed a declaration censuring magistrates for their slackness in punishing 'heresies'.[185] When, later that month, the Commons belatedly discussed the future of the armed forces and expressed a strong desire to place them under the joint control of the Lord Protector and Parliament, the Army leaders, and above all Desborough, finally lost patience. Convinced that even the Rump was preferable to this, they forced Richard Cromwell to dissolve Parliament on 22 April and recall the Rump.[186] Of the 78 Rumpers still able to attend, only 42 actually assembled in May. They refused to recognise the Protectorate and demanded Richard's resignation and the restoration of the Commonwealth. Isolated from both the Rump and the Army leadership, Richard resigned on 24 May.

However, the Army's dealings with the Rump were no happier this time than they had been previously. A shared hostility towards the Protectorate had temporarily allowed the republicans and the Army to make common cause in toppling it, but their interests remained essentially divergent. The return of the Rump was deeply unwelcome to most of the political elite: one member of the Council of State wrote that 'there is a strange contempt and hatred through the nation of this present Parliament'.[187] In such a climate, the Rump's survival inevitably depended, as before, on the Army's support, yet it seemed unable to avoid alienating the Army. It largely ignored the Humble Petition and Address of the Officers of the Army, which Lambert, Desborough and other leading officers presented on 13 May,[188] and instead set about trying to obliterate the legacy of the Protectorate. Attempts to purge supporters of the Protectorate from both the Army and local government proved highly unpopular, and the Army bitterly resented the Rump's failure to provide for their arrears or to extend religious toleration. An uneasy marriage of convenience between

Rumpers and officers survived through the summer months, partly in order to defeat the Royalist Booth's rising in the north-west. But by the autumn, as the Rump continued its endless bickering about constitutional procedures, the Army's patience was wearing thin. On 5 October, Desborough presented the Humble Representation and Petition of the Officers of the Army, forcefully reminding the Rump of the Humble Petition and Address of 13 May and urging members to safeguard the Army's interests.[189] But instead members preferred to pass an act declaring all legislation passed since April 1653 null and void, and making it high treason to collect any taxes, excise or customs without Parliament's consent.[190] This was the final straw in convincing the Army leaders that they could work with the Rump no longer: on 13 October Lambert's troops turned back members as they tried to enter the House and towards the end of that month the Army appointed a Committee of Safety to govern instead.[191]

At this point, against a background of growing anarchy, George Monck, commander of the Army in Scotland, apparently motivated by a desire to see order and stable government restored and 'the fanatical and self-seeking party' defeated, demanded the return of the Rump and began to march south.[192] Following his lead, three regiments reinstated the Rump on 26 December, but it proved wholly incapable of regaining control of events. Throughout January and early February, petitions poured in from all over the country calling for free elections or for the readmission of those members whom Pride had secluded in December 1648.[193] The Rump dithered and became increasingly paralysed by divisions as more and more members turned against Hesilrige and his allies. Monck meanwhile continued to advance southwards: he swept aside a force that Lambert sent against him, and entered London on 3 February 1660. On 11 February he demanded that elections be held to fill the seats of the secluded members, and the Rump passed a bill to that effect a week later.[194] In the meantime, however, Monck had been in secret contact with some of the most prominent secluded members and on 21 February he secured the readmission of 73 of them to Parliament, thereby reconstructing the surviving membership of the Long Parliament as it was at the beginning of December 1648.[195] As these were the people who had wished to continue negotiations with Charles I late in 1648, it was hardly surprising that over 11 years later they were overwhelmingly in favour of restoring his son. Among the first actions of the reconvened Long Parliament was to release the imprisoned Royalist rebel Sir George Booth and to appoint a Council of State dominated by leading Presbyterians, such as Denzil Holles, who were known to be sympathetic to the restoration of Charles II.[196] The Long Parliament soon bowed to the massive popular demand for 'free elections' and finally dissolved itself on 16 March 1660.[197]

Among the most striking features of the events of March and April 1660, culminating in the restoration of Charles II, was the widespread faith in the role of a 'full and free Parliament' in restoring stable and legitimate government. Events were coming full circle, constituting a revolution in the contemporary sense, and as in 1640 many regarded a settlement agreed between Crown and Parliament as the only way to achieve a lasting solution. Charles II shrewdly appealed to this mood by promising, in the Declaration of Breda (4 April 1660), to settle all controversial matters in collaboration with a 'free Parliament'.[198] The first free elections since 1640 returned a strongly pro-Royalist Convention,[199] which assembled on 25 April, together with the House of Lords (as yet comprising only the lords temporal).[200] On 8 May, the two Houses unanimously passed a declaration stating that 'it can no way be doubted but that His Majesty's right and title to his Crowns and kingdoms is and was [in] every way completed by the death of his most royal father, without the ceremony or solemnity of a proclamation'. The Convention thus affirmed Charles II to have been 'the most potent and undoubted King' of England, Scotland and Ireland since the moment of his father's execution.[201] The Houses were in effect saying that the Interregnum had officially never existed: they were neither creating nor restoring Charles as King but simply declaring that he was already the King. This recognition paved the way for the revival of the traditional parliamentary trinity, in which Crown, Lords and Commons would be knitted back together again into one body politic. But although the radical surgery and mutilation that the body politic had suffered during the previous 20 years could be cleverly disguised, they could never be forgotten, and they were to dog the Parliaments of Restoration England.

|9|

Restoration Parliaments, 1660–1689

The Restoration Settlement

During the later seventeenth century, as in earlier periods, parliamentary proceedings continued to reflect the wider relationship between the Crown and members of the political elite. In 1660, Charles and the majority of his most powerful subjects were committed to a settlement agreed by Crown and Parliament as the surest way to restore stability. Neither side wished the other to be unduly weakened: Parliament desired a strong, but not tyrannical, monarch just as Charles sought effective, but not aggressive, Parliaments. The result was a wide-ranging settlement that was implemented by means of statute. Yet it was also deeply flawed in two respects. First, the Houses refused to let Charles establish the broad-based Church that he desired: instead the settlement combined a magnanimous resolution of secular issues with a narrowly intolerant Church in a way that left religion a source of political instability. Second, in restoring many aspects of the pre-Civil War constitution, the settlement unfortunately also revived many of the tensions associated with it. Nobody could forget the crisis that those tensions had generated, and memories of the revolution haunted Restoration Parliaments. For just as Charles II and James II never forgot their father's fate, so the members of their Parliaments could neither forget how vulnerable they had felt under Charles I nor ignore the continuing threat of 'popery and arbitrary government'. The political style of individual monarchs remained crucially important, and when James II's single-minded Catholic convictions replaced Charles II's easy-going flexibility a second revolution took place, less violent than the first but with consequences that were no less profound for the nature and role of Parliaments.

The first principle of the Restoration Settlement was to reinstate legitimate government, and this was followed through with an almost obsessive thoroughness. Every statute that had received the royal assent remained in force, but all those acts and ordinances passed unilaterally by various Parliaments since 1642 were declared null and void. This meant that the reforming legislation of 1641, which Charles I had accepted, still stood as a safeguard against another Personal Rule. Prerogative taxation and the Courts of Star Chamber and High Commission remained permanently abolished. But the removal of so much other legislation of the 1640s and 1650s – about 1,200 acts and ordinances in all – necessitated the passage of more statutes during the 1660s than in any other decade of the century.[1] The insistence that Charles II had been King from the moment of his father's execution was strictly adhered to, and the numbering of statutes assumed that 1660–1 was the twelfth year of his reign.[2] A direct continuity was thus established with the Parliaments of Charles I.

The legitimacy of royal powers as they had existed in the autumn of 1641 was strongly upheld. In 1661 a Militia Act stated that 'the sole and supreme government, command and disposition of the militia' and of all the armed forces was 'the undoubted right of His Majesty and his royal predecessors', and denied that 'both or either of the Houses of Parliament' could 'pretend to the same' or lawfully raise forces against the King.[3] The following year, a further act affirmed the monarch's right to appoint whoever he chose to the lieutenancy, and required all Lords Lieutenant, Deputy Lieutenants, officers and soldiers to swear an oath that 'it is not lawful upon any pretence whatsoever to take arms against the King', and abhorring 'the traitorous position that arms may be taken by his authority against his person'.[4] In 1661 an 'Act for safety and preservation of His Majesty's person and government' condemned the 'opinion that both Houses of Parliament or either of them have a legislative power without the King'.[5] It was thus acknowledged that just as the Houses could not legitimately pass ordinances without the royal assent, neither could they assume control of the armed forces and deploy them against the monarch. The traditional procedure for parliamentary legislation was thus reaffirmed and the doctrine on which the Houses' law-making between 1642 and 1660 had rested was explicitly repudiated.

Equally, the Houses felt that to leave a monarch financially independent of Parliament was to jeopardise their own future. After 1660 the Crown therefore remained permanently stripped of prerogative taxes and feudal revenues. To compensate, the Convention voted Charles a permanent ordinary revenue estimated at about £1.2 million. However, as we have seen, this revenue depended heavily on the buoyancy of trade and it was only during the latter part of Charles's reign that the target figure was actually achieved.[6] Until his last few years, Charles was consistently short of funds. It is possible that this shortfall was deliberately contrived for political reasons, although there is also evidence that it was the result of insufficient thought and investigation.[7] The Houses' awareness that the Crown was dependent on parliamentary supply may help to explain why the new Triennial Act of 1664 only required that 'there may be a frequent calling, assembling and holding of Parliaments once in three years at the least' without establishing any formal mechanisms to guarantee this.[8] But if so, it was a short-sighted strategy, for when a trade boom boosted royal revenues in the early 1680s Charles was able to ignore the act with impunity.

The sweeping powers of statute were further demonstrated in August 1660 when the Act of Free and General Pardon, Indemnity and Oblivion was enacted.[9] Its terms were strikingly generous. The only exceptions to the general pardon were those individuals responsible for the Irish Rebellion of 1641, those who had signed Charles I's death warrant, and a handful of other named figures including Sir Henry Vane the younger. Vane and nine surviving regicides were executed, while the corpses of Cromwell, Ireton and Bradshaw were dug up, hanged and beheaded.[10] But otherwise the emphasis was on reconciliation. It was declared an offence for three years to reproach any person for their behaviour since 1638. Anxious to win over old enemies and to bring them into both national and local government, Charles deliberately avoided any attempt to impose a national land settlement by legislative means: all those former

Parliamentarians who had gained sequestered Royalist lands were declared to have sound title. It was nevertheless possible for former Royalists to regain their lands by private acts of Parliament. This turned out to be a highly appropriate and effective way to resolve individual disputes, and provides a fine example of how private bill procedure allowed subjects to take advantage of the flexibility and authority of statute in pursuing their own interests.[11]

Charles II thus worked successfully with Parliament to implement all the promises he had made in the Declaration of Breda except in one key area – religion. He had pledged a 'liberty to tender consciences', and seems to have been genuinely committed to a broad national Church with extensive toleration for those unable to subscribe to it. This would have resembled the Church under Elizabeth I and James I, and formed the natural ecclesiastical counterpart to the broad-based secular settlement. The King made his moderate views plain in the Worcester House Declaration of October 1660: however, the Convention was divided over the future of the Church, and in the summer of 1661 it was succeeded by the even more pro-Royalist Cavalier Parliament.[12] Thomas Venner's abortive Fifth Monarchist rising in January 1661 reinforced the new Parliament's determination to resist any concessions to religious radicals. It adopted a revised Prayer Book that did nothing to appease dissenters in April 1662, and the following month it passed an Act of Uniformity that required all ministers to swear their 'unfeigned assent and consent' to everything contained in the Prayer Book, and making its use compulsory in all Church of England services. Those who refused were to lose their livings, and in all nearly 2,000 of England's 9,000 parish clergy resigned or were deprived between 1660 and 1662.[13]

Opinion on the religious settlement was rather more evenly balanced in the Lords than in the Commons and the Lord Chancellor, Clarendon, who at this stage hoped to ensure 'such liberty as may be safe to men of peaceable spirits', succeeded in rallying enough support in the Upper House to diminish the penalties against nonconformists contained in the Act of Uniformity.[14] However, the years that followed saw the enactment of a systematic body of penal laws against nonconformity known, despite the Lord Chancellor's initial reservations, as the 'Clarendon Code'. The Corporation Act (December 1661) excluded from borough corporations all those who would not abjure the Solemn League and Covenant and take the Anglican sacraments;[15] the Quaker Act (May 1662) imposed fines or transportation on those who refused to take oaths or who attended gatherings of five or more Quakers;[16] the first Conventicle Act (April 1664) proscribed all meetings of five or more individuals held 'under colour or pretence of any exercise of religion';[17] and the Five Mile Act (October 1665) forbade all ministers ejected under the Act of Uniformity and other unlicensed preachers from coming within five miles of their former parish, or any corporate town or city.[18] Clarendon had originally hoped to avoid harsh penalties against nonconformity, but after Yorkshire dissenters rebelled in the autumn of 1663 he ultimately accepted the need for stern measures in order to preserve law and order.

Charles II, by contrast, still hankered after toleration for 'tender consciences'. He considered trying to suspend the Act of Uniformity, but the Bishop of London, Gilbert Sheldon, strongly opposed such a move, and he was supported by the Duke of York and possibly also by the Crown's own lawyers.[19] In December 1662 Charles therefore issued a declaration requesting Parliament to pass an act enabling him to 'exercise with a more universal satisfaction that power of dispensing which we conceive to be inherent in us'. The Commons rejected the idea of a 'dispensation act', which they felt would 'establish schism by law'.[20] As we saw in Chapter 6, they remained fearful of the royal dispensing power and resisted any attempt to give it statutory author-ity. Clarendon thought it 'a very unreasonable and unjust thing to commit such a trust to the King', and feared that it would be 'Ship Money in religion, that nobody could know the end of, or where it would rest'.[21] Charles backed down for the time being although, as we shall see, he continued to push for greater toleration periodically throughout his reign. In the meantime, the Clarendon Code constituted the great flaw in an otherwise magnanimous and far-sighted settlement. It penalised a hard core of a few hundred ministers and about 10 per cent of the laity, and although much of its effectiveness depended on the energy and zeal of local magistrates, which varied considerably from place to place,[22] it certainly destroyed any pretence that the Church was a truly national institution. The consequence was that profound religious division and mistrust permeated the politics of all Charles's Parliaments and undermined the stabil-ity so carefully fostered by other aspects of the settlement.

The Cavalier Parliament

The Cavalier Parliament sat for no fewer than 18 sessions and was not finally dissolved until January 1679. A substantial majority of members of both Houses were blindly loyal to the Crown in principle, but not necessarily to the particular policies pursued by Charles II and his advisers. As a result, the cen-tral themes running through the Parliament represented an interesting varia-tion on those that had dominated early Stuart Parliaments. Perhaps the most contentious questions were the extent to which religious toleration and/or comprehension should be extended; whether the royal suspending or dispens-ing powers could be used to counter the penal laws against nonconformists and Catholics; whether England's foreign policy should be pro-French and pro-Catholic or pro-Dutch and pro-Protestant; and the degree to which officers of state could be held accountable to Parliament, especially in financial matters. All these issues were closely connected, and behind them lay two basic prob-lems. The first was the continuing controversy over the exact relationship between the Crown and Parliament, which was no more satisfactorily defined after 1660 than it had been before 1640. The boundaries between on the one hand royal discretionary powers and, on the other, the rule of law and the rights of Parliament remained blurred and periodically caused lively debate. Second, there was the pervasive issue of 'popery and arbitrary government'. Virtually everybody agreed that they were evil, but opinion was divided over how far they presented a genuine threat to England, over what constituted symptoms of them, and over what measures might justifiably be taken against them.

The contrasting positions that members adopted on these various issues led to the gradual emergence during the Cavalier Parliament of platforms that came to be labelled 'Court' and 'Country'. These were not yet political parties in any meaningful sense; rather they were very loose groupings, often with a shifting and transient membership, that were characterised by an identifiable outlook or set of attitudes rather than a clearly defined ideology. The distinc-tion thus went deeper than a simple difference between political 'ins' and 'outs', or between office-holders and back-benchers. The 'Country' members were generally those most vehemently committed to defending Protestantism against Catholicism, both at home and abroad, to protecting the rights of Parliament against the Crown (not least to safeguard Protestantism), and to rooting out any individuals, especially among the King's advisers, who threatened these principles. Leading examples of 'Country' figures included Sir William Coventry, Sir Thomas Meres, Lord Cavendish, William Lord Russell and William Sacheverell in the Commons, and, in the Lords, Salisbury, Holles, Wharton and (after about 1674) Shaftesbury and Buckingham. The 'Court' was much more difficult to characterise, mainly because the King changed his leading ministers several times during the course of his reign and policy was shaped by figures as diverse as Clarendon (1660–7), the members of the Cabal (Clifford, Arlington, Buckingham, Ashley and Lauderdale)[23] from 1667 to 1673, and Danby between 1674 and 1679. All these people staunchly defended the Crown's powers, but they differed in their religious stance and over foreign policy. Possibly the members of the Cabal, with their sympathy for religious toleration and a pro-French foreign policy, were the closest to Charles's own heart, and it was during the period of their ascendancy that a 'Country' platform began to crystallise in opposition to them.

The fall of Clarendon which preceded the emergence of the Cabal was in some ways a rerun of the attacks on chief ministers that had taken place under the early Stuarts. The Lord Chancellor's stuffy personality and failure to build up a network of supporters within Parliament ensured that he had never been popular, and there were rumours, fuelled by his sale of Dunkirk, his building of a vast house in Piccadilly, and the marriage of his daughter to the Duke of York, that he was using his position to feather his own nest.[24] When the second Anglo-Dutch War (1665–7) went very badly for England, and culminated in the destruction of a large part of the fleet in a spectacular Dutch raid up the Medway, Clarendon was made a scapegoat for a conflict that he had actually strenuously opposed. The King sided with the Commons and against the Lords in supporting impeachment proceedings. As we saw in Chapter 6, Charles's pragmatic alignment with the Lower House was a departure from the more usual pattern in impeachments and it proved highly successful, for by thus jettisoning a political liability he made the doctrine of evil counsellors very easy to operate.[25] Only Clarendon's flight to France pre-empted his impeachment.

Many members of the Commons suspected that Clarendon was merely part of a wider problem of corruption, and in 1667 an Accounts Commission was established to examine the public accounts.[26] Although this proved only a short-lived experiment, it indicated growing concerns about the absence of procedures for ensuring the financial accountability of royal officials to Parliament. Anxiety about the lack of parliamentary control over government expenditure also prompted the insertion of 'appropriation' clauses, for example in the assessment bills of 1665 and 1667, stipulating that the money raised had to be used for particular purposes. This expedient was initially suggested by the government's financial advisers, especially Sir George Downing, as a way of raising credit for the Dutch War, but it was quickly seized on by those in the Commons who hoped to strengthen parliamentary control of government expenditure. By the late 1670s, such appropriation clauses were regularly added to bills granting supply, but there was as yet no way to enforce them in practice.[27]

The emergence of the Cabal initially calmed the restiveness of many members of the Commons. But that calm could only be temporary, for although the Cabal's outlook was attractive to Charles it did not command the support of a majority within either House. The Cabal, a name derived from the initial letters of the five 'members', was in fact a misnomer, for they agreed on little except the need for a *rapprochement* with France and greater religious toleration at home (none of them was an enthusiastic Anglican and Clifford was a covert Catholic). They displayed virtually no unity or coherence as a group, nor were they anything like equal in the political influence that they wielded. Arlington was probably the most powerful of the five, and Ronald Hutton has suggested that the period 1668–72 should be regarded as 'the ministry of Arlington'.[28] The term Cabal is also misleading because it ignores other key figures such as Sir Orlando Bridgeman, Lord Keeper and Speaker of the Lords between 1667 and 1672. Bridgeman exploited the influence of these offices – which as we saw in Chapter 5 was potentially immense – to become second only to Arlington as a political player during these years.[29]

In this period Charles embarked on a more strongly pro-French, anti-Dutch foreign policy, and in May 1670 he concluded the secret Treaty of Dover with Louis XIV which committed England and France to a joint military and naval war against the Dutch Republic two years later.[30] The treaty also included a remarkable secret clause stating that Charles, 'being convinced of the truth of the Catholic religion, [is] resolved to declare it and reconcile himself with the Church of Rome as soon as the welfare of his kingdom will permit'.[31] In fact, this 'catholicity' clause was never implemented, but had it become known to Parliament it would have caused a furore. As it was, the war against the Dutch of 1672–4 came to be widely perceived within both Houses as an unnecessary conflict against England's co-religionists.[32]

This realignment in foreign policy was accompanied by further moves towards religious toleration at home. In 1668 Charles allowed the first Conventicle Act to expire without being renewed and the following year considerable alarm was expressed in the Commons when disorderly conventicles were reported up and down the country. Anglican gentry in the Commons made common cause with like-minded bishops and peers to defend the established Church and obstruct any attempt to introduce toleration or comprehension.[33] The Commons refused to grant extraordinary supply worth more than £300,000.[34] Only after Charles accepted a second, more severe, Conventicle Act in March 1670 was further taxation voted, together with grants of new duties on imported wines for eight years and additional excise duties for nine.[35]

Charles's assent to the second Conventicle Act was a cynical manoeuvre to secure more supply, and the King's true wishes became plain on 15 March 1672 when, two days before he declared war on the Dutch, he issued a Declaration of Indulgence suspending all penal legislation for religion by virtue of his 'supreme power in ecclesiastical matters'.[36] This raised the vexed question of the royal suspending power, and we saw earlier that the Commons retaliated by denying that this power extended to religious matters and insisting that the penal statutes could only be revoked by subsequent statutes.[37] In practice, however, the only way that they could force Charles to back down was by withholding supply. We saw in Chapter 4 that in wartime the power of the purse was greatly strengthened, and in 1673–4 it was successfully used to push Charles into withdrawing the Declaration of Indulgence, accepting a Test Act that excluded Catholics from public office, and making peace with the Dutch. This episode stands out as the most effective use during Charles II's reign of the power of the purse to extract political concessions from the Crown.[38]

The King's decision to acquiesce to parliamentary pressure and reverse his recent policies left the Cabal isolated and it disintegrated shortly afterwards: Clifford was removed from the Lord Treasurership under the terms of the Test Act and later committed suicide; Shaftesbury[39] was dismissed from the Lord Chancellorship when he suggested that the King should remarry to secure a Protestant heir; and relations between Arlington and Buckingham – never good – degenerated into bitter recriminations. As with Clarendon, Charles allowed parliamentary hostility towards unpopular ministers to run its course, and vowed to 'give the people an open field in order to curb them the better when they were tired with their gallop'.[40] Once again, this strategy enabled the Houses to dislodge hated advocates of discredited policies without criticising the Crown directly.

By the sessions of 1674–5, an identifiable core of 'Country' members had emerged within both Houses. This development was evident earliest in the Upper House, where by the mid-1670s 'Country' peers formed a distinct group, committed to a Protestant foreign policy, greater toleration for Protestant dissenters, a vigorous defence of the subjects' rights and liberties, a Protestant succession, and a conviction that Parliament had a crucial role to play in protecting all these priorities against the threat of 'popery and arbitrary government'. In contrast to the very fluid and shifting parliamentary groups of the 1660s and early 1670s, which were more reminiscent of the pre-Civil War period, these 'Country' peers displayed considerable cohesion of membership and consistency in voting patterns. Andrew Swatland has argued that with their characteristic political and religious attitudes, their continuity of personnel, and their attempts to mobilise and co-ordinate support, the 'Country' peers began to display – albeit in very embryonic form – some of the traits of a party.[41] A similar process was also discernible in the Lower House, but in a slower and more untidy fashion because the Commons was so much larger than the Lords and its membership changed more regularly. In 1673, Sir Thomas Meres had allegedly spoken in the Commons of 'this side of the house, and that side', a distinction that would have been difficult to discern even a few years previously and that some of those present condemned as 'not parliamentary'.[42] Before and during the sessions of 1673–4, some 'Country' members met to co-ordinate strategy in both Houses, and the Green Ribbon Club at the King's Head Tavern in Chancery Lane, founded in 1674, became an established meeting place for opposition members.[43] As we shall see, such bicameral co-ordination became gradually more widespread and effective from the mid-1670s onwards.[44]

The 'Court' was not slow to respond to this challenge. In the early 1670s, Clifford's use of patronage to win supporters in both Lords and Commons had earned him the nickname 'Bribe Master General'. In particular, he ruthlessly exploited the financial embarrassment of some former Royalists by offering them offices and sinecures in return for their political co-operation. When the Cabal fell, Charles turned to Sir Thomas Osborne, whom he appointed Lord Treasurer in 1673 and Earl of Danby the following year, to maximise the strength of this 'Court' element. The King hoped that Danby's staunch adherence to the Church of England, his hostility to religious toleration, and his commitment to a pro-Dutch, anti-French foreign policy would coincide with the prevailing mood within the political elite.

Danby's ideological stance, together with his extensive use of patronage, helped to build up a base of support for the Crown in both Houses. In the Lords, he mobilised the Crown's natural supporters, the Anglican Royalists, who together with the bishops comprised just over half the Upper House in 1675. The first minister to make use of 'whipping' on any significant scale in the Lords, Danby instructed allies to attend and even briefed them with arguments before debates. In collaboration with successive Archbishops of Canterbury, Gilbert Sheldon and William Sancroft, Danby secured an average attendance of 13 bishops in the sessions between 1675 and 1678. He thus took full advantage of the fact that, as we saw earlier, the episcopal bench generally provided the Crown with a nucleus of reliable supporters.[45] Another important aspect of his management of the Lords was his systematic exploitation of the proxy system: in the period 1675–8, the government controlled three-quarters of registered proxies, and no less than 52 per cent of proxies were in the hands of Privy Councillors. The proxy system, described in Chapter 5,[46] was long established, but Danby harnessed it on the Crown's behalf far more extensively and methodically than had ever been attempted before. These methods were usually sufficient to secure a government majority in the Upper House, and no more than two dozen peers were in receipt of Court pensions between 1675 and 1678.[47] In the Commons, by the autumn of 1675 around 30 members were receiving pensions worth a total of over £30,000 a year derived mainly from excise revenue. As in the Lords, Danby sent personal letters to numerous members on the eve of sessions to rally further support; he also compiled management lists of likely sympathisers. Using a mixture of pensions, gifts and promises of offices and other patronage, Danby could probably rely on a hard core of about 120 to 150 loyal members in the Lower House by 1677–8, and he sometimes claimed to secure as many as 250 votes. However, the extent of his effectiveness in the Commons is difficult to assess precisely: in many cases the rewards proffered were not very great, and it is hard to determine how far members were motivated by the lure of these rather than by other considerations such as pressure from friends or constituents, or ideological sympathies.[48]

Although the exact success of Danby's managerial techniques is uncertain, it is clear that they alienated at least as many members as they won over. 'Country' members accused him of trying to create a 'Pension Parliament', and fears grew that he wished to buy Parliament off or abandon it altogether. Buckingham and Shaftesbury, who became prominent 'Country' figures after the demise of the Cabal, particularly loathed Danby, and when he introduced a Test Bill requiring all office-holders and members of Parliament to declare that taking up arms against the Crown 'on any pretence whatsoever' was unlawful, the 'Country' leaders accused him of seeking to establish arbitrary government, raise a standing army, and dispense with Parliaments. In April and May 1675 they collaborated with Arlington's clients in the Commons to launch an abortive attempt to impeach Danby.[49] Shaftesbury and his friend John Locke memorably expressed the anxieties of the 'Country' members in *A Letter from a Person of Quality to his Friend in the Country* (1675). Charles himself undermined Danby's position by a series of secret treaties with Louis XIV in which he agreed to prorogue Parliament in return for French subsidies. Parliament remained prorogued for 15 months between November 1675 and February 1677, and when it finally reassembled, Shaftesbury, Buckingham and their allies tried unsuccessfully to argue that such a long interval meant that the Parliament had legally been dissolved. Behind this spurious argument lay a belief that the Cavalier Parliament was too easily manipulated by Danby and the Crown, and that a more robust bulwark against 'arbitrary government' was needed. The 'Country' peers hoped that fresh elections would increase the number of their allies in the Lower House and thus make the Commons more resistant to government management.[50]

The 'Country' members' commitment to Protestantism, the Church of England and the survival of Parliaments was closely related to sympathy for the Dutch and hostility towards the French, whose regime they perceived as the embodiment of 'popery and arbitrary government'. Many 'Country' members shared Andrew Marvell's fears, expressed in his classic *Account of the Growth of Popery and Arbitrary Government* (1677), which claimed that 'for divers years' a 'design' had been 'carried on' to 'introduce a French slavery, and instead of so pure a religion, to establish the Roman idolatry'.[51] So potent were these fears that in 1677 the Houses voted £584,978 for the navy, and renewed for a further three years the additional excise granted in 1671, but made any further supply conditional on an alliance against France.[52] In a forceful reply that echoed James I in 1621, Charles insisted that Parliament had no brief to determine foreign policy, and this episode again highlighted the potential for dispute between the Crown and the Houses over how far the latter could advise on foreign affairs.[53] Danby helped to defuse parliamentary hostility by securing the marriage of the Duke of York's elder (Protestant) daughter, Princess Mary, who was the likely eventual heir to the throne, to the Dutch Stadholder William of Orange, whereupon the Houses voted to raise an army of 30,000 troops, but for use exclusively against France. They also agreed in principle to grant an extraordinary supply of £1 million for six months, although in the event the poll tax by which this was to be raised yielded only £300,000. It is quite possible that members consciously intended this shortfall, for as one of them told Charles 'I am for keeping the revenue from being too big, for then you'll need Parliaments.'[54]

The financial vicious circle so evident in the early Stuart Parliaments had never been resolved and was now repeating itself. The Houses were reluctant to grant the monarch generous supply lest he pursue an unpopular foreign policy and try to rule without them. Yet the more they withheld supply, or made it conditional upon an anti-Catholic foreign policy, the more likely it became that the King would turn to other sources of revenue. Deprived of prerogative taxes and feudal dues, Charles II was understandably attracted by the subsidies offered by his cousin Louis XIV, whom he liked and admired even if he did not wish to emulate. Louis's demand for the continued prorogation of Parliament (to prevent any military action against France) seemed an acceptable price to pay, especially given the truculence of some 'Country' members. Charles concluded two further secret treaties with Louis, in August 1677 and May 1678. He secured Danby's very reluctant co-operation in these clandestine negotiations at just the time when the latter was ostensibly promoting a Dutch alliance and requesting an army to be used against the French.[55]

These labyrinthine manoeuvres might not have caused Danby's downfall had it not been for the wave of 'popish plot' hysteria triggered off by the bogus allegations of Israel Tonge and Titus Oates in the autumn of 1678. So entrenched was anti-popery in seventeenth-century England that their utterly false stories – of a conspiracy to murder Charles, place James on the throne, and to eradicate English Protestantism, possibly in league with a French invasion – were very widely believed both within Parliament and in the nation at large. Such claims gained added credibility when Sir Edmund Berry Godfrey, the London magistrate before whom Oates had sworn his original deposition, was found dead: many suspected that he had been murdered by Catholics in order to silence him. On 1 November, the two Houses voted unanimously that:

> there hath been, and still is, a damnable and hellish plot contrived and carried on by the popish recusants, for the assassinating and murdering the King, and for subverting the government, and rooting out and destroying the Protestant religion.[56]

This febrile mood within Parliament had two immediate consequences. The first was that Charles had no alternative but to accept 'an Act for the more effectual preserving the King's person and government, by disabling papists from sitting in either House of Parliament'.[57] The Lords voted to grant the Duke of York a special exemption from this second Test Act, and the Commons agreed, albeit by a majority of only 158 votes to 156.[58] The second consequence was the downfall of Danby. So close was the perceived association between 'popery and arbitrary government' that Danby's authoritarian methods, including his attempts to manage Parliament and his reluctance to disband a standing army, led to accusations of 'popery' as well. When, in December 1678, the former ambassador to Paris, Ralph Montagu, revealed Danby's collusion in the secret talks with Louis XIV during 1677–8, the Commons immediately voted to draw up impeachment articles against Danby which included the absurd allegation that he was 'popishly affected'.[59] At this point, frightened at the prospect of further embarrassing disclosures, Charles prorogued Parliament and finally dissolved it on 24 January 1679.[60]

The Cavalier Parliament had met for 18 sessions, a greater number than any other Parliament in English history. At the heart of its uneven relations with the King lay the paradox that its members respected the institution of monarchy but not necessarily specific royal advisers or policies. Majorities in both Houses wished to defend not only the lawful powers of the Crown but also the restored Church of England and the privileges of Parliament. Their determination to uphold these values should not be underestimated,[61] and this was inextricably bound up with a hatred of 'popery and arbitrary government' both at home and abroad. Unfortunately, the King's predilections, especially for a greater measure of religious toleration and a *rapprochement* with France, were widely viewed as manifestations of a malign popish influence. The fact that his wife, mistress, brother and sister-in-law were all Catholics, and that his mother and favourite sister had been as well, only served to reinforce suspicions of sinister Catholic influences close to the monarch. When confronted with apparent evidence of a 'popish plot', the Houses reacted with such passionate concern that Charles finally decided he would be better off working with another Parliament.

The Exclusion Parliaments

Unfortunately for Charles, the next Parliament, which met on 6 March 1679, proved to be even more hostile to the Court than the Cavalier Parliament.[62] This was the first of the three so-called Exclusion Parliaments, although Jonathan Scott has argued that the term was something of a misnomer. The demand that the Catholic Duke of York be excluded from the line of succession only surfaced gradually, and was really a symptom of a deeper fear of 'popery and arbitrary government' in the present as much as in the future.[63] Between 1679 and 1681, this issue disrupted parliamentary politics and put the King at odds with a majority of the Commons and a substantial minority in the Lords. These years saw not only a remarkable mobilisation of public opinion outside Parliament by both the supporters and the opponents of exclusion, but also the emergence of two embryonic parties, the Whigs and the Tories, committed to ideologically contrasted visions of Church and State.

The first concern of the new Parliament was not James's exclusion but the removal of Danby. The Commons proceeded with impeachment articles, but Danby deflected the attack by resigning as Lord Treasurer on condition that he received a royal pardon. Members then considered resorting to a bill of attainder, which as we have seen was a useful and speedy alternative to impeachment because it bypassed common-law procedures.[64] However, Danby again preempted this by accepting imprisonment in the Tower for five years.[65] With Danby thus removed from the political scene, the Houses began to consider precautions that might be taken against a future Catholic monarch. They granted £200,000 towards the disbandment of the standing army, which was finally accomplished during the summer of 1679.[66] They also passed an 'Act for the better securing the liberty of the subjects, and for prevention of imprisonments beyond the seas', generally known as the Habeas Corpus Amendment Act.[67] This required that except in cases of treason or felony, prisoners had to be brought to trial and the cause of their imprisonment stated within a specified period of time. The act also made it illegal to move prisoners from one prison to another,[68] or to evade writs of habeas corpus by detaining them outside England, for example in the Scilly Isles.[69] What had long been regarded as a common-law right was thus enshrined in statute.

It was only in the final days of April 1679 that the issue of exclusion came into the open. James's former secretary Edward Coleman had been executed the previous December following the discovery in his study of correspondence with a number of Jesuits, including Louis XIV's confessor. On 27 April, part of the correspondence, which apparently implicated the Duke of York in negotiations with both France and Rome, was disclosed in the Commons, whereupon the House resolved that James's Catholicism had 'given the greatest countenance and encouragement to the present conspiracies and designs of the papists against the King, and the Protestant religion'.[70] Charles tried to calm the situation by suggesting various 'limitations' on any Catholic successor, including the temporary transference to Parliament of the Crown's rights of ecclesiastical patronage and of appointment to civil, legal and military offices whenever a Catholic occupied the throne.[71] This concession won over some, but a core of hard-liners, led by Shaftesbury, refused to settle for less than James's exclusion from the line of succession. On 15 May an exclusion bill received its first reading in the Commons, and six days later passed its second reading by 207 votes to 128.[72] Charles was furious: exclaiming that he 'would rather submit to anything than endure the gentlemen of the Commons any longer', he prorogued Parliament on 27 May and later dissolved it on 12 July.[73]

Although Charles decided to summon another Parliament in October 1679, during the summer he also resumed talks with the French in the hope of extracting sufficient funds to leave him independent of Parliament. He informed the ambassador, Barillon, that his 'one and only interest was to subsist'.[74] As the autumn approached, public opinion seemed increasingly sympathetic towards Shaftesbury, and this prompted Charles to dismiss him from the Privy Council and to prorogue Parliament until the following January.[75] Shaftesbury and his allies retaliated by calling for an immediate meeting of Parliament and tough measures to defend Protestantism. Denied the forum of Parliament, they orchestrated a petitioning campaign on an unprecedented scale, and during the winter of 1679–80 a 'monster' petition from London and several county petitions were presented to the King. Charles, however, brushed them aside as 'private petitions',[76] and instead insisted that the calling of Parliament lay entirely within his prerogative. Determined to exploit this power to the full, he prorogued Parliament again on 26 January, 15 April, 17 May, 1 July, 22 July and 23 August; not until 21 October 1680 did it finally meet.[77]

By that time, however, there were clear signs of a loyalist backlash. Many people found the mass petitions and the orchestrated campaign to exert pressure on the monarch all too reminiscent of the 1640s. Growing numbers of loyalists signed addresses 'abhorring' Shaftesbury and his followers, defending divine right monarchy and royal prerogative powers, and asserting the subjects' duty of obedience.[78] Nevertheless, when the second Exclusion Parliament eventually assembled, significant numbers in both Houses still supported exclusion.[79] Charles's offer to accept 'any new remedies which shall be proposed that may consist with the preserving the succession of the Crown in its due and legal course of descent' failed to allay doubts, and another exclusion bill quickly passed all three readings in the Commons.[80] However, when it was sent to the Lords Charles personally attended the debates and this, combined with Halifax's unflagging vigour that led him to speak no fewer than 16 times, ensured the bill's defeat by 63 votes to 30.[81] Although it has been suggested that Halifax's interventions were less decisive than has sometimes been claimed, and that they did little more than 'rally a few waverers',[82] the fact that he could speak so many times affords a striking example of how the Committee of the Whole House could work to the Crown's advantage as well as against it.[83] Thwarted by the Lords, the Commons then tried a new approach and offered a supply of £600,000 in return for exclusion. Charles flatly refused and prorogued the Parliament on 10 January 1681.[84]

Underlying the demand for exclusion was a fear of 'popery and arbitrary government' and a corresponding desire to safeguard the future of both Protestantism and Parliaments. In the eyes of many members, the two were seen as inseparably linked: as William Harbord put it, 'ever since King James [I]'s time, popery has been increased when the Parliament has been dissolved, and suppressed whilst they have been sitting'.[85] Shortly after the dissolution, 16 peers led by Essex submitted a petition to Charles expressing their 'unspeakable grief and sorrow' that Parliament had again been 'prorogued and dissolved before it could perfect what was intended for our security'.[86] Parliament was thus seen as an integral part of the nation's defences against the 'popish plot'.

When Charles did summon another Parliament, for the following March, he cleverly exploited his prerogative to determine its venue: realising the strength of exclusionist sentiment in London, he ordered Parliament to meet in the loyalist stronghold of Oxford. As with his repeated prorogations of the second Exclusion Parliament, Charles took every advantage of his prerogative powers in his handling of the crisis. His position was further reinforced on 18 March when he signed a secret treaty with France by which he secured a lump sum of

£40,000 together with further annual grants of about £115,000 for the next three years with the proviso that he did not call another Parliament during that period.[87] These sums, together with a trade boom that brought customs revenues to unprecedentedly high levels,[88] left Charles less dependent upon Parliament than ever before. As we have seen, his need for Parliament was crucially related to the buoyancy of his revenues, and these were now stronger than at any time since 1660.[89] When the Commons rejected his final offer – that when he died William and Mary would serve as regents with James as King in name only – and instead pressed ahead with another exclusion bill, Charles abruptly dissolved the Parliament after it had sat for just one week.[90]

In the end, there were three main reasons why Charles was able to face down the campaign for James's exclusion mounted in these three Parliaments. First, the King stuck to a consistent line throughout the crisis, that although prepared to contemplate some 'limitations' on the powers of a Catholic monarch, even to the extent of appointing regents, he utterly rejected the demand for exclusion. This consistency allowed the second reason to emerge, which was the loyalist backlash in support of the Crown during 1680–1. The fear that '1641 is come again' ultimately proved more potent than the exclusionists' efforts to revive memories of earlier popish plots. By 1681, the overriding memories of 40 years earlier were of petitions and demonstrations and imminent civil war rather than of the Irish Rebellion. Charles played on such feelings in his *Declaration Touching the Reasons that Moved Him to Dissolve the Two Last Parliaments*, issued on 8 April 1681, in which he reminded his subjects that 'religion, liberty and property were all lost and gone when the monarchy was shaken off, and could never be revived till that was restored'. Equally, Charles insisted that:

> no irregularities in Parliaments shall ever make us out of love with Parliaments, which we look upon as the best method for healing the distempers of the kingdom, and the only means to preserve the monarchy in that due credit and respect which it ought to have both at home and abroad.[91]

Third, the combination of financial grants from France and a surge in the Crown's ordinary revenue gave Charles the financial freedom to abandon Parliament when it persisted in demanding James's exclusion. Parliament's 'power of the purse' was thus effectively stymied, and it was the King's newfound financial independence above all which enabled him to dissolve the third Exclusion Parliament so peremptorily.

Perhaps the most lasting consequence of the Exclusion Parliaments was the emergence of the embryonic Whig and Tory parties. These groupings grew out of the 'Court' and 'Country' platforms discernible in both Houses from the mid-1670s onwards, and they displayed a clear continuity of personnel and ideas.[92] However, it was only in 1680–1 that the names Whig and Tory became widely used as labels for identifiable ideological positions, and the intensity of the political crisis served to sharpen allegiances and focus beliefs. The Tories defended the divine right of the monarchy and argued that civil authority derived directly from God; they also staunchly upheld the established Church and generally opposed attempts to introduce greater toleration or comprehension. The Whigs, by contrast, inclined towards a more contractual view of royal power, and believed that strong measures – even resistance – were justifiable against monarchs who betrayed the terms of their coronation oath. They were mostly sympathetic towards nonconformists, and urged the need for a common Protestant front against the popish menace. Each of these views was associated with a corresponding perception of the nature and role of Parliament. Many Tories believed that the greatest danger of 'arbitrary government' came not from the Crown but from republicans and nonconformists who wished to encroach on the monarch's rightful powers, subvert the legitimate succession, and create a 'tyrannous Parliament'. The Whigs, on the other hand, regarded Parliament as the guardian of Protestantism, popular liberties and property rights. The years 1679–81 saw increasingly determined efforts by Tories and especially Whigs to mobilise support both within and outside Parliament. Although these 'parties' were still very fluid, with nothing like modern structures or organisation, each possessed a dedicated core of members willing to co-ordinate strategy and rally others.[93] In particular, Shaftesbury and his followers made extensive use of mass petitioning and also sent circular letters to secure the votes of as many members as possible.[94]

The dissolution of the third Exclusion Parliament left Charles in a stronger position in relation to Parliament than at any stage since the Restoration. The trade boom continued throughout the 1680s and gave him the financial security to rule without Parliaments. In 1684, when Charles flouted the Triennial Act by not calling Parliament after an interval of three years, there was scarcely a murmur of protest. This was partly because the Exclusion Crisis had left uncomfortable memories of parliamentary attempts to put pressure on the monarch, but it also reflected a feeling within the political elite that Charles could be trusted to call another Parliament when necessary. The Whigs were defeated and discredited, and the years after 1681 saw relentless campaigns to drive them out of local government, especially by the granting of revised borough charters that excluded many of them from corporations.[95]

As Paul Halliday has recently argued, during Charles's reign partisan politics became steadily more characteristic both of urban communities and of the dynamics within Parliament.[96] In both Houses core groups of Whigs and Tories were discernible by 1681, and although these lacked many of the features of modern political parties, they nonetheless marked a significant change from the much more fluid, transient groupings of the 1660s. From the mid-1670s, 'Court' and 'Country' platforms were visible in both the Upper and Lower Houses, and these developed during the latter stages of the Exclusion Crisis into embryonic Whig and Tory parties. Bicameral collaboration and co-ordination between like-minded individuals, already evident in earlier decades, became much more frequent and systematic in these years. In general, of the two Houses the Lords remained the more naturally loyal to the Crown, and the Anglican-Royalists together with the bishops provided a base of support which royal ministers, especially Danby, could mobilise. The Commons, with its larger and more shifting membership, was altogether less easy to control, and in dissolving a Parliament the monarch was taking a calculated risk that the next one would be more amenable. The years of Danby's ascendancy saw more vigorous attempts to build up a body of support for the Crown within the Commons than any earlier period. However, this proved counter-productive because it heightened fears of authoritarian government and so helped to strengthen the 'Country'/Whig interest in the Lower House in the three Exclusion Parliaments.[97]

Eventually it was events outside Parliament – soaring royal revenues and a backlash of opinion against exclusion – that enabled Charles to regain the

initiative. He never called another Parliament, yet very few, if any, of his subjects thought that he had either the desire or the capability to establish a
lengthy period of Personal Rule, and they did not regard him as an enemy of
Parliaments. Like James I, Charles II had his specific differences with
Parliaments but was nevertheless willing to keep working with them: indeed,
he attended parliamentary sittings more frequently than any other Stuart
monarch, and declared them 'better than a play'.[98] By the same token, the vast
majority of members did not wish to curtail the royal prerogative but to defend
the nation against the threat of 'popery and arbitrary government'.[99] Several
explanations have been advanced for the docility of the political elite between
1681 and 1685. Some historians have suggested that most people essentially
trusted Charles and recognised that he lacked the energy or single-mindedness
needed to rule in a consistently authoritarian way.[100] Others have argued that
the perceived danger of 'popery and arbitrary government' was if anything
greater than before, but that the Exclusion Crisis had so discredited those most
exercised by the issue that little could be done about it.[101] Perhaps the most
plausible interpretation is that the backlash of opinion during these years of
'Tory Reaction' was sufficiently strong that most of the political elite thought
Charles less dangerous than his leading opponents. As a result, the absence of
a Parliament to resist 'popery and arbitrary government' seemed less alarming,
hence the lack of outcry when Charles flouted the Triennial Act. However, following his death in February 1685, events suddenly took a dramatic new twist,
for as in 1625 the new monarch was strikingly different from his predecessor.

James II and Parliament

James II's character was naturally authoritarian and inflexible, and this was
plainly reflected in his attitude towards Parliament. His overriding objective as
King was to remove the penal laws against Catholics, convinced that this
would unleash a wave of voluntary conversions. He recognised that such a
reform could only permanently be achieved by repealing the Test Acts, and
although he was prepared to use the Crown's dispensing and suspending powers to get round those acts in the short term, in the longer term the likelihood
(until June 1688) that he would be succeeded by a Protestant made statutory
repeal essential. To that extent he needed Parliament. But from the very beginning of his reign, he was equally determined not to become beholden to
Parliaments, and he recognised that the Crown's financial strength was crucial
in making him independent of them. Only two days after his accession he
informed the French ambassador:

> I have resolved to call a Parliament immediately and to assemble it in the
> month of May. I shall publish at the same time a declaration that I am to
> maintain myself in the enjoyment of the same revenues the King my
> brother had. Without this proclamation for a Parliament I should hazard
> too much by taking possession directly of the revenue which was estab-
> lished during the lifetime of my deceased brother. It is a decisive stroke
> for me to enter into possession and enjoyment. For hereafter it will be
> much more easy for me either to put off the assembling of Parliament or
> to maintain myself by other means which may appear more convenient
> for me.[102]

James had correctly perceived that the strength of his position in relation to Parliament was a direct function of the health of his revenues. His plan was a shrewd attempt to exploit the Crown's financial strength during Charles II's later years, and at first it went like clockwork.

Popular loyalty to the Crown remained high, and the Parliament that assembled on 19 May 1685 was overwhelmingly Tory, with only 57 Whigs in a Commons of 525. This contrasted sharply with the three Exclusion Parliaments, where the number of 'Court'/Tory members never rose above about 220.[103] Luck further strengthened James's hand during the spring as news arrived of rebellions led by Monmouth in the west country and by Argyll in the Highlands. These threats prompted Parliament in June to vote James for life all the revenues that Charles had enjoyed during his lifetime.[104] These yielded around £1.6 million a year by 1688. James was also granted other extraordinary supply in the form of various impositions for periods of five or eight years, which took his gross annual income during his reign to over £2 million.[105] This settlement ensured that, as J. P. Kenyon observed, James was 'the first monarch since Henry VIII to enjoy financial independence'.[106] The Houses also permitted James to expand the standing army, and by the end of the year it comprised nearly 20,000 troops.[107] In the light of their attempts to persuade Charles to disband his army in the late 1670s, this was a remarkable indication of the Houses' confidence in the new monarch.

Ironically, it was over the officers of that army that the first warning signs appeared during the short second session of 9–20 November 1685. In his opening speech, James calmly announced that he had used his dispensing power to exempt nearly 90 Catholics from the Test Acts and commission them as officers in his army.[108] Members of both Houses protested that such commissions were illegal, and James angrily prorogued Parliament after less than two weeks.[109] The following year he turned to the judges to uphold the dispensing power, and secured a favourable verdict in the collusive action known as Godden vs. Hales.[110] In the months that followed James made increasingly widespread use of his dispensing power. Then, in April 1687, he issued a Declaration of Indulgence that suspended the Test and Corporation Acts and all other penal laws against both Catholics and Protestant nonconformists, a suspension that was made conditional upon parliamentary approval.[111] As we have seen, the royal suspending power had already become highly contentious under Charles II, and James was justifiably convinced that his first Parliament would never agree to such use of it. He therefore dissolved that Parliament in July 1687[112] and the following autumn set about engineering the return of another which he hoped would be sympathetic to repeal.

Historians remain divided over the feasibility of James's attempt to 'pack' Parliament. At one end of the spectrum lies J. R. Jones, who sees this as perhaps the most disastrous of all James's policies and the biggest single reason why some of his subjects became 'reluctant revolutionaries'.[113] At the other end, J. R. Western argued that the campaign's failure was by no means a foregone conclusion and that James's capacity to win support, or at least acquiescence, should not be underestimated.[114] The evidence is difficult to assess. In October 1687, the King instructed Lords Lieutenant to ask JPs and Deputy Lieutenants three questions: first, 'if in case he shall be chosen knight of the shire, or burgess of a town, when the King shall think fit to call a Parliament, whether he will be for taking off the penal laws and the tests'; second, 'whether he will assist and contribute to the election of such members as shall be for taking off the penal laws and tests'; and third, 'whether he will support the King's declaration for liberty of conscience by living friendly with those of all persuasions, as subjects of the same prince and good Christians ought to do'.[115] The responses were very mixed. Over a quarter, mostly Catholics and dissenters, replied in the affirmative, about a third answered in the negative, and the remainder, the 'doubtfuls', were evasive, although some made their reservations pretty clear.[116] Nevertheless, the instinctive attitude of most of the political elite was one of deference to the Crown, and this encouraged James and his advisers to think that enough 'doubtfuls' could be manipulated or coerced to produce a pliable Parliament. When, in April 1688, special agents were sent into the localities to test opinion and assess the outcome of the elections that were being planned for the following autumn, they reported that a two-thirds majority in support of the King was a real possibility.[117]

Ironically, what finally destroyed James's attempt to 'pack' Parliament was the way in which he reacted to this promising news. For the agents' reports encouraged him to reissue the Declaration of Indulgence with instructions for it to be read in all Anglican churches on two successive Sundays. This move triggered off the disastrous publicity associated with the petition and subsequent trial of Archbishop Sancroft and six bishops.[118] That trial, and the birth of a Catholic heir in June 1688, were crucial in precipitating the invitation to William of Orange to intervene. The real importance of the attempt to 'pack' Parliament lies not so much in its viability as in the fact that it provided a vital pretext for William of Orange's invasion. William maintained that his expedition in November 1688 was 'intended for no other design but to have a free and lawful Parliament assembled as soon as is possible'.[119] In December, as William advanced towards London, James agreed to call a free Parliament for 15 January 1689. But by then it was too late. James's supporters melted away and his own state of mind deteriorated alarmingly; in the end he played into his opponents' hands by fleeing to France. An Assembly of Peers invited William to take over the reins of government and advised him to call elections for a Convention 'for the preservation of our religion, rights, laws, liberties and properties', and 'the establishment of these things upon such sure and legal foundations that they may not be in danger of being again subverted'.[120] An irregular assembly of London aldermen and former members of the Commons echoed this request, and on 29 December William duly issued the writs ordering elections.[121] It is thus a remarkable fact that no Parliament sat at any stage in the year 1688. However, Parliament was to play a central role in constructing a settlement in the wake of James II's flight.

The Revolution Settlement

The Convention which assembled on 22 January 1689 contained in the Commons roughly 319 Whigs and 232 Tories, while in the Lords there was a slight Tory majority. Both Houses were bitterly divided over both what to do next and how to interpret the events of the previous year.[122] The staunchest Whigs upheld a strictly contractual position and asserted that James had forfeited his Crown because he had 'broken the fundamental laws of the constitution'. The most hard-line Tories abhorred the idea of a breach in the legitimate line of succession and insisted that James remained King by right if not in fact. In the middle stood a large number of moderate Whigs and moderate Tories who accepted that whatever the precise legalities of the situation, James had 'abdicated' the throne. This view commanded a majority in the Commons but, as we have seen, proved offensive to the Tory majority in the Lords.[123] William finally resolved the deadlock by threatening to go home unless he was made King, and by offering two sops to Tory consciences: he accepted that Mary would share the title, although not the power, of monarch jointly with him, and he agreed that Anne would remain next in line to the throne rather than any children that he might have by a second wife if Mary died. These gestures won over enough Tories to secure majorities in both Houses behind a resolution that James had 'abdicated' and that the throne was therefore 'vacant'.[124]

That resolution formed the basis for the settlement that followed. A committee of 16 Whigs and six Tories drew up a Declaration of Rights that amounted to a 'lowest common denominator' on which most members of each House could agree. William had stated that 'he would not take the crown upon conditions', and the Declaration deliberately omitted the more contentious Whig demands, such as the repeal of the militia acts and stricter guarantees for the 'frequent sitting' of Parliaments. Had they been adopted, those demands would have strengthened parliamentary control over the armed forces and over the timing and duration of Parliament's sessions in ways that would have anticipated later developments.[125] But in an effort to minimise division both within each House and between the two Houses, the more controversial demands were left out and instead the Declaration comprised a list of 'undoubted rights and liberties' that turned out to be fairly vague. The monarch's suspending power was declared illegal. So too was the dispensing power, although here a majority in the Lords registered their loyalty to the Crown by insisting on the insertion of the qualifying phrase 'as it hath been assumed and exercised of late'.[126] It was stipulated that 'Parliaments ought to be held frequently,' and that Catholics 'shall be excluded, and be for ever incapable to inherit, possess or enjoy the crown', although no mechanisms were suggested to enforce either requirement. Tory consciences were mollified by the omission of any statement that James had broken a contract or been resisted or deposed, and William and Mary were never referred to as the 'rightful and lawful heirs' to the throne. These silences allowed Tory members to believe that James remained King by right even if William and Mary were monarchs in fact, and Whig members to believe that James had broken his contract and that a new contract had now been drawn up. The moderate majority cared more about achieving a stable settlement than about the constitutional niceties. All the most contentious issues or phrases were studiously avoided, and this was the key to the Declaration's success. Despite what some Whigs may have thought, it was never a contract. On 13 February 1689, the Declaration was simply read to William and Mary after they had already been offered the throne, and their proclamation as King and Queen the following day was not made conditional upon their agreement to it.[127] Later, in December 1689, the Declaration was enacted as the Bill of Rights. This had the force of a statute, and could be pleaded at law against the Crown.[128]

The Bill of Rights was never a binding contract in that, like any other statute, it could be amended or repealed by a subsequent statute, although in practice very little of it has been repealed. It needs stressing, however, that several other aspects of the Revolution Settlement were at least as significant in affecting the standing of Parliament and its relationship with the Crown. When William and Mary were crowned on 11 April 1689 they took a revised coronation oath in which they swore 'to govern the people of this kingdom of England ... according to *the statutes in Parliament agreed on*, and the laws and customs of the same'. This replaced the form of words taken by their predecessors, who had sworn to 'confirm to the people of England *the laws and customs to them granted by the Kings of England*'. The new coronation oath explicitly recognised the legislative supremacy of King-in-Parliament for the first time and was thus at last brought into line with what had long been the constitutional reality.[129] William and Mary also swore, unlike previous monarchs, to 'maintain the laws of God, the true profession of the gospel, and the Protestant reformed religion established by law'.[130] This ruled out the possibility of monarchs being able to overthrow the established Church or impose their personal faith on the nation as a whole, and the principle of *cuius regio, eius religio* was thus repudiated. Another contentious aspect of royal powers was curtailed by the Mutiny Act of March 1689. This confirmed and elaborated upon a clause in the Bill of Rights which stated that 'the raising or keeping [of] a standing army within this kingdom in time of peace unless it be with consent of Parliament is against the law'. The act also permitted the punishment of mutiny and the right to hold courts martial; however, this was for only a limited period and Parliament could therefore exercise considerable control over military discipline and the army's existence by refusing to pass a new act.[131] Hitherto, the only controls that Parliament had been able to exercise over the existence of a standing army consisted of attempts to 'appropriate' revenue for its maintenance or disbandment; otherwise these powers had lain entirely within the royal discretion. Henceforth, however, statute required that parliamentary consent be given for such an army to exist.

But perhaps the most important of all the ways in which the Revolution affected Parliament's relationship with the Crown was the financial settlement. Here the conscious aim was to keep the monarch dependent upon Parliament and, as we saw in Chapter 4, this was an objective shared by Tories as well as Whigs.[132] Most members of both Houses felt that settlements such as those given to Charles II and James II were too generous and that Parliament's survival could only be properly secured by keeping the monarch on a tight rein. But there was only so much that a statutory settlement could safeguard, and what really strengthened the 'power of the purse' during the final decade of the seventeenth century were the massive costs of England's involvement in an international war.

All in all, the Revolution Settlement enacted a number of significant adjustments in the relationship between the Crown and the two Houses of Parliament. If some of these – notably the reworded coronation oath – simply made explicit what was already established in reality, others, especially those concerning the Crown's military powers and its capacity to influence the nation's religion, represented genuine departures from previous arrangements. These measures were enshrined in statute, and their cumulative effect was to diminish certain powers that had hitherto lain within the royal discretion and to extend parliamentary controls over government action. It was no accident that at the heart of these changes lay a radically revised financial settlement. We have seen throughout this and earlier chapters that the financial relationship between Crown and Parliament crucially affected their political and constitutional positions. The Restoration Settlement had reconstructed, in a slightly adapted form, the pre-Civil War fiscal system. The inherent instability of these arrangements, and particularly the unpredictable fluctuations in royal revenues and expenditure, could work to the political advantage of either the monarch or the Houses depending on changing circumstances, as was evident during the reigns of Charles II and James II. But the Revolution Settlement opened the way for a fundamental overhaul of the financial system, and that in turn was intimately connected to a profound transformation of the nature and role of Parliaments.

|10|

Conclusion

Epilogue: Parliaments under William and Anne

The years immediately after the Revolution of 1688–9 saw further profound changes in the relationship between Crown and Parliament. Instead of meeting only intermittently, Parliament became a permanent institution of government that has met every year since 1689. Behind this transformation lay not just the Revolution Settlement but also the monarch's dependence on parliamentary supply in a period of almost constant war. This necessitated the abandonment of the financial system that had existed since the fourteenth century and the creation of new arrangements in which regular parliamentary grants became the basis of all royal and State finance. This in turn weakened the Crown's political position by leaving it unable to resist many of Parliament's constitutional demands. Between 1689 and 1701, a number of key statutory restrictions were imposed on powers that had hitherto been regarded as within the Crown's discretion, such as the monarch's choice of personal religion, or the determination of foreign policy. The permanence of Parliaments, and the increased regularity of general elections following the Triennial Act of 1694, also fostered a new culture in which the dichotomy between the Whig and Tory parties became the principal characteristic of parliamentary politics. At the same time, Parliament increasingly eclipsed the Court as the primary focus of political activity and intrigue. The Parliaments that emerged during these two reigns were thus significantly different from their predecessors. Characterised by a more tightly defined relationship with a constitutionally limited monarchy, and dominated by the politics of party, they began to display features that pointed the way to future developments.

We saw in Chapter 4 that the immense cost of the Nine Years War and the War of the Spanish Succession necessitated fundamental fiscal reforms that transformed England from a 'demesne state' into a 'tax state'. During the reigns of William and Anne only 3 per cent of national income was raised from non-parliamentary sources, and virtually all revenue was derived from either direct or indirect taxation voted by Parliament. This gave the Houses far more control over the Crown than hitherto. William was unable to resist demands that parliamentary supply should be 'appropriated' for the purposes for which it had been granted. The Houses also asserted their greatly strengthened 'power of the purse' by 'tacking' specific political demands onto revenue bills. From 1690 a Commission of Public Accounts investigated expenditure and mismanagement with a rigour and thoroughness far beyond the brief experiment of the later 1660s, and was able to ensure that 'appropriation' was actually enforced. From 1698 the costs of government were met by a parliamentary grant known as the 'civil list'. The ancient idea that the monarch should 'live of his own' was thus discarded, and the Crown's personal debts were subsumed within a funded National Debt underwritten by Parliament. This effectively made Parliament the guarantor of public credit, and without this the government would never have been able to borrow on the massive scale necessitated by war. Parliament's enhanced financial powers thus underpinned a mobilisation of national resources exceeded only by the Dutch Republic.[1]

These fiscal changes not only secured Parliament's permanence as an institution; they also gave the Houses the necessary leverage to wrest a series of constitutional concessions from the Crown. In 1694, after vetoing it the previous year, William finally assented to a new Triennial Act which stipulated that 'henceforth a Parliament shall be holden once in three years at the least', and that 'within three years at the farthest from and after the determination of every other Parliament, legal writs under the Great Seal shall be issued by directions of [the monarch] for calling, assembling and holding another new Parliament'.[2] This act restricted the Crown's powers of summoning and dissolving Parliament at will far more effectively than the 1664 act had done. A further act of 1696 provided for 'the continuing meeting and sitting of a Parliament in case of the death or demise of His Majesty, his heirs and successors'. This statute was prompted by Sir John Fenwick's attempt to assassinate William, and it permitted Parliament to continue sitting for up to six months after the sovereign's death rather than being automatically dissolved by it.[3] Another notable development was the sequence of 'place clauses' passed between 1694 and 1706 to exclude several thousand office-holders from Parliament.[4] These clauses were 'tacked' onto various bills after William had vetoed a place bill intended to counter 'the secret advices of particular persons who may have private interests of their own'.[5] In practice they began to introduce a separation between the executive and the legislature that had been foreign to concepts of English government until then. Henceforth, for example, no revenue official could sit in either House, and impartial parliamentary appraisal of the Crown's fiscal management was thereby promoted. Fears that offices or pensions might be used to undermine parliamentary independence were not in themselves new, and had surfaced particularly in relation to Danby's managerial techniques.[6] However, the fact that Parliament met annually after 1689 led to heightened fears that the 'influence of the Crown' could become a much more permanent problem, particularly in view of the persistent suspicions about some of William's advisers.

Perhaps the most remarkable step in this process of parliamentary restriction of the monarch's powers was the 1701 'Act for the further limitation of the Crown, and better securing the rights and liberties of the subject', usually known as the Act of Settlement.[7] The death of Princess Anne's last surviving child, William, Duke of Gloucester, in July 1700 plunged the future of the succession into doubt. The Act of Settlement bypassed 57 Catholics and vested the succession in the Protestant Electress Sophia of Hanover and her descendants. As under Henry VIII, the power of statute to determine the succession was clearly demonstrated. The Act of Settlement also imposed several highly significant constraints on royal actions that were to come into operation on Anne's death, but which actually reflected deep unhappiness with certain aspects of

William's own rule. The Houses felt that his conduct of foreign policy had been far too secretive: they had, for instance, only found out that he had signed the two international Partition Treaties of 1698 and 1700 after the second had been concluded. The suspicion lingered in some (especially Tory) circles that England had been dragged into conflicts that served Dutch interests more than her own. The Act therefore stipulated that if any future monarch were 'not . . . a native of this kingdom of England', then the nation was 'not obliged to engage in any war for the defence of any dominions or territories which do not belong to the crown of England, without the consent of Parliament'. This was a significant statutory restriction on the sovereign's powers to determine foreign policy. Many in both Houses mistrusted William's Dutch advisers, such as Hans Willem Bentinck, Duke of Portland, and feared the influence of secret advisers who did not necessarily occupy official positions. The Act stated that 'all matters and things relating to the well governing of this kingdom, which are properly cognizable in the Privy Council by the laws and customs of this realm, shall be transacted there'. The requirements of the Place Acts were further reinforced by a clause that 'no person who has an office or place of profit under the King, or receives a pension from the Crown, shall be capable of serving as a member of the House of Commons'. The Crown's control over the judiciary was also weakened. In February 1692 William had vetoed a bill stating that judges would hold office for as long as they performed their duties well (*quamdiu se bene gesserint*) rather than during the monarch's good pleasure (*durante bene placito*).[8] In practice, however, he never violated this principle, and it gained statutory authority for the first time in the Act of Settlement. It is also worth noting that although judges could not be arbitrarily removed by the sovereign, 'upon the address of both Houses of Parliament it may be lawful to remove them'. The powers of the Houses in relation to the judiciary were thus enhanced just as those of the Crown were diminished. Likewise, it was stipulated that a royal pardon could no longer 'be pleadable to an impeachment by the Commons in Parliament', a change that made Parliament's hand in such cases considerably stronger than it had been hitherto.

The Act of Settlement in addition affirmed that 'the laws of England are the birthright of the people thereof, and all the Kings and Queens, who shall ascend the throne of this realm, ought to administer the government of the same according to the said laws'. This included all the laws 'for securing the established religion', and to that end the Act required 'that whosoever shall hereafter come to the possession of this crown, shall join in communion with the Church of England, as by law established'. By the same token, all those who were reconciled to or in communion with the Church of Rome, or who married one such, were debarred from occupying the throne. This requirement – which has remained in place to the present day – marked the complete reversal of the principle of *cuius regio, eius religio*: instead of the monarch's religion determining that of the nation, the monarch had to conform to the established Protestant Church of England. The monarch's personal faith was thus directly constrained by statute in a way that abruptly ended the freedom that had previously existed in this area. It thereby also removed at a stroke one of the most intractable sources of political instability that had dogged seventeenth-century England.

The years between 1689 and 1701 thus saw a readjustment of the relationship between Crown and Parliament in ways that pointed away from the situation that had existed for most of the seventeenth century, and before. Statutes now prescribed the religion of the monarch, limited the control over foreign policy wielded by a non-English sovereign, and protected the judiciary from arbitrary royal dismissal. Regular parliamentary taxation funded civil government and guaranteed the newly established National Debt. The laws were explicitly recognised as the product of Crown-in-Parliament and the fiction that they were made by the monarch (albeit with the advice of the two Houses) largely disappeared. Parliaments became what they have remained ever since: a permanent part of the machinery of government whose continued existence was ensured not only by a Triennial Act with real teeth but also by their own financial indispensability.

These constitutional reforms were accompanied by major changes in the nature of political groupings within the Houses: henceforth parliamentary politics were shaped primarily by the dichotomy between the Whig and Tory parties. Although these terms first gained common currency during the later stages of the Exclusion Crisis,[9] the actual formation of two 'parties' was mainly a result of the Revolution of 1688–9. In part, this was because, as we saw in the previous chapter, the Revolution Settlement had succeeded in encompassing different viewpoints: as a result, Whigs and Tories supported it for different reasons, read different things into it, and hoped that it would subsequently develop further in their own preferred direction. A second reason for the growth of parties was Parliament's new-found permanence after 1689 which enabled them to acquire a more settled existence and membership than the shifting factional groups of earlier decades. Furthermore, the fact that general elections were held in 1690, 1695, 1698, 1701 (twice), 1702, 1705, 1708, 1710, 1713 and 1715, meant that party allegiances soon spread into local politics and came to influence many aspects of religious and social life.

In essence, the division between Whig and Tory members reflected different interpretations of the Revolution that were in turn associated with contrasted visions of both Church and State.[10] Most Whigs believed in a contract between ruler and subjects, and argued that rulers who breached that contract could legitimately be resisted. They regarded Parliament as a crucial defence against royal authoritarianism and a vital guarantor of popular liberties, property rights and the Protestant religion. Fervently committed to a Protestant succession, they were the principal movers behind the 1701 Act of Settlement, and the following year they promoted an Abjuration Act that required all office-holders and members of Parliament to take an oath forswearing allegiance to 'the pretended Prince of Wales'.[11] The Whigs welcomed William as a Protestant hero, and believed that all Protestants, both at home and abroad, should unite against the menace of 'popery and arbitrary government' personified by Louis XIV. This outlook made them sympathetic to dissenters and impatient with the penalties that had been imposed on them in order to safeguard the established Church. For Whigs, 1688–9 represented a 'glorious' deliverance from Catholic despotism, and they regarded limitations on the monarch, a strengthening of Parliament's position, and greater toleration for dissenters as the finest parts of the revolutionary inheritance.

The Tories took a rather different view on all these issues. Most of them still clung to the doctrine of monarchy by divine right, and they detested any idea of resisting or deposing a sovereign. They remained committed to the axiom of 'passive obedience and non-resistance' which had served to inhibit active opposition to James. Although most Tories accepted William and Anne as monarchs *de facto*, many found it difficult in conscience to recognise them as monarchs by right. In 1696, when Fenwick's assassination plot led the Whigs to propose an oath of association by which all office-holders and members of Parliament would acknowledge William as the 'rightful and lawful King of these realms', nearly 20 Tories in the Lords and over 90 in the Commons refused to take the oath. This prompted a series of purges of Tories from the county lieutenancies and the commission of the peace.[12] Many Tories still believed in the principle of an indefeasible hereditary succession, and although they went along with the Act of Settlement they did so more out of a recognition that there was no realistic alternative than out of much positive enthusiasm. They remained sceptical about William and had no desire to fight his wars for him: they preferred a 'blue-water' foreign policy in which the main emphasis lay on protecting the Atlantic seaboard and the colonies rather than the campaigns on the European mainland favoured by the Whigs. Just as Tories were suspicious of calls to help international Protestantism, so they were anxious to protect the established Church from Protestant dissenters as much as from Catholics. Tories rallied to the slogan 'the Church in danger' and were horrified at the way in which nonconformists could gain public office in return for taking the Anglican communion once a year: eventually, in 1711, they secured an act proscribing this practice of 'occasional conformity'.[13]

In each House, the Whig and Tory parties gradually crystallised around these contrasting platforms during the reigns of William and Anne. Under William they remained what John Morrill has called 'political invertebrates', fairly loose, amorphous groupings.[14] At several stages during the 1690s, especially in 1690–3 and 1697–1700, the divisions in both Houses between Whigs and Tories were overshadowed by that between Court and Country.[15] The latter were even more inchoate and transient alignments, and usually arose over issues such as the accountability (especially fiscal) of the executive, the role of placemen, the conduct of the war and the level of taxation. People's views on these questions did not necessarily coincide with Whig and Tory allegiances, and both parties had their own Court and Country wings. Only gradually did the Whigs become more associated with the Court and the Tories with the Country. Furthermore, the various constitutional reforms of William's reign largely resolved the issues over which Court/Country divisions most typically opened up, and as a result under Anne the Whig/Tory duality came to the fore.[16]

The two parties became steadily more coherent and organised. The research of Geoffrey Holmes in particular has revealed that during Anne's reign most members of both Houses had an identifiable Whig or Tory allegiance which they adhered to on the majority of occasions and on a wide range of different issues. The evidence of division lists suggests that fewer than 20 per cent of members voted across party lines. This was true of the Lords as well as the Commons, and peers can be found entrusting their proxies to others of similar outlook: out of a total of 111 entries in the Proxy Book for 1704–7, there were only five instances where a Tory peer left his proxy to a Whig or vice versa. At first the Whigs were probably the more tightly organised, and the Tories emulated their methods by co-ordinating their activities in both Houses. Each party gradually developed the practice of 'whipping' and of sending circular letters to members in order to maximise support. Although these networks lacked the tight organisation characteristic of modern political parties, they were nevertheless considerably more active, defined and consistent than the bicameral factions of earlier decades.[17]

This growth of parties within Parliament naturally affected local politics as well, and the increasingly frequent general elections were dominated by conflicts between Whigs and Tories. Growing economic prosperity meant that the electorate steadily expanded throughout these years, and it is probable that during Anne's reign at least one in four adult males in England and Wales (around 300,000 men) had the right to vote. W. A. Speck's analysis of pollbooks has shown that in parliamentary elections in this period the majority of voters cast their votes along party lines.[18] Electoral contests based on party allegiances became an accepted part of political life. Whereas in the early seventeenth century contested elections were the exception and *selections* the norm, in the years between 1660 and 1689 there were normally about 60 or 70 contests in each general election. This trend increased dramatically after the Revolution of 1688–9, and only 19 of the 269 constituencies in England and Wales saw no contest during any of the ten general elections held between 1695 and 1715. Such contests frequently led to acrimonious scenes and sometimes to actual violence. They reflected a growing popular awareness of political issues and party rivalries, albeit often in a fairly crude form.[19] In the light of all these developments, it was no wonder that contemporaries spoke in this period of the 'rage of party'.

The ways in which successive monarchs reacted to these parties in turn affected the changing relationship between Crown and Parliament. Among the most significant political consequences of James's flight and William's arrival was the fact that the Tories, hitherto the Crown's staunchest supporters, became transformed into the opposition party, while the Whigs, by nature the more sceptical about monarchy in the abstract, found themselves the more sympathetic to William's position and policies. William reportedly once told Sunderland that 'he believed the Whigs loved him best, but they did not love monarchy; and although the Tories did not like him so well as the others, yet as they were zealous for monarchy, he thought they would serve his government best'.[20] In general, William preferred to work with the Tories, but sometimes it suited his European strategy to promote Whigs, and this explains the dominance of the 'Junto', led by Somers, Wharton, Montagu and Russell, between 1694 and 1699.[21] Anne strove to remain above party conflict and once remarked: 'I pray God keep me out of the hands of both of them.'[22] However, the effect of the Crown's attempts to stay aloof was in fact to marginalise the Court and to enhance the importance of parliamentary politics. The Crown's reduced finances greatly diminished the amount of patronage on offer at Court:[23] as a result people looked elsewhere for advancement, and increasingly Parliament and the Cabinet (which came into existence as an inner circle of the Privy Council during William's prolonged absences on the continent)[24] became the principal foci of political debate and intrigue. The fact that Parliament was sitting for so much more of the time made careful management even more important than before, and the Crown came to rely increasingly on 'managers' such as Sunderland under William, and then Godolphin between 1702 and 1710, and Sir Robert Harley after 1710. These figures acted as intermediaries between the monarch and the parties in the Lords and Commons, and they played a vital role in rallying support for the Crown and steering its business through the two Houses. In order to fulfil that role, it was essential for them to enjoy the confidence of majorities in both Lords and Commons, and it was this parliamentary principle – rather than the traditional one of royal favour – that later, during the long ascendancy of Sir Robert Walpole from 1721 until 1742, became the basis of the office of Prime Minister.[25]

By the opening decade of the eighteenth century, Parliament was thus a significantly different institution from that which had existed for most of the seventeenth century. It was still, as it had always been, part of an organic system of royal government rather than something opposed to it. Yet within that body politic it was now an enlarged, more salient and more authoritative organ. Augustan Parliaments possessed an institutional permanence, founded on financial necessity, that – with the possible exception of the Long Parliament – was unknown to their early Stuart predecessors. This enabled them to secure important constitutional limitations of the Crown's powers that restricted the scope of the monarch's discretionary powers. The questions that had disrupted so many seventeenth-century Parliaments – especially financial supply, the religious sympathies of the monarch, the conduct of foreign policy, and the relationship between royal powers and the rule of law – were all subjected to statutory reform and regulation in ways that profoundly changed the nature of English political life. These constitutional limitations on the Crown were accompanied by a new political culture characterised by a Whig/Tory dichotomy that formed the basis for what became the two-party system. Whigs and Tories bickered over issues that were very different from those that had characterised the period before 1689, and their debates were conducted in relation to a Revolution Settlement that commanded wide cross-party acceptance. Party debates also took place in a context where Parliaments were increasingly the main focus of political life rather than an extension of other institutions that had the advantage of more regular meetings. All in all, the Parliaments of William and Anne usher us into a new world that had more in common with later developments than with the medieval and Tudor Parliaments. They therefore mark an appropriate place at which to conclude this book and to take stock of how far Parliaments had changed since 1603.

Assessment: change and continuity

The story of Parliaments in seventeenth-century England presents a series of variations on an institutional theme, shaped above all by the on-going relationship between successive rulers and their leading subjects. This relationship was directly reflected in parliamentary proceedings, no less during the republic than under royal government. Stuart Parliaments represented a continuation of their medieval and Tudor predecessors, in that they acted as an agency of government which brought together the diverse elements of the political nation. That remained the case throughout the seventeenth century, and a fuller appreciation of this has been among the most salutary consequences of 'revisionist' accounts of parliamentary history. Yet it is important not to lose sight of the fact that the Stuart period did leave a lasting mark on Parliament. The traumatic upheavals of the Civil Wars and Interregnum could never be forgotten and they shaped the nature of Restoration politics, while the Revolution of 1688–9 and the years that followed saw a significant reworking of the relationship between Crown and Parliament. It would be misleading to exaggerate the extent of this shift, or to see it as a linear process. It is nevertheless true that Parliament was not the same institution by the end of the century as at the beginning. Whereas the early Stuart Parliaments echoed those of the sixteenth century and the Middle Ages, Parliaments of the late seventeenth century clearly began to anticipate subsequent developments. This was a difference of emphasis rather than a dramatic watershed, yet its effects were plainly discernible. By the Augustan Age, a perceptible shift had occurred: Parliament looked less like the creation of individual monarchs, meeting and dispersing at their whim, exercising justice in their name, and acting as an extension of other conciliar bodies, and more like a permanent institution of government, an indispensable financial organ and guarantor of the National Debt, a more central arena of political action, and a more effective constraint on royal actions than before. This process involved a complex blend of continuity and change, and in order to analyse it closely we need to consider various aspects of Parliament's functions in turn.

One of the most striking developments during the final years of the seventeenth century was the tighter statutory definition of the relationship between the Crown and Parliament. This had the effect of diminishing the monarch's discretionary powers over Parliaments, especially with regard to the timing and duration of their sessions. Whereas until 1689 they had in practice been called, prorogued and dissolved at the monarch's will (regardless of the 1664 Triennial Act), thereafter they sat annually, and from 1694 a tougher Triennial Act ensured that a new Parliament met at least every three years. Parliament remained an agency of government, but one whose existence was now guaranteed rather than dependent upon royal discretion. There was thus no possibility of any repetition of Charles I's Personal Rule, and Parliament's permanence was secured more fully than those lone voices who had advocated annual Parliaments under the early Stuarts could have hoped. During the 1690s statutes limited other areas of royal authority, including those relating to the tenure of judges and the conduct of treason trials. The Act of Settlement marked the culmination of this process, and Parliament's new-found permanence enabled it to make sure that the Crown abided by statutory restrictions on such matters as choice of personal religion or the management of foreign policy. The uncertainties that had hitherto surrounded the Houses' right to discuss these issues were thus resolved, thereby removing some of the sources of tension that had dogged so many Stuart Parliaments.

These reforms, together with Parliament's permanence, meant that it began to appear less like an extension of the Crown's other conciliar bodies and more like a watchdog over them. This was not a sudden departure: the 'Great Council' had always claimed that one of its central roles was to ensure that the sovereign was rightfully advised, and one major source of political tension under the Stuarts, and especially under Charles I, stemmed from the suspicions that many members of both Houses harboured towards the monarchs' chosen advisers. Impeachment provided one way of removing 'evil counsellors', and after its revival in 1621 it was used periodically throughout the rest of the century. Where it proved problematic, a bill of attainder allowed the principles of the common law to be bypassed entirely by what amounted to a statutory death-sentence. But these weapons were deployed against those already in office; during the 1640s the Houses never secured their demands to approve the monarch's appointment of advisers, nor did those demands resurface after the Restoration. However, from 1690 onwards stricter controls were established that allowed the Houses to hold the Crown's financial officials to account. These controls were accompanied by a series of place clauses that excluded various categories of government officials from the two Houses and thus began to forge a novel distinction between the legislature and the executive.

Behind this official accountability, and indeed Parliament's new-found permanence as an institution, lay its fundamentally altered place within England's financial system. For much of the seventeenth century, relations between Crown and Parliament were bedevilled by a creaking fiscal system that had changed little since the fourteenth century. Parliamentary supply formed one of two main branches of the royal revenues, and the expectation remained that it would only be needed in particular circumstances such as wartime. This 'extraordinary' revenue declined steadily in value throughout the late Tudor and early Stuart periods, with the result that monarchs looked to alternative, non-parliamentary, sources in order to make ends meet. Parliaments faced the dilemma of granting supply and thereby reducing their bargaining power over the Crown, or withholding what was in any case a diminishing asset, thus risking driving the monarch towards extra-parliamentary levies. That tension formed a central theme throughout the Parliaments of James I and Charles I. The paper constitutions of the Interregnum began the practice of granting specified sums to the Lord Protector, and the Restoration Settlement perpetuated this principle. However, the sources voted to Charles II failed to yield the anticipated £1.2 million a year until the early 1680s, and the pre-Civil War tensions between monarch and Parliaments continued. James II's reign forcibly reminded Parliament of the dangers of giving the Crown a generous financial settlement, and William III paid the price. The stringent financial settlement that followed the Revolution, together with the unprecedented demands of two lengthy wars, swept away the old fiscal system and prompted the creation of new arrangements in which virtually all public revenues came from sources controlled by Parliament. The principle of 'appropriation', which had been unsuccessfully attempted in 1624 and again in the 1660s and 1670s, became firmly established and the Commission for Public Accounts enforced it in a way that had not been possible earlier. The Houses' 'power of the purse' was thus dramatically strengthened and was deployed to effect the constitutional reforms of William III's reign. Instead of Parliament granting one branch of the royal revenues, it now controlled virtually all of the State revenues, and underwrote the National Debt. Parliament's financial indispensability safeguarded its future: the Houses were able to monitor the government's fiscal conduct far more closely than ever before, and never again did they need to fear that their assertion of the 'power of the purse' might threaten their own extinction.

Parliament's place within a reformed financial system played a vital role in the transition from a 'demesne' state to a 'fiscal-military' state, so vividly analysed by Michael Braddick and John Brewer.[26] Behind Britain's remarkable intervention in continental warfare and later in colonial enterprise during the eighteenth century lay a mobilisation of national resources second only to the Dutch Republic. High levels of taxation and government borrowing could never have been sustained without the fact that parliamentary consent conferred legitimacy upon them. This in turn reflected a deep-rooted perception of Parliament as the 'representative of the realm' which fostered a willingness to pay taxes that had received its approval. The acute problems that arose when such public confidence was lacking had been all too apparent earlier in the century, and especially during the 1620s.

Some of this confidence in Parliament's capacity to represent the realm rested on a faith in the privileges and liberties to which the two Houses laid claim. Although these remained in principle very similar throughout the century, here again the picture was not a static one. The Commons continued to request the monarch to grant its four 'ancient' privileges at the beginning of each session, although this had been a formality since the end of the sixteenth century. One of those privileges, freedom of speech, was given a statutory basis in the Bill of Rights that it had previously lacked, with the affirmation of 'the freedom of speech and debates or proceedings in Parliament'. Similarly, in the Lords the right of the nobility to be tried by their peers, which had hitherto been merely an ancient convention, was enshrined in the 1696 Trials of Treason Act which stated that when a peer was tried for treason all peers with a right to sit in the Lords were to be summoned for the trial regardless of whether Parliament was sitting or not.[27] Another significant shift concerned the appointment of the Speaker of the Commons. For most of the century, as in earlier periods, the Commons had gone through the fiction of 'choosing' an individual who was in reality a Crown nominee. However, this issue became more controversial under the later Stuarts, and in 1695 the House actually rejected the King's nominee. Thereafter, the choice of the Speaker in practice lay with whichever party commanded a majority within the Commons, a development encouraged by the crystallisation of the Whigs and Tories under William and Anne.

These changes were symptomatic of a gradual process by which the Houses slowly became less obviously subservient to the Crown. The royal veto was not used after 1708, and various aspects of Parliaments – including some of their privileges, the timing and duration of their sessions, and the expenditure of parliamentary taxation – all of which in 1603 still lay within the monarch's discretion, were by the end of the century regulated by statute. In a very piecemeal, halting way, a number of spheres where Parliament had hitherto been subordinate to the Crown now saw both subordinated to statute. This enabled the Houses to stand up to the monarch effectively in ways that would have been deeply contentious if not impossible under the early Stuarts. A further aspect of this process was the decline of the Court as a focus for political activity and influence, and a corresponding increase in the political importance of Parliaments. The Revolution Settlement and its aftermath had the dual consequences of securing Parliament's permanence and fostering the duality of the Whig and Tory parties as the foremost characteristic of Augustan political culture. The combination of these two developments with the straitened financial circumstances of the Court made Parliament even more central to political life. By the beginning of the eighteenth century, parliamentary politics were conducted rather more in their own right, and rather less as an extension of Court politics. The Privy Council was increasingly superseded by the Cabinet, and the nature and interrelationship of the three 'points of contact' thus assumed a different character from their medieval, Tudor and early Stuart counterparts. If it was still difficult to isolate what happened in Parliaments from developments elsewhere, the Houses' position within the institutions of government had nevertheless been enhanced since 1603.

Alongside these areas of change, there were other aspects of Parliament where continuities were much more marked. First of all, the social composition of the two Houses did not alter greatly during the course of the century. Except during the bishops' exclusion between 1642 and 1661, the Lords continued to comprise the lords spiritual and temporal, together with the judges and legal assistants. The Commons remained dominated by members of the landed elite:

many members were younger sons of peers, or elected through the influence of peers, and a significant number of the merchants and lawyers in the House were scions of gentry families. Even the Parliaments of the Interregnum, whose structures sometimes differed from more 'standard' Parliaments, did not significantly depart from this pattern, and their membership marked a shift within the gentry rather than a shift away from it altogether. Indeed, it was precisely because Parliament's composition was such a faithful reflection of that of the governing elite as a whole that parliamentary proceedings mirrored the political nation's relationship with the Crown so accurately.

Parliament had evolved during the medieval and Tudor periods as an institution that brought local and national interests together. Recent research has shown the artificiality of attempting to forge a distinction between local and national politics, for many of the same personnel and issues dominated both. This was clearly the case in the closing years of the century, when Whig/Tory allegiances permeated local politics, especially during elections. But even though electoral contests became steadily more common after the middle of the century, the intertwining of local and national concerns was no less evident under the early Stuarts. The prevalence of *selections* rather than *elections* should not obscure the very real interest that people in the localities took in national affairs. It would have been as unthinkable for them not to see national issues reflected in local developments as it would have been for them not to use Parliaments to defend local interests at the centre. It was rare before the eighteenth century for constituents to issue formal instructions to their members about what they should do at Westminster, but that does not mean that there was not considerable local interest in parliamentary proceedings, and it did become gradually more difficult for 'outsiders' to be returned to the Commons. The declining proportion of 'carpetbaggers' in the Commons was a marked trend throughout the seventeenth century, and reflected a deep concern that local interests should be represented as effectively as possible in Parliament.

Another service that Parliaments performed for the nation at large was the provision of justice. This function can be traced back to Parliament's medieval origins, when the monarch's extended Council adjudicated petitions submitted to them, but it gained immensely in importance from 1621 onwards as a result of lengthy delays within the common-law courts. The revival of the Lords' appellate jurisdiction provided a very important facility for a wide range of private parties who were unable to find redress in the central law courts. The Lords discharged this duty efficiently and expeditiously, making the High Court of Parliament a reality, and the Upper House's effectiveness as a court of appeal was further enhanced after 1689 by the fact that it henceforth met each year. Some members of the Commons resented the Lords' judicature, and as a result of the cases of Skinner vs. the East India Company and Shirley vs. Fagg the Lords ceased to exercise an original jurisdiction in civil cases. Its role as an appeal court nevertheless persisted into modern times. The judicial activities of the Commons, by contrast, were confined to jurisdiction over their own members, and to joint proceedings with the Upper House in the form of impeachments and attainders. The former continued into the early nineteenth century, and there were a total of 21 cases between its revival in 1621 and 1805–6.[28] Attainder, by contrast, had fallen into disfavour by the end of the seventeenth century, mainly because it was perceived as violating common-law principles. The strong affirmation of the rule of law that followed the Revolution of

1688–9 thus served to curtail one aspect of parliamentary activity even as it reinforced others.

Parliamentary judicature was a reminder of the institution's medieval origins as an extension of the royal Court and Council: it was the monarch's High Court, exercising justice in his name. Contemporaries perceived no distinction between the administration of justice and the passing of legislation, and saw both as different facets of the making and enforcement of law. Since the Middle Ages, the Crown and the two Houses had collaborated in passing statutes, and the supremacy and omnicompetence of statute as the highest form of human positive law in England had been definitively established during the 1530s. The provision of private acts meant that parliamentary legislation was extremely useful to particular individuals and interest groups as well as to the Crown. Whereas Parliament's judicial activities tended to reinforce the image of the Crown as standing above the two Houses, legislative procedures emphasised the equipollence of Crown, Lords and Commons, collectively forming the supreme legislative authority of King-in-Parliament. Both in theory and in practice, the latter model had become rather more dominant by the end of the century. This reflected not so much the triumph of co-ordination theory or a concept of the three estates as Crown, Lords and Commons, as the growing pre-eminence of the passing of legislation among Parliament's multiple functions. The fact that Parliament sat every year led to a marked increase in the number of statutes passed, and a rise in the proportion of private acts testified to Parliament's continuing usefulness to a wide range of individuals and interest groups. Whereas in the period 1604–90, 535 (52 per cent) of a total of 1,024 acts passed were private, compared with a total of 489 (48 per cent) public acts, between 1690 and 1714, no less than 1,679 acts were passed, of which 638 (38 per cent) were public and 1,041 (62 per cent) private. The actual procedures for passing laws, and the authority of Crown-in-Parliament, were nothing new; yet after 1688–9 there was a more explicit recognition of statutes as a joint creation of Crown and Parliament that stood higher than either of them, and the fiction that they were the creation of the monarch acting with the advice of Parliament fell away. This was in large part a rhetorical change, but one that was entirely in keeping with the other developments discussed above.

The effect of this was to affirm the trend towards an equality between the three elements of the parliamentary trinity which had been emerging very gradually for many decades. As statutes became even more significant, so the position of the two Houses whose collaboration was essential for the passing of statutes naturally became stronger. This enhanced their position in relation to the Crown, and it was no accident that the royal veto was not used after 1708. Similarly, this process served to strengthen the Commons in relation to the Lords. However, it is important not to exaggerate the speed or coherence of this development, for the Lords continued to be business-like, socially dominant and politically influential. During Anne's reign in particular, the Upper House contained some of the ablest and most prominent figures in the political world, and the fact that in those years there was a slight Whig majority enabled the Lords to obstruct or delay some of the bills passed by a Tory majority in the Commons, including those against occasional conformity in 1702–4. In general, the Lords also usually remained more instinctively loyal to the Crown, and sometimes resisted the Commons' attempts to 'tack' controversial legislation to money bills. Yet these episodes again reflected the familiar pattern of interaction, and at times even conflict, between groups of members within the two Houses rather than between the two chambers as distinct entities. The seventeenth century had certainly demonstrated – more resoundingly than any earlier period – the Commons' capacity, both collectively and individually, to go their own way. Just as the later Stuarts could never forget the regicide, so the nobility always remembered the years when the Upper House had been abolished and their rights as peers abrogated. It is possible that constitutionally the Lords' position in relation to the Commons was in some ways stronger at the beginning of the century than at the end, and the declining importance of the Court, the primacy of statute, and the growing centrality of Parliament as a political arena all tended to reinforce this trend. Nevertheless, into the early eighteenth century and beyond members of the Lords continued to wield immense political influence, and neither the Crown nor the Commons could afford to alienate a majority of them.[29]

Throughout the history of the Stuart Parliaments runs the underlying theme of the relationship between the Crown and the governing elite. This was no less true of the 11 years during which the monarchy was abolished, and the parliamentary history of the Interregnum represents a variation on the central theme rather than a departure from it. In such a relationship, trust was essential, and Parliaments were ideally placed to foster such trust by periodically bringing together the monarch, royal advisers and representatives of the political nation. By the same token, any erosion of that trust was especially liable to become apparent in time of Parliament. It was this issue of trust, above all, that was the key to Parliament's political significance. But the institution's importance extended well beyond that. As an agency of government, Parliament's diverse functions gave it an organic role that was central to the processes of finance, justice, counsel and legislation. When contemporaries discussed this multi-faceted role within the body politic, they resorted again and again to biological metaphors, and these make far more sense of the institution's place in the polity than the false dichotomies between Crown and Parliament that have pervaded so much writing on the subject. Contemporaries had immense faith in Parliament as the 'physician of the realm', the panacea that would cure the nation's 'distempers'. What makes the history of the Stuart Parliaments so compelling is the fact that the body politic experienced a series of unprecedented convulsions that Parliaments proved unable to resolve without drastic surgery. The collapse of trust between Charles I and a significant number of his leading subjects worked like an infection within the body politic, and in the attempt to cure it the Long Parliament was broken apart. In the end, the infection proved so deep-rooted that the drastic solution was deployed of killing the King in order to cure the body politic. Yet to many at the time the regicide seemed like an upset of the natural order, and the various republican experiments never achieved political stability. When the monarch was restored in 1660, a systematic attempt was made to turn the clock back, but the memories of the traumas of the 1640s and 1650s could never be erased. They left a legacy of fear and division, especially in religious matters, that could not be allayed and that shaped the nature of Restoration politics both inside Parliaments and more widely. This legacy contributed to the downfall of James II and the Revolution of 1688–9, and the Parliaments that emerged in its wake differed from all their predecessors in their permanence, their enhanced financial powers, and their capacity to place statutory limitations on certain aspects of royal powers. The kaleidoscope of parliamentary history had turned once again, and

the Parliaments of the 1690s and after were the product of a complex historical process of continuity and change. They were moulded by the changing relationship between rulers and their subjects, and by a profound wish to resolve
several of the issues that had most persistently enflamed that relationship since
1603, and even since the Reformation.

Many of the historiographical controversies surrounding the Stuart
Parliaments really stem from divergent responses to two fundamental questions. The first is whether we should be more struck by the continuities
between seventeenth-century Parliaments and those of earlier periods, or by
the extent of the changes that occurred during the century. In other words,
does it make more sense to see Stuart Parliaments as the successors of medieval
and Tudor Parliaments, or as the harbingers of modern Parliaments? The second question is whether it is more important to contextualise parliamentary
history laterally (in the context of immediately contemporary events in other
spheres) or longitudinally (in the context of other events in parliamentary history in other periods). Is it more illuminating to understand parliamentary
proceedings in terms of the particular historical circumstances in which they
took place (thereby risking losing sight of their long-term significance), or
against the background of the full length of parliamentary history (thereby
running the risk of teleology)? Very generally, the Whig historians can be said
to have preferred the latter responses to both these questions, whereas the
'revisionists' have in both cases tended towards the former. Both lines of interpretation are consistent with much of the evidence, yet neither really tells the
whole story. In this book, I have attempted to sketch out what might be called
a more 'organic' approach to parliamentary history which stresses the multi-
faceted functions of Parliament and the integral role that it played in the
processes of politics and government. This interpretation involves giving due
emphasis to the ways in which Parliament's activities fused together to form an
interlocking whole, and the capacity of those activities to reflect and embody
the wider relationship between successive rulers and their subjects. Such an
interpretation acknowledges the existence of principled political conflict without losing sight of the harmony that contemporaries celebrated and that was
essential for the effective functioning of the institution. It also recognises the
complex blend of continuity and change that characterised Parliament's development, without privileging one or the other, and it gives full weight to the
complex interplay between Parliament and other institutions of government.

Such an interpretation not only offers a way of going beyond the antithesis
between Whig and 'revisionist' historians; it also connects very well with cur-
rent research into the parliamentary history of other periods. John Watts, for
example, has presented a powerful and persuasive reinterpretation of the
Parliaments of Henry VI's reign that locates them in the context of the on-
going relationship between Crown and nobility.[30] Similarly, David Dean's
account of the later Elizabethan Parliaments emphasises the workings of 'lobbies' in a way that integrates 'local' and 'national' concerns and recognises the
presence of both political conflict and harmonious decision-making.[31] Such
interpretations do not so much mediate between the Whig and 'revisionist'
positions as transcend them. For the period following the one covered in this
book, several recent accounts of eighteenth-century high political history
weave parliamentary proceedings into a wider world and consciously avoid
any artificial dichotomy between Crown and Parliament.[32] Indeed, it was the
pioneering work of Sheila Lambert on legislative procedure and the working of

lobbies that first introduced 'revisionism' into the history of eighteenth-century Parliaments rather earlier than for the medieval, Tudor and Stuart periods.[33]

All this research on other periods underlines the theme that has emerged repeatedly throughout this book, that parliamentary business reflected the various concerns of the realm as a whole and the ways in which these interacted with the Crown and its policies. It follows from this that any account of parliamentary history cannot confine itself to political and constitutional history, but must also integrate institutional and legal history, as well as the history of political thought and wider social and cultural trends. This general point holds good throughout Parliament's long history, from the thirteenth century to the twentieth. But within that story, even after the old Whig certainties have been exploded and the 'revisionist' assertions qualified, the seventeenth century must still occupy a place of central importance. For this was a genuinely transitional epoch, and the Parliaments that emerged out of its turbulent crises were significantly different from all their predecessors and pointed the way clearly towards later developments. The Stuart Parliaments suffered many blows and weathered many storms, yet they adapted and survived, and the history of seventeenth-century England demonstrated, perhaps more vividly than any other period, the continuing resilience, flexibility and essential *usefulness* of Parliaments to both the Crown and the nation.

Notes

1 Introduction

1 S. R. Gardiner, *History of England from the Accession of James I to the Outbreak of the Civil War, 1603–1642* (10 vols., 1883–4), I, 2–3.
2 J. E. Neale, *Elizabeth I and her Parliaments, 1584–1601* (1957), p. 436; J. E. Neale, *The Elizabethan House of Commons* (revised edition, 1963), p. 307.
3 J. H. Hexter (ed.), *Parliament and Liberty from the Reign of Elizabeth to the English Civil War* (Stanford, 1992). For a penetrating review of this and the succeeding volume in the series, see John Morrill, 'Taking Liberties with the Seventeenth Century', *PH*, XV (1996), 379–91.
4 As Sir Geoffrey Elton characterised this view: 'The Lords stood in the wings and made their rare appearances as a body – rather like the chorus in *Iolanthe*': G. R. Elton, *Studies in Tudor and Stuart Politics and Government* (4 vols., Cambridge, 1974–92), III, 157.
5 There is thus a significant element of what Glenn Burgess has called 'strong' teleology present in many Whiggish accounts of parliamentary history: Glenn Burgess, 'On Revisionism: An Analysis of Early Stuart Historiography in the 1970s and 1980s', *HJ*, XXXIII (1990), 609–27, especially 614–17.
6 Wallace Notestein, 'The Winning of the Initiative by the House of Commons', *Proceedings of the British Academy*, XI (1924–5), 125–75, at 175.
7 See especially Gardiner, *History of England*; S. R. Gardiner, *History of the Great Civil War, 1642–1649* (4 vols., 1893; reprinted 1987), and S. R. Gardiner, *History of the Commonwealth and Protectorate, 1649–1656* (4 vols., 1903; reprinted 1989). The story was continued in C. H. Firth, *The Last Years of the Protectorate, 1656–1658* (2 vols., 1909), and Godfrey Davies, *The Restoration of Charles II* (1955). See also David Ogg, *England in the Reign of Charles II* (2 vols., Oxford, 1934); David Ogg, *England in the Reigns of James II and William III* (Oxford, 1955); and G. M. Trevelyan, *England under the Stuarts* (1904).
8 G. W. Prothero (ed.), *Select Statutes and Other Constitutional Documents Illustrative of the Reigns of Elizabeth I and James I* (4th edition, Oxford, 1913); J. R. Tanner (ed.), *Constitutional Documents of the Reign of James I* (Cambridge, 1930); S. R. Gardiner (ed.), *Constitutional Documents of the Puritan Revolution, 1625–1660* (3rd edition, Oxford, 1906).
9 For a telling critique of Stone, see Elton, *Studies*, III, 474–9. See also the historiographical discussions in G. R. Elton, *Modern Historians on British History, 1485–1945: A Critical Bibliography, 1945–1969* (Ithaca, 1970), pp. 53–71; and John Morrill, *Revolt in the Provinces: The People of England and the Tragedies of War, 1630–1648* (2nd edition, Harlow, 1998), pp. 6–9.

10 See Pauline Croft, 'Sir John Doddridge, King James I, and the Antiquity of Parliament', *PER*, XII (1992), 95–107.

11 See below, pp. 82–6.

12 C. C. Weston and J. R. Greenberg, *Subjects and Sovereigns: The Grand Controversy over Legal Sovereignty in Stuart England* (Cambridge, 1981), pp. 183–99.

13 G. O. Sayles, *The King's Parliament of England* (1975), p. 134.

14 H. G. Richardson and G. O. Sayles, 'The Earliest Known Official Use of the Term "Parliament"', *EHR*, LXXXII (1967), 747–50.

15 Michael A. R. Graves, *Early Tudor Parliaments, 1485–1558* (Harlow, 1990), pp. 2–3. In 1366 Chief Justice Thorpe asserted that 'Parliament represents the body of all the realm': Elton, *Studies*, II, 36.

16 See below, pp. 196, 231.

17 Graves, *Early Tudor Parliaments*, p. 3; G. R. Elton, *England, 1200–1640* (1969), pp. 84–5. For the later development of the Parliament Roll, see below, p. 12.

18 See below, pp. 39–42.

19 See below, pp. 81–6.

20 For useful surveys of representative assemblies in early modern Europe, see Richard Bonney, *The European Dynastic States, 1494–1660* (Oxford, 1991), pp. 316–30; Thomas Munck, *Seventeenth Century Europe: State, Conflict and the Social Order in Europe, 1598–1700* (1990), pp. 32–5; and A. R. Myers, *Parliaments and Estates in Europe to 1789* (1975). On the Scottish Parliament, see especially Keith M. Brown, *Kingdom or Province? Scotland and the Regal Union, 1603–1715* (1992), pp. 13–20, and John R. Young, *The Scottish Parliament, 1639–1661: A Political and Constitutional Analysis* (Edinburgh, 1996). On the Irish Parliament, see T. W. Moody, F. X. Martin, and F. J. Byrne (eds.), *A New History of Ireland*, vol. 3: *Early Modern Ireland, 1534–1691* (2nd edition, Oxford, 1991), especially pp. xlv–xlvii, 22, 211–19, 247–51, 272–87. I am very grateful to Michael Graves for a helpful discussion on the comparisons and contrasts between early modern European assemblies.

21 Graves, *Early Tudor Parliaments*, p. 10.

22 J. S. Roskell, 'Perspectives in English Parliamentary History', in E. B. Fryde and Edward Miller (eds.), *Historical Studies of the English Parliament*, vol. II: *1399 to 1603* (Cambridge, 1970), p. 303.

23 See G. R. Elton, *F. W. Maitland* (1985), pp. 56–69.

24 For good summaries, see especially Sayles, *King's Parliament*; and R. G. Davies and J. H. Denton (eds.), *The English Parliament in the Middle Ages* (Manchester, 1981).

25 John Watts, *Henry VI and the Politics of Kingship* (Cambridge, 1996).

26 Roskell, 'Perspectives', especially pp. 316–21. See also W. M. Ormrod, *Political Life in Medieval England, 1300–1450* (1995), pp. 35–7; and Chapter 4, below. It is, however, worth noting that Roskell's comparison can be misleading, in that many Tudor Parliaments were summoned in peacetime and not for financial reasons. The political circumstances of the periods 1340–1440 and 1485–1603 were so contrasted that they are difficult to compare. I am most grateful to Michael Graves for a discussion on this point.

27 Elton, *Studies*, II, 26.

28 G. R. Elton (ed.), *The Tudor Constitution: Documents and Commentary* (2nd edition, Cambridge, 1982), p. 243.

29 *Ibid.*, pp. 240–1; Elton, *Studies*, IV, 37–57; G. R. Elton, *The Parliament of England, 1559–1581* (Cambridge, 1986), pp. 32–9. Cf. Conrad Russell, 'Thomas Cromwell's Doctrine of Parliamentary Sovereignty', *TRHS*, 6th series, VII (1997), 235–46.

30 Elton, *Studies*, III, 131–2.

31 See, for example, Michael A. R. Graves, *The Tudor Parliaments: Crown, Lords and Commons, 1485–1603* (Harlow, 1985), p. 58; G. R. Elton, *England under the Tudors* (3rd edition, 1991), p. 482; Elton, *Studies*, II, 35, 213.

32 Elton, *Studies*, II, 30. Some statutes received a shorter form of the enacting clause: 'be it therefore enacted by the authority of the present Parliament'. Sir Geoffrey Elton

and David Dean have shown that in the vast majority of cases, acts receiving the short formula were of official provenance whereas those that were privately promoted received the long formula: Elton, *Studies*, III, 142–55; David M. Dean, 'Enacting Clauses and Legislative Initiative, 1584–1601', *BIHR*, LVII (1984), 140–8.

33 Elton (ed.), *Tudor Constitution*, pp. 236, 277. See also Graves, *Tudor Parliaments*, p. 80.

34 Graves, *Tudor Parliaments*, pp. 65–114; J. Loach, *Parliament under the Tudors* (Oxford, 1991), pp. 78–96. See also M. A. R. Graves, *The House of Lords in the Parliaments of Edward VI and Mary* (Cambridge, 1981); J. Loach, *Parliament and the Crown in the Reign of Mary Tudor* (Oxford, 1986).

35 Graves, *Early Tudor Parliaments*, p. 81.

36 Neale, *Elizabethan House of Commons*; and the two volumes of *Elizabeth I and her Parliaments*, in which the emphasis on the 'Puritan choir' as an explanatory tool became much more pronounced. Neale's interpretation is conveniently summarised in R. K. Gilkes, *The Tudor Parliament* (1969), especially Chapter 9.

37 For this revisionist interpretation, see especially Elton, *Studies*, III, Chapters 33, 35; IV, Chapters 49, 50, 55; Elton (ed.), *Tudor Constitution*, Chapter 8; Elton, *Parliament of England*; Graves, *Tudor Parliaments*, pp. 115–58; Michael A. R. Graves, *Elizabethan Parliaments, 1559–1601* (2nd edition, Harlow, 1996).

38 M. A. R. Graves, 'Thomas Norton the Parliament Man: an Elizabethan MP, 1559–1581', *HJ*, XXIII (1980), 17–35; M. A. R. Graves, *Thomas Norton: The Parliament Man* (Oxford, 1994); Patrick Collinson, *Elizabethan Essays* (1994), pp. 59–86. See also Graves's further comments in his 'Elizabethan Men of Business Reconsidered', in S. M. Jack and B. A. Masters (eds.), *Protestants, Property, Puritans: Godly People Revisited* (*Parergon*, XIV, 1996), 111–27.

39 T. E. Hartley, *Elizabeth's Parliaments: Queen, Lords and Commons, 1559–1601* (Manchester, 1992).

40 Cf. the judicious remarks in Pauline Croft, 'The Parliament of England', *TRHS*, 6th series, VII (1997), 217–34, especially 227–33.

41 David Dean, 'Pressure Groups and Lobbies in the Elizabethan and Early Jacobean Parliaments', *PER*, XI (1991), 139–152; quotations at 139, 140. See also David Dean, 'London Lobbies and Parliament: The Case of the Brewers and Coopers in the Parliament of 1593', *PH*, VIII (1989), 341–65; David Dean, 'Public or Private? London, Leather and Legislation in Elizabethan England', *HJ*, XXXI (1988), 525–48; and Ian Archer, 'The London Lobbies in the Later Sixteenth Century', *HJ*, XXXI (1988), 17–44.

42 It is, however, worth noting one important difference, which was that the 'puritan' demands presented a direct challenge to the monarch's wishes whereas the lobbying of other interest groups, such as brewers or tanners, generally did not. I am grateful to Michael Graves for a helpful discussion on this point.

43 David Dean, *Law-making and Society in Late Elizabethan England: The Parliament of England, 1584–1601* (Cambridge, 1996).

44 For some perceptive discussions of the comparisons and contrasts between the English Parliament and continental assemblies, see especially Elton, *Studies*, II, 48–51; J. P. Cooper, *Land, Men and Beliefs: Studies in Early-Modern History*, ed. G. E. Aylmer and J. S. Morrill (1983), pp. 97–114; H. G. Koenigsberger, *Politicians and Virtuosi* (1986), pp. 1–25; and Conrad Russell, *Unrevolutionary England, 1603–1642* (1990), pp. 121–36. On continental patterns, see in addition Bonney, *European Dynastic States*, pp. 316–30; Munck, *Seventeenth Century Europe*, pp. 32–5; and Myers, *Parliaments and Estates*. See also above, p. 5. I am very grateful to Michael Graves for advice on these comparative points.

45 Collinson, *Elizabethan Essays*, pp. 53–5; Russell, *Unrevolutionary England*, pp. 24–5.

46 For the nature and history of the Parliament Roll, see Maurice F. Bond, *Guide to the Records of Parliament* (1971), p. 93; Elton, *Studies*, III, 110–42; Elton, *Parliament of England*, pp. 4–6.

47 Elizabeth Read Foster, *The Painful Labour of Mr Elsyng* (Transactions of the American Philosophical Society, new series, LXII, part viii, Philadelphia, 1972), pp. 29–35. On the revival of impeachment, see below, pp. 35–6, 109–10.

48 Elizabeth Read Foster, *The House of Lords, 1603–1649: Structure, Procedure, and the Nature of its Business* (Chapel Hill, 1983), pp. 46, 51–5.

49 A. Luders, T. E. Tomlins *et al.* (eds.), *The Statutes of the Realm from Magna Carta to the End of the Reign of Queen Anne* (11 vols., 1810–28). See Bond, *Records of Parliament*, p. 102.

50 There were a handful of exceptions to this principle, where statutes found in the sessional print are classified on the Parliament Roll as private acts: see Conrad Russell, *Parliaments and English Politics, 1621–1629* (Oxford, 1979), p. 48. The distinction between public and private bills and acts is discussed more fully below, pp. 39–42.

51 Bond, *Records of Parliament*, pp. 93–6; Maurice F. Bond, 'Acts of Parliament', *Archives*, III (1958), 201–18; Elton, *Studies*, III, 92–109; Elton, *Parliament of England*, p. 6.

52 The following discussion of the Journals of the two Houses is based on Bond, *Records of Parliament*, pp. 26–36, 205–12; Elton, *Studies*, III, 58–92; Elton, *Parliament of England*, pp. 6–9; Foster, *The Painful Labour of Mr Elsyng*, pp. 21–9; Foster, *House of Lords*, pp. 49–55; and Sheila Lambert, 'The Clerks and Records of the House of Commons, 1600–1640', *BIHR*, XLIII (1970), 215–31.

53 There is some record of debates in the Commons Journals for the early seventeenth century. However, this is very variable from session to session and virtually disappears after the opening decades of the century. I am grateful to Chris Kyle for advice on this point.

54 The volumes of the printed versions that cover the period 1603–89 are *CJ*, I–X, and *LJ*, II–XIV.

55 The Draft Journals form a largely complete series from 1621 until 1690, and the Manuscript Minutes from 1610 to date: Bond, *Records of Parliament*, pp. 33–6; HLRO, Memorandum No. 13 (revised 1957).

56 Bond, *Records of Parliament*, pp. 4, 212. A Draft Journal of the Commons was not compiled until the 1690s: *ibid.*, p. 205.

57 See below, pp. 34–8; Bond, *Records of Parliament*, pp. 106–26, 232.

58 Especially in James S. Hart, *Justice upon Petition: The House of Lords and the Reformation of Justice, 1621–1675* (1991).

59 T. C. Hansard began to use reporters to make systematic transcripts of parliamentary debates in 1830. In the period before that, various attempts were made to reconstruct debates from a variety of sources, including the Journals, newsletters, etc., and much of this material was then incorporated into *The Parliamentary History of England, 1066–1803*, ed. W. Cobbett and T. C. Hansard (36 vols., 1806–20). The first four volumes cover the years 1603–88, but they are very incomplete. For a fuller discussion, see Bond, *Records of Parliament*, pp. 36–9.

60 For example, BL, Harleian MS 6424, the diary, usually attributed to Bishop John Warner of Rochester, that covers Lords proceedings between 14 January 1641 and 4 January 1642. See Russell, *Unrevolutionary England*, pp. 111–18.

61 For example, the printed proceedings of the 1628 session of Parliament contain no fewer than eight private diaries recording events in the Commons. This and the other printed editions are listed in the Bibliography.

62 The following discussion is based on what has become an extensive body of scholarship. The initial debate can be found in Elton, *Studies*, II, 3–18, the latter part of which is a reply to J. H. Hexter's piece 'Parliament under the Lens' in *British Studies Monitor*, III (1972–3), 4–15. For Elton's views, see also *Parliament of England*, pp. 10–14. Hexter made a further contribution in 'Quoting the Commons, 1604–1642', in DeLoyd J. Guth and John W. McKenna (eds.), *Tudor Rule and Revolution* (1982), pp. 369–91. More recently, John Morrill has addressed these issues in three articles: 'Reconstructing the History of Early Stuart Parliaments', *Archives*, XXI

(1994), 67–72; 'Paying One's D'Ewes', *PH*, XIV (1995), 179–86; and 'Getting Over D'Ewes', *PH*, XV (1996), 221–30. The third of these papers is a reply to Maija Jansson, 'Dues Paid', *PH*, XV (1996), 215–20. The situation in the closing years of the seventeenth century is discussed in Colin Brooks, 'Individuals, Parties and the Parliamentary Record in the 1690s', *PER*, XVI (1996), 175–91.
63 See below, pp. 24, 32–4.
64 Morrill, 'Paying One's D'Ewes', 183.
65 A point made forcefully in Jansson, 'Dues Paid', especially 215–17, 219–20.
66 Cf. Hexter, 'Quoting the Commons', especially pp. 377–9.
67 See especially *ibid*.
68 See especially Morrill, 'Reconstructing the History of Early Stuart Parliaments', 71–2.
69 On this, see especially Richard Cust, 'News and Politics in Early Seventeenth-Century England', *PP*, CXII (1986), 60–90; Richard Cust, 'Politics and the Electorate in the 1620s', in Richard Cust and Ann Hughes (eds.), *Conflict in Early Stuart England* (1989), pp. 134–67; John Miller, 'Public Opinion in Charles II's England', *History*, LXXX (1995), 359–81.
70 A. D. T. Cromartie, 'The Printing of Parliamentary Speeches, November 1640–July 1642', *HJ*, XXXIII (1990), 23–44.
71 John Morrill, 'The Unweariableness of Mr Pym: Influence and Eloquence in the Long Parliament', in Susan D. Amussen and Mark A. Kishlansky (eds.), *Political Culture and Cultural Politics in Early Modern England: Essays Presented to David Underdown* (Manchester, 1995), pp. 19–54, especially pp. 36–9.
72 Sheila Lambert (ed.), *Printing for Parliament, 1641–1700* (List and Index Society, special series, XX, 1984). See also Sheila Lambert, 'The Beginning of Printing for the House of Commons, 1640–42', *The Library*, 6th series, III (1981), 43–61.

2 Membership, attendance and representation

1 Chris R. Kyle, 'Prince Charles in the Parliaments of 1621 and 1624', *HJ*, XLI (1998), 603–24. I am very grateful to Chris Kyle for showing me a copy of this paper prior to publication.
2 Elizabeth Read Foster, *The House of Lords, 1603–1649: Structure, Procedure, and the Nature of its Business* (Chapel Hill, 1983), pp. 13–18, 70–86.
3 Henry Elsynge, *The Manner of Holding Parliaments in England* (1768), p. 54.
4 Foster, *House of Lords*, pp. 15–18; Conrad Russell, *Parliaments and English Politics, 1621–1629* (Oxford, 1979), pp. 16, 309–11; Conrad Russell, *The Fall of the British Monarchies, 1637–1642* (Oxford, 1991), p. 100; L. O. Pike, *A Constitutional History of the House of Lords* (1894), pp. 238–9. See also below, pp. 68, 115.
5 Clyve Jones (ed.), *A Pillar of the Constitution: The House of Lords in British Politics, 1640–1784* (1989), p. 4; Lawrence Stone, *The Crisis of the Aristocracy, 1558–1641* (Oxford, 1965), pp. 758–9.
6 Richard Cust, *The Forced Loan and English Politics, 1626–1628* (Oxford, 1987), pp. 24–5.
7 Foster, *House of Lords*, pp. 15–16.
8 Maija Jansson and W. B. Bidwell (eds.), *Proceedings in Parliament, 1625* (New Haven and London, 1987), pp. 583–6; J. B. Crummett, 'The Lay Peers in Parliament, 1640–4' (unpubl. Ph.D. dissertation, University of Manchester, 1972), p. 1.
9 Foster, *House of Lords*, p. 16; J. S. A. Adamson, 'Parliamentary Management, Men-of-Business and the House of Lords, 1640–49', in Jones (ed.), *Pillar of the Constitution*, especially pp. 21–9.
10 The statute was 16 Car. I, c. 27; printed in S. R. Gardiner (ed.), *The Constitutional Documents of the Puritan Revolution, 1625–60* (3rd edition, Oxford, 1906),

pp. 241–2. The political background is analysed in Russell, *Fall of the British Monarchies*, pp. 342–4, 410–12, 442–4, 471, 475.

11 *AO*, I, 458–9.

12 C. C. Weston, *English Constitutional Theory and the House of Lords, 1556–1832* (1965), p. 49. For rates of attendance, see below, p. 21.

13 The 1642 act excluding the bishops from the Lords was repealed in 1661: 13 Car. II, c. 2.

14 Andrew Swatland, *The House of Lords in the Reign of Charles II* (Cambridge, 1996), pp. 29–34.

15 A figure calculated from the data given in E. B. Fryde, D. E. Greenway, S. Porter and I. Roy (eds.), *Handbook of British Chronology* (3rd edition, reprinted Cambridge, 1996), pp. 448–89.

16 K. H. D. Haley, 'A List of the English Peers, *c.* May 1687', *EHR*, LXIX (1954), 302–6; J. R. Western, *Monarchy and Revolution: The English State in the 1680s* (1972), p. 222.

17 J. P. Kenyon, *Robert Spencer, Earl of Sunderland, 1641–1702* (1958), pp. 147, 160, 206, 214.

18 J. S. Roskell, 'The Problem of the Attendance of the Lords in Medieval Parliaments', *BIHR*, XXIX (1956), 153–204; Michael A. R. Graves, *The Tudor Parliaments: Crown, Lords and Commons, 1485–1603* (Harlow, 1985), pp. 49–51, 74–6, 101–3, 118–20, 134–8; Pauline Croft and I. A. A. Thompson, 'Aristocracy and Representative Government in Unicameral and Bicameral Institutions: The Role of the Peers in the Castilian Cortes and the English Parliament, 1529–1664', in H. W. Blom, W. P. Blockmans and H. de Schepper (eds.), *Bicameralisme: Tweekamerstelsel vroeger en nu* (The Hague, 1992), pp. 63–86, especially pp. 65–7.

19 Angela Britton, 'The House of Lords in English Politics, 1604–1614' (unpubl. D.Phil. dissertation, University of Oxford, 1982), pp. 12–21.

20 Foster, *House of Lords*, p. 19.

21 Crummett, 'Lay Peers in Parliament', pp. 260c–260d. If the higher attendances during Strafford's trial are excluded, the upper average would be 60 rather than 63.

22 *Ibid.*

23 Their names are listed in *A Catalogue of the Names of the Knights, Citizens and Burgesses that have Served in the last four Parliaments* (1656), pp. 20–5 (Wing, C 1394; BL, TT, E 1602/6). The Oxford Parliament is discussed below, p. 131.

24 The average attendances in the Lords for 1647–9 have been calculated from the lists of those present in *LJ*, IX–X. For 1646, see C. H. Firth, *The House of Lords during the Civil War* (1910), pp. 154–5, 206. See also J. S. A. Adamson, 'The English Nobility and the Projected Settlement of 1647', *HJ*, XXX (1987), 567–602, at 569; Ian Ward, 'The English Peerage, 1649–1660: Government, Authority and Estates' (unpubl. Ph.D. dissertation, University of Cambridge, 1989), pp. 1–16.

25 Swatland, *House of Lords*, pp. 29, 35.

26 *Ibid.*, pp. 35–8.

27 J. S. Flemion, 'The Nature of Opposition in the House of Lords in the Early Seventeenth Century: A Revaluation', in Clyve Jones and David Lewis Jones (eds.), *Peers, Politics and Power: The House of Lords, 1603–1911* (1986), pp. 5–22.

28 Crummett, 'Lay Peers in Parliament', pp. 262, 265.

29 Swatland, *House of Lords*, p. 55; D. H. Willson, *The Privy Councillors in the House of Commons, 1604–1629* (Minneapolis, 1940), pp. 22, 56–63, 99–101.

30 Swatland, *House of Lords*, p. 55. For the activities of Privy Councillors in the Lords, see below, pp. 44–5. Committees and conferences are discussed more fully below, pp. 71–5.

31 Foster, *House of Lords*, p. 23; Elsynge, *Manner of Holding Parliaments*, pp. 113–18.

32 Crummett, 'Lay Peers in Parliament', pp. 5, 108.

33 Cf. Foster, *House of Lords*, p. 147.

34 Maurice F. Bond, *Guide to the Records of Parliament* (1971), p. 202; B. D. Henning (ed.), *The House of Commons, 1660–1690* (3 vols., 1983), I, 225–6. The act enfranchising Durham was 25 Car. II, c. 9, printed in Andrew Browning (ed.), *English Historical Documents, 1660–1714* (1953), pp. 210–11. The enfranchisement of Durham followed a lengthy campaign lasting several decades: see Andrew W. Foster, 'The Struggle for Parliamentary Representation for Durham, *c.* 1600–1641', in David Marcombe (ed.), *The Last Principality: Politics, Religion and Society in the Bishopric of Durham, 1494–1660* (Nottingham, 1987), pp. 176–201.

35 The lists printed in the *Return of Members of Parliaments of England, 1213–1702* (2 vols., 1878), I, 442–563 are taken from the original writs and returns of election preserved in the PRO, C 219. These are very incomplete in terms of names and returns, and even as a list of constituencies they are imperfect. As close to definitive names and figures as can be achieved for the seventeenth century are being published by the History of Parliament Trust, but to date only the volumes covering 1660–90 have appeared: see Henning (ed.), *House of Commons, 1660–1690*, I, 1–27. For the Long Parliament, see D. Brunton and D. H. Pennington, *Members of the Long Parliament* (1954), pp. 1–20. Developments under the Tudors are helpfully summarised in Graves, *Tudor Parliaments*, especially pp. 48, 132–3; and G. R. Elton (ed.), *The Tudor Constitution: Documents and Commentary* (2nd edition, Cambridge, 1982), pp. 248–9.

36 See *A Catalogue of the Names*, pp. 20–5; and below, p. 131.

37 David Underdown, *Pride's Purge: Politics in the Puritan Revolution* (Oxford, 1971), p. 220; Blair Worden, *The Rump Parliament, 1648–1653* (Cambridge, 1974), pp. 23–7.

38 The Nominated Assembly is also sometimes known as the Little Parliament, or as Barebone's Parliament (after one of its members, Praise-God Barebone).

39 Vernon F. Snow, 'Parliamentary Reapportionment Proposals in the Puritan Revolution', *EHR*, LXXIV (1959), 409–42. The revised distribution of seats is set out in the Instrument of Government, printed in Gardiner (ed.), *Constitutional Documents*, pp. 407–9. In practice, not quite all seats were taken, so that the first Protectorate Parliament comprised 456 members, and the second 458. On this, see Sarah E. Jones, 'The Composition and Activity of the Protectorate Parliaments' (unpubl. Ph.D. dissertation, University of Exeter, 1988), especially pp. 27, 42–7.

40 The Nominated Assembly also included six members from Wales, five from Scotland and six from Ireland. The Nominated Assembly and the Protectorate Parliaments were the only occasions before 1707 when Scottish and English members formed a single Parliament, and the only time until 1801 that British and Irish members sat together.

41 The English and Welsh members were returned 'according to the ancient form', and the Scottish and Irish members were subsequently admitted after lengthy and heated debate: Snow, 'Parliamentary Reapportionment Proposals', 424; and Godfrey Davies, 'The Elections to Richard Cromwell's Parliament', *EHR*, LXIII (1948), 488–501.

42 The remarkable shifts in the composition of Parliaments during the 1640s and 1650s are discussed more fully within their political contexts in Chapter 8, below.

43 Norman Ball, 'Representation in the English House of Commons: The New Boroughs, 1485–1640', *PER*, XV (1995), 117–24; J. E. Neale, *The Elizabethan House of Commons* (revised edition, 1963), pp. 140–54.

44 Elton (ed.), *Tudor Constitution*, pp. 248–9; A. D. K. Hawkyard, 'The Enfranchisement of Constituencies, 1509–1558', *PH*, X (1991), 1–26.

45 PRO, SP 14/167/10 (Sir Francis Nethersole to [Sir Dudley Carleton], 2 June 1624).

46 BL, Harleian MS 159 (diary of Sir Simonds D'Ewes), fo. 133r. I owe this reference to Chris Kyle.

47 Ball, 'Representation', 118–19; Evangeline de Villiers, 'Parliamentary Boroughs Restored by the House of Commons, 1621–41', *EHR*, LXVII (1952), 175–202. For other manifestations of this early Stuart antiquarianism, see above, p. 3; below, pp. 103–4.

48 Henning (ed.), *House of Commons, 1660–1690*, I, 104.

49 Sheila Lambert, 'Committees, Religion, and Parliamentary Encroachment on Royal Authority in Early Stuart England', *EHR*, CI (1990), 60–95, at 68.

50 Vernon F. Snow, 'Attendance Trends and Absenteeism in the Long Parliament', *HLQ*, XVIII (1954–5), 301–6.

51 Jones, 'Composition and Activity of the Protectorate Parliaments', p. 82.

52 Henning (ed.), *House of Commons, 1660–1690*, I, 79–80.

53 Lotte Glow, 'The Committee-Men in the Long Parliament, August 1642 – December 1643', *HJ*, VIII (1965), 1–15.

54 Henning (ed.), *House of Commons, 1660–1690*, I, 81.

55 T. K. Moore and H. Horwitz, 'Who Runs the House? Aspects of Parliamentary Organization in the Later Seventeenth Century', *JMH*, XLIII (1971), 205–27. The value of Parliament to private or local interests is discussed more fully below, pp. 39–42.

56 For the layout of the Palace of Westminster, see the map on p. 33. The Commons met in very cramped conditions and members were often forced to stand: this tended to favour the 'noes' in any division because the 'ayes' who went forth could never be sure of finding a seat when they returned.

57 The different types of franchise are discussed in Derek Hirst, *The Representative of the People? Voters and Voting in England under the Early Stuarts* (Cambridge, 1975), pp. 29–105. For the later seventeenth century, see Henning (ed.), *House of Commons, 1660–1690*, I, 104–7.

58 Hirst, *Representative of the People?*, pp. 223–6.

59 Hirst sees the electorate as considerably larger in the pre-Civil War period than is allowed, for example, in J. H. Plumb, 'The Growth of the Electorate in England from 1600 to 1715', *PP*, XLV (1969), 90–116.

60 Hirst, *Representative of the People?* It is possible that the figure of 13 contested elections in 1604 is an underestimate and that the number of contests was actually somewhat higher than that. I am grateful to Chris Kyle for advice on this point.

61 Mark A. Kishlansky, *Parliamentary Selection: Social and Political Choice in Early Modern England* (Cambridge, 1986), especially pp. 3–101.

62 On the electoral influence of Crown and nobility, see John K. Gruenfelder, *Influence in Early Stuart Elections, 1604–1640* (Ohio, 1981), pp. 213–14, 222–3.

63 Conrad Russell, *Unrevolutionary England, 1603–1642* (1990), pp. 209–10; John Morrill, 'The Unwear_iableness of Mr Pym: Influence and Eloquence in the Long Parliament', in Susan Amussen and Mark A. Kishlansky (eds.), *Political Culture and Cultural Politics in Early Modern England: Essays Presented to David Underdown* (Manchester, 1995), pp. 19–54, especially pp. 22–3; Mary Frear Keeler, *The Long Parliament, 1640–1641: A Biographical Study of its Members* (Memoirs of the American Philosophical Society, XXXVI, Philadelphia, 1954), p. 318; G. E. C[okayne], *The Complete Peerage* (new edition, ed. V. Gibbs *et al.*, 14 vols., 1910–59), II, 78.

64 Morrill, 'The Unweariableness of Mr Pym', p. 23. For the term 'carpetbagger', see below, p. 190.

65 Gruenfelder, *Influence*, pp. 123–32; Violet A. Rowe, 'The Influence of the Earls of Pembroke on Parliamentary Elections, 1625–41', *EHR*, L (1935), 242–56; Keeler, *Long Parliament*, p. 329; G. E. C., *Complete Peerage*, X, 412–18.

66 Kishlansky, *Parliamentary Selection*, p. 230.

67 See Derek Hirst's review of Kishlansky, *Parliamentary Selection*, in *Albion*, XIX (1987), 428–34; Richard Cust, 'Election and Selection in Stuart England', *PH*, VII (1988), 344–50; John Miller, 'Public Opinion in Charles II's England', *History*, LXXX (1995), 359–81, especially 372–3; T. E. Hartley, 'The Sheriff and County

Elections', in D. M. Dean and N. L. Jones (eds.), *The Parliaments of Elizabethan England* (Oxford and Cambridge, Mass., 1990), pp. 163–89.

68 For this point, see especially Hirst's review in *Albion*, and Cust, 'Election and Selection'.

69 Swatland, *House of Lords*, p. 38. See, for example, Centre for Kentish Studies, Sackville MS, U 269/O36/81 (Richard Sackville, fifth Earl of Dorset: 'Certain Queries concerning the ancient and legal Government and Parliaments of England').

70 John Miller, 'Representatives and Represented in England, 1660–89', *PER*, XV (1995), 125–32, at 132. Durham was nevertheless enfranchised six years later: see above, p. 22.

71 See, for example, the words of Sir Edward Coke, quoted in David Harris Sacks, 'Parliament, Liberty, and the Commonweal', in J. H. Hexter (ed.), *Parliament and Liberty from the Reign of Elizabeth to the English Civil War* (Stanford, 1992), pp. 85–121, at p. 88.

72 Keeler, *Long Parliament*, p. 23; Henning (ed.), *House of Commons, 1660–1690*, I, 16.

73 P. W. Hasler (ed.), *The House of Commons, 1558–1603* (3 vols., 1981), I, 20; Henning (ed.), *House of Commons, 1660–1690*, I, 10.

74 Keeler, *Long Parliament*, p. 21; Brunton and Pennington, *Members of the Long Parliament*, p. 5; Henning (ed.), *House of Commons, 1660–1690*, I, 8, 10.

75 Henning (ed.), *House of Commons, 1660–1690*, I, 8, 59.

76 This is a necessarily tentative conclusion because the figures for the social composition of the Commons between 1604 and 1629 currently being compiled by the History of Parliament Trust are not yet available. However, it is very unlikely that they will reveal a dramatic divergence from the pattern described here. I am grateful to Chris Kyle for advice on this point.

77 Austin Woolrych, *Commonwealth to Protectorate* (Oxford, 1982), pp. 403–33; Jones, 'Composition and Activity of the Protectorate Parliaments', p. 81. See also below, pp. 138–40, 144.

78 Keeler, *Long Parliament*, p. 18; Henning (ed.), *House of Commons, 1660–1690*, I, 25. Figures for office-holding among members of the Commons between 1604 and 1629 are currently being compiled by the History of Parliament Trust, but are not yet available. I am grateful to Chris Kyle for advice on this point.

79 Hasler (ed.), *House of Commons, 1558–1603*, I, 45–58.

80 Russell, *Parliaments*, p. 8.

81 These percentages are based on the raw figures in Gruenfelder, *Influence*, p. 226.

82 Other names frequently applied to borough members not resident in the same county were 'strangers' and 'carpetbaggers'.

83 Hasler (ed.), *House of Commons, 1558–1603*, I, 58.

84 The actual proportions fluctuated somewhat from Parliament to Parliament: these figures are rough averages based on the percentages for each Parliament tabulated in Henning (ed.), *House of Commons, 1660–1690*, I, 59–62.

85 David L. Smith, 'The Political Career of Edward Sackville, fourth Earl of Dorset (1590–1652)' (unpubl. Ph.D. dissertation, University of Cambridge, 1990), pp. 287–317. Since the 1580s the Great Yarmouth town assembly had tried to avoid the return of outsiders as members: Richard Cust, 'Parliamentary Elections in the 1620s: The Case of Great Yarmouth', *PH*, XI (1992), 179–91.

86 Gruenfelder, *Influence*, p. 225; Henning (ed.), *House of Commons, 1660–1690*, I, 62. See also Hirst, *Representative of the People?*, pp. 137–53.

87 S. A. Hipkin, 'The Economy and Social Structure of Rye, 1600–1660' (unpubl. D.Phil. dissertation, University of Oxford, 1985), especially pp. 98–108. See also Smith, 'Political Career of Dorset', pp. 297–301; Russell, *Parliaments*, pp. 37–8.

88 Cust, 'Election and Selection', 344–6. See also above, pp. 25–6.

89 Richard Cust and Peter Lake, 'Sir Richard Grosvenor and the Rhetoric of Magistracy', *BIHR*, LIV (1981), 40–53, at 50; Cust, 'Election and Selection', 349.

90 Richard Cust, 'Politics and the Electorate in the 1620s', in Richard Cust and Ann Hughes (eds.), *Conflict in Early Stuart England* (Harlow, 1989), pp. 134–67, at p. 158.

91 Richard Cust, 'News and Politics in Early Seventeenth-Century England', *PP*, CXII (1986), 60–90.

92 Cust, 'Politics and the Electorate', especially pp. 140–3; Cust, 'News and Politics', especially 79–87. On the importance of anti-popery in elections, see also Hirst, *Representative of the People?*, pp. 145–53.

93 For a case study of these perceptions at work in Great Yarmouth, see Cust, 'Parliamentary Elections'.

94 Miller, 'Public Opinion', 366.

95 Mark Knights, *Politics and Opinion in Crisis, 1678–81* (Cambridge, 1994), especially pp. 177–84. See also below, pp. 156–61.

96 W. A. Speck, 'The Electorate in the First Age of Party', in Clyve Jones (ed.), *Britain in the First Age of Party, 1680–1750: Essays Presented to Geoffrey Holmes* (1987), pp. 45–62, at p. 52. See also below, p. 172.

97 Hirst, *Representative of the People?*, pp. 183–4; Miller, 'Public Opinion', 128.

98 Cust, 'Parliamentary Elections', 182.

99 Kishlansky, *Parliamentary Selection*, p. 16; Miller, 'Public Opinion', 376–7.

100 Grey, *Debates*, VII, 407 (2 November 1680).

101 Derek Hirst, 'The Defection of Sir Edward Dering, 1640–1641', *HJ*, XV (1972), 193–208. See also below, p. 126.

102 Russell, *Parliaments*, p. 21. See also Russell, *Unrevolutionary England*, pp. 56–7; Miller, 'Representatives', 127.

103 Quoted in Cust, 'Politics and the Electorate', p. 141.

104 Miller, 'Public Opinion', 376. He adds in a footnote: 'It could perhaps be argued that the Swedish Diet was more representative, not least because peasants were represented by peasants'. Cf. Richard Bonney, *The European Dynastic States, 1494–1660* (Oxford, 1991), pp. 326–7.

105 See pp. 134–5, below.

106 Quoted in Miller, 'Representatives', 126.

107 Quoted in Russell, *Unrevolutionary England*, p. 134.

108 *Ibid.*, pp. 134–5; see also pp. 13–14.

3 Functions I: High Court and Great Council

1 Quoted in John Guy, 'The Rhetoric of Counsel in Early Modern England', in Dale Hoak (ed.), *Tudor Political Culture* (Cambridge, 1995), pp. 292–310, at p. 304.

2 The following two paragraphs are greatly indebted to H. M. Colvin (ed.), *The History of the King's Works* (6 vols., 1963–82), I, 491–552; IV, 286–300; Plan III.

3 On this, see in particular Charles Howard McIlwain, *The High Court of Parliament and its Supremacy* (New Haven, 1910), especially pp. 121–4.

4 J. P. Cooper, *Land, Men and Beliefs: Studies in Early-Modern History*, ed. G. E. Aylmer and J. S. Morrill (1983), p. 99.

5 Sir Thomas Smith, *De Republica Anglorum*, ed. Mary Dewar (Cambridge, 1982), p. 85 (Book II, Chapter 2); Edward Coke, *The Fourth Part of the Institutes of the Laws of England* (1797 edition), pp. 1–52.

6 Elizabeth Read Foster, *The House of Lords, 1603–1649: Structure, Procedure, and the Nature of its Business* (Chapel Hill, 1983), pp. 162–79; Andrew Swatland, *The House of Lords in the Reign of Charles II* (Cambridge, 1996), p. 76.

7 See below, pp. 36–8.

8 For a brief outline of attainder, see G. R. Elton (ed.), *The Tudor Constitution: Documents and Commentary* (2nd edition, Cambridge, 1982), p. 82. On the medieval and Tudor background, see especially J. R. Lander, 'Attainder and Forfeiture, 1453 to 1509', *HJ*, IV (1961), 119–51; S. E. Lehmberg, 'Parliamentary

Attainder in the Reign of Henry VIII', *HJ*, XVIII (1975), 675–702; W. R. Stacy, 'Richard Roose and the Use of Parliamentary Attainder in the Reign of Henry VIII', *HJ*, XXIX (1986), 1–15.

9 On this, see particularly Colin G. C. Tite, *Impeachment and Parliamentary Judicature in Early Stuart England* (1974), pp. 212–13, 216; William R. Stacy, 'Impeachment, Attainder, and the "Revival" of Parliamentary Judicature under the Early Stuarts', *PH*, XI (1992), 40–56; W. R. Stacy, 'The Bill of Attainder in English History' (unpubl. Ph.D. dissertation, University of Wisconsin-Madison, 1986), pp. 239–96. I am grateful to Alan Orr for alerting me to this dissertation.

10 Conrad Russell, *Unrevolutionary England, 1603–1642* (1990), pp. 89–109; John H. Timmis, *Thine is the Kingdom* (Alabama, 1974); W. R. Stacy, 'Matter of Fact, Matter of Law, and the Attainder of the Earl of Strafford', *American Journal of Legal History*, XXIX (1985), 323–47; Stacy, 'Bill of Attainder', pp. 297–363. The point about speed being the primary motive in a Parliament that was fearful for its own future is made very convincingly in D. Alan Orr, 'Sovereignty, State and the Law of Treason in England, 1641–1649' (unpubl. Ph.D. dissertation, University of Cambridge, 1997), pp. 56–105. I am most grateful to Alan Orr for showing me his dissertation prior to submission, and for several very valuable discussions on this subject.

11 Stacy, 'Bill of Attainder', pp. 364–465.

12 *Ibid.*, pp. 466–586. The act to attaint Fenwick was 8 & 9 Gul. III, c. 4, printed in Andrew Browning (ed.), *English Historical Documents, 1660–1714* (1953), p. 204.

13 For the revival of impeachment after 1621, see especially Tite, *Impeachment, passim*, and Stacy, 'Impeachment, Attainder, and the "Revival" of Parliamentary Judicature'.

14 See below, pp. 88–9, 93, 109–11, 115.

15 Maurice F. Bond, *Guide to the Records of Parliament* (1971), p. 109.

16 *Ibid.* The variations in the procedures that have generally been lumped together as 'impeachments' are clearly laid out in Tite, *Impeachment*, especially pp. 224–7.

17 See below, pp. 26–31.

18 Quoted in Tite, *Impeachment*, p. 158.

19 This point is particularly well made in Conrad Russell, *Parliaments and English Politics, 1621–1629* (Oxford, 1979), pp. 15–17, 103–18, 198–202.

20 For example, the Lords heard only five cases of error in King's Bench between 1514 and 1589, and none between 1589 and 1621: Foster, *House of Lords*, p. 179. Between 1621 and 1649, nearly 400 writs of error were brought into the Lords: Swatland, *House of Lords*, pp. 74–5.

21 This and the following paragraph are heavily indebted to James S. Hart, *Justice upon Petition: The House of Lords and the Reformation of Justice, 1621–1675* (1991); J. Stoddart Flemion, 'Slow Process, Due Process, and the High Court of Parliament: A Reinterpretation of the Revival of Judicature in the House of Lords in 1621', *HJ*, XVII (1974), 3–16; and Allen Horstman, 'A New *Curia Regis*: The Judicature of the House of Lords in the 1620s', *HJ*, XXV (1982), 411–22.

22 Hart, *Justice upon Petition*, p. 142.

23 See below, p. 126.

24 See above, p. 21.

25 Hart, *Justice upon Petition*, p. 175.

26 These violations are discussed more fully below, pp. 133–4.

27 Mary Cotterell, 'Interregnum Law Reform: The Hale Commission of 1652', *EHR*, LXXXIII (1968), 689–704; Ivan Roots, '"The Other House": Bicamerism in the Protectorate Parliaments', in H. W. Blom, W. P. Blockmans and H. de Schepper (eds.), *Bicameralisme: Tweekamerstelsel vroeger en nu* (The Hague, 1992), pp. 249–60, especially pp. 251–2.

28 William Prynne, for example, had made a powerful polemical case that the Lords' judicature was useful as well as rightful in his *A Plea for the Lords, and House of Peers*, originally published in 1648 (Wing, P 4032; BL, TT, E 430/8) and republished in 1658 (Wing, P 4034; BL, TT, E 749/1).

29 Swatland, *House of Lords*, pp. 128–41; Hart, *Justice upon Petition*, pp. 242–58. See also below, pp. 66, 91–2.
30 *CJ*, IX, 347. It is likely that the Commons' prime motive was not to attack the Lords' appellate judicature *per se*, but to defend the immunity of their members from law suits during time of Parliament: Swatland, *House of Lords*, p. 74.
31 *LJ*, XII, 718; quoted in Hart, *Justice upon Petition*, p. 254.
32 Swatland, *House of Lords*, pp. 90, 140; Flemion, 'Slow Process, Due Process, and the High Court of Parliament', 16; Bond, *Records of Parliament*, pp. 106–7, 114–15.
33 Foster, *House of Lords*, p. 149.
34 BL, Harleian MS 6810, fo. 127; quoted in Swatland, *House of Lords*, p. 79.
35 The intermittent nature of parliamentary sessions is discussed more fully below, pp. 75–6.
36 Bond, *Records of Parliament*, p. 115.
37 See above, p. 9.
38 Russell, *Unrevolutionary England*, p. 134.
39 Cooper, *Land, Men and Beliefs*, pp. 106–7.
40 For contemporary accounts of bill procedure, see William Hakewill, *The Manner how Statutes are Enacted in Parliament by Passing of Bills* (1641), pp. 1–102 (written in about 1610–11); Henry Elsynge, *The Method of Passing Bills in Parliament* (1685), reprinted in *The Harleian Miscellany* (10 vols., 1808–13), V, 226–34 (written in about 1625); Henry Scobell, *Memorials of the Method and Manner of Proceedings in Parliament in Passing Bills* (1658), pp. 40–69; C. S. Sims, 'The Speaker of the House of Commons: An Early Seventeenth-Century Tractate', *AHR*, XLV (1939–40), 90–5; C. S. Sims, '"The Moderne Forme of the Parliaments of England"', *AHR*, LIII (1947–8), 288–305. There are particularly helpful summaries of the procedure in G. R. Elton, *The Parliament of England, 1559–1581* (Cambridge, 1986), pp. 43–61, 88–130; Bond, *Records of Parliament*, pp. 59–64, 70–82; David Dean, *Law-making and Society in Late Elizabethan England: The Parliament of England, 1584–1601* (Cambridge, 1996), pp. 19–33; David Dean, 'Bills and Acts, 1584–1601' (unpubl. Ph.D. dissertation, University of Cambridge, 1984), pp. 31–85; and Foster, *House of Lords*, pp. 189–202.
41 Restitution bills are discussed below, p. 41. It was also usual for naturalisation bills (see below, p. 41) to originate in the Commons.
42 For a more detailed examination of parliamentary committees, see below, pp. 71–3.
43 The transfer formula, in Law French, was 'ceste bille soit baillé aux seigneurs' if it was being forwarded from the Commons to the Lords, or 'ceste bille soit baillé aux communes' if from Lords to Commons.
44 The royal assent – and the occasional use of the royal veto – are analysed more fully below, pp. 95–6. For conferences between the two Houses, see below, pp. 74–5.
45 Elton, *Parliament of England*, pp. 44–5.
46 Hakewill, *The Manner how Statutes are Enacted in Parliament*, pp. 78–9.
47 Elton, *Parliament of England*, pp. 52–5, 128–9.
48 *Ibid.*, pp. 55–61. I am very grateful to Chris Kyle for advice on this point.
49 HLRO, Braye MS 52, fos. 261–5; O. C. Williams, *The Clerical Organisation of the House of Commons* (Oxford, 1954), pp. 299–300; Foster, *House of Lords*, p. 30.
50 These acts were, respectively, 3 Jac. I, OA 37; 7 Jac. I, OA 28; 16 & 17 Car. I, OA 31; 22 Car. II, OA 29.
51 These acts were, respectively, 3 Jac. I, c. 23; 21 Jac. I, c. 31; 12 Car. II, c. 22; 13 & 14 Car. II, c. 28; 29 Car. II, c. 10.
52 See especially Dean, *Law-making and Society in Late Elizabethan England*; also David Dean, 'Parliament and Locality', in D. M. Dean and N. L. Jones (eds.), *The Parliaments of Elizabethan England* (Oxford and Cambridge, Mass., 1990), pp. 139–62; David Dean, 'Pressure Groups and Lobbies in the Elizabethan and Early Jacobean Parliaments', *PER*, XI (1991), 139–152; David Dean, 'London

Lobbies and Parliament: The Case of the Brewers and Coopers in the Parliament of 1593', *PH*, VIII (1989), 341–65; David Dean, 'Public or Private? London, Leather and Legislation in Elizabethan England', *HJ*, XXXI (1988), 525–48; and Ian Archer, 'The London Lobbies in the Later Sixteenth Century', *HJ*, XXXI (1988), 17–44.

53 The following account is based on Clive Holmes, 'Drainers and Fenmen: The Problem of Popular Political Consciousness in the Seventeenth Century', in Anthony Fletcher and John Stevenson (eds.), *Order and Disorder in Early Modern England* (Cambridge, 1985), pp. 166–95.

54 Smith, *De Republica Anglorum*, ed. Dewar, p. 79 (Book II, Chapter 1); quoted in Dean, *Law-making and Society in Late Elizabethan England*, p. 17.

55 See Russell, *Unrevolutionary England*, p. 6.

56 See Appendix 2, pp. 239–40, below.

57 The figures for 1571–97 are derived from Michael A. R. Graves, *The Tudor Parliaments: Crown, Lords and Commons, 1485–1603* (Harlow, 1985), pp. 139, 141; those for the period after 1660 from Swatland, *House of Lords*, p. 53, and Julian Hoppit (ed.), *Failed Legislation, 1660–1800, Extracted from the Commons and Lords Journals* (1997), pp. 4–5, 22. I am very grateful to Kurt Fryklund for kindly supplying figures for the period 1603–25.

58 R. W. K. Hinton, 'The Decline of Parliamentary Government under Elizabeth I and the Early Stuarts', *CHJ*, XIII (1957), 116–32.

59 Russell, *Unrevolutionary England*, p. 217; Russell, *Parliaments*, pp. 181, 190, 233–4.

60 Quoted in Russell, *Unrevolutionary England*, p. 24. Cf. Russell, *Parliaments*, p. 45.

61 See Guy, 'Rhetoric of Counsel', p. 302; P. J. Holmes, 'The Last Tudor Great Councils', *HJ*, XXXIII (1990), 1–22.

62 Russell, *Unrevolutionary England*, p. 8. Rehoboam was the son of Solomon whose doings as King of Israel and then of Judah are told in I Kings, 11–14, and II Chronicles, 10–12.

63 Edward Coke, *The First Part of the Institutes of the Lawes of England* (1629), p. 110 (Book 2, Chapter 10, section 164).

64 James Spedding (ed.), *The Letters and the Life of Francis Bacon* (7 vols., 1861–74), VI, 38.

65 Francis Hargrave (ed.), *A Complete Collection of State-Trials* (11 vols. in 7, 1776), I, 517.

66 Quoted in Guy, 'Rhetoric of Counsel', p. 298; see also H. M. Jewel, 'The Value of *Fleta* as Evidence about Parliament', *EHR*, CVII (1992), 90–4.

67 D. H. Willson, *The Privy Councillors in the House of Commons, 1604–1629* (Minneapolis, 1940), pp. 56–63, 99–101, 236–45; R. C. Munden, '"All the Privy Council Being Members of this House": A Note on the Constitutional Significance of Procedure in the House of Commons, 1589–1614', *PH*, XII (1993), 115–25.

68 Andrew Swatland, 'The Role of Privy Councillors in the House of Lords, 1660–1681', in Clyve Jones (ed.), *A Pillar of the Constitution: The House of Lords in British Politics, 1640–1784* (1989), pp. 51–77, especially pp. 52–3, 56, 62–6; Swatland, *House of Lords*, pp. 55–6, 60. The Committee of the Whole House is discussed more fully below, pp. 73–4.

69 The system of proxies in the Lords is discussed below, p. 68.

70 There is a growing literature on the nature of these political groupings and how they reflected the bicameral structure of Parliament: for a cross-section of some of the most significant contributions, see Blom, Blockmans and de Schepper (eds.), *Bicameralisme*, especially the papers by Pauline Croft and I. A. A. Thompson, David Dean, G. A. Harrison and Ivan Roots; Russell, *Unrevolutionary England*, pp. xi–xiii; Swatland, *House of Lords*, Chapters 6–7; J. S. A. Adamson, 'Parliamentary Management, Men-of-Business and the House of Lords, 1640–49', and Swatland, 'The Role of Privy Councillors', in Jones (ed.), *Pillar of the Constitution*, pp. 21–77; Simon Adams, 'Foreign Policy and the Parliaments of 1621 and 1624', in Kevin

Sharpe (ed.), *Faction and Parliament: Essays on Early Stuart History* (Oxford, 1978), pp. 139–71.

71 These exchanges are conveniently printed in J. R. Tanner (ed.), *Constitutional Documents of the Reign of James I* (Cambridge, 1930), pp. 276–89, from which the following quotations are taken.

72 The full form of words in the writ of summons called members '*ad tractandum et consentiendum pro quibusdam arduis et urgentibus negotiis statum et defensionem regni et ecclesiae Anglicanae tangentibus*' ('to treat and consent about difficult and urgent business concerning the state and defence of the kingdom and the Church of England'); quoted in Russell, *Unrevolutionary England*, p. 7.

73 *LJ*, III, 209–10. See also Thomas Cogswell, *The Blessed Revolution: English Politics and the Coming of War, 1621–1624* (Cambridge, 1989), pp. 167–8.

74 Richard Cust, *The Forced Loan and English Politics, 1626–1628* (Oxford, 1987), p. 82.

75 Richard Cust, 'Charles I and a Draft Declaration for the 1628 Parliament', *HR*, LXIII (1990), 143–61, at 159.

76 J. P. Kenyon (ed.), *The Stuart Constitution: Documents and Commentary* (2nd edition, Cambridge, 1986), pp. 28, 46.

77 This clause comes from the second of the *Nineteen Propositions*, printed in S. R. Gardiner (ed.), *Constitutional Documents of the Puritan Revolution, 1625–1660* (3rd edition, Oxford, 1906), pp. 250–1.

78 Declaration of the Houses in Defence of the Militia Ordinance, 6 June 1642, printed in Gardiner (ed.), *Constitutional Documents*, pp. 256–7.

79 In exploring the origins of ordinances, Michael Mendle's otherwise convincing article 'The Great Council of Parliament and the First Ordinances: The Constitutional Theory of the Civil War', *JBS*, XXXI (1992), 133–62, seems to me to over-emphasise Parliament's role as Great Council at the expense of that as High Court: the crucial rationale for ordinances rested on Parliament's fusion of both functions. Cf. Elizabeth R. Foster, 'The House of Lords and Ordinances, 1641–1649', *American Journal of Legal History*, XXI (1977), 157–73.

80 *CJ*, VI, 111.

81 Gardiner (ed.), *Constitutional Documents*, pp. 384–8.

82 *LJ*, XII, 166.

83 John Miller, 'Charles II and his Parliaments', *TRHS*, 5th series, XXXII (1982), 1–23, especially 4–5.

84 *CJ*, IX, 426.

85 *His Majesty's Declaration to all his loving subjects, touching the causes and reasons that moved him to dissolve the two last Parliaments* (1681), printed in Browning (ed.), *English Historical Documents*, pp. 185–8 (quotations at p. 186).

86 See below, pp. 162–3.

87 Quoted in David Harris Sacks, 'Parliament, Liberty, and the Commonweal', in J. H. Hexter (ed.), *Parliament and Liberty from the Reign of Elizabeth to the English Civil War* (Stanford, 1992), pp. 85–121, at p. 116.

88 For this claim, see in particular William's Declaration of 30 September 1688, printed in E. N. Williams (ed.), *The Eighteenth-Century Constitution, 1688–1815: Documents and Commentary* (Cambridge, 1960), pp. 10–16 (quotation at p. 15).

89 The Bill of Rights (1 Gul. & Mar., sess. 2, c. 2) is printed in Browning (ed.), *English Historical Documents*, pp. 122–8 (quotations at pp. 123–4).

90 These privileges are discussed more fully below, pp. 64–8.

4 Functions II: the power of the purse

1 For an extremely clear summary of this system, see G. R. Elton (ed.), *The Tudor Constitution: Documents and Commentary* (2nd edition, Cambridge, 1982), pp. 39–45. The medieval background is set out in G. L. Harriss, 'Medieval Doctrines

in the Debates on Supply, 1610–1629', in Kevin Sharpe (ed.), *Faction and Parliament: Essays on Early Stuart History* (Oxford, 1978), pp. 73–103. Another excellent overview is Clive Holmes, 'Parliament, Liberty, Taxation, and Property', in J. H. Hexter (ed.), *Parliament and Liberty from the Reign of Elizabeth to the English Civil War* (Stanford, 1992), pp. 122–54.

2 Conrad Russell, *The Addled Parliament of 1614: The Limits of Revision* (Reading, 1992), p. 10.

3 There were two Convocations of the clergy, one for the southern province of Canterbury, which met concurrently with Parliament, the other for the northern province of York, which usually met immediately after the end of the parliamentary session. See also p. 231, below.

4 *CJ*, I, 448.

5 For analyses of the fifteenth and tenth, see G. R. Elton, *The Parliament of England, 1559–1581* (Cambridge, 1986), pp. 153–5; Michael J. Braddick, *The Nerves of State: Taxation and the Financing of the English State, 1558–1714* (Manchester, 1996), pp. 91–3; Michael J. Braddick, *Parliamentary Taxation in Seventeenth-Century England: Local Administration and Response* (Woodbridge, 1994), pp. 23–63; Conrad Russell, 'Parliament and the King's Finances', in Conrad Russell (ed.), *The Origins of the English Civil War* (1973), pp. 98, 103.

6 Conrad Russell, *Unrevolutionary England, 1603–1642* (1990), pp. 22, 42; Braddick, *Parliamentary Taxation*, pp. 64–125. For the problem of under-assessment in the Tudor period, see Roger Schofield, 'Taxation and the Political Limits of the Tudor State', in Claire Cross, David Loades and J. J. Scarisbrick (eds.), *Law and Government under the Tudors: Essays Presented to Sir Geoffrey Elton on his Retirement* (Cambridge, 1988), pp. 227–55.

7 Quoted in John Guy, *Tudor England* (Oxford, 1988), p. 384. I am grateful to Graham Seel for drawing my attention to this reference.

8 Conrad Russell, *Parliaments and English Politics, 1621–1629* (Oxford, 1979), pp. 49–50; Felicity Heal and Clive Holmes, *The Gentry in England and Wales, 1500–1700* (1994), pp. 157–8.

9 Braddick, *Nerves of State*, p. 94.

10 *Ibid.*, p. 12.

11 J. S. Roskell, 'Perspectives in English Parliamentary History', in E. B. Fryde and Edward Miller (eds.), *Historical Studies of the English Parliament*, vol. II: *1399 to 1603* (Cambridge, 1970), p. 318.

12 H. G. Koenigsberger, *Politicians and Virtuosi* (1986), p. 24.

13 See, in particular, Russell, *Unrevolutionary England*, pp. 20–3, 35–47; Russell, *Parliaments*, pp. 49–53; Russell, 'Parliament and the King's Finances'; Conrad Russell, *The Causes of the English Civil War* (Oxford, 1990), pp. 178–83.

14 Russell, *Unrevolutionary England*, p. 42.

15 Russell, *Parliaments*, p. 53.

16 Russell, *Unrevolutionary England*, p. 36; Russell, *Causes*, p. 183.

17 Thomas Cogswell, 'A Low Road to Extinction? Supply and Redress of Grievances in the Parliaments of the 1620s', *HJ*, XXXIII (1990), 283–303 (quotations at 301, 303). For another penetrating critique of Russell's interpretation, see Christopher Thompson, *Parliamentary History in the 1620s: In or Out of Perspective?* (Wivenhoe, 1986). I am very grateful to Christopher Thompson for providing me with a copy of this paper.

18 Russell, *Unrevolutionary England*, pp. 41–2; Russell, *Parliaments*, pp. 323–89; Cogswell, 'Low Road to Extinction?', 296–300.

19 Russell, *Unrevolutionary England*, pp. 38–9; Russell, *Parliaments*, pp. 260–322; Russell, *Causes*, p. 178; Cogswell, 'Low Road to Extinction?', 291–5.

20 Conrad Russell, 'English Parliaments 1593–1606: One Epoch or Two?', in D. M. Dean and N. L. Jones (eds.), *The Parliaments of Elizabethan England* (Oxford and Cambridge, Mass., 1990), pp. 191–213, at p. 204.

21 Russell, *Unrevolutionary England*, p. 36.

22 *Ibid.*, pp. 36–7; Russell, *Parliaments*, pp. 85–144; Cogswell, 'Low Road to Extinction?', 285–9; Thomas Cogswell, 'War and the Liberties of the Subject', in Hexter (ed.), *Parliament and Liberty*, pp. 229–31.

23 Russell, *Unrevolutionary England*, pp. 37–8; Russell, *Parliaments*, pp. 145–203; Russell, *Causes*, p. 180; Cogswell, 'Low Road to Extinction?', 289–91. See also Mark E. Kennedy, 'Legislation, Foreign Policy, and the "Proper Business" of the Parliament of 1624', *Albion*, XXIII (1991), 41–60.

24 Thomas Cogswell, *The Blessed Revolution: English Politics and the Coming of War, 1621–1624* (Cambridge, 1989), pp. 227–61; Cogswell, 'War and the Liberties of the Subject', pp. 234–5.

25 Chris R. Kyle, '*Lex Loquens*: Legislation in the Parliament of 1624' (unpubl. Ph.D. dissertation, University of Auckland, 1993), pp. 484–97.

26 J. P. Kenyon (ed.), *The Stuart Constitution: Documents and Commentary* (2nd edition, Cambridge, 1986), pp. 51, 64–7; Kyle, '*Lex Loquens*', pp. 485–6. See also below, p. 111.

27 *Procs., 1628*, II, 58–9.

28 Chris R. Kyle, 'Prince Charles in the Parliaments of 1621 and 1624', *HJ*, XLI (1998), 603–24. I am very grateful to Chris Kyle for showing me a copy of this paper prior to publication. See also below, pp. 93, 111.

29 John Reeve has argued convincingly that the problem was not that England was inherently incapable of fighting a war but that Charles's personality and policies led to a loss of trust between himself and the political elite which greatly impeded the war effort: John Reeve, 'The Politics of War Finance in an Age of Confessional Strife: A Comparative Anglo-European View', in S. M. Jack and B. A. Masters (eds.), *Protestants, Property, Puritans: Godly People Revisited* (*Parergon*, XIV, 1996), 85–109. I am most grateful to John Reeve for letting me see a copy of this paper prior to publication, and for a stimulating discussion on this subject.

30 For example, the five subsidies voted by the Parliament of 1628 raised £275,000: Richard Cust, *The Forced Loan and English Politics, 1626–1628* (Oxford, 1987), p. 4.

31 On this, see especially Cust, *Forced Loan*, pp. 58–62.

32 Quoted in Harriss, 'Medieval Doctrines', p. 83.

33 Quoted in Cogswell, 'Low Road to Extinction?', 295, 302.

34 Quoted in Cogswell, 'War and the Liberties of the Subject', p. 247.

35 Richard Cust, 'Charles I and a Draft Declaration for the 1628 Parliament', *HR*, LXIII (1990), 143–61, at 153, 156, 158.

36 Braddick, *Nerves of State*, pp. 50–1.

37 On Bate's Case, see especially Pauline Croft, 'Fresh Light on Bate's Case', *HJ*, XXX (1987), 523–39; Glenn Burgess, *The Politics of the Ancient Constitution: An Introduction to English Political Thought, 1603–1642* (1992), pp. 140–4; Braddick, *Nerves of State*, pp. 132–7; Holmes, 'Parliament, Liberty, Taxation, and Property', pp. 129–37, 141–3.

38 Braddick, *Nerves of State*, pp. 53–5; Russell, *Unrevolutionary England*, pp. 38–9.

39 Russell, *Unrevolutionary England*, pp. 38–9; Russell, *Parliaments*, pp. 49–53, 136, 150–1, 198–9, 227–9, 278–9.

40 Burgess, *Politics of the Ancient Constitution*, pp. 140–4; Braddick, *Nerves of State*, pp. 132–7.

41 Russell, *Parliaments*, pp. 227–9, 386–8, 400–406, 413–16; Russell, *Unrevolutionary England*, pp. 39–40; Braddick, *Nerves of State*, pp. 51–5, 139–40.

42 Gardiner (ed.), *Constitutional Documents*, p. 83.

43 Cust, 'Charles I and a Draft Declaration', especially 150–9.

44 Quoted in Cust, *Forced Loan*, p. 33.

45 Russell, *Causes*, pp. 182–3; Russell, 'Parliament and the King's Finances', pp. 103–4.

46 Russell, 'Parliament and the King's Finances', pp. 100–1; Eric Lindquist, 'The Failure of the Great Contract', *JMH*, LVII (1985), 617–51; Harriss, 'Medieval Doctrines', pp. 89–90; Alan G. R. Smith, 'Crown, Parliament and Finance: The Great Contract of 1610', in Peter Clark, Alan G. R. Smith and Nicholas Tyacke (eds.), *The English Commonwealth, 1547–1640: Essays in Politics and Society Presented to Joel Hurstfield* (Leicester, 1979), pp. 111–27.
47 Quoted in Lindquist, 'Failure of the Great Contract', 639.
48 *Ibid.*, 648.
49 Russell, 'Parliament and the King's Finances', pp. 105–8; Russell, *Parliaments*, especially pp. 282–5, 382–5, 406.
50 Braddick, *Nerves of State*, Chapters 3 and 4; Kevin Sharpe, *The Personal Rule of Charles I* (New Haven and London, 1992), Chapters 3 and 9.
51 Centre for Kentish Studies, uncatalogued Cranfield Papers: Edward Sackville, fourth Earl of Dorset, to Lionel Cranfield, first Earl of Middlesex, 1 October 1636.
52 Conrad Russell, *The Fall of the British Monarchies, 1637–42* (Oxford, 1991), pp. 90–123; Sharpe, *Personal Rule*, pp. 851–77; Holmes, 'Parliament, Liberty, Taxation, and Property', p. 152.
53 These acts were 16 Car. I, c. 8; 16 Car. I, c. 14; 16 Car. I, c. 16; 16 Car. I, c. 20; printed in Gardiner (ed.), *Constitutional Documents*, pp. 159–62, 189–97. At about the same time, a bill was introduced declaring purveyance illegal. However, this was lost during the parliamentary recess of September–October 1641, and it was not until December 1642 that a resolution of the Houses suspended purveyance. On this, see G. E. Aylmer, 'The Last Years of Purveyance, 1610–1660', *EcHR*, X (1957–8), 81–93; Russell, *Fall of the British Monarchies*, pp. 363–4.
54 Russell, 'Parliament and the King's Finances', pp. 111–16; Russell, *Fall of the British Monarchies*, pp. 252–7. See also below, pp. 124–5.
55 See below, pp. 124–5.
56 Russell, *Fall of the British Monarchies*, pp. 256–7, 346–50, 357–62, 436–7.
57 Russell, *Unrevolutionary England*, p. 175.
58 The classic statement of these terms is found in the *Nineteen Propositions* of 1 June 1642, printed in Gardiner (ed.), *Constitutional Documents*, pp. 249–54.
59 Quoted in Russell, *Causes*, p. 23.
60 *AO*, I, 85–100.
61 *Ibid.*, 630–46.
62 Braddick, *Nerves of State*, pp. 95–6; Braddick, *Parliamentary Taxation*, pp. 126–67.
63 This act had been one of the last to receive Charles I's assent: 16 Car. I, c. 32.
64 John Morrill, *Revolt in the Provinces: The People of England and the Tragedies of War, 1630–1648* (2nd edition, Harlow, 1998), pp. 118–19.
65 Braddick, *Nerves of State*, p. 99; J. P. Cooper, *Land, Men and Beliefs: Studies in Early-Modern History*, ed. G. E. Aylmer and J. S. Morrill (1983), pp. 105–6.
66 *AO*, I, 202–14.
67 *Ibid.*, 274–83, 364–6, 466–8.
68 *Ibid.*, 1004–7; Braddick, *Nerves of State*, pp. 99–100, 220–4; Braddick, *Parliamentary Taxation*, pp. 178–92; David Underdown, *Revel, Riot and Rebellion: Popular Politics and Culture in England, 1603–1660* (Oxford, 1985), pp. 149, 216, 270.
69 *AO*, II, 213–35, 845–53.
70 Morrill, *Revolt in the Provinces*, pp. 80–2.
71 M. A. E. Green (ed.), *Calendar of the Proceedings of the Committee for the Advance of Money* (3 vols., 1888), I, v–xviii.
72 M. A. E. Green (ed.), *Calendar of the Proceedings of the Committee for Compounding with Delinquents* (5 vols., 1889–93), I, v–xxiv; V, v–xlii.
73 *AO*, I, 16–20, 627–30.
74 Morrill, *Revolt in the Provinces*, p. 75.
75 On this backlash, see especially *ibid.*, Chapters 2 and 3; Robert Ashton, 'From

Cavalier to Roundhead Tyranny, 1642–9', in John Morrill (ed.), *Reactions to the English Civil War, 1642–1649* (1982), pp. 185–207.

76 The text of this petition is printed in John Morrill, *The Revolt of the Provinces: Conservatives and Radicals in the English Civil War, 1630–1650* (Longman edition, Harlow, 1980), pp. 207–8.

77 Morrill, *Revolt in the Provinces*, pp. 111–14.

78 The King's final speeches are conveniently printed in David Lagomarsino and Charles J. Wood (eds.), *The Trial of Charles I: A Documentary History* (Hanover, NH, and London, 1989), especially pp. 64–6, 79–82, 140–3.

79 Maurice Ashley, *Financial and Commercial Policy under the Cromwellian Protectorate* (2nd edition, 1962), pp. 72–83.

80 See, for example, the grievances voiced in the debate of 12–13 June 1657: J. T. Rutt (ed.), *Diary of Thomas Burton, Esq.* (4 vols., 1828), II, 229–47.

81 Ashley, *Financial and Commercial Policy*, pp. 62–70; Braddick, *Parliamentary Taxation*, pp. 168–201.

82 BL, TT, 669.f.21(58); quoted in Braddick, *Parliamentary Taxation*, p. 199.

83 Quoted in Braddick, *Parliamentary Taxation*, p. 198; Ashley, *Financial and Commercial Policy*, p. 67.

84 AO, II, 845–53 (at 849).

85 On Cony's Case and its significance, see especially Braddick, *Nerves of State*, pp. 144–6; Alan Cromartie, *Sir Matthew Hale, 1609–1676: Law, Religion and Natural Philosophy* (Cambridge, 1995), pp. 82–3.

86 Timothy Venning, *Cromwellian Foreign Policy* (1995), pp. 125–6, 145–6, 182–5, 249–50. See also below, p. 141.

87 S. R. Gardiner, *History of the Commonwealth and Protectorate* (4 vols., 1903), III, 299–302; Christopher Durston, 'The Fall of Cromwell's Major-Generals', *EHR*, CXIII (1998), 18–37.

88 See, for example, Rutt (ed.), *Diary of Burton*, II, 29.

89 The Instrument of Government, § XXVII; printed in Gardiner (ed.), *Constitutional Documents*, p. 414.

90 The Humble Petition and Advice, § 7; printed in *ibid.*, pp. 452–3.

91 The Crown was voted in perpetuity the so-called 'hereditary excise', worth roughly half the excise of the 1640s and 1650s. In addition, Charles was also granted for his lifetime the other half of the excise together with the customs revenues: C. D. Chandaman, *The English Public Revenue, 1660–1688* (Oxford, 1975), pp. 37–43; Braddick, *Parliamentary Taxation*, pp. 201–3.

92 Much the most detailed account of the financial settlement, and of Restoration finance in general, is Chandaman, *Public Revenue*. See also Paul Seaward, *The Cavalier Parliament and the Reconstruction of the Old Regime, 1661–1667* (Cambridge, 1989), pp. 103–30.

93 On the hearth tax, see Chandaman, *Public Revenue*, pp. 77–109; Braddick, *Parliamentary Taxation*, pp. 241–70.

94 Chandaman, *Public Revenue*, p. 332.

95 *Ibid.*, pp. 138–95; Braddick, *Parliamentary Taxation*, pp. 158–67.

96 The sums that these sources generated are tabulated in Chandaman, *Public Revenue*, p. 332.

97 This problem was to some extent aggravated by his habitual extravagance, although the precise extent remains a source of controversy: for contrasting assessments, see *ibid.*, pp. 269–72, and Lionel K. J. Glassey, 'Politics, Finance and Government', in Lionel K. J. Glassey (ed.), *The Reigns of Charles II and James VII & II* (1997), pp. 47–8.

98 Grey, *Debates*, IV, 115.

99 Quoted in Chandaman, *Public Revenue*, p. 279.

100 Quoted in Derek M. Hirst, 'Freedom, Revolution, and Beyond', in Hexter (ed.), *Parliament and Liberty*, p. 269. For an example of a failed attempt at appropriation, see Seaward, *Cavalier Parliament*, p. 124.

101 Hirst, 'Freedom, Revolution, and Beyond', p. 270.
102 D. T. Witcombe, *Charles II and the Cavalier House of Commons, 1663–1674* (Manchester, 1966), pp. 127–40; John Miller, 'Charles II and his Parliaments', *TRHS*, 5th series, XXXII (1982), 1–23, especially 15–16. Cf. Hirst, 'Freedom, Revolution, and Beyond', pp. 268–70; and Derek Hirst, 'The Conciliatoriness of the Cavalier Commons Reconsidered', *PH*, VI (1987), 221–35, at 228–9.
103 Miller, 'Charles II and his Parliaments', 15–16; Hirst, 'Freedom, Revolution, and Beyond', pp. 269–70; Hirst, 'Conciliatoriness of the Cavalier Commons', 229.
104 Chandaman, *Public Revenue*, pp. 303–4.
105 See below, pp. 77, 160–1.
106 1 Jac. II, c. 1.
107 1 Jac. II, c. 3; 1 Jac. II, c. 4; 1 Jac. II, c. 5.
108 Chandaman, *Public Revenue*, pp. 48–9, 256–61, 332–3.
109 Kenyon (ed.), *Stuart Constitution*, p. 364. Cf. Glassey, 'Politics, Finance and Government', p. 50.
110 Quoted in W. A. Speck, *Reluctant Revolutionaries: Englishmen and the Revolution of 1688* (Oxford, 1988), p. 43.
111 Quoted in John Miller, *The Glorious Revolution* (Harlow, 1983), pp. 40, 42.
112 Gilbert Burnet, *History of my Own Time* (6 vols., Oxford, 1833), IV, 60–1.
113 The grant was made up of the hereditary excise, other hereditary revenues (such as the Crown lands), the temporary excise, which was voted to William and Mary for their lives, and the customs. However, the customs, which were worth over £500,000 a year, were initially voted for only four years. On the financial settlement, see especially Clayton Roberts, 'The Constitutional Significance of the Financial Settlement of 1690', *HJ*, XX (1977), 59–76; E. A. Reitan, 'From Revenue to Civil List, 1689–1702: The Revolution Settlement and the "Mixed and Balanced" Constitution', *HJ*, XIII (1970), 571–88; John Brewer, *The Sinews of Power: War, Money and the English State, 1688–1783* (1989), pp. 144–9.
114 Quoted in Miller, *Glorious Revolution*, pp. 40–1.
115 The Bill of Rights is printed in Andrew Browning (ed.), *English Historical Documents, 1660–1714* (1953), pp. 122–8 (quotation at p. 123).
116 Miller, *Glorious Revolution*, p. 59.
117 Braddick, *Nerves of State*, pp. 12–16.
118 *Ibid.*, p. 13.
119 Brewer, *Sinews of Power*, Chapter 4; Miller, *Glorious Revolution*, pp. 55–61; Colin Brooks, 'Public Finance and Political Stability: The Administration of the Land Tax, 1688–1720', *HJ*, XVII (1974), 281–300.
120 See below, pp. 167–70, 174–6.
121 Brewer, *Sinews of Power*, pp. 149–61; J. A. Downie, 'The Commission of Public Accounts and the Formation of the Country Party', *EHR*, XCI (1976), 33–51.
122 Chandaman, *Public Revenue*, pp. 295–300; Seaward, *Cavalier Parliament*, pp. 124–8; Henry Roseveare, *The Treasury, 1660–1870: The Foundations of Control* (1973), pp. 20–45.
123 Braddick, *Nerves of State*, pp. 41–5.
124 Reitan, 'From Revenue to Civil List'.
125 Edward, Earl of Clarendon, *The Life of Edward, Earl of Clarendon . . . written by himself* (2 vols., Oxford, 1760), I, 440.

5 Procedure

1 See, in particular, Sheila Lambert, 'Procedure in the House of Commons in the Early Stuart Period', *EHR*, XCV (1980), 753–81.
2 The office of Speaker is discussed in more detail below, pp. 68–70.
3 Henry Elsynge, *The Manner of Holding Parliaments in England* (1768), pp. 173–4; G. R. Elton (ed.), *The Tudor Constitution: Documents and Commentary*

(2nd edition, Cambridge, 1982), pp. 260–1; Johann P. Sommerville, 'Parliaments, Privilege, and the Liberties of the Subject', in J. H. Hexter (ed.), *Parliament and Liberty from the Reign of Elizabeth to the English Civil War* (Stanford, 1992), pp. 56–84, at p. 59.

4 Sommerville, 'Parliaments, Privilege, and the Liberties of the Subject', p. 59.

5 E. R. Turner, *The Privy Council of England in the Seventeenth and Eighteenth Centuries, 1603-1784* (2 vols., Baltimore, 1927–8), I, especially Chapters 4–5; Allen Horstman, 'A New *Curia Regis*: The Judicature of the House of Lords in the 1620s', *HJ*, XXV (1982), 411–22, especially 414, 421.

6 Elizabeth Read Foster, *The House of Lords, 1603-1649: Structure, Procedure, and the Nature of its Business* (Chapel Hill, 1983), pp. 140–1; Andrew Swatland, *The House of Lords in the Reign of Charles II* (Cambridge, 1996), pp. 42–3.

7 Quoted in Sommerville, 'Parliaments, Privilege, and the Liberties of the Subject', p. 60.

8 Elton (ed.), *Tudor Constitution*, pp. 261–2; Foster, *House of Lords*, pp. 140–1.

9 For the details of Shirley's Case, see J. R. Tanner (ed.), *Constitutional Documents of the Reign of James I* (Cambridge, 1930), pp. 302–17. The statute was 1 & 2 Jac. I, c. 13, printed at p. 317.

10 J. P. Kenyon (ed.), *The Stuart Constitution: Documents and Commentary* (2nd edition, Cambridge, 1986), p. 24; Tanner (ed.), *Constitutional Documents*, p. 279.

11 S. R. Gardiner, *History of England from the Accession of James I to the Outbreak of the Civil War, 1603-1642* (10 vols., 1883–4), IV, 133–7, 267; Conrad Russell, *Unrevolutionary England, 1603-1642* (1990), pp. 81–8.

12 On the Arundel case, see Elsynge, *Manner of Holding Parliaments*, pp. 192–254, which prints extracts from *LJ*, III, 526–682. See also Kevin Sharpe, 'The Earl of Arundel, his Circle and the Opposition to the Duke of Buckingham, 1618–1628', in Kevin Sharpe (ed.), *Faction and Parliament: Essays on Early Stuart History* (Oxford, 1978), pp. 209–44; Vernon F. Snow, 'The Arundel Case, 1626', *The Historian*, XXVI (1964), 323–49; Conrad Russell, *Parliaments and English Politics, 1621-1629* (Oxford, 1979), pp. 287, 312–14, 317–19; Foster, *House of Lords*, p. 145.

13 Sommerville, 'Parliaments, Privilege, and the Liberties of the Subject', p. 71. The King imprisoned Digges and Eliot following their speeches on the article in Buckingham's impeachment alleging the Duke's responsibility for James's death. They had also apparently implied Charles's complicity. They were released when members of both Houses signed a protestation to the King insisting that neither of them had spoken the words to which Charles objected: Russell, *Parliaments*, pp. 306–7.

14 Gardiner, *History of England*, X, 132–41.

15 David Underdown, *Pride's Purge: Politics in the Puritan Revolution* (Oxford, 1971), pp. 162–3.

16 Peter Gaunt, 'Cromwell's Purge? Exclusions and the first Protectorate Parliament', *PH*, VI (1987), 1–22. See also below, p. 141.

17 S. R. Gardiner (ed.), *Constitutional Documents of the Puritan Revolution, 1625-1660* (3rd edition, Oxford, 1906), pp. 388–9.

18 Derek Hirst, 'The Conciliatoriness of the Cavalier Commons Reconsidered', *PH*, VI (1987), 221–35, at 223.

19 See especially Swatland, *House of Lords*, pp. 72–4, 110–11, 130–5, 214–15. These two cases are also discussed above, p. 38, and below, p. 91–2.

20 Elton (ed.), *Tudor Constitution*, p. 264.

21 Tanner (ed.), *Constitutional Documents*, pp. 317–18.

22 Maurice F. Bond, *Guide to the Records of Parliament* (1971), pp. 238–9. The history of this committee under Elizabeth I is analysed in Mary Frear Keeler, 'The Emergence of Standing Committees for Privileges and Returns', *PH*, I (1982), 25–46. For the development of the Committee of the Whole House, see below, pp. 73–4.

23 The literature on the Buckinghamshire case is extensive. On the fudged, interim nature of the settlement, see Derek Hirst, 'Elections and the Privileges of the House of Commons in the Early Seventeenth Century: Confrontation or Compromise?', *HJ*, XVIII (1975), 851–62; and Eric N. Lindquist, 'The Case of Sir Francis Goodwin', *EHR*, CIV (1989), 670–7. The impact of Court politics is analysed in R. C. Munden, 'James I and "the growth of mutual distrust": King, Commons, and Reform, 1603–1604', in Sharpe (ed.), *Faction and Parliament*, pp. 43–72; and R. C. Munden, 'The Defeat of Sir John Fortescue: Court versus Country at the Hustings?', *EHR*, XCIII (1978), 811–16. The roots of the conflict in long-standing local rivalries are discussed in Linda Levy Peck, 'Goodwin v. Fortescue: The Local Context of Parliamentary Controversy', *PH*, III (1984), 33–56. A more traditional view of the case's constitutional significance is presented in J. H. Hexter, 'Parliament, Liberty, and Freedom of Elections', in Hexter (ed.), *Parliament and Liberty*, pp. 21–55.

24 See above, pp. 45–8.

25 For example, *Procs., 1628*, II, 18.

26 Edward Coke, *The Fourth Part of the Institutes of the Laws of England* (1797 edition), p. 50.

27 Foster, *House of Lords*, pp. 32, 147.

28 *Ibid.*, p. 146.

29 Gardiner, *History of England*, VII, 32–3, 63–4; Sommerville, 'Parliaments, Privilege, and the Liberties of the Subject', pp. 65–6; L. J. Reeve, *Charles I and the Road to Personal Rule* (Cambridge, 1989), pp. 32, 84, 92, 106.

30 Elton (ed.), *Tudor Constitution*, pp. 265, 289; Tanner (ed.), *Constitutional Documents*, pp. 319–21.

31 Donald Pennington, 'The War and the People', and Robert Ashton, 'From Cavalier to Roundhead Tyranny, 1642–9', both in John Morrill (ed.), *Reactions to the English Civil War, 1642–1649* (1982), pp. 115–35, 185–207; John Morrill, *Revolt in the Provinces: The People of England and the Tragedies of War, 1630–1648* (2nd edition, Harlow, 1998), pp. 90–3.

32 See above, p. 20.

33 On the proxy system, see especially Elsynge, *Manner of Holding Parliaments*, pp. 119–36; Foster, *House of Lords*, pp. 19–22; Swatland, *House of Lords*, pp. 44–6.

34 Russell, *Parliaments*, pp. 285–6.

35 *LJ*, III, 507.

36 *LJ*, VII, 276–7; VIII, 319, 331–2; C. H. Firth, *The House of Lords During the Civil War* (1910), p. 154; J. S. A. Adamson, 'The Peerage in Politics, 1645–49' (unpubl. Ph.D. dissertation, University of Cambridge, 1986), especially pp. 294–5.

37 On dissents and protests, see Swatland, *House of Lords*, pp. 46–8.

38 Foster, *House of Lords*, pp. 138–40; Swatland, *House of Lords*, pp. 40–1.

39 John C. Lassiter, 'Defamation of Peers: The Rise and Decline of the Action for Scandalum Magnatum, 1497–1773', *American Journal of Legal History*, XXII (1978), 216–36.

40 L. O. Pike, *A Constitutional History of the House of Lords* (1894), p. 267.

41 For a list of Lord Chancellors and Lord Keepers of the Great Seal in this period, see Appendix 3. For the sake of brevity, the term Lord Chancellor alone will be used throughout the following discussion.

42 Foster, *House of Lords*, p. 43.

43 *Ibid.*, pp. 32–3; Swatland, *House of Lords*, pp. 98–100.

44 Foster, *House of Lords*, p. 28. This claim is also found in the Triennial Act of February 1641: Gardiner (ed.), *Constitutional Documents*, p. 153.

45 For a list of Speakers of the Commons in this period, see Appendix 4.

46 Hirst, 'Conciliatoriness of the Cavalier Commons', 222.

47 No previous seventeenth-century Speaker of the Commons had been a Privy Councillor, and the same was also true of their Elizabethan predecessors. I am grateful to Michael Graves and Chris Kyle for advice on this point.

48 Grey, *Debates*, II, 186–8; VI, 402–39; VII, 1–4; Andrew Browning (ed.), *English Historical Documents, 1660–1714* (1953), pp. 165–8; Philip Laundy, *The Office of Speaker* (1964), pp. 241–2.

49 Laundy, *Office of Speaker*, pp. 244–5.

50 *Ibid.*, pp. 250–60; E. N. Williams (ed.), *The Eighteenth-Century Constitution, 1688–1815: Documents and Commentary* (Cambridge, 1960), pp. 177–8, 252; Kathryn Ellis, '"The Squint from the Chair": Speaker Sir John Trevor, *c.* 1637–1717', *PH*, XVII (1998), 198–214; Geoffrey Holmes, *British Politics in the Age of Anne* (revised edition, 1987), pp. 301–3.

51 D. H. Willson, *The Privy Councillors in the House of Commons, 1604–1629* (Minneapolis, 1940), pp. 220–5.

52 Willson, *Privy Councillors*, pp. 217–25; Lambert, 'Procedure', 773–5.

53 Gardiner, *History of England*, VII, 67–76; Russell, *Parliaments*, pp. 415–16; Laundy, *Office of Speaker*, pp. 198–201; Ian H. C. Fraser, 'The Agitation in the Commons, 2 March 1629, and the Interrogation of the Leaders of the Anti-Court Group', *BIHR*, XXX (1957), 86–95.

54 Gardiner, *History of England*, X, 140; Laundy, *Office of Speaker*, pp. 208–13.

55 The Clerks of the Parliaments in this period are listed in Appendix 5. The title 'Clerk of the Parliaments' became fixed, with 'Parliaments' in the plural form, in the early seventeenth century: Maurice F. Bond, 'Clerks of the Parliaments, 1509–1953', *EHR*, LXXIII (1958), 78–85, at 81. The plural form emphasises the continuity of the office from Parliament to Parliament. See also Maurice F. Bond, 'The Office of Clerk of the Parliaments', *Parliamentary Affairs*, XII (1958–9), 297–310.

56 For a discussion of these sources, see above, pp. 12–13.

57 No fewer than four Clerks of the Parliaments held office during the course of Charles I's Personal Rule: see Appendix 5. Various fees were charged for requests for copies of parliamentary documents: HLRO, Braye MS 52, fos. 261–5.

58 Foster, *House of Lords*, pp. 57–61; J. C. Sainty, *The Parliament Office in the Seventeenth and Eighteenth Centuries* (HLRO, 1977), pp. 4–5, 9, 15, 21.

59 Bond, *Records of Parliament*, p. 243. The Clerks of the House of Commons in this period are listed in Appendix 6. I am grateful to Chris Kyle for information about John Wright.

60 This paragraph is based in particular on Maurice F. Bond, 'The Formation of the Archives of Parliament, 1497–1691', *Journal of the Society of Archivists*, I (1955–9), 151–8.

61 Foster, *House of Lords*, pp. 45–55.

62 See above, pp. 36–7.

63 Sheila Lambert, 'The Clerks and Records of the House of Commons, 1600–1640', *BIHR*, XLIII (1970), 215–31, especially 223; HMC, *The Manuscripts of the House of Lords*, new series, X, ed. Maurice F. Bond (1953), pp. xl–xliii; Foster, *House of Lords*, pp. 207–9.

64 Foster, *House of Lords*, pp. 87–92; J. L. Beatty, 'Committee Appointments in the House of Lords in Early Seventeenth-Century England', *HLQ*, XXIX (1965–6), 117–26.

65 Kevin Sharpe, 'Introduction: Parliamentary History 1603–1629: In or Out of Perspective?', in Sharpe (ed.), *Faction and Parliament*, pp. 1–42, especially p. 27; Lotte Glow, 'The Manipulation of Committees in the Long Parliament, 1641–1642', *JBS*, V (1965–6), 31–52.

66 Foster, *House of Lords*, pp. 89–90. The earls' bench included dukes and marquesses as well as earls; the barons' bench also included viscounts. The most typical composition of early seventeenth-century Lords committees was either two from the bishops' bench, two from the earls' bench, and four from the barons' bench, or four, four, and eight respectively.

67 Swatland, *House of Lords*, p. 61; Richard W. Davis, 'Committee and Other Procedures in the House of Lords, 1660–1685', *HLQ*, XLV (1982), 20–35; Foster, *House of Lords*, p. 90.

68 C. S. Sims, '"Policies in Parliaments": An Early Seventeenth-Century Tractate on House of Commons Procedure', *HLQ*, XV (1951–2), 45–58, at 53; Foster, *House of Lords*, p. 94. For the location of these venues, see the map on p. 33.

69 Foster, *House of Lords*, p. 93; Swatland, *House of Lords*, pp. 63–4.

70 This account of Commons committees is greatly indebted to Chris R. Kyle, '"All that come are to have Voice": An Analysis of House of Commons Committees in Early Stuart England' (forthcoming). I am very grateful to Chris Kyle for showing me a copy of this paper prior to publication, and for a helpful discussion on this subject.

71 Foster, *House of Lords*, pp. 87–96; Lambert, 'Procedure', 759–62.

72 Foster, *House of Lords*, pp. 88–92.

73 See above, pp. 21–2; Foster, *House of Lords*, p. 92; J. S. Flemion, 'The Nature of Opposition in the House of Lords in the Early Seventeenth Century: A Revaluation', in Clyve Jones and David Lewis Jones (eds.), *Peers, Politics and Power: The House of Lords, 1603–1911* (1986), pp. 5–22.

74 Willson, *Privy Councillors*, pp. 236–45; R. C. Munden, '"All the Privy Council Being Members of this House": A Note on the Constitutional Significance of Procedure in the House of Commons, 1589–1614', *PH*, XII (1993), 115–25.

75 The role of the Receivers and Triers of Petitions is discussed in Elsynge, *Manner of Holding Parliaments*, pp. 262–98.

76 Keeler, 'Emergence of Standing Committees', 36; Lambert, 'Procedure', 759–60.

77 On the development of the Committee of the Whole House, see especially Russell, *Parliaments*, pp. 38–41; Foster, *House of Lords*, pp. 111–16; Bond, *Records of Parliament*, pp. 218–19; Swatland, *House of Lords*, pp. 58–60.

78 Sheila Lambert, 'Committees, Religion, and Parliamentary Encroachment on Royal Authority in Early Stuart England', *EHR*, CI (1990), 60–95, especially 79–80.

79 Russell, *Parliaments*, pp. 38–9; Willson, *Privy Councillors*, pp. 241–6.

80 W. R. Stacy, 'The Bill of Attainder in English History' (unpubl. Ph.D. dissertation, University of Wisconsin-Madison, 1986), pp. 297–363; Foster, *House of Lords*, pp. 115–16; Swatland, *House of Lords*, pp. 207–9.

81 See above, p. 35.

82 See, for example, Lotte Mulligan, 'Peace Negotiations, Politics and the Committee of Both Kingdoms, 1644–1646', *HJ*, XII (1969), 3–22.

83 The development and decline of joint committees is analysed in Foster, *House of Lords*, pp. 116–25; Bond, *Records of Parliament*, p. 57; Swatland, *House of Lords*, pp. 119–20.

84 Joint committees were later revived from 1864 onwards: Bond, *Records of Parliament*, p. 57.

85 On the development of conferences during the sixteenth century, see in particular David Dean, 'Patrons, Clients and Conferences: The Workings of Bicamerism in the Sixteenth Century English Parliament', in H. W. Blom, W. P. Blockmans and H. de Schepper (eds.), *Bicameralisme: Tweekamerstelsel vroeger en nu* (The Hague, 1992), pp. 209–27, especially pp. 210–17.

86 Dean, 'Patrons, Clients and Conferences', p. 217.

87 Swatland, *House of Lords*, p. 119.

88 On conferences, see especially Sims, '"Policies in Parliaments"', 55–7; Foster, *House of Lords*, pp. 126–33; Bond, *Records of Parliament*, p. 58; Swatland, *House of Lords*, pp. 117–19; Willson, *Privy Councillors*, pp. 124–5, 225–36.

89 Cf. Michael Graves, 'Managing Elizabethan Parliaments', in D. M. Dean and N. L. Jones (eds.), *The Parliaments of Elizabethan England* (Oxford and Cambridge, Mass., 1990), pp. 37–63, at p. 53; and Sheila Lambert, *Bills and Acts: Legislative Procedure in Eighteenth-Century England* (Cambridge, 1971), pp. 55–8.

90 J. E. Neale, *The Elizabethan House of Commons* (revised edition, 1963), p. 388.

91 Willson H. Coates (ed.), *The Journal of Sir Simonds D'Ewes from the First Recess of the Long Parliament to the Withdrawal of King Charles from London* (New Haven, 1942; reprinted Hamden, 1970), p. 187.

92 *CJ*, I, 139–256; *LJ*, II, 263–344.

93 *CJ*, I, 872–920; *LJ*, III, 686–879.

94 Three out of 50 in the Commons and 3 out of 39 in the Lords: *CJ*, II, 20–61; *LJ*, IV, 82–122.

95 *CJ*, II, 300–28; *LJ*, IV, 412–57.

96 *CJ*, VIII, 534–66; *LJ*, XI, 581–621.

97 *CJ*, IX, 713–55; *LJ*, XIV, 1–71.

98 These figures are derived from the dates of parliamentary sessions listed in Appendix 1.

99 Conrad Russell's famous dictum that a Parliament in this period was 'an event and not an institution' (Russell, *Parliaments*, p. 3) possibly underestimates the extent to which Parliament displayed many of the characteristics of a settled institution. It possessed a permanent meeting place, some permanent officials, and established procedures, as well as continuous records. It might be more accurate to call it, as Chris Kyle has done, an 'institutional event': Chris R. Kyle, 'Prince Charles in the Parliaments of 1621 and 1624', *HJ*, XLI (1998), 603–24 at 622. I am grateful to Chris Kyle for showing me a copy of this paper prior to publication, and to both him and Michael Graves for discussions on this point.

100 The death of a monarch also brought the automatic dissolution of any Parliament in existence at that moment.

101 On this theme, see especially three articles by G. A. Harrison: 'Parliaments and Sessions: The Case of 1621', *PH*, XII (1993), 19–28; 'Innovation and Precedent: A Procedural Reappraisal of the 1625 Parliament', *EHR*, CII (1987), 31–62; and '"Abuses of Power and Power Itself": Adjournments, Forbearances, and the Petition of Right, 1628', *PH*, VII (1988), 1–23. See also Sommerville, 'Parliaments, Privilege, and the Liberties of the Subject', pp. 64–6.

102 What follows is based in large part on Pauline Croft, 'The Debate on Annual Parliaments in the Early Seventeenth Century', *PER*, XVI (1996), 163–74.

103 36 Edw. III, c. 10; 40 Edw. III, c. 14.

104 Extensive extracts from this tract are printed, together with an introduction and commentary, in Pauline Croft, 'Annual Parliaments and the Long Parliament', *BIHR*, LIX (1986), 155–71.

105 16 Car. I, c. 1; printed in Gardiner (ed.), *Constitutional Documents*, pp. 144–55. For the Scottish act, see C. Innes and T. Thomson (eds.), *The Acts of the Parliaments of Scotland, 1124–1707* (12 vols., Edinburgh, 1814–75), V, 303.

106 16 Car. I, c. 7; printed in Gardiner (ed.), *Constitutional Documents*, pp. 158–9.

107 *CJ*, VII, 880.

108 16 Car. II, c. 1; printed in Browning (ed.), *English Historical Documents*, pp. 153–4. The political context of this act is analysed in Caroline Robbins, 'The Repeal of the Triennial Act in 1664', *HLQ*, XII (1948–9), 121–40; and Paul Seaward, *The Cavalier Parliament and the Reconstruction of the Old Regime, 1661–1667* (Cambridge, 1989), pp. 137–40.

109 D. T. Witcombe, *Charles II and the Cavalier House of Commons, 1663–1674* (Manchester, 1966), p. 81.

110 6 & 7 Gul. & Mar., c. 2; printed in Browning (ed.), *English Historical Documents*, pp. 159–60.

111 This is discussed more fully above, pp. 61–3, and below, pp. 167–70, 174–6.

112 Elizabeth Read Foster, 'Staging a Parliament in Early Stuart England', in Peter Clark, Alan G. R. Smith and Nicholas Tyacke (eds.), *The English Commonwealth, 1547–1640: Essays in Politics and Society Presented to Joel Hurstfield* (Leicester, 1979), pp. 129–46, at p. 129. See also Foster, *House of Lords*, pp. 3–5.

113 David Dean, 'Image and Ritual in the Tudor Parliaments', in Dale Hoak (ed.), *Tudor Political Culture* (Cambridge, 1995), pp. 243–71, especially pp. 258–62. See also Pauline Croft and I. A. A. Thompson, 'Aristocracy and Representative Government in Unicameral and Bicameral Institutions: The Role of the Peers in the

Castilian Cortes and the English Parliament, 1529–1664', in Blom, Blockmans and de Schepper (eds.), *Bicameralisme*, pp. 63–86, especially pp. 67–9.

114 Foster, *House of Lords*, p. 4; Dean, 'Image and Ritual', pp. 262–5.

115 Foster, *House of Lords*, pp. 8–11; Elsynge, *Manner of Holding Parliaments*, pp. 106–12.

116 See above, p. 65.

117 Foster, *House of Lords*, p. 7; Elsynge, *Manner of Holding Parliaments*, pp. 159–74; Dean, 'Image and Ritual', pp. 265–7.

118 Russell, *Unrevolutionary England*, p. 11.

119 Cf. James Daly, *Cosmic Harmony and Political Thinking in Early Stuart England* (Transactions of the American Philosophical Society, new series, LXIX, part vii, Philadelphia, 1979), pp. 18–19.

120 For the forms of words used to grant the royal assent, see above, p. 40. The formula for the royal veto was 'le roi s'avisera'. The use of the royal veto is discussed below, pp. 95–6.

121 Foster, *House of Lords*, pp. 205–6; Dean, 'Image and Ritual', pp. 268–70.

122 Sheila Lambert, 'The Opening of the Long Parliament', *HJ*, XXVII (1984), 265–87, at 265; John Morrill, *The Nature of the English Revolution* (Harlow, 1993), p. 46.

123 Pauline Croft, 'The Parliamentary Installation of Henry, Prince of Wales', *HR*, LXV (1992), 177–93; Croft and Thompson, 'Aristocracy and Representative Government', p. 69; Kyle, 'Prince Charles in Parliament', 604–6.

6 The parliamentary trinity

1 G. R. Elton, *England under the Tudors* (3rd edition, 1991), p. 482; G. R. Elton, *Studies in Tudor and Stuart Politics and Government* (4 vols., Cambridge, 1974–92), II, 35, 213.

2 Sheila Lambert, 'Committees, Religion, and Parliamentary Encroachment on Royal Authority in Early Stuart England', *EHR*, CI (1990), 60–95, at 69.

3 See above, pp. 6–7.

4 See especially Georges Duby, *The Three Orders: Feudal Society Imagined*, trans. Arthur Goldhammer (Chicago, 1980).

5 The English Parliament had closer affinities with the bicameral Diets of Poland, Hungary and Bohemia – in which the upper chamber was drawn from the magnates and the lower from the nobility as a whole – than it did with the pattern in much of Western Europe: Richard Bonney, *The European Dynastic States, 1494–1660* (Oxford, 1991), pp. 317–18. The Irish Parliament had a bicameral structure based on the English model, but the Scottish Parliament consisted of a single chamber in which peers, burgesses, bishops and officers of state sat together: see above, p. 5.

6 J. P. Cooper, *Land, Men and Beliefs: Studies in Early–Modern History*, ed. G. E. Aylmer and J. S. Morrill (1983), pp. 106–7, 115–33; H. G. Koenigsberger, *Politicians and Virtuosi* (1986), pp. 6–12.

7 Cited above, p. 7.

8 G. R. Elton, *The Parliament of England, 1559–1581* (Cambridge, 1986), pp. 16–23; C. C. Weston, *English Constitutional Theory and the House of Lords, 1556–1832* (1965), pp. 9–23; David Dean, 'Patrons, Clients and Conferences: The Workings of Bicamerism in the Sixteenth Century English Parliament', in H. W. Blom, W. P. Blockmans and H. de Schepper (eds.), *Bicameralisme: Tweekamerstelsel vroeger en nu* (The Hague, 1992), pp. 209–27, especially p. 209.

9 See, for example, G. R. Elton (ed.), *The Tudor Constitution: Documents and Commentary* (2nd edition, Cambridge, 1982), p. 16.

10 *CD, 1621*, IV, 2–3; quoted in David Harris Sacks, 'Parliament, Liberty, and the

Commonweal', in J. H. Hexter (ed.), *Parliament and Liberty from the Reign of Elizabeth to the English Civil War* (Stanford, 1992), at p. 88.

11 Edward Coke, *The Fourth Part of the Institutes of the Laws of England* (1797 edition), pp. 1–2.

12 J. P. Sommerville, *Politics and Ideology in England, 1603–1640* (Harlow, 1986), pp. 174–5.

13 William Prynne, *The Soveraigne Power of Parliaments and Kingdomes* (1643), Part I, p. 110; quoted in C. C. Weston, 'Concepts of Estates in Stuart Political Thought', *Studies Presented to the International Commission for the History of Representative and Parliamentary Institutions*, XXXIX (1970), at 105. I am very grateful to Professor Weston for sending me an offprint of this paper.

14 Weston, 'Concepts of Estates'; Weston, *English Constitutional Theory*, pp. 35–6; C. C. Weston and J. R. Greenberg, *Subjects and Sovereigns: The Grand Controversy over Legal Sovereignty in Stuart England* (Cambridge, 1981), pp. 52–66.

15 See, in particular, Michael Mendle, *Henry Parker and the English Civil War: The Political Thought of the Public's 'Privado'* (Cambridge, 1995); Michael Mendle, 'Parliamentary Sovereignty: A Very English Absolutism', in Nicholas Phillipson and Quentin Skinner (eds.), *Political Discourse in Early Modern Britain* (Cambridge, 1993), pp. 97–119; Margaret A. Judson, *The Crisis of the Constitution: An Essay in Constitutional and Political Thought in England, 1603–1645* (New Brunswick, 1949), pp. 396–436.

16 The text of the *Answer to the Nineteen Propositions*, from which the above quotations are taken, is conveniently printed in John Rushworth, *Historical Collections of Private Passages of State* (8 vols., 1680–1701), IV, 725–35. See also the discussions in Michael Mendle, *Dangerous Positions: Mixed Government, the Estates of the Realm, and the Making of the Answer to the XIX Propositions* (Alabama, 1985), especially pp. 5–20, 171–83; David L. Smith, *Constitutional Royalism and the Search for Settlement, c. 1640–1649* (Cambridge, 1994), pp. 90–1, 177–8, 184–6, 230–1; Weston and Greenberg, *Subjects and Sovereigns*, pp. 35–86; Weston, *English Constitutional Theory*, pp. 23–33, 263–5.

17 Weston, *English Constitutional Theory*, pp. 23–33; Smith, *Constitutional Royalism*, p. 91.

18 Smith, *Constitutional Royalism*, pp. 244–7.

19 H[enry] F[erne], *A Reply unto severall treatises pleading for the armes now taken up by subjects in the pretended defence of religion and liberty* (Oxford, 1643), p. 32 (Wing, F 799; BL, TT, E 74/9). See also Smith, *Constitutional Royalism*, pp. 228–31; Weston, *English Constitutional Theory*, pp. 34–6; Weston and Greenberg, *Subjects and Sovereigns*, pp. 99–102.

20 [Sir John Spelman], *The Case of our Affaires, in law, religion, and other circumstances briefly examined, and presented to the conscience* (Oxford, 1643), pp. 1, 5 (Wing, S 4936; BL, TT, E 30/14).

21 Smith, *Constitutional Royalism*, p. 228; Weston, 'Concepts of Estates', 112–15; Weston and Greenberg, *Subjects and Sovereigns*, pp. 108–13.

22 [Dudley Digges], *A Review of the Observations upon some of His Majesties late answers and expresses, written by a gentleman of quality* (Oxford, 1643), pp. 9, 24 (Wing, D 1459; BL, TT, E 97/11).

23 [Dudley Digges], *The Unlawfulnesse of Subjects taking up armes against their Soveraigne, in what case soever* (Oxford, 1643[/4]), pp. 59, 138–9 (Wing, D 1462; BL, TT, E 128/42); Smith, *Constitutional Royalism*, pp. 224–5.

24 *AO*, II, 325–9.

25 Weston, *English Constitutional Theory*, pp. 70–8.

26 *CJ*, VIII, 8.

27 Quoted in Elton, *Parliament of England*, p. 20.

28 Weston, 'Concepts of Estates', 120.

29 Quoted in Weston and Greenberg, *Subjects and Sovereigns*, p. 157. See also Weston, *English Constitutional Theory*, pp. 83–6.

30 Weston and Greenberg, *Subjects and Sovereigns*, p. 159.

31 *Ibid.*, pp. 159–60.

32 Weston, *English Constitutional Theory*, pp. 92–9.

33 Weston and Greenberg, *Subjects and Sovereigns*, pp. 182–92; for Petyt, see also above, p. 3.

34 Weston and Greenberg, *Subjects and Sovereigns*, pp. 192–205.

35 Weston, 'Concepts of Estates', 93; Weston, *English Constitutional Theory*, pp. 111–13.

36 Weston and Greenberg, *Subjects and Sovereigns*, pp. 226–30.

37 Quoted in Weston, 'Concepts of Estates', 123.

38 See especially Weston, *English Constitutional Theory*, pp. 87–137.

39 Andrew Browning (ed.), *English Historical Documents, 1660–1714* (1953), p. 122.

40 E. N. Williams (ed.), *The Eighteenth-Century Constitution, 1688–1815: Documents and Commentary* (Cambridge, 1960), p. 37.

41 Sir William Blackstone, *Commentaries on the Laws of England* (4 vols., Oxford, 1765–9), I, 153.

42 Weston, *English Constitutional Theory*, p. 87.

43 Quoted in Weston, 'Concepts of Estates', 129–30.

44 On this development, see for example Weston, *English Constitutional Theory*, Chapters 4–6.

45 See above, pp. 36–8.

46 This was a point that Henry Elsynge drew out in his *Expeditio Billarum Antiquitus*, ed. Catherine Strateman Sims (Louvain, 1954). See also above, pp. 3–5, 78–9.

47 M. A. R. Graves, 'Managing Elizabethan Parliaments', in D. M. Dean and N. L. Jones (eds.), *The Parliaments of Elizabethan England* (Oxford and Cambridge, Mass., 1990), pp. 37–63, at p. 49.

48 See above, p. 42.

49 See above, pp. 71–5.

50 See above, pp. 25–6, 28; Conrad Russell, *Parliaments and English Politics, 1621–1629* (Oxford, 1979), p. 17.

51 For some examples, see above, pp. 25–6, 28.

52 J. T. Peacey, 'Led by the Hand: Manucaptors and Patronage at Lincoln's Inn in the Seventeenth Century', *The Journal of Legal History*, XVIII (1997), 26–44. I am grateful to Michael Graves for drawing this article to my attention.

53 Conrad Russell, *Unrevolutionary England, 1603–1642* (1990), pp. 209–12. See also below, pp. 88–9, 115, 124–5.

54 Russell, *Parliaments*, pp. 12–14, 131–2, 163, 171–3, 184, 187–8, 224–5, 254–6, 293–300, 326–7, 342–3; Richard Cust, *The Forced Loan and English Politics, 1626–1628* (Oxford, 1987), pp. 101, 204, 332; J. A. Manning (ed.), *Memoirs of Sir Benjamin Rudyerd* (1841).

55 For example, on 9 July 1642 both Rudyerd and Pembroke made pleas for an 'accommodation': *A Worthy Speech spoken in the Honourable House of Commons, by Sir Benjamin Rudyerd, this present July, 1642* (1642), Wing, R 2206; *A Perfect Diurnall of the Passages in Parliament* [4–11 July 1642], p. 6 (BL, TT, E 202/14).

56 For the nature of these ties in sixteenth-century Parliaments, see Dean, 'Patrons, Clients and Conferences'. I am grateful to Chris Kyle for advice on this point.

57 For an excellent survey, see Dean, 'Patrons, Clients and Conferences'.

58 *Oxford English Dictionary*, *sub* Faction, 3.

59 Russell, *Parliaments*, pp. 260–322; J. S. Flemion, 'The Dissolution of Parliament in 1626: A Revaluation', in Clyve Jones and David Lewis Jones (eds.), *Peers, Politics and Power: The House of Lords, 1603–1911* (1986), pp. 23–9; G. A. Harrison, '"A good correspondence between Lords and Commons": Bicameral Politics in the English Parliaments of 1621 to 1629', in Blom, Blockmans and de Schepper (eds.),

Bicameralisme, pp. 229–48, especially pp. 236, 239–40; Kevin Sharpe, 'The Earl of Arundel, his Circle and the Opposition to the Duke of Buckingham, 1618–1628', in Kevin Sharpe (ed.), *Faction and Parliament: Essays on Early Stuart History* (Oxford, 1978), pp. 209–44; Roger Lockyer, *Buckingham: The Life and Political Career of George Villiers, first Duke of Buckingham, 1592–1628* (Harlow, 1981), pp. 308–33; D. H. Willson, *The Privy Councillors in the House of Commons, 1604–1629* (Minneapolis, 1940), pp. 179–89.

60 Russell, *Parliaments*, pp. 340–89; Harrison, '"A good correspondency"', pp. 240–2; J. S. Flemion, 'The Struggle for the Petition of Right in the House of Lords: The Study of an Opposition Party Victory', in Jones and Jones (eds.), *Peers, Politics and Power*, pp. 31–48; J. S. Flemion, 'A Saving to Satisfy All: The House of Lords and the Meaning of the Petition of Right', *PH*, X (1991), 27–44.

61 J. S. A. Adamson, 'Parliamentary Management, Men-of-Business and the House of Lords, 1640–49', in Clyve Jones (ed.), *A Pillar of the Constitution: The House of Lords in British Politics, 1640–1784* (1989), pp. 21–50, especially pp. 29–31.

62 Adamson, 'Parliamentary Management', pp. 31–50; J. S. A. Adamson, 'Oliver Cromwell and the Long Parliament', in John Morrill (ed.), *Oliver Cromwell and the English Revolution* (Harlow, 1990), pp. 49–92; J. S. A. Adamson, 'The Baronial Context of the English Civil War', *TRHS*, 5th series, XL (1990), 93–120; Valerie Pearl, 'The "Royal Independents" in the English Civil War', *TRHS*, 5th series, XVIII (1968), 69–96; David Underdown, *Pride's Purge: Politics in the Puritan Revolution* (Oxford, 1971), pp. 45–105.

63 Adamson, 'Parliamentary Management', pp. 31–50; Adamson, 'Baronial Context', especially 109–14; J. S. A. Adamson, 'The Peerage in Politics, 1645–49' (unpubl. Ph.D. dissertation, University of Cambridge, 1986), especially pp. 17–58, 115–32.

64 The texts of these propositions are printed in S. R. Gardiner (ed.), *Constitutional Documents of the Puritan Revolution, 1625–1660* (3rd edition, Oxford, 1906), pp. 262–7, 275–86, 290–306. For the peace treaties conducted on the basis of them, see Smith, *Constitutional Royalism*, Chapters 5 and 6.

65 The text of the *Heads of the Proposals* is printed in Gardiner (ed.), *Constitutional Documents*, pp. 316–26. Although it seems agreed that a bicameral grouping supported the *Heads*, the balance of responsibility between the Independents in the two Houses and their Army allies remains controversial: see J. S. A. Adamson, 'The English Nobility and the Projected Settlement of 1647', *HJ*, XXX (1987), 567–602; Mark A. Kishlansky, 'Saye What?', *HJ*, XXXIII (1990), 917–37; J. S. A. Adamson, 'Politics and the Nobility in Civil-War England', *HJ*, XXXIV (1991), 231–55; Mark A. Kishlansky, 'Saye No More', *JBS*, XXX (1991), 399–448.

66 Underdown, *Pride's Purge*, p. 69.

67 Gardiner (ed.), *Constitutional Documents*, p. 466.

68 Andrew Swatland, *The House of Lords in the Reign of Charles II* (Cambridge, 1996), pp. 159–72; Paul Seaward, *The Cavalier Parliament and the Reconstruction of the Old Regime, 1661–1667* (Cambridge, 1989), pp. 162–95. See also below, p. 149.

69 Swatland, *House of Lords*, pp. 124–7, 135–6; Tim Harris, *Politics under the Later Stuarts: Party Conflict in a Divided Society, 1660–1715* (Harlow, 1993), pp. 61–5; Andrew Browning, *Thomas Osborne, Earl of Danby and Duke of Leeds, 1632–1712* (3 vols., Glasgow, 1944–51), I, 185–246; III, 33–151. See also below, pp. 153–5.

70 D. L. Jones (ed.), *A Parliamentary History of the Glorious Revolution* (1988), passim. See also Weston and Greenberg, *Subjects and Sovereigns*, pp. 255–7; W. A. Speck, *Reluctant Revolutionaries: Englishmen and the Revolution of 1688* (Oxford, 1988), pp. 94–114.

71 The case and the dispute that it caused are discussed in Swatland, *House of Lords*, pp. 72–3, 110–11, 130–4; J. P. Kenyon (ed.), *The Stuart Constitution: Documents and Commentary* (2nd edition, Cambridge, 1986), pp. 419, 422–3. See also above, pp. 38, 66.

72 Quoted in Kenyon (ed.), *Stuart Constitution*, p. 422.

73 *LJ*, XII, 694.

74 Swatland, *House of Lords*, pp. 134–5, 214–15; Kenyon (ed.), *Stuart Constitution*, pp. 419, 425–6. See also above, pp. 38, 66.

75 Swatland, *House of Lords*, pp. 134–6.

76 Russell, *Unrevolutionary England*, p. 48.

77 Menna Prestwich, *Cranfield: Politics and Profits under the Early Stuarts* (Oxford, 1966), pp. 423–68; Thomas Cogswell, *The Blessed Revolution: English Politics and the Coming of War, 1621–1624* (Cambridge, 1989), especially pp. 268–73; Russell, *Parliaments*, pp. 198–202.

78 Edward, Earl of Clarendon, *The History of the Rebellion and Civil Wars in England*, ed. W. Dunn Macray (6 vols., Oxford, 1888), I, 28 (Book I, § 44).

79 Swatland, *House of Lords*, pp. 137–8; Seaward, *Cavalier Parliament*, pp. 306–27; D. T. Witcombe, *Charles II and the Cavalier House of Commons, 1663–1674* (Manchester, 1966), pp. 61–77; Clayton Roberts, 'The Impeachment of the Earl of Clarendon', *CHJ*, XIII (1957), 1–18.

80 Quoted in Swatland, *House of Lords*, p. 137.

81 See, in particular, M. A. R. Graves, 'The Management of the Elizabethan House of Commons: The Council's "Men-of-Business"', *PH*, II (1983), 11–38; M. A. R. Graves, 'The Commons Lawyers and the Privy Council's Parliamentary Men-of-Business, 1584–1601', *PH*, VIII (1989), 189–215; M. A. R. Graves, 'Elizabethan Men of Business Reconsidered', in S. M. Jack and B. A. Masters (eds.), *Protestants, Property, Puritans: Godly People Revisited (Parergon*, XIV, 1996), 111–27.

82 Cf. Graves, 'Managing Elizabethan Parliaments'.

83 Esther S. Cope, 'The Bishops and Parliamentary Politics in Early Stuart England', *PH*, IX (1990), 1–13, at 9.

84 Swatland, *House of Lords*, pp. 31–2, 169–70, 174, 232, 245, 254–5.

85 See above, pp. 19–21.

86 Cope, 'Bishops and Parliamentary Politics', 2.

87 Adamson, 'Parliamentary Management', pp. 22–8. See also above, p. 20.

88 Swatland, *House of Lords*, pp. 254–5.

89 See above, pp. 76–8.

90 Maija Jansson and W. B. Bidwell (eds.), *Proceedings in Parliament, 1626* (4 vols., New Haven and London, 1991–6), II, 395.

91 Conrad Russell, *The Addled Parliament of 1614: The Limits of Revision* (Reading, 1992), p. 25.

92 See below, pp. 158–61, 167–70, 174–6.

93 Elton, *Parliament of England*, pp. 123–6.

94 Dean and Jones (eds.), *Parliaments of Elizabethan England*, pp. 39, 194.

95 *LJ*, II, 352–3. I am most grateful to Chris Kyle for this information, and for a helpful discussion on the use of the veto.

96 A bill for observance of the sabbath, and a bill for the obtaining of licences of alienation. These became 3 Car. I, c. 1, and 1 Car. I, c. 3, respectively.

97 See above, pp. 22–3.

98 Conrad Russell has suggested that James vetoed six bills in 1624: Russell, *English Parliaments*, p. 44. However, Chris Kyle has shown that there was only one bill against Catholic recusants, rather than the two listed by Russell: Chris R. Kyle, '*Lex Loquens*: Legislation in the Parliament of 1624' (unpubl. Ph.D. dissertation, University of Auckland, 1993), pp. 315–23. I am very grateful to Chris Kyle for advice on this point, and for lending me a copy of his dissertation.

99 Russell, *English Parliaments*, pp. 44–5.

100 *LJ*, XIII, 394.

101 J. P. Kenyon, *The Popish Plot* (1972), pp. 102, 104–5, 109. The 1661 Militia Act is discussed below, p. 148.

102 *CJ*, XI, 72.

103 See below, pp. 168, 174–5.

104 Strictly speaking, the dispensing and suspending powers were separate and distinct, but in contemporary usage the term 'dispensing power' was sometimes used as an umbrella term to cover both powers. For an example, see Kenyon (ed.), *Stuart Constitution*, pp. 407–11.
105 Paul Birdsall, '"Non Obstante": A Study of the Dispensing Power of English Kings', in Carl Wittke (ed.), *Essays in History and Political Theory in Honor of Charles H. McIlwain* (New York, 1936), pp. 37–76; Weston and Greenberg, *Subjects and Sovereigns*, pp. 22–32, 257–8.
106 Swatland, *House of Lords*, pp. 173–6; Kenyon (ed.), *Stuart Constitution*, pp. 375–6, 379–82.
107 *CJ*, IX, 257.
108 Kenyon (ed.), *Stuart Constitution*, pp. 376–7, 382–7.
109 *Ibid.*, pp. 377, 395, 403–4; A.F. Havighurst, 'James II and the Twelve Men in Scarlet', *Law Quarterly Review*, LXIX (1953), 522–46; Weston and Greenberg, *Subjects and Sovereigns*, pp. 234–7.
110 Kenyon (ed.), *Stuart Constitution*, pp. 396–7, 407–11.
111 Browning (ed.), *English Historical Documents*, p. 123. My italics.
112 Weston and Greenberg, *Subjects and Sovereigns*, pp. 253–9.

7 Early Stuart Parliaments, 1603–1640

1 Johann P. Sommerville (ed.), *King James VI and I: Political Writings* (Cambridge, 1994), pp. 155–6.
2 *Ibid.*, p. 157.
3 J. R. Tanner (ed.), *Constitutional Documents of the Reign of James I* (Cambridge, 1930), p. 221.
4 See below, pp. 106–7.
5 G. R. Elton, *Studies in Tudor and Stuart Politics and Government* (4 vols., Cambridge, 1974–92), II, 164–82.
6 Sommerville (ed.), *James VI and I: Political Writings*, pp. 183–4.
7 *Ibid.*, p. 186.
8 *Ibid.*, p. 74; J. P. Kenyon (ed.), *The Stuart Constitution: Documents and Commentary* (2nd edition, Cambridge, 1986), p. 8.
9 In Scotland at the beginning of the seventeenth century there was no exact equivalent to the supremacy of parliamentary statute. Laws could equally well be enacted by proclamation of the King and Council, or by conventions of the estates or of the nobility. It was possible for the government to enforce laws almost indefinitely that had not received Parliament's consent. See, for example, Keith M. Brown, *Kingdom or Province? Scotland and the Regal Union, 1603–1715* (1992), pp. 13–20. I am very grateful to Michael Graves for advice about the Scottish Parliament.
10 Kenyon (ed.), *Stuart Constitution*, p. 11.
11 Tanner (ed.), *Constitutional Documents*, p. 202.
12 S. R. Gardiner, *History of England from the Accession of James I to the Outbreak of the Civil War, 1603–1642* (10 vols., 1883–4), II, 251.
13 Pauline Croft, 'The Debate on Annual Parliaments in the Early Seventeenth Century', *PER*, XVI (1996), 163–74, at 168.
14 See above, p. 3.
15 Tanner (ed.), *Constitutional Documents*, p. 222.
16 *Ibid.*, pp. 26–7.
17 Jenny Wormald, 'James VI, James I and the Identity of Britain', in Brendan Bradshaw and John Morrill (eds.), *The British Problem, c. 1534–1707: State Formation in the Atlantic Archipelago* (1996), pp. 148–71. See also Jenny Wormald, 'The Creation of Britain: Multiple Kingdoms or Core and Colonies?', *TRHS*, 6th series, II (1992), 175–94; Jenny Wormald, 'One King, Two Kingdoms',

in A. Grant and K. J. Stringer (eds.), *Uniting the Kingdom? The Making of British History* (1995), pp. 123–32.

18 Sommerville (ed.), *James VI and I: Political Writings*, pp. 161, 162, 166–8, 173.

19 See above, p. 41.

20 Sommerville (ed.), *James VI and I: Political Writings*, pp. 170–1.

21 *Ibid.*, p. 209 (20 June 1616).

22 Quoted in Bruce Galloway, *The Union of England and Scotland, 1603–1608* (Edinburgh, 1986), p. 22.

23 This commission was created by 1 & 2 Jac. I, c. 2.

24 By far the most detailed account of these debates is found in Galloway, *Union*, pp. 93–130. The fullest primary source is D. H. Willson (ed.), *The Parliamentary Diary of Robert Bowyer, 1606–1607* (Minneapolis, 1931; reprinted New York, 1971), especially pp. 187–320.

25 *CJ*, I, 334.

26 See especially above, pp. 6–7, 9, 38–43.

27 On this point, see Conrad Russell, 'Thomas Cromwell's Doctrine of Parliamentary Sovereignty', *TRHS*, 6th series, VII (1997), 235–46, especially 241–2.

28 See above, pp. 73–4.

29 4 Jac. I, c. 1. For the debates on this bill, see Willson (ed.), *Diary of Robert Bowyer*, especially pp. 297–330, 350–62, 376–87.

30 See above, pp. 49–56.

31 Tanner (ed.), *Constitutional Documents*, pp. 227–9; Pauline Croft, 'Wardship in the Parliament of 1604', *PH*, II (1983), 39–48.

32 See, for example, Willson (ed.), *Diary of Robert Bowyer*, pp. 53–77. On wardship and purveyance in the first three sessions of James's first Parliament, see especially Croft, 'Wardship in the Parliament of 1604'; Pauline Croft, 'Parliament, Purveyance and the City of London, 1589–1608', *PH*, IV (1985), 9–34; and Nicholas Tyacke, 'Wroth, Cecil and the Parliamentary Session of 1604', *BIHR*, L (1977), 120–4.

33 See above, p. 55.

34 H. S. Scott (ed.), 'The Journal of Sir Roger Wilbraham', in *Camden Miscellany*, X (Camden Society, 3rd series, IV, 1902), 3–129, at 102.

35 G. P. V. Akrigg (ed.), *Letters of King James VI & I* (Berkeley, 1984), p. 317 (James I to Robert Cecil, Earl of Salisbury [?6 December 1610]).

36 For the debates on the Great Contract, see E. R. Foster (ed.), *Proceedings in Parliament, 1610* (2 vols., New Haven and London, 1966), I, 56–60, 67–70, 90–3, 104–10, 113–20, 140–5, 152–65, 196–205, 211–19, 250–3, 299–305, 309–11; II, 31–2, 46–8, 64–70, 73–80, 135–41, 166–70, 276–9, 283–94, 309–23, 392–400.

37 See above, pp. 53–4.

38 See above, pp. 53–4.

39 See, for example, the Commons' petition of right against impositions in May 1610: Tanner (ed.), *Constitutional Documents*, pp. 245–7.

40 Conrad Russell, *The Addled Parliament of 1614: The Limits of Revision* (Reading, 1992), p. 9.

41 Akrigg (ed.), *Letters of James VI & I*, p. 291 (James I to the Privy Council [?19 October 1607]).

42 Sommerville (ed.), *James VI and I: Political Writings*, p. 166 (31 March 1607).

43 Menna Prestwich, *Cranfield: Politics and Profits under the Early Stuarts* (Oxford, 1966), pp. 12–17.

44 Tanner (ed.), *Constitutional Documents*, p. 359.

45 For the debates on impositions in 1610, see Foster (ed.), *Proceedings*, especially I, 82–6, 130–3; II, 93–5, 108–16, 151–65, 170–250, 266–8, 272–7, 317–19, 396–8, 409–20. For 1614, see Maija Jansson (ed.), *Proceedings in Parliament, 1614* (Philadelphia, 1988), pp. 146–54, 156–60, 166, 224–7, 258–66.

46 Linda Levy Peck, *Northampton: Patronage and Policy at the Court of James I* (1982), pp. 205–12.

47 See above, pp. 51–2. Jansson (ed.), *Proceedings, 1614*, pp. 110, 116, 146–54, 155–9, 437–40, 442.

48 Russell, *Addled Parliament*, p. 17.

49 On this depression, see B. E. Supple, *Commercial Crisis and Change in England, 1600–1642* (Cambridge, 1964), pp. 52–72.

50 Gardiner, *History of England*, III, 373, 380–1; Roger Lockyer, *Buckingham: The Life and Political Career of George Villiers, first Duke of Buckingham, 1592–1628* (1981), pp. 82–6.

51 *CD, 1621*, II, 1–13; IV, 1–6; V, 424–30.

52 18 Jac. I, c. 2; *CD, 1621*, II, 93–4, 163, 177, 209, 244, 257; IV, 132–3, 143–7, 169, 183; V, 466–7, 498–9.

53 On the revival of impeachment, see above, pp. 35–6.

54 *CD, 1621*, II, 112–14, 127–32, 149–50, 157–99, 209–12, 220–1, 232–5, 267–9, 346–7; IV, 78–87, 111–17, 121–8, 131–49, 157–8, 162–4, 184–5; V, 257–8, 275–88, 293–4, 323–8, 366–7, 483–6; VI, 39–45, 69–71, 249–57, 260–70, 286–7, 301–4, 308–11, 378–83; VII, 366–70, 501–2.

55 Conrad Russell, *Parliaments and English Politics, 1621–1629* (Oxford, 1979), pp. 106–8, 122.

56 It was characteristic of James that although he had claimed that he was 'very free and able to punish any man's misdemeanours in Parliament, as well during their sitting as after', he wisely did not put this to the test, and waited until the parliamentary recess before detaining Sandys together with the Earls of Oxford and Southampton: see above, p. 65.

57 *CD, 1621*, II, 224–7, 237–49, 251–2, 341–2; III, 152–4; IV, 155–7, 160–1, 166–9, 173–4, 296–7; V, 55–9, 76–8, 298–9, 306–10, 364–5; VI, 64–8, 384–7.

58 Russell, *Parliaments*, pp. 103–12.

59 J. F. Larkin and P. L. Hughes (eds.), *Stuart Royal Proclamations*, vol. I: *Royal Proclamations of King James I, 1603–25* (Oxford, 1973), 511–19.

60 Gardiner, *History of England*, IV, 186–231.

61 On how this misunderstanding arose, see Conrad Russell, *Unrevolutionary England, 1603–1642* (1990), pp. 59–79; and Russell, *Parliaments*, pp. 121–44.

62 See above, pp. 45–6, 67.

63 Russell, *Unrevolutionary England*, pp. 81–8.

64 Controversy surrounds exactly how genuine, explicit and widespread anti-Spanish sentiment was: see Thomas Cogswell, 'Phaeton's Chariot: The Parliament-Men and the Continental Crisis in 1621', and Conrad Russell, 'Sir Thomas Wentworth and Anti-Spanish Sentiment, 1621–1624', both in J. F. Merritt (ed.), *The Political World of Thomas Wentworth, Earl of Strafford, 1621–1641* (Cambridge, 1996), pp. 24–62.

65 Tanner (ed.), *Constitutional Documents*, pp. 290, 295.

66 Thomas Cogswell, *The Blessed Revolution: English Politics and the Coming of War, 1621–1624* (Cambridge, 1989), especially pp. 77–105.

67 See above, p. 46.

68 Tanner (ed.), *Constitutional Documents*, p. 299.

69 21 Jac. I, c. 3. Robert Ashton, *The City and the Court, 1603–1643* (Cambridge, 1979), pp. 106–20.

70 For a fine analysis of this legislation, see Chris R. Kyle, 'Lex Loquens: Legislation in the Parliament of 1624' (unpubl. Ph.D. dissertation, University of Auckland, 1993).

71 See above, p. 52.

72 On this aspect of James's kingship, see above all Kenneth Fincham and Peter Lake, 'The Ecclesiastical Policy of King James I', *JBS*, XXIV (1985), 169–207.

73 Gardiner, *History of England*, III, 260; V, 351–5.

74 Russell, *Parliaments*, p. 420.

75 *LJ*, III, 424.

76 Russell, *Parliaments*, p. 419.

77 See above, pp. 93, 104–6, 109–12.
78 *LJ*, III, 435.
79 Richard Cust, 'Charles I and a Draft Declaration for the 1628 Parliament', *HR*, LXIII (1990), 143–61.
80 *Ibid.*, especially 150–7.
81 Maija Jansson and W. B. Bidwell (eds.), *Proceedings in Parliament, 1625* (New Haven and London, 1987), p. 449.
82 *LJ*, III, 436.
83 Christopher Thompson, 'Court Politics and Parliamentary Conflict in 1625', in Richard Cust and Ann Hughes (eds.), *Conflict in Early Stuart England* (Harlow, 1989), pp. 168–92; Russell, *Parliaments*, pp. 204–59.
84 Russell, *Parliaments*, pp. 227–9; see also above, p. 54.
85 Jansson and Bidwell (eds.), *Proceedings, 1625*, pp. 330–4, 336–44; Russell, *Parliaments*, pp. 231–3, 240–1.
86 Jansson and Bidwell (eds.), *Proceedings, 1625*, pp. 359–61, 364, 526, 532.
87 *LJ*, III, 470–1.
88 *Ibid.*, 477–81.
89 Jansson and Bidwell (eds.), *Proceedings, 1625*, pp. 472–83.
90 Lockyer, *Buckingham*, pp. 281–5.
91 The six pricked as sheriffs were Sir Edward Coke, Sir Francis Seymour, Sir Robert Phelips, Sir Guy Palmes, Edward Alford and Sir Thomas Wentworth: Gardiner, *History of England*, VI, 33–4; Russell, *Parliaments*, p. 20.
92 Russell, *Parliaments*, pp. 268–9; Richard Cust, *The Forced Loan and English Politics, 1626–1628* (Oxford, 1987), pp. 24–5. See also above, pp. 000–000.
93 Barbara Donagan, 'The York House Conference Revisited: Laymen, Calvinism and Arminianism', *HR*, LXIV (1991), 312–30.
94 Maija Jansson and W. B. Bidwell (eds.), *Proceedings in Parliament, 1626* (4 vols., New Haven and London, 1991–6), II, 375–83.
95 The principal documents relating to the attempted impeachment of Buckingham are printed in Gardiner (ed.), *Constitutional Documents*, pp. 2–44.
96 See above, pp. 88–9.
97 See above, pp. 20, 88–9.
98 See above, pp. 20, 65–6, 68.
99 On impeachment, see above, pp. 35–6, 93, 109–11.
100 Jansson and Bidwell (eds.), *Proceedings, 1626*, III, 219, 223. For early seventeenth-century images of Sejanus, especially as found in Ben Jonson's *Sejanus his Fall*, see Blair Worden, 'Ben Jonson among the Historians', in Kevin Sharpe and Peter Lake (eds.), *Culture and Politics in Early Stuart England* (1994), pp. 67–89.
101 Cust, *Forced Loan*, pp. 24–6; Lockyer, *Buckingham*, pp. 275–6, 331–2, 414–15.
102 On the policies described in this paragraph, and their impact, see especially Cust, *Forced Loan*; Lockyer, *Buckingham*, pp. 356–415; John Guy, 'The Origins of the Petition of Right Reconsidered', *HJ*, XXV (1982), 289–312.
103 Cust, *Forced Loan*, pp. 24–5.
104 See above, p. 52.
105 The Petition of Right is most conveniently printed in Kenyon (ed.), *Stuart Constitution*, pp. 68–71. Of the vast literature on the Petition, see especially E. R. Foster, 'Petitions and the Petition of Right', *JBS*, XIV (1974), 21–45; Russell, *Parliaments*, pp. 342–84; L. J. Reeve, 'The Legal Status of the Petition of Right', *HJ*, XXIX (1986), 257–77; L. J. Reeve, *Charles I and the Road to Personal Rule* (Cambridge, 1989), pp. 118–71; Glenn Burgess, *The Politics of the Ancient Constitution: An Introduction to English Political Thought, 1603–1642* (1992), pp. 194–9; and Glenn Burgess, *Absolute Monarchy and the Stuart Constitution* (New Haven and London, 1996), pp. 202–7.
106 See above, pp. 87–92.
107 See above, p. 89.
108 Gardiner (ed.), *Constitutional Documents*, p. 70; *Procs., 1628*, IV, 51–6.

109 *Procs., 1628*, IV, 177–94. This formula of assent for petitions of right was slightly different from that used for private bills or petitions of grace ('soit fait comme il est désiré'): Foster, 'Petitions and the Petition of Right', 24–6.
110 *CJ*, II, 151.
111 Reeve, 'Legal Status'; E. R. Foster, 'Printing the Petition of Right', *HLQ*, XXXVIII (1974–5), 81–3.
112 *Procs., 1628*, IV, 311–17, 351–7.
113 *Ibid.*, 354–7.
114 *Ibid.*, 470–1.
115 *LJ*, III, 879; Kenyon (ed.), *Stuart Constitution*, pp. 89–90.
116 *LJ*, III, 879.
117 *Ibid.*
118 See above, pp. 67–8.
119 Gardiner, *History of England*, VI, 312, 329–30.
120 Russell, *Parliaments*, pp. 379–81, 384.
121 *LJ*, IV, 12. For accounts of the 1629 session, see Russell, *Parliaments*, pp. 396–416; Reeve, *Road to Personal Rule*, pp. 58–98.
122 *LJ*, IV, 5–43. Cf. Russell, *Parliaments*, pp. 408–9.
123 Reeve, *Road to Personal Rule*, pp. 80–1.
124 Gardiner (ed.), *Constitutional Documents*, pp. 77–82 (quotations at pp. 79, 82).
125 *Ibid.*, pp. 82–3. For this episode see above, pp. 70, 77; also Gardiner, *History of England*, VII, 67–76; Russell, *Parliaments*, pp. 415–16; Ian H. C. Fraser, 'The Agitation in the Commons, 2 March 1629, and the Interrogation of the Leaders of the Anti-Court Group', *BIHR*, XXX (1957), 86–95.
126 *LJ*, IV, 43.
127 Charles's declaration of 10 March 1629 is printed in Gardiner (ed.), *Constitutional Documents*, pp. 83–99 (quotations at pp. 84, 86, 93, 95, 97–8).
128 Reeve, *Road to Personal Rule*, pp. 118–71; John Reeve, 'The Arguments in King's Bench Concerning the Imprisonment of John Selden and Other Members of the House of Commons', *JBS*, XXV (1986), 264–87.
129 Reeve, *Road to Personal Rule*, pp. 275–96.
130 J. F. Larkin (ed.), *Stuart Royal Proclamations*, vol. II: *Royal Proclamations of King Charles I, 1625–46* (Oxford, 1983), 226–8 (quotations at 228).
131 See above, pp. 88–9, 112–13.
132 Esther S. Cope, 'Public Images of Parliament during its Absence', *Legislative Studies Quarterly*, VII (1982), 221–34.
133 *LJ*, IV, 47–8; Esther S. Cope (ed.), *Proceedings of the Short Parliament of 1640* (Camden Society, 4th series, XIX, 1977), 115–21.
134 PRO, SP 16/451/39 (Sir Francis Windebank's notes, 24 April 1640); *LJ*, IV, 67.
135 Conrad Russell, *The Fall of the British Monarchies, 1637–1642* (Oxford, 1991), pp. 90–123; Sharpe, *Personal Rule*, pp. 858–77.
136 Cope (ed.), *Proceedings*, 140–1, 149–50.
137 *LJ*, IV, 66.
138 Russell, *Fall of the British Monarchies*, p. 115. By far the fullest source for this debate, as for much of the rest of the Short Parliament, is Judith D. Maltby (ed.), *The Short Parliament (1640) Diary of Sir Thomas Aston* (Camden Society, 4th series, XXXV, 1988), 85–97.
139 Cope (ed.), *Proceedings*, 209; Maltby (ed.), *Diary of Aston*, 132. Vane was speaking from personal experience of the Addled Parliament: Russell, *Fall of the British Monarchies*, p. 118.
140 *LJ*, IV, 81.
141 John Morrill, *The Nature of the English Revolution* (Harlow, 1993), pp. 7, 46.
142 The petition of the 12 peers is printed in Gardiner (ed.), *Constitutional Documents*, pp. 134–6 (quotation at p. 135).

8 Revolutionary Parliaments, 1640–1660

1 For the dates of parliamentary sessions after 1689, see E. B. Fryde, D. E. Greenway, S. Porter and I. Roy (eds.), *Handbook of British Chronology* (3rd edition, reprinted Cambridge, 1996), pp. 577–81.

2 Wallace Notestein (ed.), *The Journal of Sir Simonds D'Ewes from the Beginning of the Long Parliament to the Opening of the Trial of the Earl of Strafford* (New Haven, 1923), p. 7.

3 Daniel Parsons (ed.), *The Diary of Sir Henry Slingsby of Scriven, Bart.* (1836), p. 66.

4 *Sir Iohn Culpeper His Speech in Parliament, concerning the Grievances of the Church and Common-wealth* (1641), Wing, C 5058; BL, TT, E 196/8; Notestein (ed.), *Journal of D'Ewes*, p. 8.

5 J. A. Manning (ed.), *Memoirs of Sir Benjamin Rudyerd* (1841), p. 162.

6 Conrad Russell, *The Fall of the British Monarchies, 1637–1642* (Oxford, 1991), pp. 230–1; David L. Smith, *Constitutional Royalism and the Search for Settlement, c. 1640–1649* (Cambridge, 1994), pp. 70–1.

7 *CJ*, II, 54.

8 D. Alan Orr, 'Sovereignty, State and the Law of Treason in England, 1641–1649' (unpubl. Ph.D. dissertation, University of Cambridge, 1997), pp. 106–55.

9 Russell, *Fall of the British Monarchies*, p. 126.

10 On attainder, see above, p. 35.

11 Russell, *Fall of the British Monarchies*, pp. 288–300.

12 The act of attainder is printed in S. R. Gardiner (ed.), *Constitutional Documents of the Puritan Revolution, 1625–1660* (3rd edition, Oxford, 1906), pp. 156–8.

13 Conrad Russell, *Unrevolutionary England, 1603–1642* (1990), pp. 281–302; Russell, *Fall of the British Monarchies*, pp. 291–4, 330–7.

14 Orr, 'Sovereignty, State and the Law of Treason', pp. 56–105.

15 16 Car. I, c. 1; printed in Gardiner (ed.), *Constitutional Documents*, pp. 144–55. See above, p. 77.

16 These petitions are discussed more fully above, p. 37, and below, p. 126.

17 16 Car. I, c. 7; printed in Gardiner (ed.), *Constitutional Documents*, pp. 158–9.

18 16 Car. I, c. 8; printed in *ibid.*, pp. 159–62.

19 16 Car. I, c. 12; 16 Car. I, c. 22; 16 Car. I, c. 25; 16 Car. I, c. 29; 16 Car. I, c. 31; 16 Car. I, c. 35.

20 See above, pp. 55–6, and below, pp. 124–5.

21 16 Car. I, c. 10 and 16 Car. I, c. 11; printed in Gardiner (ed.), *Constitutional Documents*, pp. 179–89.

22 16 Car. I, c. 14; 16 Car. I, c. 16; 16 Car. I, c. 20; printed in *ibid.*, pp. 189–97.

23 See above, pp. 55–6.

24 Russell, *Fall of the British Monarchies*, pp. 346–50, 357–64.

25 *Ibid.*, pp. 252–7. See above, pp. 55–6, 87–8.

26 Russell, *Fall of the British Monarchies*, p. 351.

27 The Ten Propositions are printed in Gardiner (ed.), *Constitutional Documents*, pp. 163–6 (quotations at p. 164).

28 Russell, *Fall of the British Monarchies*, p. 353.

29 *LJ*, IV, 306, 310–11.

30 BL, Harleian MS 164 (diary of Sir Simonds D'Ewes), fo. 217r.

31 *CJ*, II, 159.

32 Conrad Russell, 'Issues in the House of Commons, 1621–1629: Predictors of Civil War Allegiance', *Albion*, XXIII (1991), 23–39; together with the reply by Wilfrid Prest, 'Predicting Civil War Allegiances: The Lawyers' Case Considered', *Albion*, XXIV (1992), 225–36. See also Conrad Russell, *The Causes of the English Civil War* (Oxford, 1990), especially pp. 220–6.

33 Smith, *Constitutional Royalism*, pp. 71–3.

34 *LJ*, IV, 142.

35 *CJ*, II, 72.
36 John Morrill, *Revolt in the Provinces: The People of England and the Tragedies of War, 1630–1648* (2nd edition, Harlow, 1998), pp. 47–74; Anthony Fletcher, *The Outbreak of the English Civil War* (1981), pp. 91–124, 208–27; David Underdown, *Revel, Riot and Rebellion* (Oxford, 1985), pp. 136–41. See also Jacqueline Eales, 'Iconoclasm, Iconography, and the Altar in the English Civil War', in Diana Wood (ed.), *The Church and the Arts* (Studies in Church History, XXVIII, 1992), 313–27.
37 Derek Hirst, 'The Defection of Sir Edward Dering, 1640–1641', *HJ*, XV (1972), 193–208; see above, p. 30.
38 BL, Harleian MS 164, fo. 89r.
39 Sir Thomas Aston, *A Remonstrance against Presbytery* (1641), p. 62 (Wing, A 4078; BL, TT, E 163/1, E 163/2). On Aston, see especially Judith Maltby, *Prayer Book and People in Elizabethan and Early Stuart England* (Cambridge, 1998), Chapter 4.
40 *CJ*, II, 279–81; Russell, *Fall of the British Monarchies*, pp. 368–70.
41 James S. Hart, *Justice upon Petition: The House of Lords and the Reformation of Justice, 1621–1675* (1991), pp. 69–87; see also above, p. 37.
42 The text of the London root and branch petition is printed in Gardiner (ed.), *Constitutional Documents*, pp. 137–44. For a fuller discussion, see David L. Smith, 'From Petition to Remonstrance', and Richard Strier, 'From Diagnosis to Operation', both in David L. Smith, Richard Strier and David Bevington (eds.), *The Theatrical City: Culture, Theatre and Politics in London, 1576–1649* (Cambridge, 1995), pp. 209–43.
43 Fletcher, *Outbreak*, pp. 92–6; John Morrill, *The Nature of the English Revolution* (Harlow, 1993), pp. 177–8.
44 Fletcher, *Outbreak*, pp. 283–91; Judith Maltby, '"By this Book": Parishioners, the Prayer Book and the Established Church', in Kenneth Fincham (ed.), *The Early Stuart Church, 1603–1642* (1993), pp. 115–37; Maltby, *Prayer Book and People*, especially pp. 83–129, 238–47.
45 Fletcher, *Outbreak*, pp. 191–227.
46 Russell, *Unrevolutionary England*, pp. 263–4; Russell, *Fall of the British Monarchies*, pp. 366–7.
47 The text of the Grand Remonstrance is printed in Gardiner (ed.), *Constitutional Documents*, pp. 202–32, from which the following quotations are taken. See also Smith, 'From Petition to Remonstrance', and Strier, 'From Diagnosis to Operation'.
48 For this debate, see Willson H. Coates (ed.), *The Journal of Sir Simonds D'Ewes from the first Recess of the Long Parliament to the Withdrawal of King Charles from London* (New Haven, 1942; reprinted Hamden, 1970), pp. 183–7; *CJ*, II, 322.
49 Russell, *Fall of the British Monarchies*, p. 424.
50 For Charles's answer to the Grand Remonstrance, see Gardiner (ed.), *Constitutional Documents*, pp. 233–6.
51 *CJ*, II, 379; Willson H. Coates, Anne Steele Young and Vernon F. Snow (eds.), *The Private Journals of the Long Parliament* (3 vols., New Haven and London, 1982–92), I, 67.
52 Most of the Militia Ordinance is printed in Gardiner (ed.), *Constitutional Documents*, pp. 245–7, although for the complete list of those proposed as Lords Lieutenant and Deputy Lieutenants, see the full text in *LJ*, IV, 625–7.
53 J. B. Crummett, 'The Lay Peers in Parliament, 1640–4' (unpubl. Ph.D. dissertation, University of Manchester, 1972), pp. 260c–260d.
54 The monthly averages for attendance revealed in Commons division lists for the first eight months of 1642 are as follows: January 276, February 168, March 120, April 159, May 172, June 149, July 123, August 76. These figures are derived from *CJ*, II, 368–739. See also Mary Frear Keeler, *The Long Parliament, 1640–1641: A*

Biographical Study of its Members (Memoirs of the American Philosophical Society, XXXVI, Philadelphia, 1954), p. 6.

55 Russell, *Causes*, pp. 222–4.

56 Russell, *Fall of the British Monarchies*, pp. 470–4; J. S. A. Adamson, 'The Baronial Context of the English Civil War', *TRHS*, 5th series, XL (1990), 93–120.

57 Smith, *Constitutional Royalism*, especially pp. 80–96.

58 See above, pp. 46–7.

59 This decline in the return of carpetbaggers marked a dramatic acceleration of a trend already visible before the outbreak of the Civil War: see above, p. 28. On the recruiter elections, see D. Brunton and D. H. Pennington, *Members of the Long Parliament* (1954), pp. 21–37; David Underdown, 'Party Management in the Recruiter Elections, 1645–1648', *EHR*, LXXXIII (1968), 235–64; Morrill, *Revolt in the Provinces*, pp. 166–9 (quotation at p. 168). On the rival groups within the Long Parliament, see also above, pp. 89–90, and below, pp. 132–3.

60 Michael Mendle, 'The Great Council of Parliament and the First Ordinances: The Constitutional Theory of the Civil War', *JBS*, XXXI (1992), 133–62; Elizabeth R. Foster, 'The House of Lords and Ordinances, 1641–1649', *American Journal of Legal History*, XXI (1977), 157–73. See also above, pp. 46–7.

61 Approximate annual totals of 'public' ordinances passed between March 1642 and December 1648 are as follows: 45 in 1642, 155 in 1643, 134 in 1644, 147 in 1645, 78 in 1646, 111 in 1647, and 92 in 1648. These figures are derived from the chronological table of ordinances in *AO*, III, i–cix. I have not counted those directives entitled 'order' or 'declaration'. But this distinction is an imperfect one, and *AO*, although very full, is not a definitive collection: see Sheila Lambert (ed.), *Printing for Parliament, 1641–1700* (List and Index Society, special series, XX, 1984), iii–iv. *AO* does not include 'private' ordinances: these can be reconstructed from *LJ* and *CJ*, and from eight manuscript 'Books of Ordinances' at the HLRO.

62 See above, pp. 32–43.

63 Smith, *Constitutional Royalism*, pp. 186–7.

64 See above, pp. 56–7.

65 See above, p. 74.

66 Morrill, *Revolt in the Provinces*, pp. 80–2, 93–101.

67 Gardiner (ed.), *Constitutional Documents*, p. 274.

68 Morrill, *Revolt in the Provinces*, pp. 83–4.

69 Edward, Earl of Clarendon, *The History of the Rebellion and Civil Wars in England*, ed. W. Dunn Macray (6 vols., Oxford, 1888), II, 195 (Book V, § 361).

70 *His Majesties Declaration to all his Loving Subjects* [12 August 1642], p. 57 (Wing, C 2241; BL, TT, E 115/11).

71 Clarendon, *History*, III, 294 (Book VII, § 370).

72 John Rushworth, *Historical Collections of Private Passages of State* (8 vols., 1680–1701), V, 589, 594–5.

73 Rushworth, *Historical Collections*, V, 894. For further discussions of the Oxford Parliament, see S. R. Gardiner, *History of the Great Civil War, 1642–1649* (4 vols., 1893; reprinted 1987), I, 259, 299–300, 307–8, 331, 335; II, 114, 181; and Smith, *Constitutional Royalism*, especially pp. 117–18, 169–74, 208–10.

74 [Edward Hyde], *A Full Answer to an Infamous and Trayterous Pamphlet* (1648), p. 105 (Wing, C 4423; BL, TT, E 455/5).

75 Gardiner (ed.), *Constitutional Documents*, pp. 300–1.

76 These documents are printed in Gardiner (ed.), *Constitutional Documents*, pp. 249–54, 262–7, 275–86, 290–306, 335–47. For a fuller discussion of these issues, see Smith, *Constitutional Royalism*, Chapters 5 and 6.

77 The numbers included in these categories rose steadily until 1644, when they became stabilised at 48 and 58 respectively.

78 Clarendon, *History*, II, 149 (Book V, § 280).

79 See especially J. H. Hexter, 'The Problem of the Presbyterian Independents', in J. H.

Hexter, *Reappraisals in History* (1961), pp. 163–84; Valerie Pearl, 'The "Royal Independents" in the English Civil War', *TRHS*, 5th series, XVIII (1968), 69–96; David Underdown, *Pride's Purge: Politics in the Puritan Revolution* (Oxford, 1971), pp. 45–105.

80 See above, pp. 89–90.

81 Underdown, *Pride's Purge*, pp. 45–105; Morrill, *Revolt in the Provinces*, pp. 166–9, 199–200; Adamson, 'Parliamentary Management', pp. 31–50; J. S. A. Adamson, 'The Peerage in Politics, 1645–49' (unpubl. Ph.D. dissertation, University of Cambridge, 1986).

82 On this, see in particular Adamson, 'Parliamentary Management', pp. 31–50; Adamson, 'Baronial Context', especially 109–14; Adamson, 'The Peerage in Politics', especially pp. 17–58, 115–32; and J. S. A. Adamson, 'Of Armies and Architecture: The Employments of Robert Scawen', in Ian Gentles, John Morrill and Blair Worden (eds.), *Soldiers, Writers and Statesmen of the English Revolution* (Cambridge, 1998), pp. 36–67, especially pp. 50–63.

83 Adamson, 'Parliamentary Management', pp. 34–8; Adamson, 'Baronial Context', 109–116; Patricia Crawford, *Denzil Holles, 1598–1680: A Study of his Political Career* (1979), pp. 105–20.

84 See especially Adamson, 'Parliamentary Management', pp. 45–50; also above, pp. 87–90.

85 These phrases are taken from the Army's *Declaration* of 14 June 1647, quoted in Mark Kishlansky, 'Ideology and Politics in the Parliamentary Armies, 1645–9', in John Morrill (ed.), *Reactions to the English Civil War, 1642–1649* (1982), pp. 163–83, at p. 171.

86 The best recent account of these events is found in Ian Gentles, *The New Model Army in England, Ireland and Scotland, 1645–1653* (Oxford, 1992), pp. 176–97.

87 The text of the *Heads* is printed in Gardiner (ed.), *Constitutional Documents*, pp. 316–26. For the debate over the relationship between the Army officers and the Independents within the two Houses, see: J. S. A. Adamson, 'The English Nobility and the Projected Settlement of 1647', *HJ*, XXX (1987), 567–602; Mark A. Kishlansky, 'Saye What?', *HJ*, XXXIII (1990), 917–37; J. S. A. Adamson, 'Politics and the Nobility in Civil-War England', *HJ*, XXXIV (1991), 231–55; Mark A. Kishlansky, 'Saye No More', *JBS*, XXX (1991), 399–448.

88 On the growth of 'Parliamentarian tyranny', see especially Robert Ashton, 'From Cavalier to Roundhead Tyranny, 1642–9', in Morrill (ed.), *Reactions to the English Civil War*, pp. 185–207; and Morrill, *Revolt in the Provinces*, Chapter 2.

89 Quoted in Morrill, *Revolt in the Provinces*, p. 75.

90 See above, pp. 37, 74.

91 See above, pp. 56–7.

92 Morrill, *Revolt in the Provinces*, pp. 77–9, 111–18; Smith, *Constitutional Royalism*, especially pp. 178–89.

93 On these petitions in general, see Morrill, *Revolt in the Provinces*, pp. 169–74; Robert Ashton, *Counter-Revolution: The Second Civil War and its Origins, 1646–8* (New Haven and London, 1994), pp. 117–58.

94 Quoted in John Morrill, *The Revolt of the Provinces: Conservatives and Radicals in the English Civil War, 1630–1650* (Longman edition, Harlow, 1980), pp. 207–8.

95 *AO*, I, 582–607, 749–57, 879–83.

96 See especially John Morrill, 'The Church in England, 1642–9', in Morrill (ed.), *Reactions to the English Civil War*, pp. 89–114.

97 Morrill, *Revolt in the Provinces*, pp. 143–7, 208.

98 The texts of the *Agreements of the People* are printed in Don M. Wolfe (ed.), *Leveller Manifestos of the Puritan Revolution* (1944), pp. 223–34, 291–303, 397–410.

99 Gardiner (ed.), *Constitutional Documents*, pp. 360–3. These proposals were partially implemented during the Cromwellian Protectorate: see above, p. 23.

100 These phrases are taken from the Army's *Remonstrance* of 16 November 1648,

printed in J. P. Kenyon (ed.), *The Stuart Constitution: Documents and Commentary* (2nd edition, Cambridge, 1986), pp. 281–92 (quotations at pp. 289–90). The best surveys of Leveller thought are G. E. Aylmer, *The Levellers in the English Revolution* (1975), and David Wootton, 'Leveller Democracy and the Puritan Revolution', in J. H. Burns and Mark Goldie (eds.), *The Cambridge History of Political Thought, 1450–1700* (Cambridge, 1991), pp. 412–42.

101 On the context and events of the second Civil War, see especially Ashton, *Counter-Revolution*; and Morrill, *Revolt in the Provinces*, pp. 204–8.

102 This conviction was dramatically expressed at the officers' prayer meeting at Windsor Castle at the end of April 1648: William Allen, *A Faithful Memorial of that Remarkable Meeting of Many Officers of the Army* (1659), reprinted in John, Baron Somers, *A Collection of Scarce and Valuable Tracts*, ed. Sir Walter Scott, VI (1811), 501.

103 Kenyon (ed.), *Stuart Constitution*, pp. 288–9.

104 The finest account of the Purge remains Underdown, *Pride's Purge*, Chapter 6. See also above, p. 66.

105 Blair Worden, *The Rump Parliament, 1648–1653* (Cambridge, 1974), pp. 23, 387–92; Underdown, *Pride's Purge*, pp. 208–56, 361–98.

106 *CJ*, VI, 111.

107 Gardiner (ed.), *Constitutional Documents*, p. 380.

108 *Ibid.*, pp. 384–8 (quotations at pp. 385, 387).

109 *Ibid.*, p. 388.

110 *Ibid.*

111 Quentin Skinner, 'Conquest and Consent: Thomas Hobbes and the Engagement Controversy', in G. E. Aylmer (ed.), *The Interregnum: The Quest for Settlement, 1646–1660* (1972), pp. 79–98; Glenn Burgess, 'Usurpation, Obligation and Obedience in the Thought of the Engagement Controversy', *HJ*, XXIX (1986), 515–36.

112 Worden, *Rump Parliament*, pp. 23–32, 387–94.

113 *Ibid.*, p. 92. These figures, derived from the list in *AO*, III, lxvi–xci, are a slight underestimate. Sheila Lambert calculates that the Rump in fact passed 355 public acts rather than the 311 listed in *AO*, together with 33 private acts: Lambert (ed.), *Printing for Parliament*, iv.

114 Worden, *Rump Parliament*, p. 92.

115 *AO*, II, 387–9, 409–12; Worden, *Rump Parliament*, pp. 232–6.

116 *AO*, II, 423–5; Gardiner (ed.), *Constitutional Documents*, pp. 391–4; Worden, *Rump Parliament*, pp. 238–40.

117 *AO*, II, 342–8.

118 Worden, *Rump Parliament*, pp. 234–6, 327–8.

119 Mary Cotterell, 'Interregnum Law Reform: The Hale Commission of 1652', *EHR*, LXXXIII (1968), 689–704; Worden, *Rump Parliament*, pp. 105–18.

120 *AO*, III, lxvi–lxxi, lxxxii–lxxxiv, xc–xci.

121 S. C. Lomas (ed.), *The Letters and Speeches of Oliver Cromwell, with Elucidations by Thomas Carlyle* (3 vols., 1904), II, 226.

122 Gardiner (ed.), *Constitutional Documents*, p. 400.

123 Lomas (ed.), *Letters and Speeches of Cromwell*, II, 279.

124 Gardiner (ed.), *Constitutional Documents*, p. 401.

125 Lomas (ed.), *Letters and Speeches of Cromwell*, II, 279–80.

126 Cromwell's motives for expelling the Rump are unravelled in Worden, *Rump Parliament*, pp. 317–84; and Austin Woolrych, *Commonwealth to Protectorate* (Oxford, 1982), pp. 25–102.

127 G. C. Moore Smith (ed.), *The Letters of Dorothy Osborne to William Temple* (Oxford, 1928), p. 39 (23 April 1653).

128 Much the best account of the Assembly is Woolrych, *Commonwealth to Protectorate*.

129 This phrase is taken from the summons to members of the Assembly, printed in

Gardiner (ed.), *Constitutional Documents*, p. 405. Five more members (including Cromwell) were later co-opted: a full list of all 144 is given in Woolrych, *Commonwealth to Protectorate*, pp. 410–33.

130 Lomas (ed.), *Letters and Speeches of Cromwell*, II, 272–303 (quotations at 273, 282, 298).

131 Woolrych, *Commonwealth to Protectorate*, pp. 165–93.

132 *AO*, II, 715–18, 753–64, 772–3.

133 *CJ*, VII, 336, 340, 352, 358, 361.

134 *Ibid.*, 363.

135 Woolrych, *Commonwealth to Protectorate*, pp. 352–90; David Farr, 'The Military and Political Career of John Lambert, 1619–57' (unpubl. Ph.D. dissertation, University of Cambridge, 1996), pp. 270–3.

136 The text of the Instrument of Government is printed in Gardiner (ed.), *Constitutional Documents*, pp. 405–17.

137 Quoted in Kenyon (ed.), *Stuart Constitution*, p. 299.

138 Lomas (ed.), *Letters and Speeches of Cromwell*, II, 381.

139 See above, p. 27.

140 Lomas (ed.), *Letters and Speeches of Cromwell*, III, 101.

141 I develop these points at greater length in David L. Smith, 'Oliver Cromwell, the first Protectorate Parliament and Religious Reform', *PH* (forthcoming).

142 Lomas (ed.), *Letters and Speeches of Cromwell*, II, 339–59 (quotations at 339, 340).

143 *Ibid.*, 366–90.

144 Peter Gaunt, 'Cromwell's Purge? Exclusions and the First Protectorate Parliament', *PH*, VI (1987), 1–22; J. T. Rutt (ed.), *Diary of Thomas Burton, Esq.* (4 vols., 1828), I, xxxii–xxxvi; *CJ*, VII, 367–8.

145 Ruth Spalding (ed.), *The Diary of Bulstrode Whitelocke, 1605–1675* (British Academy, Records of Social and Economic History, new series, XIII, Oxford, 1990), p. 400 (3 February 1655).

146 Lomas (ed.), *Letters and Speeches of Cromwell*, II, 407–9.

147 Peter Gaunt, *Oliver Cromwell* (Oxford and Cambridge, Mass., 1996), pp. 181–2; Peter Gaunt, 'The Councils of the Protectorate, from December 1653 to September 1658' (unpubl. Ph.D. dissertation, University of Exeter, 1983), pp. 129–42.

148 Peter Gaunt, 'Law-Making in the First Protectorate Parliament', in Colin Jones, Malyn Newitt and Stephen Roberts (eds.), *Politics and People in Revolutionary England: Essays in Honour of Ivan Roots* (Oxford and New York, 1986), pp. 163–86. For a draft list of bills intended for the first Protectorate Parliament, see BL, Stowe MS 322 (Revenue Papers), fo. 74r–v.

149 The text of this bill is printed in Gardiner (ed.), *Constitutional Documents*, pp. 427–47.

150 *Ibid.*, pp. 431–2.

151 *Ibid.*, pp. 443–5; *CJ*, VII, 403, 405, 408.

152 Gardiner (ed.), *Constitutional Documents*, p. 443.

153 Blair Worden, 'Toleration and the Cromwellian Protectorate', in W. J. Sheils (ed.), *Persecution and Toleration* (Studies in Church History, XXI, 1984), 199–233, especially 218–22; J. C. Davis, 'Cromwell's Religion', in John Morrill (ed.), *Oliver Cromwell and the English Revolution* (Harlow, 1990), pp. 196–7.

154 Ivan Roots, 'Cromwell's Ordinances: The Early Legislation of the Protectorate', in Aylmer (ed.), *The Interregnum*, pp. 143–64.

155 Lomas (ed.), *Letters and Speeches of Cromwell*, II, 404–30 (quotations at 409, 416–17, 422, 430).

156 See above, p. 59.

157 C. H. Firth, *The Last Years of the Protectorate, 1656–1658* (2 vols., 1909), I, 11–22; Carol S. Egloff, 'The Search for a Cromwellian Settlement: Exclusions from the Second Protectorate Parliament. Part 1: The Process and its Architects', and 'Part 2: The Excluded Members and the Reactions to the Exclusion', *PH*, XVII (1998), 178–97, 301–21.

158 Ivan Roots, 'Lawmaking in the Second Protectorate Parliament', in H. Hearder and H. R. Loyn (eds.), *British Government and Administration: Essays Presented to S. B. Chrimes* (Cardiff, 1974), pp. 132–43.

159 Rutt (ed.), *Diary of Burton*, I, 20–174; *CJ*, VII, 468–9.

160 Lomas (ed.), *Letters and Speeches of Cromwell*, III, 20. On the issue of the Commons' judicature, see above, pp. 34–6.

161 As he put it in his letter to the Speaker on 25 December 1656: 'we detest and abhor the giving or occasioning the least countenance to persons of such opinions and practices, or who are under the guilt of such crimes as are commonly imputed to the said person': Lomas (ed.), *Letters and Speeches of Cromwell*, III, 20.

162 *Ibid.*, 24.

163 Rutt (ed.), *Diary of Burton*, I, 175–372; *CJ*, VII, 483–4; Christopher Durston, 'The Fall of Cromwell's Major-Generals', *EHR*, CXIII (1998), 18–37.

164 Lomas (ed.), *Letters and Speeches of Cromwell*, II, 543.

165 The fullest account of the offer of the kingship to Cromwell and his subsequent refusal remains C. H. Firth, 'Cromwell and the Crown', *EHR*, XVII (1902), 429–42; XVIII (1903), 52–80. I am very grateful to Patrick Little for a helpful discussion on this subject.

166 Lomas (ed.), *Letters and Speeches of Cromwell*, III, 125–9.

167 *Ibid.*, 71.

168 A despatch from the Venetian ambassador in Paris, Francesco Giustiniani, throws interesting light on this question. He reported that, according to Cromwell's ambassador in Paris, Cromwell was reluctant to accept the kingship 'since he wields more authority in his present position than he would as King, because he would be obliged to concede and renew many privileges and jurisdictions to Parliament such as were granted by Henry VIII': *CSPV*, XXXI (1657–9), 32–3.

169 The text of the Humble Petition and Advice is printed in Gardiner (ed.), *Constitutional Documents*, pp. 447–59.

170 *CJ*, VII, 578. For the ceremonial surrounding Cromwell's second installation as Lord Protector, see Roy Sherwood, *The Court of Oliver Cromwell* (1977), pp. 158–67.

171 *CSPV*, XXXI (1657–9), 157–8. Cf. above, pp. 78–9.

172 Cromwell's hopes were expressed particularly in speeches on 20 and 25 January: Lomas (ed.), *Letters and Speeches of Cromwell*, III, 150–8, 162–85 (quotation at 165).

173 Firth, *Last Years*, II, 7–16. For an example of the writ of summons, see Gardiner (ed.), *Constitutional Documents*, p. 464.

174 Kenyon (ed.), *Stuart Constitution*, pp. 420–1. The two peers who accepted were Lord Fauconberg and Lord Eure: Firth, *Last Years*, II, 14.

175 Rutt (ed.), *Diary of Burton*, II, 374–464.

176 Gardiner (ed.), *Constitutional Documents*, p. 449.

177 Firth, *Last Years*, II, 7–24.

178 Lomas (ed.), *Letters and Speeches of Cromwell*, III, 162–85.

179 Firth, *Last Years*, II, 30–5.

180 Lomas (ed.), *Letters and Speeches of Cromwell*, III, 187–92 (quotation at 192).

181 The best accounts of the years 1658–60 are Austin Woolrych, 'Historical Introduction (1659–1660)', in Robert W. Ayers (ed.), *The Complete Prose Works of John Milton*, VII (revised edition, New Haven and London, 1980), 1–228, and Ronald Hutton, *The Restoration: A Political and Religious History of England and Wales, 1658–1667* (Oxford, 1985), pp. 3–123.

182 Godfrey Davies, 'The Elections to Richard Cromwell's Parliament', *EHR*, LXIII (1948), 488–501.

183 *CJ*, VII, 621; Rutt (ed.), *Diary of Burton*, IV, 277–93.

184 *CJ*, VII, 604; Rutt (ed.), *Diary of Burton*, III, 288–96; Woolrych, 'Historical Introduction', 19–22.

185 *CJ*, VII, 625–6; Rutt (ed.), *Diary of Burton*, IV, 334–49.

186 Hutton, *The Restoration*, pp. 30–40; *CJ*, VII, 644; Rutt (ed.), *Diary of Burton*, IV, 469–86.

187 Quoted in Austin Woolrych, 'Last Quests for a Settlement, 1657–1660', in Aylmer (ed.), *The Interregnum*, pp. 183–204, at p. 196.

188 *CJ*, VII, 651.

189 *Ibid.*, 792.

190 *Ibid.*, 795; *AO*, II, 1351–2.

191 For general accounts of the Rump between May and October 1659, see especially Woolrych, 'Historical Introduction', 70–6, 96–117; and Hutton, *The Restoration*, pp. 42–67.

192 See his revealing letter to John Owen of 29 November 1659, in C. H. Firth (ed.), *The Clarke Papers*, IV (Camden Society, 2nd series, LXII, 1901), 151–4.

193 Woolrych, 'Historical Introduction', 160–2.

194 *CJ*, VII, 846; Woolrych, 'Historical Introduction', 170–4; Hutton, *The Restoration*, pp. 93–7.

195 *CJ*, VII, 846–7; Woolrych, 'Historical Introduction', 173–6; Hutton, *The Restoration*, pp. 95–8.

196 *CJ*, VII, 848–9.

197 *Ibid.*, 876, 880; *AO*, II, 1469–72; Woolrych, 'Historical Introduction', 192–4; Hutton, *The Restoration*, pp. 96–104.

198 Gardiner (ed.), *Constitutional Documents*, pp. 465–7.

199 A Convention was an extraordinary assembly of Parliament which took place without a royal summons having been issued, for example in 1660 and 1689. During the first half of the century, the term had been used to describe a Parliament, legitimately summoned by the monarch, that failed to pass any acts. See also below, p. 231.

200 *LJ*, XI, 3; *CJ*, VIII, 1.

201 *LJ*, XI, 19; *CJ*, VIII, 16–17.

9 Restoration Parliaments, 1660–1689

1 See Appendix 2, below. The total number of parliamentary acts and ordinances passed between 1642 and 1660 has been calculated from the table in *AO*, III, i–cix. It is probable that this slightly underestimates the actual figure: see above, p. 218.

2 Thus, the first public act of Charles II's reign, an 'Act for removing and preventing all questions and disputes concerning the assembling and sitting of this present Parliament', was numbered 12 Car. II, c. 1.

3 13 Car. II, stat. 1, c. 6; printed in Andrew Browning (ed.), *English Historical Documents, 1660–1714* (1953), p. 793.

4 14 Car. II, c. 3; printed in *ibid.*, pp. 793–5.

5 13 Car. II, stat. 1, c. 1; printed in *ibid.*, pp. 63–5 (quotation at p. 64).

6 See above, pp. 60–1.

7 C. D. Chandaman, *The English Public Revenue, 1660–1688* (Oxford, 1975), pp. 196–206; Paul Seaward, *The Cavalier Parliament and the Reconstruction of the Old Regime, 1661–1667* (Cambridge, 1989), pp. 103–30.

8 16 Car. II, c. 1; printed in Browning (ed.), *English Historical Documents*, pp. 153–4. See above, pp. 60–1, 77.

9 12 Car. II, c. 11; printed in *ibid.*, pp. 164–5.

10 *LJ*, XI, 205.

11 J. P. Kenyon (ed.), *The Stuart Constitution: Documents and Commentary* (2nd edition, Cambridge, 1986), p. 416; Maxwell P. Schoenfeld, *The Restored House of Lords* (The Hague, 1967), pp. 104–26. On private bill procedure, see above, pp. 39–42.

12 For the composition and outlook of the Cavalier Parliament, see especially Seaward, *Cavalier Parliament*, pp. 35–70; B. D. Henning (ed.), *The House of Commons, 1660–1690* (3 vols., 1983), I, 11–13, 32–3, 45.

13 14 Car. II, c. 4; printed in Browning (ed.), *English Historical Documents*, pp. 377–82.

14 Andrew Swatland, *The House of Lords in the Reign of Charles II* (Cambrdige, 1996), pp. 159–72; Seaward, *Cavalier Parliament*, pp. 162–95. See also above, p. 90.

15 13 Car. II, stat. 2, c. 1; printed in Browning (ed.), *English Historical Documents*, pp. 375–6.

16 13 & 14 Car. II, c. 1.

17 16 Car. II, c. 1.

18 17 Car. II, c. 2; printed in Browning (ed.), *English Historical Documents*, pp. 382–4.

19 Seaward, *Cavalier Parliament*, pp. 180–1. I am grateful to Paul Seaward for advice on this point.

20 Kenyon (ed.), *Stuart Constitution*, p. 375.

21 Edward, Earl of Clarendon, *The Life of Edward, Earl of Clarendon . . . written by himself* (3 vols., Oxford, 1827), II, 348.

22 See, for example, the recent analysis of the implementation of the Corporation Act in Paul D. Halliday, *Dismembering the Body Politic: Partisan Politics in England's Towns, 1650–1730* (Cambridge, 1998), pp. 92–105, 354–61.

23 Clifford was Treasurer of the Household from 1668 and Lord Treasurer from 1672; Arlington was Secretary of State from 1662; Buckingham held no major state office but was on good personal terms with the King; Ashley was Chancellor of the Exchequer from 1661 and Lord Chancellor from 1672; and Lauderdale was Secretary for Scottish affairs on and off from 1660.

24 Seaward, *Cavalier Parliament*, pp. 217–35.

25 *CJ*, IX, 4–42; Grey, *Debates*, I, 1–70. See also Ronald Hutton, *The Restoration: A Political and Religious History of England and Wales, 1658–1667* (Oxford, 1985), pp. 268–90; Seaward, *Cavalier Parliament*, pp. 276–327; D. T. Witcombe, *Charles II and the Cavalier House of Commons, 1663–1674* (Manchester, 1966), pp. 61–77; Swatland, *House of Lords*, pp. 137–8; and above, p. 93.

26 19 & 20 Car. II, c. 1; printed in Browning (ed.), *English Historical Documents*, pp. 176–8.

27 Paul Seaward, *The Restoration, 1660–1688* (1991), pp. 21–2; Seaward, *Cavalier Parliament*, pp. 124–8; Chandaman, *Public Revenue*, pp. 155, 236, 278–9, 295; Witcombe, *Charles II and the Cavalier House of Commons*, pp. 34–6; Henry Roseveare, *The Treasury, 1660–1870: The Foundations of Control* (1973), pp. 20–45.

28 Ronald Hutton, *Charles II: King of England, Scotland, and Ireland* (Oxford, 1989), pp. 254–86.

29 *Ibid.*, pp. 258–60. See also above, pp. 68–70.

30 Ronald Hutton, 'The Making of the Secret Treaty of Dover, 1668–1670', *HJ*, XXIX (1986), 297–318. See also Hutton, *Charles II*, pp. 263–73; Ronald Hutton, 'The Religion of Charles II', in R. Malcolm Smuts (ed.), *The Stuart Court and Europe: Essays in Politics and Political Culture* (Cambridge, 1996), pp. 228–46; and John Miller, *Charles II* (1991), pp. 142–82.

31 The text of the secret Treaty of Dover is printed in Browning (ed.), *English Historical Documents*, pp. 863–7 (quotation at p. 864).

32 Grey, *Debates*, II, 228–33, 239–40, 245–8.

33 *Ibid.*, I, 146–7, 159–63, 174–6, 220–3; Tim Harris, *Politics under the Later Stuarts: Party Conflict in a Divided Society, 1660–1715* (1993), pp. 68–70.

34 This supply was granted by 20 Car. II, c. 1; for the debates on it, see Grey, *Debates*, I, 148–50, 176–7, 186–9.

35 The second Conventicle Act was 22 Car. II, c. 1; printed in Browning (ed.), *English Historical Documents*, pp. 384–6. The various financial grants that followed were

made in 22 Car. II, c. 3; 22 Car. II, c. 4; 22 & 23 Car. II, c. 3; 22 & 23 Car. II, c. 5. See also Grey, *Debates*, I, 272–93, 310–32, 355–68.

36 Browning (ed.), *English Historical Documents*, pp. 387–8.

37 See above, pp. 96–7.

38 See above, p. 60. The first Test Act of 1673 was 25 Car. II, c. 2; printed in Browning (ed.), *English Historical Documents*, pp. 389–91. This, together with the other concessions, was the price that Charles paid for securing extraordinary supply worth about £1.2 million (25 Car. II, c. 1).

39 Ashley had been created Earl of Shaftesbury in April 1672.

40 Quoted in Hutton, *Charles II*, p. 316. For the Commons' assault on the Cabal in 1674 see Grey, *Debates*, II, 223–454; *CJ*, IX, 286–314; Witcombe, *Charles II and the Cavalier House of Commons*, pp. 127–65.

41 Swatland, *House of Lords*, pp. 203–33.

42 Henning (ed.), *House of Commons, 1660–1690*, I, 29.

43 Harris, *Politics under the Later Stuarts*, pp. 84–7; Swatland, *House of Lords*, pp. 211–13. See also above, pp. 90–1.

44 Swatland, *House of Lords*, pp. 227–8.

45 See above, p. 94. See also Mark Goldie, 'Danby, the Bishops and the Whigs', in Tim Harris, Paul Seaward and Mark Goldie (eds.), *The Politics of Religion in Restoration England* (Oxford and Cambridge, Mass., 1990), pp. 75–105.

46 See above, p. 68.

47 For Danby's management of the Upper House, see especially Swatland, *House of Lords*, pp. 242–50.

48 Harris, *Politics under the Later Stuarts*, pp. 61–5; Andrew Browning, *Thomas Osborne, Earl of Danby and Duke of Leeds, 1632–1712* (3 vols., Glasgow, 1944–51), I, 146–283; III, 33–151; Seaward, *The Restoration*, p. 26; Henning (ed.), *House of Commons, 1660–1690*, I, 34–5. See also above, pp. 90–1.

49 The impeachment articles are found in *CJ*, IX, 324. See also Browning, *Danby*, I, 152–60; Grey, *Debates*, III, 49–51, 58–96; Swatland, *House of Lords*, pp. 135–6, 213–16, 224, 230–2.

50 Grey, *Debates*, IV, 63–95; Swatland, *House of Lords*, pp. 221–3.

51 Alexander B. Grosart (ed.), *The Complete Works in Verse and Prose of Andrew Marvell* (4 vols., 1872–5), IV, 248, 261.

52 29 Car. II, c. 1; 29 Car. II, c. 2. For the debates on this grant of supply, see Grey, *Debates*, IV, 103–30, 149–59, 173–7, 225–37; *CJ*, IX, 390–1, 398.

53 See above, p. 47.

54 Quoted in Roger Lockyer, *Tudor and Stuart Britain, 1471–1714* (2nd edition, Harlow, 1985), p. 341. The poll tax was raised by 29 & 30 Car. II, c. 1. For the debates on it, see Grey, *Debates*, V, 77–122, 150–3, 164–223; *CJ*, IX, 432–4, 446–51. For its yield, see Chandaman, *Public Revenue*, pp. 169–70, 188, 330, 356–7, 360–1.

55 Miller, *Charles II*, pp. 256–87.

56 *CJ*, IX, 530; Grey, *Debates*, VI, 128–30; *LJ*, XIII, 333. The finest account of the 'popish plot' and the hysteria that it provoked remains John Kenyon, *The Popish Plot* (1972).

57 30 Car. II, stat. 2, c. 1; printed in Browning (ed.), *English Historical Documents*, pp. 391–4.

58 Grey, *Debates*, VI, 240–54; *CJ*, IX, 543; *LJ*, XIII, 365.

59 Browning, *Danby*, I, 284–314; Grey, *Debates*, VI, 337–401; *CJ*, IX, 559–66; *LJ*, XIII, 433.

60 Grey, *Debates*, VI, 400–1; *CJ*, IX, 566; *LJ*, XIII, 447–8.

61 Derek Hirst, 'The Conciliatoriness of the Cavalier Commons Reconsidered', *PH*, VI (1987), 221–35.

62 For its composition, see Henning (ed.), *House of Commons, 1660–1690*, I, 46–7, 52–3.

63 Jonathan Scott, *Algernon Sidney and the Restoration Crisis, 1677–1683* (Cambridge, 1991).
64 See above, p. 35.
65 Browning, *Danby*, I, 314–41; Grey, *Debates*, VII, 55–63, 85–90, 92–7, 103–5, 116, 133–7, 152–7, 167–87, 199–213, 219–28, 292–303; *CJ*, IX, 574–9, 588–90, 597, 606, 612–13, 615–16; *LJ*, XIII, 514–16, 521, 537–41, 545, 552–3, 556–7, 564–5, 573, 579–80, 591–3; Swatland, *House of Lords*, pp. 253, 255–6.
66 31 Car. II, c. 1; Grey, *Debates*, VII, 118–21.
67 31 Car. II, c. 2; printed in Browning (ed.), *English Historical Documents*, pp. 92–6.
68 As Charles I had done in 1629: see above, p. 119.
69 As Cromwell had done with the Socinian John Biddle in 1655: J. C. Davis, 'Cromwell's Religion', in John Morrill (ed.), *Oliver Cromwell and the English Revolution* (Harlow, 1990), pp. 196–7; Barry Coward, *Oliver Cromwell* (Harlow, 1991), pp. 122–3. See also above, p. 140.
70 Grey, *Debates*, VII, 137–52; *CJ*, IX, 605.
71 Grey, *Debates*, VII, 236–60; *CJ*, IX, 607–8; *LJ*, XIII, 547.
72 Grey, *Debates*, VII, 285–91, 313–14; *CJ*, IX, 623, 626–7.
73 Grey, *Debates*, VII, 344–6; *CJ*, IX, 634; *LJ*, XIII, 595–6.
74 Mark Knights, *Politics and Opinion in Crisis, 1678–81* (Cambridge, 1994), p. 58.
75 Hutton, *Charles II*, p. 383.
76 Knights, *Politics and Opinion*, pp. 193–257.
77 *CJ*, IX, 635–6; *LJ*, XIII, 597–610.
78 Knights, *Politics and Opinion*, pp. 258–75.
79 Henning (ed.), *House of Commons, 1660–1690*, I, 46–7, 52–3.
80 Grey, *Debates*, VII, 348, 396–413, 418–21, 425–30, 431–59; *CJ*, IX, 646, 647, 651. The text of the exclusion bill is printed in Browning (ed.), *English Historical Documents*, pp. 113–14.
81 Swatland, *House of Lords*, pp. 256–8. Twenty-four peers entered their dissents from this vote: *LJ*, XIII, 666.
82 Swatland, *House of Lords*, p. 258.
83 See above, pp. 73–4.
84 Grey, *Debates*, VIII, 290; *CJ*, IX, 704. The Parliament was subsequently dissolved on 18 January 1681: *LJ*, XIII, 742–3.
85 Grey, *Debates*, VII, 380.
86 Quoted in Scott, *Algernon Sidney and the Restoration Crisis*, pp. 72–3.
87 Miller, *Charles II*, pp. 342–4.
88 See above, pp. 60–1.
89 See above, pp. 60–1.
90 Grey, *Debates*, VIII, 291–343; *CJ*, IX, 705–12; *LJ*, XIII, 745–57.
91 The text of this *Declaration* is conveniently printed in Browning (ed.), *English Historical Documents*, pp. 185–8 (quotations at pp. 187–8). See also Knights, *Politics and Opinion*, pp. 316–29.
92 Swatland, *House of Lords*, pp. 203–59; Richard Davis, 'The "Presbyterian" Opposition and the Emergence of Party in the House of Lords in the Reign of Charles II', in Clyve Jones (ed.), *Party and Management in Parliament, 1660–1784* (Leicester, 1984), pp. 1–35. See also above, pp. 90–1, 153–4.
93 Knights, *Politics and Opinion*, especially pp. 107–45.
94 See, for example, Shaftesbury's letter to his allies in the third Exclusion Parliament, printed in Browning (ed.), *English Historical Documents*, pp. 256–8.
95 See especially John Miller, 'The Crown and the Borough Charters in the Reign of Charles II', *EHR*, C (1985), 53–84; Halliday, *Dismembering the Body Politic*, pp. 189–236.
96 Halliday, *Dismembering the Body Politic*, especially pp. 106–45. On the changing nature of local politics, see also above, pp. 26, 29.
97 Henning (ed.), *House of Commons, 1660–1690*, I, 34–40.

98 *The Oxford Dictionary of Quotations* (3rd edition, Oxford, 1979), p. 140 ('King Charles II', no. 22).

99 John Miller, 'Charles II and his Parliaments', *TRHS*, 5th series, XXXII (1982), 1–23.

100 For this view, see in particular John Miller's writings, especially 'The Potential for "Absolutism" in Later Stuart England', *History*, LXIX (1984), 187–207.

101 J. R. Western, *Monarchy and Revolution: The English State in the 1680s* (1972), especially pp. 34–77.

102 Quoted in W. A. Speck, *Reluctant Revolutionaries: Englishmen and the Revolution of 1688* (Oxford, 1988), p. 43.

103 Henning (ed.), *House of Commons, 1660–1690*, I, 47, 53.

104 1 Jac. II, c. 1.

105 1 Jac. II, c. 3; 1 Jac. II, c. 4; 1 Jac. II, c. 5; Grey, *Debates*, VIII, 361–72; *LJ*, XIV, 19–21; *CJ*, IX, 739, 756–60. See also Chandaman, *Public Revenue*, pp. 256–61; C. D. Chandaman, 'The Financial Settlement in the Parliament of 1685', in H. Hearder and H. R. Loyn (eds.), *British Government and Administration: Essays presented to S. B. Chrimes* (Cardiff, 1974), pp. 144–54.

106 Kenyon (ed.), *Stuart Constitution*, p. 364.

107 Harris, *Politics under the Later Stuarts*, p. 124.

108 *LJ*, XIV, 73–4; *CJ*, IX, 756.

109 *LJ*, XIV, 88; *CJ*, IX, 756–61; Grey, *Debates*, VIII, 353–72.

110 See above, p. 97.

111 See the discussion above, p. 97.

112 *LJ*, XIV, 99.

113 J. R. Jones, *The Revolution of 1688 in England* (1972), pp. 128–75.

114 Western, *Monarchy and Revolution*, especially pp. 210–29.

115 Browning (ed.), *English Historical Documents*, p. 192.

116 Western, *Monarchy and Revolution*, pp. 212–22.

117 *Ibid.*, pp. 223–9; J. P. Kenyon, *Robert Spencer, Earl of Sunderland, 1641–1702* (1958), pp. 171–4, 187–95. For the instructions to these agents, see Kenyon (ed.), *Stuart Constitution*, pp. 466–8.

118 See above, p. 97.

119 For this claim, see in particular William's Declaration of 30 September 1688, printed in E. N. Williams (ed.), *The Eighteenth-Century Constitution, 1688–1815: Documents and Commentary* (Cambridge, 1960), pp. 10–16 (quotation at p. 15).

120 Robert Beddard (ed.), *A Kingdom without a King: The Journal of the Provisional Government in the Revolution of 1688* (Oxford, 1988), pp. 166–7.

121 *Ibid.*, p. 65.

122 Henning (ed.), *House of Commons, 1660–1690*, I, 47, 54.

123 For these debates, see *LJ*, XIV, 110–201; *CJ*, X, 14; and D. L. Jones (ed.), *A Parliamentary History of the Glorious Revolution* (1988), especially pp. 24–32. See also above, p. 91

124 *LJ*, XIV, 122–7; *CJ*, X, 21–4.

125 See below, pp. 167–70, 174–6.

126 Jones (ed.), *Parliamentary History*, pp. 40–1, 48–9.

127 *LJ*, XIV, 127; *CJ*, X, 26–30; Jones (ed.), *Parliamentary History*, pp. 41–6.

128 The Bill of Rights was enacted as 1 Gul. & Mar., sess. 2, c. 2. The full text is printed in Browning (ed.), *English Historical Documents*, pp. 122–8.

129 See above, pp. 6–7, 38–9.

130 Williams (ed.), *Eighteenth-Century Constitution*, pp. 37–9 (my emphasis).

131 1 Gul. & Mar., c. 5; printed in Browning (ed.), *English Historical Documents*, pp. 812–13.

132 See above, p. 61.

10 Conclusion

1 On these developments, see also above, pp. 61–3.

2 6 & 7 Gul. & Mar., c. 2; printed in Andrew Browning (ed.), *English Historical Documents, 1660–1714* (1953), pp. 159–60. William had previously vetoed the bill in March 1693: *LJ*, XV, 289.

3 7 & 8 Gul. III, c. 15; printed in Browning (ed.), *English Historical Documents*, pp. 160–1.

4 Geoffrey Holmes, *British Politics in the Age of Anne* (revised edition, 1987), pp. 130–6, 145–9; G. S. Holmes, 'The Attack on "The Influence of the Crown", 1702–16', *BIHR*, XXXIX (1966), 47–68; David Hayton, 'The Reorientation of Place Legislation in England in the 1690s', *PER*, V (1985), 103–8. For examples of place clauses, see E. N. Williams (ed.), *The Eighteenth-Century Constitution, 1688–1815: Documents and Commentary* (Cambridge, 1960), pp. 190–1.

5 *CJ*, XI, 72; *LJ*, XV, 351.

6 See above, pp. 90–1, 153–5.

7 The Act of Settlement was 12 Gul. III, c. 2; printed in Browning (ed.), *English Historical Documents*, pp. 129–34, from which the quotations in this and the following paragraph are taken.

8 *LJ*, XV, 92.

9 See above, pp. 159–60.

10 There are good overviews of the characteristic beliefs of Whigs and Tories in Tim Harris, *Politics under the Later Stuarts: Party Conflict in a Divided Society, 1660–1715* (1993), pp. 152–61; and Geoffrey Holmes, *The Making of a Great Power: Late Stuart and Early Georgian Britain, 1660–1722* (Harlow, 1993), pp. 334–42. J. P. Kenyon, *Revolution Principles: The Politics of Party, 1689–1720* (Cambridge, 1977) is an outstanding study of the development of these ideologies, and for the Tories see also Mark Goldie, 'Tory Political Thought, 1689–1714' (unpubl. Ph.D. dissertation, University of Cambridge, 1978).

11 For the Whigs' promotion of the Act of Settlement and the Abjuration Act, see especially Henry Horwitz, *Parliament, Policy and Politics in the Reign of William III* (Manchester, 1977), pp. 276–84, 291–4, 301–4; and W. A. Speck, *The Birth of Britain: A New Nation, 1700–1710* (Oxford and Cambridge, Mass., 1994), pp. 24–6, 32–3, 49. The Abjuration Act was 13 Gul. III, c. 6.

12 Horwitz, *Parliament, Policy and Politics*, pp. 214–18, 238–9. The oath of association was imposed by 7 & 8 Gul. III, c. 27 ('An Act for the better security of His Majesty's royal person and government'); printed in Browning (ed.), *English Historical Documents*, pp. 74–6.

13 On these occasional conformity bills, see Holmes, *British Politics in the Age of Anne*, especially pp. 100–4, 273–6, 308–10, 373–4; Henry L. Snyder, 'The Defeat of the Occasional Conformity Bill and the Tack: A Study in the Techniques of Parliamentary Management in the Reign of Queen Anne', in Clyve Jones and David Lewis Jones (eds.), *Peers, Politics and Power: The House of Lords, 1603–1911* (1986), pp. 111–31. The Occasional Conformity Act of 1711 was 10 Annae, c. 6; printed in Browning (ed.), *English Historical Documents*, pp. 406–8.

14 John Morrill, *The Nature of the English Revolution* (Harlow, 1993), p. 439.

15 Harris, *Politics under the Later Stuarts*, pp. 161–9; Horwitz, *Parliament, Policy and Politics*, pp. 50–122, 222–74; D. Rubini, *Court and Country, 1688–1702* (1968).

16 David Hayton, 'The "Country" Interest and the Party System, 1689–c. 1720', in Clyve Jones (ed.), *Party and Management in Parliament, 1660–1784* (Leicester, 1984), pp. 37–85.

17 The classic account of the development of party structures during Anne's reign is Holmes, *British Politics in the Age of Anne*. Useful summaries are also found in Harris, *Politics under the Later Stuarts*, pp. 149–52; Holmes, *Making of a Great Power*, pp. 342–8; and Henry Horwitz, 'The Structure of Parliamentary Politics', in Geoffrey Holmes (ed.), *Britain after the Glorious Revolution, 1689–1714* (1969),

pp. 96–114. On the Lords, see also Eveline Cruickshanks, David Hayton and Clyve Jones, 'Divisions in the House of Lords on the Transfer of the Crown and other Issues, 1689–94: Ten New Lists', in Jones and Jones (eds.), *Peers, Politics and Power*, pp. 79–110.

18 See above, p. 29.

19 On elections and the electorate, see especially Harris, *Politics under the Later Stuarts*, pp. 188–96; Holmes, *Making of a Great Power*, pp. 322–33; W. A. Speck, 'The Electorate in the First Age of Party', in Clyve Jones (ed.), *Britain in the First Age of Party, 1680–1750: Essays Presented to Geoffrey Holmes* (1987), pp. 45–62; W. A. Speck, *Tory and Whig: The Struggle in the Constituencies, 1701–1715* (1970); and Paul D. Halliday, *Dismembering the Body Politic: Partisan Politics in England's Towns, 1650–1730* (Cambridge, 1998), especially pp. 276–303.

20 Gilbert Burnet, *History of his own Time* (6 vols., Oxford, 1833), IV, 5.

21 J. P. Kenyon, *Robert Spencer, Earl of Sunderland, 1641–1702* (1958), pp. 247–318.

22 Quoted in Mark Kishlansky, *A Monarchy Transformed: Britain, 1603–1714* (1996), p. 319.

23 On the declining political importance of the Court, see especially R. O. Bucholz, *The Augustan Court: Queen Anne and the Decline of Court Culture* (Stanford, 1993); and John Cannon, *Aristocratic Century: The Peerage of Eighteenth-Century England* (Cambridge, 1984), pp. 93–125.

24 On the development of the Cabinet, see especially Holmes, *British Politics in the Age of Anne*, pp. 111–12, 255–6, 348, 375–6, 436–7; Williams (ed.), *Eighteenth-Century Constitution*, pp. 108–9, 111–16; J. H. Plumb, *The Growth of Political Stability in England, 1675–1725* (1967), pp. 99–103.

25 Holmes, *Making of a Great Power*, pp. 322–4; Holmes, *British Politics in the Age of Anne*, pp. 188–94, 345–53, 367–81, 414–18.

26 See especially Michael J. Braddick, *The Nerves of State: Taxation and the Financing of the English State, 1558–1714* (Manchester, 1996); and John Brewer, *The Sinews of Power: War, Money and the English State, 1688–1783* (1989).

27 7 Gul. III, c. 3; printed in Browning (ed.), *English Historical Documents*, pp. 89–91.

28 Maurice F. Bond, *Guide to the Records of Parliament* (1971), p. 109.

29 See especially Holmes, *British Politics in the Age of Anne*, pp. 382–403; Snyder, 'The Defeat of the Occasional Conformity Bill'.

30 John Watts, *Henry VI and the Politics of Kingship* (Cambridge, 1996).

31 David Dean, *Law-making and Society in Late Elizabethan England: The Parliament of England, 1584–1601* (Cambridge, 1996).

32 See, for example, Jonathan Clark, 'A General Theory of Party, Opposition and Government, 1688–1832', *HJ*, XXIII (1980), 295–325; Jeremy Black, *Robert Walpole and the Nature of Politics in Early Eighteenth-Century England* (1990), especially pp. 51–5; and Frank O'Gorman, *The Long Eighteenth Century: British Political and Social History, 1688–1832* (1997), especially pp. 26–30, 36–51, 129–34, 172–4.

33 Sheila Lambert, *Bills and Acts: Legislative Procedure in Eighteenth-Century England* (Cambridge, 1971).

Glossary

Note: Words in italics denote terms that are themselves defined in this glossary.

adjournment   the postponement of the next meeting of either House of Parliament until a fixed day. Such an interval, known as a 'recess', could last anything from a day or two to over a year. The decision to adjourn could be taken by either the monarch or the relevant House, although the latter was usually only on a daily or short-term basis. Some members of the Commons claimed that the House could not be adjourned without its own consent. When a House was adjourned, the progress of all bills was frozen and could be resumed when the House reconvened. After an adjournment, the House began a new sitting, but this was a continuation of the same session. Cf. *prorogue*.

appellate jurisdiction   the authority of a court to hear and adjudicate appeals against the decisions of an inferior court.

assessment   a land tax, introduced by the Houses of Parliament in February 1643. It was levied weekly (later monthly) at a rate roughly equivalent to a parliamentary *subsidy* every fortnight.

attainder   an act of Parliament declaring an individual guilty of treason or a *felony* without the requirement of a formal trial.

benevolences (or free gifts)   levies, raised by English monarchs in national emergencies. They were raised under *prerogative* powers and payment was voluntary (although informal pressure was sometimes exerted to persuade subjects to pay). The meagre yield of the benevolence of 1626 led Charles I to levy a *Forced Loan*, payment of which was compulsory.

Books of Rates   these contained the official valuations of items that were liable to *customs* duties. Most goods paid a fixed sum, or a percentage of their nominal value, with the result that *customs* duties failed to keep pace with inflation. In 1608, Salisbury issued a new Book of Rates – the first since 1558 – which extended *impositions* to most imports and increased the rates of payment. Another Book of Rates increased duties still further in 1635.

Clarendon Code the name later applied, somewhat misleadingly, to the body of legislation enacted between 1661 and 1665 to penalise those who refused to conform to the Church of England or who attended unauthorised services. In fact, Clarendon initially tried to moderate such penal laws, and only accepted them reluctantly. The principal acts were the Corporation Act (December 1661), the Act of Uniformity (May 1662), the Quaker Act (May 1662), the first Conventicle Act (April 1664), and the Five Mile Act (October 1665).

common law the system of case law, precedent and custom which formed the basis of English criminal law and much civil law. It could be changed only by acts of Parliament.

comprehension the belief that the doctrines and practices of the Church of England should be broad enough to enable as many people as possible to be members of it.

Convention during the early seventeenth century the term was applied to a meeting of Parliament summoned by the monarch, but which passed no acts. During the second half of the century, the term was used to describe an extraordinary meeting of the Houses of Parliament without the issuing of writs of summons by the sovereign, such as met in 1660 and 1689–90. These later seventeenth-century Conventions proclaimed themselves Parliaments and the next ensuing Parliament passed acts giving blanket approval to all bills passed by them.

Convocation within the Church of England, there was an assembly of clergy known as Convocation for each of the two 'provinces', Canterbury and York. The former was the more important, and was often referred to simply as 'Convocation'. It met at the same time as Parliament, whereas the York Convocation usually met immediately after Parliament. Each Convocation had two Houses, an Upper made up of the bishops and a Lower made up of 'proctors' of the presbyters of every diocese.

court of record a court of the sovereign whose proceedings are enrolled on parchment as a permanent record and can be cited as valid evidence of fact. Such courts have the authority both to fine and to imprison.

customs duties levied by the Crown on imports according to rates laid down in the *Books of Rates*. Some of these were 'ancient customs' (or 'great customs') that had been granted to the Crown in perpetuity during the Middle Ages. Other customs duties, such as *tonnage and poundage,* were traditionally voted to the monarch by Parliament at the beginning of each reign.

dissenters usually applied to those Protestants who refused to conform to the practices and discipline of the established Church; often also referred to as *nonconformists*.

durante bene placito literally, 'during [the King's] good pleasure'. Commissions issued to judges *durante bene placito* meant that the

monarch could dismiss them at will. Such commissions were last issued
during the reign of James II.

excise   a sales tax, introduced by the Houses of Parliament in July 1643. It
was imposed on such vital commodities as beer, meat and salt, and
extended to more and more products during the course of the Civil Wars.
Although widely unpopular, it was retained after the Restoration.

extraordinary revenue   tax revenue granted to the Crown by Parliament from
time to time to meet a special need, such as a war or some other national
emergency. The principal forms of parliamentary taxation were the *subsidy* and *fifteenths and tenths*.

felonies   crimes that carried the death penalty.

fifteenths and tenths   a form of parliamentary taxation, first introduced in the
fourteenth century. It was levied on land and movable property, and
became increasingly burdensome for smaller landowners.

Forced Loans   levies, raised from the mid-fifteenth century by English monarchs in national emergencies. They were raised under *prerogative* powers
and then retrospectively turned into taxes by Parliament, but Charles I's
Loan of 1627 proved extremely controversial.

forest fines   as a way of raising revenue, from the summer of 1634 onwards
Charles I sought to reassert the medieval boundaries of royal forests, and
to fine landowners whose estates had inadvertently encroached upon
them.

Great Council   a term applied during the Middle Ages to the monarch's
Council afforced by a full assembly of peers; sometimes representatives of
the shires and boroughs were included as well. Such Great Councils continued to be called from time to time under the Tudors, but they had
largely disappeared by the reign of Elizabeth I. By the end of the sixteenth
century, 'Great Council' was almost invariably used as an alternative
name for Parliament (or occasionally for *Star Chamber*).

impeachment   a trial in Parliament in which the Commons acted as prosecu-
tors and the Lords as judges. It fell into disuse after 1459 but was revived
in 1621. After 1621 there were attempted impeachments in most
Parliaments for the rest of the seventeenth century.

impositions   additional duties on imports, imposed by royal *prerogative*
powers, and charged over and above the *customs* granted to the Crown in
perpetuity or at the beginning of each reign. The Crown's right to levy
them was upheld in Bate's Case (1606), but remained a cause of controversy.

Independents   those Protestants who opposed a coercive national church, and
believed that each congregation should be independent and free to

organise its own style of worship. They advocated a wide measure of toleration for religious radicals.

knighthood fines in January 1630, Charles I appointed a commission to fine those who owned freehold land worth £40 a year, and were thus eligible for knighthood, but who had ignored the sixteenth-century precedents requiring them to present themselves to be knighted at the King's coronation. The practice was declared illegal in 1641.

nonconformists usually applied to those Protestants who refused to conform to the practices and discipline of the established Church; often also referred to as *dissenters*.

ordinance between 1642 and 1649, the English Houses of Parliament claimed the right, in time of emergency, to pass ordinances which had the force of *statute* law even though they had not received the royal assent. The term was also applied to measures enacted by Cromwell as Lord Protector when Parliament was not sitting, but which required Parliament's subsequent ratification.

ordinary revenue the income that the Crown derived on a regular basis from its lands, from feudal revenues, from the profits of justice, and from a range of duties such as *customs*.

original jurisdiction the authority of a court to hear and adjudicate legal cases being initiated for the first time.

prerogative the general term applied to royal discretionary powers; sometimes sub-divided into the 'ordinary' (or legal) prerogative, exercised through Parliament and the *common law*, and the 'extraordinary' (or absolute) prerogative which could supplement (but not contravene) the law in order to safeguard the public good.

Presbyterians those who saw all ministers as equal and opposed clerical hierarchies. They envisaged a rigid structure of discipline based on the Calvinist institutions of a national synod, regional assemblies, and local groupings of parishes (called 'presbyteries' in Scotland and 'classes' in England). English Presbyterians regarded the churches of Scotland and Geneva as models and tried (unsuccessfully) to introduce a similar system in England.

Privy Council the inner body of royal advisers, selected by the monarch, that emerged out of the King's *Great Council* (or Parliament). It usually numbered somewhere between 15 and 45, and discharged a wide range of political, administrative and judicial functions in addition to its advisory role.

proclamation an edict issued by the King or the King and Council. Proclamations were less powerful than *statutes* in that they could not touch life or limb, or affect *common-law* rights of property.

prorogue the royal right to end a particular parliamentary session without actually dissolving the Parliament, thus keeping it in existence for further sessions. When a session was prorogued, all bills and committees then in progress were automatically terminated and had to begin again in the next session. Cf. *adjournment*.

puritans those who regarded the Church of England as 'but halfly reformed', and wished to purify it of the legacies of Catholicism, such as bishops, vestments and the Prayer Book. They were sometimes also called 'the hotter sort of Protestants' or 'the godly'.

purveyance the traditional royal right to purchase transport, food and other supplies for the royal household at prices well below market level.

quamdiu se bene gesserint literally, 'for as long as they shall do good'. Commissions issued to judges *quamdiu se bene gesserint* meant that they in effect had security of tenure, except on evidence of complete incompetence, corruption or gross moral turpitude.

quo warranto literally, 'by what warrant'. Writs of *quo warranto* called for the legal scrutiny and surrender of a charter of rights, and were used extensively during the reigns of Charles II and James II to rescind borough charters of incorporation.

sheriff an officer appointed annually by the Crown in each county to collect royal revenues and to preserve public order. They also acted as returning officers in parliamentary elections, and were therefore debarred from serving as members of Parliament themselves.

Ship Money from Edward III's reign, the Crown had raised money on royal writs from coastal regions during national emergencies to build a fleet. Such levies were normally imposed every few decades, but between 1634 and 1639 Charles raised them every year, and from 1635 he extended Ship Money to the whole of England and Wales. It produced a high financial yield but at heavy political cost, and it was abolished in 1641.

Star Chamber the *Privy Council* and the Chief Justices of King's Bench and Common Pleas sitting as a court of law that dealt with criminal offences, especially those involving breaches of public order. It became widely unpopular during the 1630s because of the savage penalties imposed on *puritan* critics of royal policies, and was abolished in 1641.

statute an act of Parliament, i.e. a bill passed by both Houses of Parliament and assented to by the Crown. Statute was the highest form of human law, and its omnicompetence was definitively established during the Reformation Parliament (1529–36).

subsidy a form of parliamentary taxation, first introduced in 1523. It was a tax on land and the capital value of property, but its yield diminished with time because outdated assessments led to the rich being increasingly under-assessed.

tonnage and poundage   duties imposed on every tun of wine imported, and every pound's worth of goods that was either imported or exported. Traditionally, the first Parliament of each reign granted these duties to a new monarch for life. When the 1625 Parliament failed to grant them to Charles I, his continued collection of them without parliamentary consent proved highly controversial.

Tories   the name originally given to Irish (Catholic) cattle rustlers. From around 1680 it was applied to those who upheld the principle of divine right monarchy and believed that civil authority derived directly from God. Most Tories strongly defended the established Church and were hostile towards *dissenters* and republicans.

wardship   the Crown's feudal right to assume the guardianship of those of its tenants-in-chief who inherited estates as minors. It involved both the management of the wards' lands and the right to arrange their marriages. This highly profitable right was either administered by the Crown through the Court of Wards or sold off to interested parties.

Whigs   a name originally given to Scottish *Presbyterian* rebels of the late 1640s. From around 1680 it was applied to those who believed that civil authority derived from the people, and that rulers who did not govern for the public good could be resisted. They saw Parliament as an essential safeguard of Protestantism, liberties and property. Most Whigs opposed the intolerance of the Church of England and were sympathetic towards *dissenters*.

Appendix 1

Dates of parliamentary sessions, 1604–1689

Parliament		Dates of sessions	Date of dissolution
James I			
1604–10	(1)	19 March–7 July 1604	
	(2)	5 Nov. 1605–27 May 1606	
	(3)	18 Nov. 1606–4 July 1607	
	(4)	9 Feb.–23 July 1610	
	(5)	16 Oct.–6 Dec. 1610	9 Feb. 1611
1614		5 April–7 June 1614	7 June 1614
1621[1]		30 Jan.–18 Dec. 1621	6 Jan. 1622
1624		19 Feb.–29 May 1624	27 March 1625 (automatically dissolved by the King's death)
Charles I			
1625[2]		18 June–12 Aug. 1625	12 Aug. 1625
1626		6 Feb.–15 June 1626	15 June 1626
1628–9	(1)	17 March–26 June 1628	
	(2)	20 Jan.–10 March 1629	10 March 1629
1640 [Short Parlt.]		13 April–5 May 1640	5 May 1640
1640–53 [Long Parlt.]		3 Nov. 1640–20 April 1653	Rump Parlt. after Pride's Purge on 6 Dec. 1648
[1644–5 (Oxford Parlt.)	(1)	22 Jan.–16 April 1644	
	(2)	8 Oct. 1644–10 March 1645	Never formally diss.]
The Interregnum			
1648–53 [Rump Parlt.]		6 Dec. 1648–20 April 1653	20 April 1653

1653 [Nominated Ass.]		4 July–12 Dec. 1653	12 Dec. 1653
1654–5 [1st Prot. Parlt.]		3 Sept. 1654–22 Jan. 1655	22 Jan. 1655
1656–8³ [2nd Prot. Parlt.]		17 Sept. 1656–4 Feb. 1658	4 Feb. 1658
1659 [3rd Prot. Parlt.]		27 Jan.–22 April 1659	22 April 1659
1659–60 [Rump Parlt.; Long Parlt. from 21 Feb.–16 March 1660]		7 May–13 Oct. 1659 26 Dec. 1659–16 March 1660	16 March 1660

Charles II

1660⁴ [Convention]		25 April–29 Dec. 1660	29 Dec. 1660
1661–79 [Cavalier Parlt.]	(1)	8 May 1661–19 May 1662	
	(2)	18 Feb.–27 July 1663	
	(3)	16 March–17 May 1664	
	(4)	24 Nov. 1664–2 March 1665	
	(5)	9–31 Oct. 1665	
	(6)	18 Sept. 1666–8 Feb. 1667	
	(7)	25–29 July 1667	
	(8)	10 Oct. 1667–1 March 1669	
	(9)	19 Oct. –11 Dec. 1669	
	(10)	14 Feb. 1670–22 April 1671	
	(11)	4 Feb.–20 Oct. 1673	
	(12)	27 Oct.–4 Nov. 1673	
	(13)	7 Jan.–24 Feb. 1674	
	(14)	13 April–9 June 1675	
	(15)	13 Oct.–22 Nov. 1675	
	(16)	15 Feb. 1677–13 May 1678	
	(17)	23 May–15 July 1678	
	(18)	21 Oct.–30 Dec. 1678	24 Jan. 1679
1679		6 March–27 May 1679	12 July 1679
1680–81		21 Oct. 1680–10 Jan. 1681	18 Jan. 1681
1681		21–28 March 1681	28 March 1681

James II

1685	(1)	19 May–2 July 1685	
	(2)	9–20 Nov. 1685	2 July 1687
1689–90 [Convention]	(1)	22 Jan.–20 Aug. 1689 [recognised as a Parlt., 23 Feb. 1689]	
	(2)	19 Oct. 1689–27 Jan. 1690	6 Feb. 1690

Notes:

1 The 1621 Parliament consisted of two sittings (30 January–4 June, and 20 November–18 December 1621). These were separated by an adjournment rather than a prorogation, and thus constitute two sittings of a single session.

2 The 1625 Parliament consisted of two sittings (18 June–11 July, at Westminster, and 1–12 August, at Oxford). As with the 1621 Parliament, these were separated by an adjournment rather than a prorogation, and thus constitute two sittings of a single session.

3 The second Protectorate Parliament consisted of two sittings (17 September 1656–26 June 1657, and 20 January–4 February 1658), separated by an adjournment rather than a prorogation.

4 The 1660 Convention consisted of two sittings (25 April–13 September, and 6 November–29 December), separated by an adjournment rather than a prorogation.

Main sources: E. B. Fryde, D. E. Greenway, S. Porter and I. Roy (eds.), *Handbook of British Chronology* (3rd edition, reprinted Cambridge, 1996), pp. 574–7; B. D. Henning (ed.), *The House of Commons, 1660–1690* (3 vols., 1983), I, 85–7.

Appendix 2

Sessional totals of public and private acts, 1604–1689

Session	Public	Private	Total
1604	33	38	71
1605–6	27	29	56
1606–7	13	20	33
1610 (1)	24	42	66
1610 (2)	0	0	0
1614	0	0	0
1621	2	0	2
1624	35	38	73
1625	7	2	9
1626	0	0	0
1628	8	19	27
1629	0	0	0
1640	0	0	0
1640–2	37	13	50
1660	37	32	69
1661–2	52	60	112
1663	17	19	36
1664	8	10	18
1664–5	12	17	29
1665	9	1	10
1666–7	13	19	32
1667	0	0	0
1667–9	13	15	28
1669	13	25	38
1670–1	26	30	56
1673 (1)	10	11	21
1673 (2)	0	0	0
1674	0	0	0
1675 (1)	0	5	5
1675 (2)	1	2	3
1677–8	12	35	47
1678 (1)	9	12	21

Session	Public	Private	Total
1678 (2)	1	0	1
1679	3	2	5
1680–1	2	1	3
1681	0	0	0
1685 (1)	22	8	30
1685 (2)	0	0	0
1689	34	22	56
1689–90	9	8	17
Totals	489 (48%)	535 (52%)	1,024

Appendix 3

Lord Chancellors and Lord Keepers of the Great Seal, 1603–1689

Note: A Lord Keeper (LK) exercised the same authority as a Lord Chancellor (LC), but his office was of less dignity.

Sir Thomas Egerton, later Lord Ellesmere	LK May 1596 LC July 1603	d. March 1617
Sir Francis Bacon, later Lord Verulam and Viscount St Albans	LK March 1617 LC Jan. 1618	dism. May 1621
John Williams, later Bishop of Lincoln	LK July 1621	dism. Oct. 1625
Sir Thomas Coventry, later Lord Coventry	LK Nov. 1625	d. Jan. 1640
Sir John Finch, later Lord Finch	LK Jan. 1640	fled abroad Dec. 1640
Sir Edward Lyttleton, later Lord Lyttleton	LK Jan. 1641	d. Aug. 1645
Sir Richard Lane	LK Aug. 1645	d. April 1650
Sir Edward Herbert	LK April 1653	res. June 1654

In November 1643, the Houses of Parliament authorised a new Great Seal which they entrusted to commissioners. In January 1649 a new Commonwealth Seal was created. This was again entrusted to commissioners, who finally ceased to act in May 1660. The Commonwealth Seal was defaced and then broken up.

Sir Edward Hyde, later Lord Hyde, then Earl of Clarendon	LC Jan. 1658	dism. Aug. 1667
Sir Orlando Bridgeman	LK Aug. 1667	dism. Nov. 1672
Anthony Ashley Cooper, Lord Ashley, later Earl of Shaftesbury	LC Nov. 1672	dism. Nov. 1673

Sir Heneage Finch, later Lord Finch, then Earl of Nottingham	LK Nov. 1673 LC Dec. 1675	d. Dec. 1682
Sir Francis North, later Lord Guilford	LK Dec. 1682	d. Sept. 1685
Sir George Jeffreys, later Lord Jeffreys	LC Sept. 1685	depr. Dec. 1688

The Seal was then placed in commission until Sir John Somers, later Lord Somers, was appointed Lord Keeper in March 1693.

Main source: E. B. Fryde, D. E. Greenway, S. Porter and I. Roy (eds.), *Handbook of British Chronology* (3rd edition, reprinted Cambridge, 1996), pp. 89–90.

Appendix 4

Speakers of the House of Commons, 1604–1689

March 1604–February 1611	Sir Edward Phelips
April–June 1614	Sir Randolph Crew
January 1621–January 1622	Sir Thomas Richardson
February 1624–August 1625	Sir Thomas Crew
February–June 1626	Sir Heneage Finch
March 1628–March 1629	Sir John Finch
April–May 1640	Sir John Glanville
November 1640–April 1653	William Lenthall*
July–December 1653	Francis Rous
September 1654–January 1655	William Lenthall
September 1656–February 1658	Sir Thomas Widdrington
January–March 1659	Chaloner Chute
March 1659	Sir Lislebone Long
March–April 1659	Thomas Bampfylde
May 1659–January 1660	William Lenthall
January 1660	William Say
January–March 1660	William Lenthall
April–December 1660	Sir Harbottle Grimston

May 1661–May 1671	Sir Edward Turnor
February 1673	Sir Job Charlton
February 1673–April 1678	Sir Edward Seymour
April–May 1678	Sir Robert Sawyer
May 1678–March 1679	Sir Edward Seymour
March–July 1679	Sir William Gregory
October 1680–March 1681	Sir William Williams
May 1685–July 1687	Sir John Trevor
January–February 1689	Henry Powle

* Henry Pelham briefly acted as Speaker from 30 July to 5 August 1647 while Lenthall and 57 other members of the Commons fled to the Army to seek refuge from Presbyterian demonstrators.

Source: A. I. Dasent, *The Speakers of the House of Commons* (1911), pp. 382–91.

Appendix 5

Clerks of the Parliaments, 1603–1691

1597–1609	Sir Thomas Smith
1609–21	Robert Bowyer
1621–35	Henry Elsynge
1635–7	Thomas Knyvett
1637	Daniel Bedingfield
1638–49	John Browne
1644–5	Edward Norgate (Clerk of the Upper House at the Oxford Parliament)
1649–60	Henry Scobell
1660–91	John Browne

Sources: Maurice F. Bond, *Guide to the Records of Parliament* (1971), pp. 303–4; Maurice F. Bond, 'Clerks of the Parliaments, 1509–1953', *EHR*, LXXIII (1958), 78–85, especially 83–4.

Appendix 6

Clerks of the House of Commons, 1603–1689

Note: The Clerk of the House of Commons was also sometimes known as the Under-Clerk of the Parliaments.

1603–11	Ralph Ewens
1611–12	William Pynches
1612–33	John Wright
1639–48	Henry Elsynge (the younger)
1649–58	Henry Scobell
1658–9	John Smythe
1659	John Phelpes
1659–60	Thomas St Nicholas
1660	William Jessop
1661–78	William Goldsborough (the elder)
1678–83	William Goldsborough (the younger)
1683–1727	Paul Jodrell

Source: Maurice F. Bond, *Guide to the Records of Parliament* (1971), p. 305.

Select bibliography

Throughout the notes to this book, full details of primary and secondary sources are given the first time they are cited in each chapter, and there is thus no need to provide a comprehensive bibliography here. Instead, what follows is intended as a brief guide to some of the salient works in which the study of seventeenth-century Parliaments can be taken further. It is divided into two sections, dealing with primary and secondary sources respectively.

1 Printed primary sources

A General

There is an excellent survey of the sources for parliamentary history, including those in manuscript, in Maurice F. Bond, *Guide to the Records of Parliament* (1971). For comprehensive collections of the acts and ordinances passed by successive Parliaments, see: C. H. Firth and R. S. Rait (eds.), *Acts and Ordinances of the Interregnum, 1642–1660* (3 vols., 1911); and A. Luders, T. E. Tomlins *et al.* (eds.), *The Statutes of the Realm from Magna Carta to the End of the Reign of Queen Anne* (11 vols., 1810–28). The Journals of both Houses were printed as: *Journals of the House of Commons* (1803–), and *Journals of the House of Lords* (1846).

Four collections of documents also contain extensive material relating to parliamentary history:

Prothero, G. W. (ed.), *Select Statutes and Other Constitutional Documents Illustrative of the Reigns of Elizabeth I and James I* (4th edition, Oxford, 1913)
Tanner, J. R. (ed.), *Constitutional Documents of the Reign of James I* (Cambridge, 1930)
Gardiner, S. R. (ed.), *Constitutional Documents of the Puritan Revolution, 1625–1660* (3rd edition, Oxford, 1906)
Browning, Andrew (ed.), *English Historical Documents, 1660–1714* (1953)

B Parliamentary proceedings

The following are the main printed editions of parliamentary proceedings during the seventeenth century. This list is not exhaustive: for further guidance on the earlier part of the century, see Robert C. Johnson, 'Parliamentary Diaries of the Early Stuart Period', *BIHR*, XLIV (1971), 293–300. The first item below covers the whole period; the remainder are listed chronologically for ease of reference.

Cobbett, W. and Hansard, T. C. (eds.), *The Parliamentary History of England, 1066–1803* (36 vols., 1806–20)

[Various editors], *The Parliamentary or Constitutional History of England* [often referred to as the 'Old Parliamentary History'] (24 vols., 1751–61) [covers 1066–1660]

Willson, D. H. (ed.), *The Parliamentary Diary of Robert Bowyer, 1606–1607* (Minneapolis, 1931; reprinted New York, 1971)

Foster, E. R. (ed.), *Proceedings in Parliament, 1610* (2 vols., New Haven and London, 1966)

Jansson, Maija (ed.), *Proceedings in Parliament, 1614* (Philadelphia, 1988)

Notestein, Wallace, Relf, F. H. and Simpson, H. (eds.), *Commons Debates, 1621* (7 vols., New Haven, 1935)

Relf, F. H. (ed.), *Notes of the Debates in the House of Lords, 1621–9* (Camden Society, 3rd series, XLII, 1929)

Gardiner, S. R. (ed.), *Notes of the Debates in the House of Lords in 1624 and 1626* (Camden Society, 2nd series, XXIV, 1879)

Jansson, Maija, and Bidwell, W. B. (eds.), *Proceedings in Parliament, 1625* (New Haven and London, 1987)

Jansson, Maija, and Bidwell, W. B. (eds.), *Proceedings in Parliament, 1626* (4 vols., New Haven and London, 1991–6)

Keeler, M. F., Cole, M. J. and Bidwell, W. B. (eds.), *Proceedings in Parliament, 1628* (6 vols., New Haven, 1977–83)

Notestein, Wallace, and Relf, F. H. (eds.), *Commons Debates for 1629* (Minneapolis, 1921)

Cope, Esther S. (ed.), *Proceedings of the Short Parliament of 1640* (Camden Society, 4th series, XIX, 1977)

Maltby, Judith D. (ed.), *The Short Parliament (1640) Diary of Sir Thomas Aston* (Camden Society, 4th series, XXXV, 1988)

Notestein, Wallace (ed.), *The Journal of Sir Simonds D'Ewes from the Beginning of the Long Parliament to the Opening of the Trial of the Earl of Strafford* (New Haven, 1923)

Coates, Willson H. (ed.), *The Journal of Sir Simonds D'Ewes from the Final Recess of the Long Parliament to the Withdrawal of King Charles from London* (New Haven, 1942; reprinted Hamden, 1970)

Coates, Willson H., Young, A. S. and Snow, V. F. (eds.), *The Private Journals of the Long Parliament* (3 vols., New Haven and London, 1982–92)

Hamilton, A. H. A. (ed.), *Note Book of Sir John Northcote* (1877)

Jansson, Maija (ed.), *Two Diaries of the Long Parliament* (Gloucester and New York, 1984)

Verney, H. (ed.), *Notes of Proceedings in the Long Parliament . . . by Sir Ralph Verney* (Camden Society, 1st series, XXXI, 1845)

Rutt, J. T. (ed.), *Diary of Thomas Burton, Esq.* (4 vols., 1828) [covers 1654–9]

Chandler, R. (ed.), *The History and Proceedings of the House of Commons, from the Restoration to the Present Time* (14 vols., 1741–4) [covers 1660–1743]

Timberland, E. (ed.), *The History and Proceedings of the House of Lords, from the Restoration to the Present Time* (8 vols., 1742–3) [covers 1660–1742]

Robbins, Caroline (ed.), *The Diary of John Milward, Esq.* (Cambridge, 1938) [covers 1666–8]

Grey, Anchitell (ed.), *Debates of the House of Commons from the Year 1667 to the Year 1694* (10 vols., 1763)

Henning, B. D. (ed.), *The Parliamentary Diary of Sir Edward Dering, 1670–1673* (New Haven, 1940)

Jones, D. L. (ed.), *A Parliamentary History of the Glorious Revolution* (1988)

2   Secondary sources

This section contains a highly selective list of books and articles relating to Stuart Parliaments. A few works on the parliamentary history of earlier periods are also included because they provide useful background. Many of the books listed below contain valuable bibliographies that point the reader towards further works. Fuller bibliographical guidance can be found in the relevant sections of *The Royal Historical Society Bibliography on CD-ROM: The History of Britain, Ireland and the British Overseas* (Oxford, 1998). It is still worth consulting G. Davies and M. F. Keeler (eds.), *Bibliography of British History: Stuart Period, 1603–1714* (Oxford, 1970) as well.

Blom, H. W., Blockmans, W. P. and de Schepper, H. (eds.), *Bicameralisme: Tweekamerstelsel vroeger en nu* (The Hague, 1992), especially the chapters by Croft and Thompson, Dean, Harrison and Roots

Braddick, Michael J., *The Nerves of State: Taxation and the Financing of the English State, 1558–1714* (Manchester, 1996)

Braddick, Michael J., *Parliamentary Taxation in Seventeenth-Century England: Local Administration and Response* (Woodbridge, 1994)

Brunton, D. and Pennington, D. H., *Members of the Long Parliament* (1954)

Chandaman, C. D., *The English Public Revenue, 1660–1688* (Oxford, 1975)

Cogswell, Thomas, *The Blessed Revolution: English Politics and the Coming of War, 1621–1624* (Cambridge, 1989)

Cogswell, Thomas, 'A Low Road to Extinction? Supply and Redress of Grievances in the Parliaments of the 1620s', *HJ*, XXXIII (1990), 283–303

Cust, Richard, 'Charles I and a Draft Declaration for the 1628 Parliament', *HR*, LXIII (1990), 143–61

Cust, Richard, *The Forced Loan and English Politics, 1626–1628* (Oxford, 1987)

Cust, Richard, and Hughes, Ann (eds.), *Conflict in Early Stuart England* (Harlow, 1989), especially the chapters by Cust and Thompson

Dean, David, *Law-making and Society in Late Elizabethan England: The Parliament of England, 1584–1601* (Cambridge, 1996)

Dean, D. M. and Jones, N. L. (eds.), *The Parliaments of Elizabethan England* (Oxford and Cambridge, Mass., 1990)

Elton, G. R., *The Parliament of England, 1559–1581* (Cambridge, 1986)

Elton, G. R., *Studies in Tudor and Stuart Politics and Government* (4 vols., Cambridge, 1974–92)

Elton, G. R. (ed.), *The Tudor Constitution: Documents and Commentary* (2nd edition, Cambridge, 1982)

Foster, Elizabeth Read, *The House of Lords, 1603–1649: Structure, Procedure, and the Nature of its Business* (Chapel Hill, 1983)

Foster, Elizabeth Read, *The Painful Labour of Mr Elsyng* (Transactions of the American Philosophical Society, new series, LXII, part viii, Philadelphia, 1972)

Graves, Michael A. R., *Elizabethan Parliaments, 1559–1601* (2nd edition, Harlow, 1996)

Graves, Michael A. R., *The Tudor Parliaments: Crown, Lords and Commons, 1485–1603* (Harlow, 1985)

Gruenfelder, John K., *Influence in Early Stuart Elections, 1604–1640* (Ohio, 1981)

Hart, James S., *Justice upon Petition: The House of Lords and the Reformation of Justice, 1621–1675* (1991)

Hartley, T. E., *Elizabeth's Parliaments: Queen, Lords and Commons, 1559–1601* (Manchester, 1992)

Henning, B. D. (ed.), *The House of Commons, 1660–1690* (3 vols., 1983)

Hexter, J. H. (ed.), *Parliament and Liberty from the Reign of Elizabeth to the English Civil War* (Stanford, 1992), especially the chapters by Hexter, Sommerville, Holmes, Cogswell and Hirst

Hinton, R. W. K., 'The Decline of Parliamentary Government under Elizabeth I and the Early Stuarts', *CHJ*, XIII (1957), 116–32

Hirst, Derek, 'The Conciliatoriness of the Cavalier Commons Reconsidered', *PH*, VI (1987), 221–35

Hirst, Derek, *The Representative of the People? Voters and Voting in England under the Early Stuarts* (Cambridge, 1975)

Holmes, Geoffrey, *British Politics in the Age of Anne* (revised edition, 1987)

Hoppit, Julian (ed.), *Failed Legislation, 1660–1800, Extracted from the Commons and Lords Journals* (1997)

Jones, Clyve (ed.), *A Pillar of the Constitution: The House of Lords in British Politics, 1640–1784* (1989), especially the chapters by Adamson and Swatland

Jones, Clyve and Jones, David Lewis (eds.), *Peers, Politics and Power: The House of Lords, 1603–1911* (1986), especially the chapters by Flemion and Christianson

Judson, Margaret A., *The Crisis of the Constitution: An Essay in Constitutional and Political Thought in England, 1603–1645* (New Brunswick, NJ, 1949)

Keeler, Mary Frear, *The Long Parliament, 1640–1641: A Biographical Study of its Members* (Memoirs of the American Philosophical Society, XXXVI, Philadelphia, 1954)

Kenyon, J. P. (ed.), *The Stuart Constitution: Documents and Commentary* (2nd edition, Cambridge, 1986)

Kishlansky, Mark A., *Parliamentary Selection: Social and Political Choice in Early Modern England* (Cambridge, 1986)

Knights, Mark, *Politics and Opinion in Crisis, 1678–81* (Cambridge, 1994)

Lambert, Sheila, *Bills and Acts: Legislative Procedure in Eighteenth-Century England* (Cambridge, 1971)

Lambert, Sheila (ed.), *Printing for Parliament, 1641–1700* (List and Index Society, special series, XX, 1984)

Lambert, Sheila, 'Procedure in the House of Commons in the Early Stuart Period', *EHR*, XCV (1980), 753–81

Loach, J., *Parliament under the Tudors* (Oxford, 1991)

McIlwain, Charles Howard, *The High Court of Parliament and its Supremacy* (New Haven, 1910)

Mendle, Michael, *Dangerous Positions: Mixed Government, the Estates of the Realm, and the Making of the Answer to the XIX Propositions* (Alabama, 1985)

Miller, John, 'Charles II and his Parliaments', *TRHS*, 5th series, XXXII (1982), 1–23

Miller, John, 'Representatives and Represented in England, 1660–89', *PER*, XV (1995), 125–32

Moir, Thomas L., *The Addled Parliament of 1614* (Oxford, 1958)

Morrill, John (ed.), *Reactions to the English Civil War, 1642–1649* (1982), especially the chapters by Pennington and Ashton

Notestein, Wallace, *The House of Commons, 1604–1610* (New Haven, 1971)

Notestein, Wallace, 'The Winning of the Initiative by the House of Commons', *Proceedings of the British Academy*, XI (1924–5), 125–75

Plumb, J. H., 'The Growth of the Electorate in England from 1600 to 1715', *PP*, XLV (1969), 90–116

Reeve, L. J., *Charles I and the Road to Personal Rule* (Cambridge, 1989)

Ruigh, Robert, *The Parliament of 1624* (Cambridge, Mass., 1971)

Russell, Conrad, *The Addled Parliament of 1614: The Limits of Revision* (Reading, 1992)

Russell, Conrad, *The Causes of the English Civil War* (Oxford, 1990)

Russell, Conrad, *The Fall of the British Monarchies, 1637–1642* (Oxford, 1991)

Russell, Conrad (ed.), *The Origins of the English Civil War* (1973), especially the chapter by Russell

Russell, Conrad, *Parliaments and English Politics, 1621–1629* (Oxford, 1979)

Russell, Conrad, *Unrevolutionary England, 1603–1642* (1990)

Seaward, Paul, *The Cavalier Parliament and the Reconstruction of the Old Regime, 1661–1667* (Cambridge, 1989)

Sharpe, Kevin (ed.), *Faction and Parliament: Essays on Early Stuart History* (Oxford, 1978)

Swatland, Andrew, *The House of Lords in the Reign of Charles II* (Cambridge, 1996)

Tite, Colin G. C., *Impeachment and Parliamentary Judicature in Early Stuart England* (1974)

Underdown, David, *Pride's Purge: Politics in the Puritan Revolution* (Oxford, 1971)

Weston, C. C., 'Concepts of Estates in Stuart Political Thought', *Studies presented to the International Commission for the History of Representative and Parliamentary Institutions*, XXXIX (1970)

Weston, C. C., *English Constitutional Theory and the House of Lords, 1556–1832* (1965)

Weston, C. C. and Greenberg, J. R., *Subjects and Sovereigns: The Grand Controversy over Legal Sovereignty in Stuart England* (Cambridge, 1981)

Williams, E. N. (ed.), *The Eighteenth-Century Constitution, 1688–1815: Documents and Commentary* (Cambridge, 1960)

Witcombe, D. T., *Charles II and the Cavalier House of Commons, 1663–1674* (Manchester, 1966)

Woolrych, Austin, *Commonwealth to Protectorate* (Oxford, 1982)

Worden, Blair, *The Rump Parliament, 1648–1653* (Cambridge, 1974)

Zaller, Robert, *The Parliament of 1621* (Berkeley, 1971)

Index

Printed in the United States
18798LVS00001B/67